Passing and the

Fictions of Identity

NEW AMERICANISTS

A Series Edited by Donald E. Pease

PASSING

AND THE FICTIONS

OF IDENTITY

Edited by Elaine K. Ginsberg

Duke University Press   Durham and London

1996

© 1996 Duke University Press

All rights reserved

Printed in the United States of America on acid-free paper ∞

Designed by Cherie H. Westmoreland

Typeset in Monotype Fournier by Keystone Typesetting, Inc.

Library of Congress Cataloging-in-Publication Data

appear on the last printed page of this book.

Contents

Acknowledgments   vii

Introduction: The Politics of Passing   ELAINE K. GINSBERG   1

I. Passing to Freedom   19

The Subaltern as Imperialist: Speaking of Olaudah Equiano
MARION RUST   21

"A Most Respectable Looking Gentleman": Passing, Possession,
and Transgression in *Running a Thousand Miles for Freedom*
ELLEN M. WEINAUER   37

II. The (Re)Construction of Race   57

The Autobiography of an Ex-Coloured Man: (Passing for)
Black Passing for White   SAMIRA KAWASH   59

Sliding Significations: Passing as a Narrative and Textual
Strategy in Nella Larsen's Fiction   MARTHA J. CUTTER   75

III. Blackness and the White Imagination   101

Spanish Masquerade and the Drama of Racial Identity in
Uncle Tom's Cabin   JULIA STERN   103

Blackness and the Literary Imagination: Uncovering *The Hidden
Hand*   KATHARINE NICHOLSON INGS   131

"A Most Disagreeable Mirror": Reflections on White Identity
in *Black Like Me*   GAYLE WALD   151

IV. Creating the Self   179

Confederate Counterfeit: The Case of the Cross-Dressed Civil
War Soldier   ELIZABETH YOUNG   181

Displacing Desire: Passing, Nostalgia, and *Giovanni's Room*
VALERIE ROHY   218

Passing for White, Passing for Black   ADRIAN PIPER   234

Works Cited   271

Index   285

Contributors   297

Acknowledgments

*T*his collection of essays on the subject of "passing" originated in a call for papers for the annual Modern Language Association convention. The overwhelming number of submissions was evidence that the topic interested a wide range of scholars, and that those scholars were producing some of the most exciting work in the field of literary and cultural studies. I am appreciative of the interest of the many who responded to that call, and especially to those who submitted essays for possible inclusion in this collection.

For contributing the idea for that session, and for her early assistance in this project, I want to thank my colleague Anna Shannon Elfenbein. Dennis Allen, Laura Brady, and Judith Stitzel offered careful readings and sound advice. The anonymous readers for Duke University Press provided invaluable criticism and suggestions. Ken Wissoker of the Press was all that anyone could ask an editor to be—committed, helpful, and patient. For their diligence and persistence, and especially for the clarity and intelligence of their critical insights, I am most grateful to the authors of the essays contained herein; finally, this volume is theirs.

Introduction:

The Politics of Passing

ELAINE K. GINSBERG

100 DOLLARS REWARD. Will be given for the apprehension of my negro Edmund Kenney. He has straight hair, and complexion so nearly white that it is believed a stranger would suppose there was no African blood in him. He was with my boy Dick a short time since in Norfolk, and offered for sale . . . , but escaped under the pretence of being a white man. — Richmond *Whig*, 6 January 1836

Love Hurts: Brandon Teena was a woman who lived and loved as a man. She was killed for carrying it off. — *Village Voice*, 19 April 1994

*T*he slave owner placing the above ad, typical of many seen in antebellum newspapers, announces two aspects of Edmund Kenney's identity in the phrase "my negro": Kenney's legal status as property and his legal race as Negro. That Kenney's legal status was an imposed, socially constructed identity is self-evident; that his race was also imposed and socially constructed is not. To his owner, and under Virginia law, Kenney's race was Negro. No matter that Kenney's physical appearance made it obvious that his legally invisible white ancestors likely outnumbered the African and that "a stranger" would see a white, and presumably free, man. The law and the social custom that defined Kenney as a Negro and a slave privileged that "African blood"—invisible on the surface of the body—over the obviously dominant and visible heritage that would cause a "stranger" to assume Kenney is both white and free. Thus Kenney's creation of a new "white" identity—that is, his "passing"—was a transgression not only of legal boundaries (that is, from slave to freeman) but of cultural boundaries as well. Kenney and the unknown thousands of others who passed out of slavery moved from a category of subordination and oppression to one of freedom and privilege, a movement that interrogated and thus threatened the system of

racial categories and hierarchies established by social custom and legiti-
mated by the law.

Teena Brandon, biologically and legally female, wanted to live as a man. As
Brandon Teena, he moved in early fall 1993 to Falls City, Nebraska, where,
with no knowledge of Brandon's origins, the young people saw a slightly
built but interesting young man who was attractive to women. Ironically,
Brandon's passing was definitively revealed upon his arrest for forgery. The
arresting sheriff remarked that Brandon's gender was ambiguous: "When
you looked at her you couldn't really tell. She was a good looking person
either way." Yet Brandon's passing was convincing enough that, even after
the local law enforcement officers and some angry men exposed him, both
legally and literally, women still insisted that he was "one of the nicest men"
they had ever met and the "best boyfriend" they had ever dated. Gender
identity in this instance, like racial identity in the case of Edmund Kenney,
has a dual aspect. It is from one perspective performative, neither constituted by nor indicating the existence of a "true self" or core identity. But,
like racial identity, gender identity is bound by social and legal constraints
related to the physical body. Brandon was able for a time to pass successfully; and the young women who dated Brandon remember "him" (they
continue to use the male pronoun) as an attentive and loving young man.
But the law and social custom insist on the relationship between an individual's gender identity and his or her physical being, and when that relationship is subverted, the cultural logic of gender categories—and privileges—is
threatened. The two young men who, at a party on Christmas Eve, angrily
exposed Brandon's female body allegedly shot and killed Brandon on New
Year's Day. Thus it seems that Brandon's murder was a tragic consequence
of a female's transgression and usurpation of male gender and sexual roles.[1]

As the stories of Edmund Kenney and Brandon Teena illustrate, passing is about identities: their creation or imposition, their adoption or rejection, their accompanying rewards or penalties. Passing is also about the
boundaries established between identity categories and about the individual and cultural anxieties induced by boundary crossing. Finally, passing
is about specularity: the visible and the invisible, the seen and the unseen.

The genealogy of the term *passing* in American history associates it with
the discourse of racial difference and especially with the assumption of a

fraudulent "white" identity by an individual culturally and legally defined as "Negro" or black by virtue of a percentage of African ancestry. As the term metaphorically implies, such an individual crossed or passed through a racial line or boundary—indeed *trespassed*—to assume a new identity, escaping the subordination and oppression accompanying one identity and accessing the privileges and status of the other. Enabled by a physical appearance emphasizing "white" features, this metaphysical passing necessarily involved geographical movement as well; the individual had to leave an environment where his or her "true identity"—that is, parentage, legal status, and the like—was known to find a place where it was unknown. By extension, "passing" has been applied discursively to disguises of other elements of an individual's presumed "natural" or "essential" identity, including class, ethnicity, and sexuality, as well as gender, the latter usually effected by deliberate alterations of physical appearance and behavior, including cross-dressing. Not always associated with a simple binary, some instances of passing, as illustrated by the "Spanish masquerade" of George Harris in *Uncle Tom's Cabin*, demonstrate the multiplicity of racial or related identity categories into which one might pass. Nor is the pass always permanent; it may be brief, situational, or intermittent, as in the case of Nella Larsen's protagonists, James Weldon Johnson's "ex-coloured man," or women, such as Loreta Velazquez, the "Woman in Battle," who cross-dressed temporarily to enter professions or occupations or to seek experiences barred to them as females. And although the cultural logic of passing suggests that passing is usually motivated by a desire to shed the identity of an oppressed group to gain access to social and economic opportunities, the rationale for passing may be more or less complex or ambiguous and motivated by other kinds of perceived rewards. Both history and literature present numerous examples. Jazz musician Billy Tipton, whose female sex was revealed only upon his death in 1989 at the age of seventy-four, lived his professional life as a man, presumably because his chosen profession was not open to women, but lived his personal life as a man as well, concealing the fact of his female sex even from his three adopted sons. John Howard Griffin and Grace Halsell, both white journalists, passed for black by temporarily darkening their skin to write exposés of racism. Adrian Piper, who tells her own story in the last essay in this collection, prefers to identify with the cultural heritage of her black ancestry although her visible appearance leads most people to assume that she is white "passing for black." Ann Powers, writing in the *Village Voice*, has chronicled the emergence of "the queer straight," a product of the "political impact of a rejuvenated gay and lesbian movement" (74) which in some quarters has made an androgynous and sexually ambiguous look "chic."[2]

Whatever the rationale, both the process and the discourse of passing interrogate the ontology of identity categories and their construction. For the possibility of passing challenges a number of problematic and even antithetical assumptions about identities, the first of which is that some identity categories are inherent and unalterable essences: presumably one cannot pass for something one *is not* unless there is some other, pre-passing, identity that one *is*.[3] Further, passing forces reconsideration of the cultural logic that the physical body is the site of identic intelligibility; as noted by Amy Robinson, "The 'problem' of identity, a problem to which passing owes the very possibility of its practice, is predicated on the false promise of the visible as an epistemological guarantee" (716). Finally, allowing the possibility that "maleness" or "whiteness" or ethnicity can be performed or enacted, donned or discarded, exposes the anxieties about status and hierarchy created by the potential of boundary trespassing. For both the process and the discourse of passing challenge the essentialism that is often the foundation of identity politics, a challenge that may be seen as either threatening or liberating but in either instance discloses the truth that identities are not singularly true or false but multiple and contingent.

As illustrated by the ease with which assimilation has so often been accomplished, class, ethnic origin, and sexual orientation are not difficult to enact or to disguise. Race and gender, however, present other complications. First, cultural logic presupposes a biological foundation of race visibly evident in physical features such as facial structures, hair color and texture, and skin color—what Frantz Fanon has called the "epidermal schema" of racial difference (112). Gender, even when recognized as a pattern of culturally constructed behaviors discursively produced, has been assumed linked to biological features that distinguish the binary set male / female. Cultural associations of the physical body with both race and gender, and the putative visibility of these two identity categories, thus make race and gender passing seem more problematic than other instances of passing. Second, the status and privilege accompanying "whiteness" and "maleness" highlight the similarities of black-to-white race passing and female-to-male gender passing as sources of cultural anxiety, for both "not-white" and "woman" are sites of difference that affirm the priority of "white" and "man" in the hegemonic ideology.[4] Further, both visibility and difference (or "otherness") are linked by what Marjorie Garber describes as the necessity for the "hegemonic cultural imaginary" to *see* difference to interpret it and "to guard against a difference that might otherwise put the identity of one's own position in question" (130). Finally, the genealogy of the concept in American culture reveals the origins of passing in the sexual exploitation of black slave women by white men. The children born of these encounters inherited the abject status of the mother even as, through successive generations, a visible, albeit culturally inauthentic, "whiteness" was reproduced from "black" female bodies. At the same time, to insure the reproduction as well as the purity of his whiteness, the white man also needed to exert control over the sexuality of both the white woman and the black man, effectively enslaving the former and emasculating the latter. Consequently, in American history, race, sex, and gender have been inextricably linked, first through a system of slavery that placed white men in control of the productive labor of black men and the productive and reproductive labor of both black and white women, and then nationally through an economic and political system and a cultural ideology that established a fundamentally racist and sexist hierarchy of privilege and oppression. Thus, although the essays in this volume consider, in addition to black / white and female / male passing, some issues of national identification and of sexuality where those issues impinge on the political questions related to race and gender, the assumption underlying this volume is that critical to the process and discourse of "passing" in American history and in the American cultural imaginary are the status and privileges associated with being white and being male. Focusing on race and gender and demonstrating in addition the ways that race, gender, nationality, and sexuality are imbricated, the essays in this collection therefore expose the contingencies of all identities as well as the "politics" inherent in their construction and imposition.

The epistemology of the concept of "race" and its specific deployment in American history reveal the discursive process that has operated in the construction of that identity category and the ways putative racial differences have served social and political ends. Historians of race remind us that, although some concept of race has existed throughout time as "an organizing, explanatory principle, what the term refers to—that is, the origin and basis of 'racial differences'—has not remained constant" (Outlaw 61–62).[5] In popular discourse, racial categories refer not only to persons with discernible and visible physical characteristics such as skin color but also to persons who share language, nationality, and religion. Often used as "ethnic intensifiers,"[6] racial categories have throughout history been created for the deliberate purpose of exploitation, domination, or persecution of one group by another. In the American colonies, as the English imported more and more Africans as slave labor, it became important not only to emphasize the physical differences between themselves and the Africans but also to fuse these differences with religion, nationality, and morality. According to Winthrop Jordan, for the English, "vis-à-vis the Negro . . . to be Christian was to be civilized rather than barbarous, English rather than African, white rather than black" (94). Christian, English, and white supremacy were thus all affirmed and justified.[7]

Marion Rust's discussion in this collection of the autobiography of Olaudah Equiano, an early (1789) example of the slave narrative, demonstrates the process through which that African in particular internalized the dominant ideology described by Jordan. Initially viewing whiteness as disfigurement and the English as monsters, Equiano comes not only to accept the ideologies of his imperialist masters but also to employ and articulate their economic ethics. The former slave becomes slave owner, and the African, Englishman, substituting national identification for complexion as he passes from slave to imperialist. The ruptures in the text, however, as Rust suggests, are warnings that for the African, integral subjectivity is not so easily maintained; the danger is always that Equiano's self-mastery will disintegrate, forcing him back into subalternity and silence.

In a study of the legal history of race identity in the United States, Cheryl Harris observes:

By the 1660's, the especially degraded status of Blacks as chattel slaves was recognized by law. Between 1680 and 1682, the first slave codes appeared, codifying the extreme deprivations of liberty already existing in social practice. . . . Racial identity was further merged with stratified social and legal status: "Black" racial identity marked who was subject to enslavement; "white" racial identity marked who was "free" or, at minimum, not a slave. The ideological and rhetorical move from "slave" and "free" to "Black" and "white" as polar constructs marked an important step in the social construction of race. (1718)

The ideological and rhetorical equivalence of slave / black and free / white was undermined, however, by the generations of miscegenation that made invisible in some individuals those ever smaller percentages of African heritage that would have visibly marked them as "slave," enabling legally "black" men and women, like Edmund Kenney or Ellen Craft, to pass as white and free.[8] Had emancipation brought full social and legal equality, the story of race passing might have ended in the 1860s. But in the aftermath of the Civil War, numerous legal as well as cultural barriers were erected to full citizenship for persons defined as "Negro." And well past the middle of the twentieth century, some states defined Negro as someone with a single Negro great-grandparent; in three states, one great-great-grandparent was sufficient.[9] As Harris observes, "In a society structured on racial subordination, white privilege became an expectation and . . . whiteness became the quintessential property for personhood" (1730). Accompanying any such privilege, like the right to join an exclusive club, is the right to determine who else shall be permitted to join or, to put it another way, the right to exclude, the right to define who would be deemed "not white." The Supreme Court of the United States, in the 1896 *Plessy v. Ferguson* decision, confirmed that a person with one-eighth Negro ancestry could be legally defined as Negro under Louisiana law, even though, as in the case of Plessy, that ancestry was not physically visible.[10] For the white majority, that decision had important consequences.

At the individual level, recognizing oneself as "white" necessarily assumes premises based on white supremacy: It assumes that Black ancestry in any degree, extending to generations far removed, automatically disqualifies claims to white identity, thereby privileging "white" as unadulterated, exclusive, and rare. Inherent in the concept of "being white" was the right to own or hold whiteness to the exclusion and subordination of Blacks. (Harris 1737)

Although little is documented about the actual extent of race passing by blacks in the United States, the specter of passing derives its power not from the number of instances of passing but as a signification that embodies the anxieties and contradictions of a racially stratified society. This specter of race passing—enabled by what Joel Williamson calls "invisible blackness"—threatened the security of white identity, on both a societal and an individual level. Although for the legally or culturally black individual race passing is an attempt to move from the cultural margin to the center, from the perspective of a dominant race, passing is deception, an attempt to claim status and privilege falsely. But when "race" is no longer visible, it is no longer intelligible: if "white" can be "black," what is white? Race passing thus not only creates, to use Garber's term, a *category crisis* (16) but also destabilizes the grounds of privilege founded on racial identity. "Identity only becomes an issue," Kobena Mercer has written, "when it is in crisis, when something assumed to be fixed, coherent and stable is displaced by the experience of doubt and uncertainty" (43). William Craft, for example, in his account of his and his wife's escape from slavery, *Running a Thousand Miles for Freedom* (1860), plays on white anxieties about racial identity by interpolating into his story accounts of white children deceptively sold into slavery on the pretense that they were "black." Harriet Beecher Stowe also warns of this possibility, suggesting in the *Key to Uncle Tom's Cabin* that a system that traded in light-skinned slaves would eventually tempt an enterprising entrepreneur to sell white orphans as octoroons.

The arbitrariness of racial classifications as well as their political motivation lead Henry Louis Gates Jr. to define race as merely a metaphor, "the ultimate trope of difference" ("Writing 'Race'" 5). Nevertheless, the reality of *racism* and its effects cannot be denied. According to Toni Morrison, who echoes Gates, "Race has become metaphorical—a way of referring to and disguising forces, events, classes and expressions of social decay and economic division far more threatening to the body politic than biological 'race' ever was" (63). Morrison argues that one effect of such threats was the use of the Africanist character and the Africanist presence as surrogate to enable white authors "to limn out and enforce the invention and implications of whiteness" (52). In a different approach to similar issues, Katharine Nicholson Ings's discussion of E. D. E. N. Southworth's *The Hidden Hand, or, Capitola the Madcap* (1888) demonstrates how that white Southerner and prolific writer of sentimental novels, in a book replete with masquerades and disguises, resemanticizes "whiteness" as "blackness" through the old black woman "Hat" and the novel's white heroine, Capitola Black ("Cap"). The novel also represents a meditation on identity and specularity and thus, perhaps unconsciously, on the visibility of race and gender identity. As such, Southworth's novel destabilizes both racial and gender expectations as well as the moral order of sentimental fiction. Written almost three quarters of a century later, John Howard Griffin's autobiographical account of his experiment in race passing, *Black Like Me* (1961), is a conscious meditation on black oppression and white privilege. For that white author, however, as Gayle Wald argues, passing becomes also an unconscious journey to self-knowledge, a way of discovering the meanings of his own white racial identity and his own implication in the system of oppression he sets out to expose. Wald foregrounds Griffin's internalization of the "Southern economy of spectatorship under the dominant social order" and demonstrates how his experiment in passing "proves instructive in these 'invisible' laws of looking, under which spectatorship is a function of economic and social power and hence dependent on race, class, and gender."

One of the assumed effects of a racist society is the internalization, by members of the oppressed race, of the dominant culture's definitions and characterizations. This is the context in which the literature of race passing has most often been read. This body of literature as traditionally discussed includes the narratives of those who escaped slavery by passing as white, in addition to works of fiction and nonfiction by both white and black authors, some of which complicate identity issues with multiple boundary crossings, both literal and figurative. Although some critics have accused black authors who write passing fiction of pandering to white audiences by portraying passing as a source of anxiety and alienation for the passer,[11] it is significant that most of these authors were individuals for whom the ambiguity of their racial identity was likely the source of their creative concern.[12] As one of the characters in Nella Larsen's *Passing* observes, perhaps echoing her creator's thoughts: "It's funny about 'passing.' We disapprove of it and at the same time condone it. It excites our contempt and yet we rather admire it. We shy away from it with an odd kind of revulsion, but we protect it" (185–86). Samira Kawash foregrounds the fallacy of any singular interpretation of the passing narrative; she argues that "blackness or whiteness as they emerge in the passing narrative belie the possibility of identity or authenticity that would allow one to be unequivocally black or white." Her essay on James Weldon Johnson's *Autobiography of an Ex-Coloured Man* (1912) demonstrates that neither the "blackness" nor the "whiteness" of the narrator of that novel is intrinsic; both are merely specular identifications, acts of volition accomplished through "studious spectatorship." Following this view, "all race identity is . . . the product of passing." Nevertheless, once raised, the specter of "blackness" haunts Johnson's narrator, so that he fears "that something invisible in himself will give him away." That something, Kawash argues, is "the mark of difference itself, the empty signifier of race." Marrying a white woman and fathering white children paradoxically insures the "authenticity" of his white identity, even as he expresses some regret for "having sold [his] birthright for a mess of pottage."

Although at first glance James Baldwin's *Giovanni's Room* (1956) might not seem appropriately a passing narrative, in her discussion of that novel and its central (white) character Valerie Rohy argues that Baldwin's novel is a passing narrative in that it "articulates the ways in which identities, including 'nationality,' 'race,' and 'sexuality,' are retrospective, indeed nostalgic constructions." In this novel, race is figured as nationality, Giovanni's swarthy color, his Italian nationality, and marginalized class status contrasting with David's blonde whiteness and American privilege. David's conflicted sexuality alludes to the homosexual subtexts of Nella Larsen's *Passing* as well as the erotic connections between Johnson's narrator and his white patron. The knowing glance of a sailor who "reads" David as gay and David's panicked reaction recall the specular identification of the passing black. As David considers his return to America, "home" represents a "nostalgic ideal of secure gender and sexual identity," a coherence that can never be attained. Baldwin's novel, writes Rohy, is a text that "poses questions of nationalism, nostalgia, and the constitution of racial and sexual subjects in terms that are particularly resonant for contemporary identity politics."

As a psychoanalytic concept, nostalgia suggests an imaginary pre-Oedipal and prediscursive state of subjective wholeness, an originary identity that cannot be recovered. As a longing for a lost culture or sense of belonging, nostalgia is an element in Nella Larsen's novels *Quicksand*

(1928) and *Passing* (1929) as well as in Johnson's *Autobiography of an Ex-Coloured Man*. While in Europe, both Helga Crane and "Ex-Coloured Man" experience a strong desire to return "home" to the black community. To suggest that fictional race passing may be read as a metaphor for alienation and self-denial, however, is to ignore the rich complexity of this genre and its permutations. "Home," a mythical place of coherent identity, turns out to be for these characters, as for Baldwin's David, a phantasm. And although the nostalgia of *Passing*'s fair-skinned, blond-haired Clare Kendry for her black community would seem to confirm the equation of passing with loss, Martha Cutter's essay on passing as a narrative and textual strategy in Larsen's fiction persuasively argues that for Larsen, passing is a tactic that allows an individual creative subjectivity. Helga Crane, protagonist of Larsen's first novel, *Quicksand,* seeking an elusive unitary identity corresponding to her essential self, becomes trapped in a stifling role as the wife of a country preacher. Clare Kendry, on the other hand, refuses the constraints of a singular identity and uses passing as a subversive strategy to transcend the limitations of a racist, classist, and sexist society. Although some have pointed to Clare's death as demonstrating the penalties of passing for what one is not, the two novels may be read as inverse images of each other: *Quicksand* illustrates the consequences of a fixed and limited identity; *Passing* leaves its characters and its readers in a destabilized universe in which identities, and texts, refuse suffocating closure.

Although the discourse of race passing and discussions of race-passing narratives traditionally assume a black / white binary and a related class system, complications of that dichotomy in fiction belie any such simple assumptions. In Larsen's *Passing,* for example, Irene Redfield comments that she is often assumed to be "an Italian, a Spaniard, a Mexican or a gipsy" (150), any one of which identities might enable access to social privileges that her black identity would not. A vignette in an earlier text, however—the Spanish masquerade of George Harris in *Uncle Tom's Cabin* (1852)—more pointedly exposes the fictions grounding rigid racist and classist assumptions. Possessed of a "fine set of European features" and light-skinned enough to pass as white, George confounds the logic of passing and *darkens* his skin to pass as a "Spanish" gentleman in order to help his wife and child to freedom. Julia Stern argues that this brief episode in Harriet Beecher Stowe's novel presents that author's "most subtle meditation on race and domination in America." George's masquerade exposes the inability of his audience—representative of the rural antebellum South—to read "otherness" in anything but black/white terms. All that is needed for George's performance to be convincing are the accoutrements of social status, which include, ironically, the attendance of a "slave" who in reality is a free black. Stern reminds us, however, that America's most famous abolitionist author was also a supporter of the plan to establish a colony in Africa for freed slaves. In George's last speech in *Uncle Tom's Cabin*, he declaims: "I have no wish to be an American, or to identify myself with them. It is with the oppressed, enslaved African race that I cast my lot" (608). It seems that Stowe could not consciously envision an American society constructed on the lesson taught by her own narrative—that racial identity is not only a social construction but also unrelated to an individual's worthiness.

The sex-gender system of American society is a subtext in many passing narratives, beginning with slave narratives such as Harriet Jacobs's *Incidents in the Life of a Slave Girl* (1861), which records how the gender of Harriet's light-skinned uncle allows him the mobility of flight in contrast to her freedom/confinement in her grandmother's attic. It is reflected as well in stories such as Kate Chopin's "Désirée's Baby," in which it is the mother who is mistakenly branded with the presumption of racial impurity. Charles Chesnutt's *The House behind the Cedars* (1900) demonstrates the inability of Rena Walden to overcome the passivity of her learned gender role to pass as white in South Carolina society along with her brother. The complex imbrications of race and gender are reflected in a number of passing narratives that combine race passing with cross-dressing. Eliza Harris in *Uncle Tom's Cabin*, light enough to pass for white, dons boy's clothing and dresses her son as a girl to effect a dangerous and courageous flight to freedom. But this subplot ends with Eliza being recuperated in her appropriate gender role as George Harris's wife. *Running a Thousand Miles for Freedom* chronicles the real escape from slavery of William Craft and his wife Ellen, whose light skin enabled her disguise as an invalid (or in/valid) white man attended by a Negro slave—in reality, her husband. Discussed by Ellen Weinauer in this book, Ellen Craft's passing is a multiple boundary crossing, from black to white, slave to freewoman, woman to man, wife to master. That a black woman could make "a most respectable-looking [white] gentleman" confounds utterly the cultural logic of specular identification and reveals the performative fictions at the center of such categories. A close reading of William Craft's narrative makes it clear, however, that for William to claim his manhood, indeed his subjectivity, Ellen must return to her "true" identity as "woman," a gender identity William underscores in recounting the "feminine" fears and frailties she displays both before and after the successful escape. Freed from the legal system of slavery (and from the legal prohibition against slave marriages), Ellen can inhabit the subject position of "wife" to her true master, her husband.

Thus, although Henry Louis Gates wants to insist that race is "the ultimate trope of difference," it can be argued that gender, in the arbitrariness of its cultural prescriptions, is a trope of difference that shares with race (especially in the context of black/white passing) a similar structure of identity categories whose enactments and boundaries are culturally policed. In most cultures, it is assumed that the distinctions between "man" and "woman" are not only visible and readily discernible but also inextricably related to the binary set male/female. Nevertheless, just as the ontology of race exposes the contingencies of the categories "white" and "black," so the ontology of gender exposes the essential inauthenticity of "man" and "woman."[13] Like race, gender is defined "within the terms of a hegemonic cultural discourse" (Butler, *Gender Trouble* 9). Further, like race passing, gender passing creates category crisis as Garber defines it: "a failure of definitional distinction, a borderline that becomes permeable, that permits of border crossings from one (apparently distinct) category to another" (16). The very real possibility of gender passing—cross-dressing—thus is likely to threaten not only the security of male identity, as race passing threatens the security of white identity, but also, as does race passing, the certainties of identity categories and boundaries. It is perhaps these threats that were responsible for the violent reaction to Brandon Teena's passing. The recorded history of numerous instances of cross-dressing women being prosecuted for fraud and deception illustrates the more usual cultural response to female "usurpation of [male] rights and privileges" (Friedli 237).[14]

Given the asymmetry of privilege and power in most societies, it is not difficult to understand the rationale for most female cross-dressing. When women cross-dress, they usually do so to gain access to professional and economic opportunities or to experiences seen as available only to men.

Two examples are jazz musician Billy Tipton and Salvador Sanchez, a bullfighter, both of whom were revealed to be women, Tipton at his death and Sanchez when he was gored by a bull in Pamplona. Although male transvestites, like some women cross-dressers, may be committed to subverting phallocentric gender constructions and constraints, their motivations for cross-dressing obviously may also be more varied and complex. There are those who, like Venus Xtravaganza in Jennie Livingston's 1992 film *Paris Is Burning,* express the essentialist notion that they are female "inside." Yet some theorists have suggested that "drag" not only is not expressive of a desire to be a woman but may in reality be motivated by a misogynistic impulse. Others have argued that, rather than being subversive of gender binarism, male transvestism in reality reinscribes gender norms and hierarchies. Madeline Kahn claims, however, that male transvestites generally do not create a permanent female persona; the male transvestite's interest is in the success of the illusion, which is not complete until it is revealed as an illusion (14).[15] Finally, no discussion of gender identity can ignore the ways sexuality is implicated in gender ambiguity—from the assumption that both female and male cross-dressers are homosexual to the accusation that cross-dressing merely reinscribes heterosexual norms, to the homophobia that is incited by the "unveiling" of a cross-dressed individual.[16]

Seeking access to economic opportunities, or even to the excitement of adventures unavailable to them, some of the most famous cross-dressing females in history have masqueraded as men to fight as soldiers, that most masculine of professions.[17] *The Female Review; or, Memoirs of an American Young Lady* (1797) tells the story of Deborah Sampson who fought for eighteen months in the American Revolution until her sex was discovered. The presentation of Sampson's story by Herman Mann illustrates how historically an attempt on the part of a female to transgress categories, by assuming either the privileges or the visible accoutrements of masculinity, has been seen as a subversive act that threatens the stability of the social structures perpetuating male dominance. Mann "compares enlisting as a soldier, an unnatural act in a woman, with *civil* war, an unnatural event in society" (qtd. in Friedli 243). Thus, appropriately, the American Civil War provides the context for the narrative of a cross-dressing woman discussed in this collection by Elizabeth Young, Loreta

Velazquez's *The Woman in Battle* (1876). Young argues that the importance of cross-dressing in this text "inheres in its figurative as well as literal meanings" and that the "military masquerade functions . . . as a metaphorical point of exchange for intersections among individual bodies and the body politic in Civil War and Reconstruction America." Masquerading at various times as a Confederate soldier, a spy, or a pro-Union woman, Velazquez crosses boundaries and borders between armies and regions—North and South—as well as genders. Significantly, in her Confederate masquerade, Velazquez needs the presence of her male black slave to authenticate "Lt. Buford's" "masculinity" as well as his social position. Also embedded within this narrative of Civil War cross-dressing is a protolesbian plot of same-sex seduction. Thus, read as a burlesque of both Confederate manhood and virtuous Southern womanhood, *The Woman in Battle* "makes visible the gender mythologies of the postwar South." It exposes the truth that Southern masculinity is authenticated only through the subordination and abjection of white women and black men. Framing her discussion of Velazquez's narrative, Young also demonstrates how the 1993 sex discrimination suit of Lauren Burgess against the U.S. Department of the Interior for barring her participation in a Civil War reenactment brings the complex implications of Velazquez's story home to present-day America.

The historical occasion of the Civil War appropriately brings the discussion of passing back full circle to issues of race and identity. Adrian Piper's autobiographical essay that closes this book relates her experiences as a light-skinned woman who chooses to identify with her black ancestry although she "looks," and is generally assumed to be, white. In effect a mirror image of the traditional passing narrative, her account foregrounds the threats to white complacency and security, as well as to social privilege, that passing represents, for Piper's decision to "pass" as black, to self-construct an identity perceived by a white majority as less desirable, disrupts the assumptions of superiority that buttress white privilege and self-esteem. Piper demonstrates how challenging racial categories threatens those whose sense of self-worth depends on their racial identity and the social status that accompanies it. She concludes that not until "we have faced the full human and personal consequences of self-serving, historically entrenched social and legal conventions that in fact undermine the privileged interests they were designed to protect will we be in a position to decide whether the very idea of racial classification is a viable one in the first place."

In their focus on the phenomenon of passing, the essays in this collection reveal the political motivations inherent in the origins and maintenance of identity categories and boundaries. And they suggest as well the especially well guarded boundaries demarcating race and gender. What these essays also make clear, however, is the positive potential of passing as a way of challenging those categories and boundaries. In its interrogation of the essentialism that is the foundation of identity politics, passing has the potential to create a space for creative self-determination and agency: the opportunity to construct new identities, to experiment with multiple subject positions, and to cross social and economic boundaries that exclude or oppress.

Notes

1. Facts about the life and murder of Teena Brandon / Brandon Teena, as well as quotes, are based on stories in the following news sources: *New York Times* 4 January 1994: A6; *Des Moines Register* 9 January 1994: 1; *Advocate* 8 March 1994: 28–30; *Village Voice* 19 April 1994: 24–30. These sources, plus letters in subsequent issues of the *Voice*, variously characterize Brandon and Brandon's life, generally reflecting societal uncertainty about transgendered individuals: Brandon is referred to as a transvestite, cross-dresser, transsexual, or "stone butch," and headlines featured such words as "charade" or "masquerade."

2. This discussion suggests the seriousness of purpose behind what I am calling "passing"; it therefore does not include such performances as minstrelsy. Nor does it consider instances of "camp" or "drag," parodies of gender in which the performer intends for the viewer to finally "read," or see through, the performance. This discussion also does not consider the case of transsexuals, those who wish to alter their physical body surgically so that it more closely conforms to their felt gender identity.

3. The *OED* defines "pass (for)" as "to be taken for, to be accepted, received, or held in repute as. Often with the implication of being something else." The implication of this definition is that the vague "something else" is an irreducible "being" or essence, a "true identity."

4. This is not to deny that other identities, such as "Christian" and "heterosex-

Introduction

ual," do not have great cultural exchange value. The focus here, however, is on identity categories as they are related not only to privilege and status but also to putative visibility.

5. For extensive discussions of the concept of "race," see Stepan, *The Idea of Race in Science*; Guillaumin, "The Idea of Race and Its Elevation to Autonomous, Scientific, and Legal Status"; and Outlaw, "Toward a Critical Theory of 'Race,'" and other essays in Goldberg, ed., *Anatomy of Racism*.

6. I take this phrase from an essay by Lawrence Wright, "One Drop of Blood," in which he discusses the U.S. census and the political forces that have through the two centuries of its existence affected the racial categories by which respondents were classified.

7. Winthrop Jordan's massive study of race in America, *White over Black*, is the most extensive history of black / white social and legal relations before the 1960s. See also Gossett, *Race: The History of an Idea in America*. Cheryl I. Harris, "Whiteness as Property," discusses the legal history of definitions of black and white and their implications.

8. Jordan observes that it is impossible to know how many slaves escaped by passing as white; passing depended on a "conspiracy of silence not only for the individual but for a biracial society which had drawn a rigid color line based on visibility" (174). Nevertheless, enough testimonies exist to suggest that it was not a rare phenomenon. See also Williamson, *New People*, and Harris, "Whiteness as Property."

9. This asymmetrical definition of race came to be known as the "one-drop rule"; its function, according to Paul Spickard, was to maintain "an absolute wall surrounding white dominance" (16).

10. *Plessy v. Ferguson* (1896) involved the claim of Plessy, whose heritage was "seven eighths Caucasian and one eighth African . . . that the mixture of colored blood was not discernible in him, and that he was entitled to every recognition, right, privilege and immunity secured to citizens of the United States of the white race." The Supreme Court upheld Louisiana law defining Plessy as Negro and at the same time sanctioned the constitutionality of "separate but equal" (Harris 1710).

11. Early examples are Bone, *The Negro Novel in America*, and Arthur Davis, *From the Dark Tower: Afro-American Writers, 1900–1960*. See also Washington, "The Mulatta Trap: Nella Larsen's Women of the 1920's," in *Invented Lives*.

12. Charles W. Chesnutt, James Weldon Johnson, Nella Larsen, and Jessie Fauset, for example, were all of mixed racial heritage.

13. On the ontology of "sex" and "gender," see Laqueur, *Making Sex*, and Fuss,

Essentially Speaking. On gender as cultural construction, see Butler, *Gender Trouble;* de Lauretis, *Technologies of Gender*; and Nicholson, "Interpreting *Gender.*"

14. At times in the past, even when women were not attempting to pass as men but merely adapting an item of men's clothing for ease and convenience, they have been accused of usurping male privilege. For example, in America in the 1850s, when numbers of women began wearing trousers (called "bloomers," after Amelia Bloomer, who popularized them), "there was a strong suspicion that trousers represented a usurpation of men's rights and prerogatives, and, as such, were an instrument of the newly organized Women's Rights movement" (Luck 200).

15. For extensive discussions of cross-dressing, see Bullough and Bullough, *Cross Dressing, Sex, and Gender,* and Garber, *Vested Interests.* Butler's discussion of *Paris Is Burning* in *Bodies That Matter* also addresses the issue of the readability of drag.

16. In Neil Jordan's 1992 film *The Crying Game,* the unveiling of Dil's male body causes in Fergus perhaps an extreme homophobic reaction: he becomes physically ill.

17. See Wheelwright, *Amazons and Military Maids*; Garber, *Vested Interests*; and Bullough and Bullough, *Cross Dressing.*

PART I

Passing

to Freedom

The Subaltern as Imperialist:

Speaking of Olaudah Equiano

MARION RUST

I

I have invoked my positionality in this awkward way so as to accentuate the fact that calling the place of the investigator into question remains a meaningless piety in many recent critiques of the sovereign subject. Thus, although I will attempt to foreground the precariousness of my position throughout, I know such gestures can never suffice. — Gayatri Chakravorty Spivak, "Can the Subaltern Speak?" 1988

If, then, the following narrative does not appear sufficiently interesting to engage general attention, let my motive be some excuse for its publication. I am not so foolishly vain as to expect from it either immortality or literary reputation. . . . Let it therefore be remembered that, in wishing to avoid censure, I do not aspire to praise. — Olaudah Equiano, *The Life of Olaudah Equiano*, 1789

*P*ositionality, place, foreground: one would think Gayatri Spivak were writing a travel narrative. A narrative, perhaps, like that of Olaudah Equiano, an Igbo African and a former British slave who served sea captains most of his life. Instead, Spivak sidles up to the "theoretical," whereas Equiano heads for the "conversational," to cite an opposition Spivak invokes (to undo) in the same essay (272). But the geographical lilt to the first epigraph is an excuse for suggesting that her project echoes his. Clearly, both writers share a melancholy anticipation of errors yet to come, endeavors for which they've risked their "I."

And for both, divided as they are by two hundred years, one danger is that "I" will come to stand for "Imperialist." Equiano's narrative, ostensibly intended to convince the British Parliament to make slavery a crime throughout its territories, is fodder for the premise that "abolition contained the seeds of empire," in the words of Patrick Brantlinger (186).

Spivak's theorization drags that premise into the present by suggesting that *all* Western intellectual discourse is imperialistic, in the sense that it silences those it would represent. Does "the subaltern cannot speak" (Spivak 308) mean that anyone who speaks is no longer a subaltern? It is the purpose of this essay to "use" *The Interesting Narrative of the Life of Olaudah Equiano, or Gustavus Vassa, the African, Written By Himself* to consider this question as it relates to the phenomenon of passing in its original sense—passing for white.[1] I conclude that Equiano's text, while it may pass as an imperialist production, also exists outside the category of imperialist discourse.

This is not to claim the same status for the argument here. Quotation marks around my "use" of this "prototype" (Gates, "Introduction" xiv) do not redeem this effort's exploitative aspect. The self-incriminatory edge to Spivak's conclusion that "the subaltern cannot speak" thus adds an element of discomfort to the attempt to speak about it. To consider one's disquisition implicated in another's silence should be upsetting for anyone who does more than listen.

How, then, is somebody who has committed herself to a discursive act, newly discomfited by its hazards, to do the right thing? Can an introductory apology, like the two that open this essay, manage to stick to "regret" without turning into apology's other meaning, "defense," further evidence of the aggression for which one is apologizing?

Both the "awkward" Spivak and the "not so vain as to expect" Equiano exclude the latter definition to the extent that they foreground humility and vulnerability. As a result, however, both end up proclaiming their modesty, an oxymoronic venture if ever there was one. But while these initial displays can't prevent the silencings that subsequent textual politics will bring about—they aren't much good as amulets—they do invite me, as reader, to remember that something is lost as I proceed and that, being lost, the reader is not to know what it was. I would like to invoke the same privilege for what follows.

II

"Passing" is possessed of many likenesses: impersonation, masquerade, drag, crossing over. Why, then, has recent criticism displayed a need to appropriate this abbreviation for "passing for white," resituating it in contexts of sexual as well as racial trauma? How does passing satisfy us in a way no other word can? One answer, I think, is that it evokes something the others with the possible exception of crossing over, revoke: namely, a quality of loss. Like its overlapping signs, passing describes an act of simulation, in which two states, being and not-being, assumption and revocation, inhere. But although words like the above synonyms enfranchise the former—the act of putting on, be it a mask or a pair of women's stockings or men's suspenders—it is the melancholy privilege of passing to foreground the latter—what is lost that's there. Indeed, as Judith Butler notes in a gloss of Nella Larsen's novel *Passing,* the word itself is a pun, which in addition to the common definition of "cross . . . the color line undetected" (Madigan 524) also signifies the ultimate turning away, death (Butler, *Bodies That Matter* 183). When one thinks of passing in this light, its recent adoption seems less strange than the persistent, almost manic euphemism of terms once employed in its stead. Passing also mocks our melancholy, ridiculing essentialist notions of a "true" self preceding, and corrupted by, its subsequent enactments.[2] In a sense, passing foregrounds what is *between*—between origin and enactment, body and gesture— calling into question all such fixed ways of determining identity.

As such, passing is like the water in Olaudah Equiano's text. Equiano— ex-slave and purchaser of slaves; African and Englishman; slave cargo turned sailor—is consistently engaged in the phenomenon we call passing. He is also consistently passing through the oceans that divide one geographic homeland from another. Water becomes the most important place in his *Life* not only because that's where he spends the most time but also because it's where he obtains the greatest authority. Rules that exclude him from full membership in London society don't apply there; for instance, black men and white women can marry "on the water," but not on land (86). Thus when he labels a ship called the *Royal George* "a little world" (65) because it has everything on it that he could find on land, one is also reminded that it's the only world where, occasionally, he gets called "Captain." Equiano may learn navigation so as to find his way to "Old England" (89), but through it, he also navigates a subjectivity that Old England would have inaugurated into oblivion.

The synecdochic relationship of water to this essay is reflected in the religious and philosophical import of water in Equiano's West African

Igbo homeland. The Igbo, like many other West African peoples, attribute divine characteristics to what John Mbiti calls "major objects of nature," among them, seas, rivers, and lakes. As forms of spiritual being, these bodies of water are thus part of an intermediate sphere between the "Sasa" realm of the living and the "Zamani" realm of the afterlife: Mbiti claims that such objects "are 'closer' to men, than is God." For Equiano, then, water may have served as a transitional medium in both physical and spiritual terms and a semidivine one where his greater powers might be understood as concordant with his greater nearness to an omnipotent Creator (Mbiti 77, 163).

Whatever its spiritual associations, however, water's pragmatic function—as a medium for the transportation of goods to buyers—seems to have predominated in Equiano's motivations as he records them. Near the end of his seafaring days, he even includes slaves in the bargain, which suggests the degree to which he has approximated imperialist economic ethics: "Our vessel being ready to sail for the Musquito shore, I went with the Doctor on board a Guineaman, to purchase some slaves to carry with us, and cultivate a plantation" (*Life* 154). In so doing, he approaches the limit of his precarious self-articulation as both African and European. But no matter how skilled Equiano's articulation of English imperialist ideologies, enough ruptures and silences remain in his text finally to subvert those same ideologies. Silence becomes a form of speech in Equiano's *Life*; and it is that silence we must read to gain fully his significance to an understanding of the effect of imperialist ethics on those who both benefit from and despise them.

III

Olaudah Equiano's case is an interesting one because he plays the role of the speaker and of the silenced. As a former slave and a black man, denied privileges accorded whites even after purchasing his freedom, he is an obvious candidate for subalternity. As a writer representing himself to thousands (the *Life* appeared in eight British editions and one American during his lifetime [Gates, "Introduction" ix]), as a black who repeatedly exercises authority over other blacks, as an international merchant who includes slaves in his cargo, and as a man who perceives women as means to the fulfillment of his sex, he closely approximates the elitist ideologies of his white male mentors. Equiano positions himself as a student, when not a servant, throughout the text: while he is quick to credit all the masters from whom he has learned everything from hairdressing to the French horn, he never mentions teaching anyone else. Nevertheless, in "dedicating" the narrative, "the chief design of which is to excite in your august assemblies a sense of compassion for the miseries which the Slave-Trade has entailed on my unfortunate countrymen," to the lords and commons of the Parliament of Britain (3), Equiano educates; he participates in the "Western intellectual production" that Spivak acknowledges is, "in many ways, complicit with Western international economic interests" (294, 297). That this transition occurs in the name of ending oppression reaffirms the difficulty of speaking from a position of innocence. That it is never complete but results in an uneasy tug-of-war that fractures subjectivity suggests that the snail-like "track of ideology" glimpsed by Spivak is more than a single line (272): viewed, perhaps impossibly, from the seat of oppressor and subaltern simultaneously, it is a web.

Maybe the most obvious symbol of the interdependence of abolition and imperialism in this text is the means by which Equiano obtains "freedom": he buys it. In so doing, he takes a step from the mode of production characteristic of his African homeland (which as he describes it is consistent with Marx's definition of "use-value") to the capitalist dependence on "exchange value" (that is, profit) of his European destination. Another way to view these two economic realms is through Samir Amin's differentiation between capitalism and everything prior: "In all earlier social systems, the economic phenomenon is transparent. By this I mean that the destination of that which is produced is immediately visible: The major part of production is directly consumed by the producers themselves. . . . Market exchange and wage labor are, of course, not entirely absent, but they remain limited in their range and marginal in their social and economic scope" (1). Equiano himself suggests a metaphor for the economic community he leaves behind as the space defined by the Igbo "New Year" celebration: "We compute the year from the day on which the sun crosses the line, and on its setting that evening, there is a general shout throughout the land; at least I can speak from my own knowledge, throughout our vicinity" (20). Igbo economic exchange extended, similarly, as far as one could make actual human contact: there were few, if any, middlepeople. It was a form of interaction for which "science of economics," in Amin's language (1), or "philosophy," in V. Y. Mudimbe's, would not be as accurate as Mudimbe's word for African precolonial or "traditional" ways of knowing, *gnosis*, which includes the element of "acquaintance with someone" (ix).

In *The Invention of Africa*, Mudimbe links colonialism with imperialism, alternately considering the latter the cause of the former or the two as a single phenomenon, "colonial imperialism" (2–3).[3] It seems fair, then, to use one of the three "main keys" he devises to account for "colonial organization" in a discussion of Equiano's insertion into the imperialist order. Number three is "the manner of managing ancient organizations and implementing new modes of production" or "the integration of local economic histories into the Western perspective" (Mudimbe 2), and Equiano demonstrates precisely this when he discusses his purchase of freedom after describing the economic ways of his homeland. In sharp contrast to the international exchange market already characteristic of late-eighteenth-century Europe, Equiano depicts the Igbo economy as local, dependent on trade rather than purchase, and dedicated to "improving," rather than transforming / exploiting, natural resources: "As we live in a country where nature is prodigal of her favors, our wants are few, and easily supplied; of course we have few manufactures. . . . In such a state money is of little use. . . . All our industry is exerted to improve those blessings of nature" (16–17). The Igbo "mode of production" is also communal rather than competitive: when a house is to be built, "the whole neighborhood afford their unanimous assistance" (16). Even their dealings with slaves seemed, by contrast with those of the European, oriented to "acquaintance" rather than profit: "How different was their condition from that of the slaves in the West Indies! With us they do no more work than other members of the community, than even their master: their food, clothing, and lodging, were nearly the same as theirs" (19). Equiano shares the "shock" of his master, then, to see slaves sold by the pound in the European-controlled islands (79).

To escape being weighed, Equiano learns the way of the masters, which is to view objects as signs, markers in an international economy. It is only by learning the difference between "provisions" and "cargo" that Equiano "acquires a sum of money sufficient to purchase" his manumission (96). His last owner is the first to point out the change a "thing" undergoes when it is exchanged for cash: "He thought by carrying one little thing or other to different places to sell I might make money" (92). In fact, Equiano has already been doing just that, starting with a glass tumbler that he bought for a half bit in St. Eustatia and sold for a bit in Montserrat and working his way up to "near three hundred percent, by four barrels of pork I brought from Charlestown" (97).

The loving detail Equiano bestows on each transaction suggests the significance to him of his "mastery" of international capitalism: when he exclaims at "finding myself master of about forty-seven pounds" (99), the choice of label suggests that he is not only purchasing manumission but also legitimacy within the world into which he has been kidnapped. Simultaneously, he is coming to see his former peers as distinct from him, calling them by the names used by the imperialist traders whom he now includes in his own syntactic subjecthood: "We took in a live cargo, as we call a cargo of slaves" (98). Merchanthood continues to serve as the shield between him and slavery, as he dedicates page after page to his skill at turning a profit.

Not only does active participation in colonial imperialism enable Equiano to purchase his own freedom, but it is also key to his argument for an end to British trade in African slaves. Equiano gives the lie to the self-satisfaction of those British who view abolition as a utopian aim, a step away from crass mercantile interests, when he concludes his narrative with a direct appeal to the pocketbooks, and not the hearts, of the lords and commons and their charge. Africans can't be "civilized," he argues, until they are no longer victims of "the inhuman traffic of slavery" (175). The trick is, that once they are, they will become willing participants in all other forms of British "traffic."

I doubt not, if a system of commerce was established in Africa, the demand for manufactures will most rapidly augment, as the native inhabitants will insensibly adopt the British fashions, manners, customs, &c. In proportion to the civilization, so will be the consumption of British manufactures. . . . A commercial intercourse with Africa opens an inexhaustible source of wealth to the manufacturing interests of Great Britain; and to all which the slave-trade is an objection. (175–76)

Brantlinger writes that "the British began to see themselves less and less as perpetrators of the slave trade and more and more as the potential saviors of the African" (192). Equiano makes clear that such self-deceptive complacency required merely that one form of trade be supplanted by another, one more profitable because it depended on a need that all Africans could be assumed to develop, rather than making enemies of the many for the benefit of a few. Abolition of the African slave trade would make consumers out of former potential slaves: that is, Parliament would do well by doing good.

Mudimbe includes "the reformation of natives' minds" on his list of forms of colonial organization (2). And it is in this category, more than any other, that Equiano at times assumes the voice of an imperialist speaking for abolition. Here, imperialism is renamed "refinement" and is acquired through such things as "manners and customs," another phrase for capitalist modes of consumption. If the British would only free the Africans, Equiano asserts, they would find them equally capable of refined manners. "Are there not causes enough to which the apparent inferiority of an African may be ascribed," he asks,

without limiting the goodness of God, and supposing He forebore to stamp understanding on what is certainly his own image, because "carved in ebony"? Might it not naturally be ascribed to their situation? . . . But above all, what advantages do not a refined people possess over those who are rude and uncultivated! Let the polished and haughty European recollect that his ancestors were once like the Africans, uncivilized and even barbarous. (24)

By placing the African and the European on a continuum and offering the British a view of themselves as children, Equiano accomplishes one of his most extraordinary rhetorical feats, one perhaps even more effective than the appeal to mercy or greed, in that it brings the problem closer to home, turning the slave from a "he" or an "it" into an "I" for the European reader, asking Europeans to take care of themselves, rather than some distant other. But how stable is Equiano's place in this classificatory scheme? How certain is his claim to the "new" world? Equiano is at constant risk of being pushed "backward" into the land of the slave;

and his ambivalence about the "monsters" he has come to call friends reveals itself by several forms of rupture in what might otherwise seem a masterpiece of Western imperialist discourse.

IV

Among the unheard-of wonders Equiano witnesses after being kidnapped from his place of birth are flying fish, snow, clocks, portraits, and slaves who dine with their masters. According to the custom of his youth, only one practice divided slaves from the families to which they belonged: "They were not permitted to eat with those who were free-born" (19). Thus, while Equiano is still in Africa, traveling with his captors, his determination to escape home is "strengthened by the mortifying circumstance of not daring to eat with the free-born children, although I was mostly their companion" (27). Just about the time he stops trying to escape, deciding "that any attempt to return home would be hopeless" (27), he is astonished to find that when "mealtime came, I was led into the presence of my mistress, and ate and drank before her with her son. This filled me with astonishment; and I could scarcely avoid expressing my surprise that the young gentleman should suffer me, who was bound, to eat with him who was free" (30).

Equiano's astonishment soon changes its tenor, however; despite "the Enlightenment belief that all people should be treated equally under the law" (Brantlinger 192), Equiano repeatedly encounters distinctions made between him and his surrounding Europeans, many of them written into the law, even after he has bought his way into "people." As a result of this dislocation and subsequent oppression, the character he makes of himself in this narrative maintains a sense of having just sat down to a dinner to which he doesn't know why he was invited, with people he doesn't quite trust. In the following discussion of the way Equiano's subalternity pushes against his imperialist pass, the emphasis will be on his mode of self-construction: to be crude, it will be on the "style," rather than the "content," of his discourse. As such, it will echo chapter 2 of Mudimbe's *The Invention of Africa,* which introduces marginality as a way of speaking, rather than, or at the very least coeval with, a condition of the spoken-about.

Equiano introduces the topic of his exclusion from the rights of his white neighbors by describing his sale, without warning, from one master to another.

Captain Doran asked me if I knew him; I answered I did not. "Then," said he, "you are now my slave." I told him my master could not sell me to him or anyone else. "Why," said he, "did not your master buy you?" I confessed he did. "But I have served him," said I, "many years, and he has taken all my wages and prize-money, for I only got six-pence during the war. Besides this, I have been baptized; and, by the laws of the land, no one has a right to sell me:" And I added, that I had heard a lawyer, and others, at different times tell my master so. They both then said, that those people were not my friends: but I replied—it was very extraordinary that other people did not know the law as well as they. Upon this, Captain Doran said I talked too much English, and if I did not behave myself well and be quiet, he had a method on board to make me. (65)

The progression of this passage from a discussion of legal rights to a resort to force is characteristic of subsequent outrages against Equiano, most of which have to do with being ripped off during commercial trans-actions. Clearly, the fact that Equiano "talks English" cannot turn him into an Englishman—and things improve little upon his manumission. After being freed, Equiano is, in order, almost flogged for beating another man's slave (102); excluded from testifying to his master's having reneged on a loan because "throughout the West Indies, no Black man's testimony is admitted, on any occasion, against any white person whatever" (119); forced, on his would-be way from the "Grenades" (now French Guyana) to Montserrat, to "advertise myself, and give notice of my going off the island . . . this degrading necessity . . . every Black man is under, of advertising himself like a slave, when he leaves an island" (120); denied payment by a "white man" who "threatened me and another Black man he had bought goods of, so that we found we were like to get more blows than payment" (127); and threatened with prison by "one Mr. Smith," who refused to pay twenty-five pounds, offering instead to "say I was going to set his house on fire; at another [time] he would swear I was going to run away with his slaves. I was astonished at this usage from a person who was in the situation of a gentleman; but I had no alternative, and was therefore obliged to submit" (128).

After this passage, the accounts of misuse for being black dwindle;

perhaps Equiano has learned, with his developing skill at navigating this white, seafaring culture, to avoid them, or perhaps he has simply become more used to having "no alternative" and forbears to mention them. Perhaps he suspects they would diminish the coherency of a narrative increasingly dedicated to modeling all society on the British pattern. Whatever the reason, they are enough to inform other, less explicit, silences—I equate being forced to "submit" with silence—in the text.

Gates speaks of "two distinct voices" in *The Life of Olaudah Equiano* ("Introduction" xiv). What might be most interesting about these voices is the space between them, which on the page is almost nil. Yet one wonders by what course a mind gets from a lament of the horrors of the Middle Passage to a quiet report on fish. The following example begins with a surge of captured Africans attempting to throw themselves overboard:

Two of the wretches were drowned; but they got the other, and afterward flogged him unmercifully, for thus attempting to prefer death to slavery. In this manner we continued to undergo more hardships than I can now relate. . . . Many a time we were near suffocation from the want of fresh air, being deprived thereof for days together.

During our passage I first saw flying fishes, which surprised me very much; they used frequently to fly across the ship, and many of them fell on deck. (36)

This passage is remarkable for its reverse symbolic beauty: some creatures throw themselves over, others into. And this is certainly an attractive way to view the ubiquitous shifts from the "revelation of atrocities" Brantlinger considers characteristic of antislavery writing to the more detached reportage on climates natural and social (189). Another might be Equiano's stated desire to spare the reader what might otherwise become a limitless, and deadening, description of torture. But the shifts from anguished collective autobiography to apparently neutral nature writing offer neither sufficient symbolic coherence nor relief from atrocity to complete either explanation.

These shifts seem to enact, perhaps more "coherently" than smoother passages, the paradox of a black man trying to make himself understood to the predominantly white culture responsible for his enslavement. Equiano's most repeated description of his emotional state bolsters this attempt at an explanation: in the style of the American captivity narrative popular shortly before publication of this work, Equiano repeatedly describes being cast from one extreme to another, as in "Thus, at the very moment I dreamed of the greatest happiness, I found myself most miserable" (31). Silence may be the most accurate depiction of what appears a ruptured, random existence: to the extent that language is, and depicts, meaning as order, it is already a lie, an inauguration of a subject that is other than the "I" undergoing representation.

If one attempts to view the entire narrative in one glance and to make the space in which Equiano's "distinct voices" are contained not sentences or paragraphs but chapters or beginning and end, a no less mystifying series of ruptures appears in his representation of whites. The horror with which Equiano describes his initial encounters with a creature entirely unknown to him seems irreconcilable with his final positing of the white as a model that the black may hope to attain. And it is only by a fascinating act of transposition that he manages it at all.

Whiteness, according to the child Equiano, is the same as disfigurement: "I remember while in Africa to have seen three Negro children, who were tawny, and another quite white, who were universally regarded as deformed by myself and the natives in general" (17). On first meeting the crew of sailors who are to carry him away from Africa, who prod and toss him around to see if he is worth the space on board, Equiano adds evil and danger to the list of qualities associated with whiteness, being "persuaded that I had got into a world of bad spirits, and that they were going to kill me. Their complexions too, differing so much from ours, their long hair, and the language they spoke, which was very different from any I had ever heard, united to confirm me in this belief" (33). Everything the crew does increases its diabolic power: "The white men had some spell or magic they put in the water, when they liked, in order to stop the vessel. I . . . really thought they were spirits" (34). Nothing that happens to him during the Middle Passage improves this opinion: "Every circumstance I met with served only to render my state more painful, and heighten my apprehension and my opinion of the cruelty of the whites" (36).

How, then, is one to account for the difference between a group of monsters whose habits "debauch the taste" of natives (15) and one whose "civilization" Equiano comes to hope will serve them as a guiding light

(176)? Equiano accomplishes the feat in two stages. First, he perceives that whites are not all the same; among their differences, some are less monstrous than others. The "white men" who originally represent uniform power, being equated with the king of Benin as the only thing in Equiano's childhood to which he was subjected without acquaintance (12), begin to assume distinct visages during his second voyage: "Every body on board used me very kindly, quite contrary to what I had seen of any white people before; I therefore began to think that they were not all of the same disposition" (40).

Second, he employs a brilliant metonymy, by which membership in a nation is substituted for "complexion." When Equiano is speaking about "white men," he has little good to say; but once they are divided into "Europeans" and "British," the euphemisms begin to attract compliments. Equiano achieves at least two things by this shift: he is able to distinguish between bad whites, who are mostly Europeans living in the West Indies, and good ones, possessed of "the freedom which diffuses health and prosperity throughout Britain" (80). And he is able to qualify for membership in the latter group and thus find a place for himself, to himself, in previously entirely hostile surroundings.

Thus Equiano preserves meaning for his existence and dignity for himself by making geography coeval with moral states. He can thereby turn a forced, meaningless journey into a pilgrimage, in which "the poor man came over the sea to London" (139). And he is able to smooth over ruptures in his past that would otherwise threaten to turn him into at least two entirely distinct and antagonistic beings, African and Englishman, slave and purchaser of slaves. Equiano creates continuity by phrasing his future as his coming full circle rather than drifting off the horizon, with the dream of "returning to England, where my heart had always been" (107).

To the extent that this dream comes true, Equiano uses nationness to escape racism, invoking precisely the quality in nationalism that Benedict Anderson finds crucial: "It is the magic of nationalism to turn chance into destiny" (12). For Equiano probably more obviously than for most nationalists, the nation is an act of imagination, an alternative assertion of membership in a community now that the communal New Year's shout of his Igbo homeland is no longer an option. His is a textbook case of Anderson's thesis:

The nation . . . is an imagined political community . . . *imagined* because the members of even the smallest nation will never know most of their fellow-members, meet them, or even hear of them, yet in the minds of each lives the image of their communion. . . . It is imagined as a *community*, because, regardless of the actual inequality and exploitation that may prevail in each, the nation is always conceived as a deep, horizontal comradeship. (7)

But Equiano's example also indicates the dangers of resting too long in the imagination. For, regardless of his seeming optimism, the above-described instances of oppression indicate that the sense of "comradeship" is not generally shared by his fellow Westerners, including the British. Equiano may use "nationness" to turn a kidnapping into a pilgrimage, but this does not erase the fact that his journey away from Africa was clearly not chosen, nor was the death of others on board or that of slaves throughout the Americas and Europe. While his rhetorical feat may reveal a need to impose "coherency" on the narratives that people make of their pasts, it shouldn't trick one into ignoring the necessary incompletion of any such attempt in the face of what Spivak labels the "macrological . . . relationship between global capitalism . . . and nation-state alliances" (279).

That Equiano allows his terrified child's voice, so contrary to everything the adult utters, to remain in this text and that he doesn't smooth over the bumpy tracks between descriptions of torture and scenes of tranquillity indicate that he does not excuse colonial imperialists, which to a certain extent also means he's not excusing himself. Neither, however, is he pronouncing judgment. Instead, Equiano allows contradiction to keep its place in the text; mediation takes the place of either / or. In regard to nationality, this mediation becomes nostalgia; having learned to think in terms of places to which one belongs and having identified himself as belonging to England, he can still turn back to Africa with the words, "Whether the love of one's country be real or imaginary, a lesson of reason or an instinct of nature, I still look back with pleasure on the first scenes of my life" (25).

It has been my goal to affirm the claim that "the relationship between global capitalism (exploitation in economics) and nation-state alliances (dominance in geopolitics) is so macrological that it cannot account for the micrological texture of power" (Spivak 279), in other words, that

Equiano's *Life,* while testimony to the alliance between British abolition-ism and British imperialism, also engages another dimension in which Equiano's self-constitution as an agent of national imperialism does not undo his resistance to those same forces. Equiano's narrative thus be-comes an example of that "radical practice" Spivak suggests should "at-tend to this double session of representations [by proxy and by portrait] rather than reintroduce the individual subject through totalizing concepts of power and desire." In arguing for an end to slavery, Equiano is de-manding that blacks obtain "representation in the political context" into which they have been kidnapped. In refusing the play of black African and British subject to allow his "representation as staging," his "portrait" rather than his "proxy," to make him "transparent," in denying the pos-sibility that one could cancel out the other, he is denying the capacity of "desire as the determining interest" to "restore the category of the sov-ereign subject." Rather than become the monolithic "other" that theorists from his time to ours would have him be, he enacts the faceted subjec-tivity that those "who are named and differentiated" would have be ex-clusively theirs. In so doing, he undoes this essay's introductory opposi-tion between theory and conversation to become a "responsible critic," refusing "the refusal of the sign-system" so "that the impossibility of . . . interested individualistic refusals of the institutional privileges of power bestowed on the subject is taken seriously" (Spivak 272–80 passim). In his printed word, fear, courtesy, love, anger, optimism, and despair over-lie each other in such a mass of discontinuity that not one can be ignored in its specificity or merely pitted as opposite to another, destined to be subsumed into it on the text's way to harmonious resolution. In sum, the text is itself a rupture, a niche in the wall of monolithic Western imperi-alistic discourse, despite the fact that it pleads for the refinement of Africa.

If Olaudah Equiano's journey shows us anything about the phenome-non we now call "passing," it is that we must resist collapsing its doubling into the racist paradigm that pits integrity against compromise, identity against simulation. Rather, passing is merely one more indication that subjectivity involves fracture—that no true self exists apart from its mul-tiple, simultaneous enactments. Equiano does not become less of a revo-lutionary by becoming more of an imperialist; in fact, it is only by becoming a successful trader and subsequent propagandist for abolition phrased as the victory of empire that he is able to articulate—and have heard—his imperturbable dissatisfaction with European intrusions on African identities. Equiano passes for civilized European imperialist trader to mark that frame as inherently self-deluded, complicating its simplistic self-articulation with yet another proof that, in Terry Eagleton's summation of Walter Benjamin's words, "there was no document of civilization that was not also a record of barbarism" (32).

That the correlations between civilized/barbaric and African/European become so tortured in Equiano's document as to elude any final classification goes to show only that the paradigms themselves are inadequate. Of course, it is tempting to align the civilized with the African and have done with it; but after reading the *Life,* any such reversal of the cardinal hierarchy of imperialist discourse seems almost criminally simplistic. An informed reading of Equiano's text refuses such easy answers, scraping them away to reveal underlying structures of power that serve to make any uniform notion of subjectivity nonsensical and almost charmingly naïve.

Notes

1. George M. Fredrickson dates this phrase and phenomenon to at least the late eighteenth century, where it was an "institutionalized . . . characteristic of the Cape Colony of South Africa" (245, 247).

2. As Judith Butler writes in regard to gender, passing "fully subverts the distinction between inner and outer psychic space and effectively mocks both the expressive model of [race] and the notion of a true [racial] identity" (*Gender Trouble* 137). In substituting race for gender in the above citation, I engage a question articulated in her next book: "What would it mean, on the other hand, to consider the assumption of sexual positions, the disjunctive ordering of the human as 'masculine' or 'feminine' as taking place not only through a heterosexualizing symbolic with its taboo on homosexuality, but through a complex set of racial injunctions which operate in part through the taboo on miscegenation?" (*Bodies That Matter* 167).

3. On Grover Clark's *The Balance Sheet of Imperialism,* for instance, Mudimbe comments, "Grover Clark demonstrated that colonialism was not only economically irrational but also ruinous for the colonial powers" (2).

"A Most Respectable Looking Gentleman":

Passing, Possession, and Transgression in

Running a Thousand Miles for Freedom

ELLEN M. WEINAUER

*I*n a 1992 *Elle* article entitled "Life's a Drag," performance artist RuPaul asserted: "The truth is that I'm a man. The illusion is I look like a woman. But the illusion is truer" (33). *Elle* magazine is, perhaps, an unlikely place to find the way into and through an antebellum slave narrative. But in this remark, RuPaul offers a formulation that illuminates the complex dynamics of the narrative this essay addresses: William Craft's *Running a Thousand Miles for Freedom*. RuPaul suggests that in drag, the very notions of truth and illusion are caught up in an intimate and endlessly mirroring relation. In *Mother Camp*, a study of female impersonators and the cultural practice of drag, Esther Newton argues that "at the most complex, [drag] is a double inversion that says, 'appearance is an illusion.' Drag says, 'my "outside" appearance is feminine, but my essence "inside" . . . is masculine.' At the same time it symbolizes the opposite inversion: 'my appearance "outside" . . . is masculine but my essence "inside" . . . is feminine'" (103). But, Judith Butler points out in citing Newton's observation, since these "claims to truth contradict one another," "gender significations" are "displace[d] . . . from the discourse of truth and falsity" (*Gender Trouble* 137). It is on this level that RuPaul's formulation becomes especially challenging: in asserting that the illusion of appearing like a woman is truer than the truth of being a man, she puts the ostensibly discrete categories of "man" and "woman" into play. RuPaul denaturalizes the naturalized essences called *sex* and *gender*, giving the lie to the notion that gender identity is a prediscursive truth grounded in clearly legible bodies.

Such contemporary theorizing about the practice of drag provides a lens through which to read William Craft's 1860 narrative, although the cross-dressing that occurs in this text goes to very different ends — namely, escape from slavery: "[I]t occurred to me that, as my wife was nearly white, I might get her to disguise herself as an invalid gentleman, and assume to be my master, while I could attend as his slave, and that in this manner we might effect our escape" (29). Thus does William Craft introduce his readers to the elaborate, double-passing plot by which he and his wife, Ellen, eventually reach the free states. And from this introduction to the plan of escape it becomes clear that, as Marjorie Garber has observed, in *Running a Thousand Miles for Freedom* "transvestism" is "deployed strategically as disguise": for Ellen Craft, male attire serves to secure a literal freedom from the bonds of slavery (282).

But if the aims of Ellen Craft's cross-dressing are quite different from those of RuPaul, some of the effects prove to be the same. For the Crafts, the crossing of the boundary from South to North becomes contingent on the crossing of other boundaries, of the limits whereby identity is conventionally fixed: gender, race, class—Ellen traverses the dividing lines of each, becoming in the course of the narrative black and white, slave and owner, woman and man, wife and master. Drawing the lines of these categories in order to (double-)cross them, Ellen sets in motion questions about authentic, essential identity. Like RuPaul's transvestism, Ellen Craft's cross-dressing serves ultimately to challenge the status of (only apparently) "natural" categories.

Running a Thousand Miles for Freedom thus becomes a disruptive text— a text that attempts to unsettle not only the legal institution of slavery but also the normative categories that underwrite it. But, even as we watch Craft the narrator turn this maze of articulated identities to his ideological use, we witness a reemergence of one "pure" category, one fixed boundary: Craft insists, finally, on the natural status of gendered categories, writing Ellen into her proper place within them. Unlike the meanings assigned to race and class memberships, meanings that Craft presents as discursive, interested constructions, "woman" is assigned a meaning that is fixed, immutable, and presumably disinterested. Ellen's masculine persona is an illusion, Craft tries to insist; she is "true" only as a "woman"— only as a true woman and an antebellum wife.

Craft makes quite obvious efforts to vouch for Ellen's true womanly nature: having applauded the fact that, in her disguise, she "made a most respectable looking gentleman," Craft moves to offer quick reassurance that "my wife had no ambition whatever to assume this disguise, and would not have done so had it been possible to have obtained her liberty by more simple means" (35). For Garber, this move suggests that "respectability" is "very much on William Craft's mind" (284) throughout the narrative. Indeed, as much as Craft is interested in assuring his readers of Ellen's fundamental respectability, he wants to bear witness to his own. Craft seeks acknowledgment not only as a "respectable looking gentleman" but also as a man, as a person.

Placed in the context of the antebellum slave narrative, this desire is not in itself surprising. For, as James Olney has argued, the slave narrative constitutes, by definition, the slave narrator's effort to "underwrite" his "very being": in the "lettered utterance" of the narrative is "assertion of identity, and in identity is freedom—freedom from slavery, . . . freedom from non-being" (157). Thus, *Running a Thousand Miles for Freedom* is necessarily the story of a fugitive slave struggling to locate identity, to find some ground on which to effect his transformation from legal nonbeing to being. But what is surprising—or, perhaps more precise, what is telling—is how that transformation is at last effected: on the figure of an explicitly gendered Ellen Craft; more fundamental, on the legalized figure of the antebellum wife. Finally, Craft relies on some of the very categories that his own text seeks to complicate and from which he would free both himself and his wife. The fact that he does so—that his narrative thus comes to argue against itself—bears witness not to Craft's failures but rather to the tenacity of (white and male) legal norms in the production of subjectivity in antebellum America.

In the winter of 1836–37, feminist activist Ernestine Rose circulated a petition demanding that the New York State Legislature amend the law that prevented married women from holding property in their own name. Although this early petition was largely unsuccessful ("After a good deal of trouble, I obtained five signatures," Rose herself later reported [Stanton, Anthony, and Gage 99]), Rose remained committed to the crusade for legislative reform of marital property rights. And, at a time when organized agitation on behalf of women was in its fledgling stages and was borrowing much from the more established—if no less marginalized—antislavery movement, Rose insisted on the significance of this early feminist issue by uniting her claims about married women's proprietary disenfranchisement to the issue of chattel slavery in the United States. "Woman is a slave from the cradle to the grave," she once asserted. "Father, guardian, husband—master still. One conveys her, like a piece of property, over to the other" (qtd. in Basch 162).

In presenting woman's condition as a form of slavery, in suggesting that both marriage and slavery are property relations that effectively convert (black and female) subjects into objects of exchange, Rose makes use of a trope that was to become common in antebellum feminist rhetoric. Many of the early leaders in the American feminist movement—Elizabeth Cady Stanton, Lucy Stone, Abby Kelley—had first entered the realm of political activism and agitation through their work in the antislavery movement.[1] And many of these women contended that it was precisely their antislavery work that led them to an initial awareness of what they took to be the imprisoning shackles of American womanhood. In 1838, in fact, Abby Kelley acknowledged this ideological debt explicitly, asserting that "in striving to strike [the slave's] irons off, we found most surely that we were manacled ourselves" (qtd. in Hersh 34).

The exploitation at work in the woman-as-slave analogy is clear. By insisting that their condition was akin to that of slaves, white women subsumed difference and, with it, the much more tangible experience of literal enslavement. For the slaves on whose behalf Abby Kelley agitated, for example, "irons" had a material rather than simply a figurative existence.[2] Ernestine Rose's remark exhibits a similar conflation. Her initial assertion that a "woman is a slave" is undercut in the slippage that follows: woman's enslavement is manifested, Rose says, in her passage, "like a piece of property," from one man to another. The slave, however, is not "like" a piece of property—by definition, he or she *is* a piece of property.

In overlooking (and so, simultaneously, marking) the distinction between the situation of the married woman and the slave, Rose's declaration begs a crucial question: What happens when the married woman is a slave, when the two figures—the wife and the slave—are one and the same? An analogue assumes separation; it is an assertion of the likeness between two separate entities. But in the body of the slave-wife, the analogy collapses. And in the body of the slave-wife, two separate juridical systems—matrimony and slavery—enter into competition and collide in their claims. As each system claims an absolute proprietary control over its subject, the subject who is both female *and* black is displaced, exiled from any normative subject-position. The slave-wife thus incorporates a collision of mutually exclusive subject-positions—she is a virtually impossible subjectivity, a subjectivity for which the law does not account.

In *Democracy in America,* Alexis de Tocqueville identified what he understood to be the "profound and natural antipathy between the institution of marriage and that of slavery" (qtd. in Grossberg 132). This antipathy was recognized and codified by Southern slaveholders, who disallowed civil marriage between slaves. In his study of domestic and family law, Michael Grossberg argues that the prohibition on slave marriage was based not only on the "denial of consensual ability to slaves" but also on the perception that, should a slave marry, the "duties" of matrimony, or "coverture," would compete with the "duties" of slavery (130). Among the duties that both slavery and marriage conferred on their black / female subjects was a surrender of the notion of subjectivity itself. The slave, for example, was deemed to acquire "meaning" only in relation to his or her master: "The slave was . . . a body with natural movements, but without its own reason, an existence entirely absorbed in another. The proprietor of this thing, . . . the soul and the reason of this body, the source of this life, was the master," historian Henri Wallon wrote in 1879 (qtd. in Patterson 4). Such a process of legal absorption has parallels in the structure of antebellum marriage. According to William Blackstone, whose *Commentaries on the Laws of England* became a virtual handbook of the common law for American legal practitioners, "the very being or legal existence of the woman is suspended during the marriage, or at least is incorporated and consolidated into that of her husband, under whose wing, protection, and *cover,* she performs every thing" (1:430). Thus, in the words of legal historian Norma Basch, laws of coverture "created an equation in which one plus one equaled one" by "erasing the female one" (17). Having been absorbed into her husband, the married woman, or *feme covert,* lost all rights of property and procedure: her spouse owned her personal estate, gained the rights to manage her real property, and could claim her wages. She could not make contracts, incur debt, engage in trade, or execute a will.

An alienation of self from self thus becomes the modus operandi of laws of coverture as well as laws of slavery. If the antislavery feminists' use of the woman-as-slave analogy veered into appropriation, then, it nonetheless came of an awareness that, as Karen Sanchez-Eppler has written, "personhood can be annihilated and a person owned, absorbed, and un-named" (31). Under the guise of the allegedly "natural" subjugation of those both black and female to those white and male, the law worked to deny to both slaves and married women any sort of recogniz-able subject-position. And this continuity leads, in the instance of the female slave who considers herself a wife, to an inevitable confrontation. When brought together to describe one body—the body of the woman who is at once slave *and* wife—the systems of slavery and marriage enter into competition, each one seeking to exert an absolute proprietary con-trol over the female subject.

An early Pennsylvania Supreme Court case reveals the ways in which matrimony and slavery make these absolute claims. In 1814, George Stephens, a free black man, attempted to win the legal freedom of his fugitive slave wife by exploiting antebellum laws of coverture. Stephens's wife had escaped slavery in Maryland and fled to Pennsylvania, where she and George Stephens married. When Mrs. Stephens's master, Mr. Clements, came north to find and reclaim her, he struck a bargain with his fugitive slave: she agreed to return to Maryland as an indentured servant, with his promise that after three years, she would be emancipated. George Stephens, however, sought a writ of habeas corpus on behalf of his wife, contesting Clements's right to take her to Maryland. In court, he chal-lenged the agreement between master and slave, arguing that "his wife's legal subservience to him . . . precluded her from making a contract without his consent" (Grossberg 130). Despite its ingenuity, Stephens's bid for his wife's freedom was unsuccessful: the court decided against him, on the basis that his wife's status " 'is totally different from that of a free woman' and that therefore the common-law disabilities [of cover-ture] did not apply to her" (130). Recognizing that the husband's claims cannot be reconciled to those of the master, the court made the predictable choice as to whose claims to the slave-wife ought to triumph.

The notion of "consent" that is so central to this case dramatizes the slave-wife's double displacement in law. Neither slave nor *feme covert* can consent to a contract without authorization from master or husband. Since both husband and slaveholder have the legal capacity to decide on the woman's behalf, the issue becomes the woman herself and whose right of consent—that of Mr. Stephens or Mr. Clements—is primary. Significantly, Mrs. Stephens can be released from her bargain with her master only on the basis of her *un*freedom: her inability to make a con-tract, to consent, to choose in her own name. She must exist as the property of her husband to escape existence as the property of her master.[3] Willed out of the case as willful subject, the slave-wife becomes instead the site of a battle between two juridical systems, each seeking the exclusive right to identify and represent her.

Thus, what de Tocqueville called the "antipathy" between marriage and slavery is a product of the conflict between the two systems—a product of a continuity of claims based on gender on the one hand and race on the other. The slave-wife experiences a subordination that is impossibly redundant: she cannot be a wife because she is "by nature" black and a slave; she cannot be a slave because she is "by nature" female and a wife. The slave-wife, doubly negated, acquires a complex status: a legal nonentity twice over, she is structured by categories that fail, finally, to account for her.

Ironically, though, in embodying multiple (and legally contradictory) identities, the slave-wife becomes a figure who disturbs the smooth functioning of the same legal structures that would define and delimit her. The law would have her be either black/slave or female/wife: according to Kimberle Crenshaw, the law seeks to "treat race and gender as mutually exclusive categories of experience and analysis" (57). The law operates, Crenshaw argues, along a "single-axis framework" (57). But the black woman's experience does not situate itself along such a "single categorical axis" (57)—and it is this that the slave-wife's multidimensionality foregrounds. In the slave wife, the single axis systems of race and gender collide, intersecting in their efforts to structure her absolutely. And so, if the case of Mrs. Stephens clearly indicates both the displacement of the black woman at law (her will is a moot point) and the hegemony of white masculinity (the court's judgment favors the white master, not the black husband), this case simultaneously indicates the law's insistence on singularity, on bounded categories; this case indicates, in short, the law's "antipathy" to multiple, articulated categories of identity. By incorporating precisely such articulated identities, the slave-wife unsettles the smooth surface of a legal system which works along single lines of analysis and which treats identity as one-dimensional, unicategorical.

It is just such an act of destabilization that Ellen Craft performs in *Running a Thousand Miles for Freedom*. According to William Craft, Ellen realizes that the law seeks to structure her along a single-axis framework: she "saw," Craft reports, that "the laws under which we lived did not recognize her to be a woman, but a mere chattel, to be bought and sold, or

43

otherwise dealt with as her owner might see fit" (30). As in the case of Mrs. Stephens, the law would have Ellen be not "woman"—and so, "naturally," wife, mother—but "black"—and so, "naturally," slave, chattel. Indeed, it is precisely because "the laws under which she lives" will not allow her to be both "black" and "woman" that Ellen agrees to the plan of escape. Thus, Ellen's willingness to assume the disguise of a white slave owner is simultaneously born of and a challenge to the law's insistence on her singularity, its efforts to confine her in a sole, unarticulated category.

Throughout *Running a Thousand Miles for Freedom*, William Craft plays upon Ellen Craft's multiple significations—and, ultimately, the disturbances they create. Ellen is herself fluidly transformative: she is fair-skinned enough to "pass" for white; and although she had, by all accounts, "the appearance of a well-bred and educated lady" (Josephine Brown 81), she could easily become the counterpart to that lady—the gentleman of property and distinction. In his book *The Underground Rail Road*, William Still gives a telling account of the Crafts' arrival in Philadelphia: "[I]t is easy to picture them in a private room . . . —Ellen in her fine suit of black, with her cloak and high-heeled boots, looking, in every respect, like a young gentleman; in an hour after having dropped her male attire, and assumed the habiliments of her sex[,] the feminine only was visible in every line and feature of her structure" (370). Readily, then, Ellen transforms herself from a piece of (black and female) property to a (white) man of property. Here, clothing appears to make the man—or the woman. The relationship between what is "true" and what is "illusion"— between appearance and reality—is complicated: Ellen Craft becomes increasingly multivalent, and gender and race begin to emerge as matters of performance.

William Craft recognizes this notion of performance and rhetorically applauds it. If, Garber has observed, it was William Craft who "conceived of the plan and persuaded [Ellen] to go along," "it was Ellen Craft who invented the persona of the young invalid gentleman that was to prove so effective" (284).[4] Fearing that "the smoothness of her face might betray her" (34–35) or that her status as slave will be revealed when she is unable to sign hotel registers or William's transport documents, Ellen devises strategic props: a poultice "worn under the chin, up the cheeks, and . . . tie[d] over the head . . . hid the expression of the countenance, as well as the beardless chin"; another poultice tied around her right hand conceals her illiteracy under the guise of injury; and green spectacles enable her to "get on better" in the "company of gentlemen" (35). With boots and a top hat for height, cropped hair and trousers, the transformation is complete: Ellen Craft is now "Mr. William Johnson" (35).[5]

In his narrative, Craft recounts the often harrowing eight days that it takes the couple to execute their plan of escape. The close encounters the fugitives have on their journey from Macon, Georgia, to Philadelphia provide Craft with opportunities to remark not only on Ellen's multiple significations but also on the dissonance that her multivalence creates.[6] From the distanced perspective of the narrative—the couple escaped in 1848, twelve years before *Running a Thousand Miles for Freedom* was published—Craft can present the escape as a sort of great adventure / hoax. Thus, the narrative's tone is often urbane and ironic, its humor fueled by the different ways that Ellen / Mr. Johnson can "read." At times, such incidents of signification are treated with gentle irony: when Mr. Johnson is placed in a cabin with a gentleman and his two young daughters, for example, one of the ladies is completely taken by him. " 'I never felt so much for a gentleman in my life!' " the woman tells her father, as Craft offers a winking aside: "To use an American expression, 'they fell in love with the wrong chap' " (60). But other incidents are treated more sardonically: at one of the "best" of Southern hotels—a hotel known to be a "head-quarters" for "great southern fire-eating statesmen" and their proslavery views—Mr. Johnson is treated as a great gentleman: "The proprietor made me stand on one side, while he paid my master the attention and homage he thought a gentleman of his high position merited" (52). Here, Craft mocks the obsequious landlord and his "fire-eating" patrons, men who would insist on the unmistakable, always evident inferiority of "black blood" but who, unbeknownst to themselves, bow and scrape to a fugitive slave.

Craft facilitates Ellen's imposture on the level of his own language, employing a rhetoric appropriate to the disguise in order to recount the "run for freedom": "[I] got into the negro car in which I knew I should have to ride; but my *master* (as I will now call my wife) took a longer way around, and only arrived there with the bulk of the passengers. He obtained a ticket for himself and one for his slave to Savannah" (42). Craft maintains this language throughout his retelling of their "run," altering his rhetorical mode only when the couple gets off the train in Philadelphia (79). For much of the narrative, then, this "she" becomes a "he," "my master." As Craft playfully recalls, one man "gave me a ten-cent piece, and requested me to be attentive to my good master. I promised that I would do so, and have ever since endeavoured to keep my pledge" (59).

As Craft teases his audience with the notion of a wife's "mastery" over a husband's life and affections, troping on the notion of the "sovereign female," he seems to be merely deploying the dissonance between what appears and what is, between the real and the illusory. The joke is—and has to be—on those who witness (but do not detect) Ellen Craft's performance. Thus, the narrative itself plays on the distinction between what is real and what is apparent: what we, the audience of the narrative, know is that Mr. Johnson is not what he seems to be. That is the joke; and that is the key to the success of the plan of escape.

But there is more to the appearance / reality issue than this interpretation would suggest, for Craft is up to something more complicated and far reaching: he is interested in exploring the very idea of the "real"—of where the boundary between appearance and reality collapses. When Craft caricatures the Southern men who, duped by a complacent faith in their own powers of perception, lavish attention on one who appears to be a "gentleman of distinction" (55), for example, he engages a question that he has introduced much earlier in the text—a question he asks, indeed, on the narrative's second page: What do racial categories "truly" mean? In a sketch of Ellen Craft's early life, Craft states that "notwithstanding my wife being of African extraction on her mother's side, she is almost white" (2). This announcement of Ellen's "mulatta" status—she is the child of master and slave—leads him into a five-page digression in which he considers slavery's long, indiscriminate arm. "It may be remembered," he writes, "that slavery in America is not at all confined to persons of any particular complexion; there are a very large number of slaves as white as any one; but as the evidence of a slave is not admitted in court against a free white person, it is almost impossible for a white child, after having been kidnapped and sold into or reduced to slavery, . . . ever to recover its freedom" (2–3).

This rhetorical sidetrack is in part a bid for the sympathetic attention of white readers, who will presumably be drawn into the narrative by his stories of people "kidnapped or sold into or reduced to slavery" though their "parents were white and free" (3). Craft exploits white self-interest through such reminders that we are all vulnerable to seizure, no matter how fair our skin.[7] As he asserts when he launches into a story about "Salome Muller," a white German woman kidnapped into slavery, "he who has the power, and is inhuman enough to trample upon the sacred rights of the weak, cares nothing for race or colour" (3).

Such remarks suggest that Craft accepts his culture's divisions of "race or colour": he appears to attack "inhuman" abuses of "power" above all and to maintain the essential meaning of racial categories by intimating, merely, that some oppressors ignore the appropriate distinctions. But implicit here is a more challenging exploration into those distinctions themselves: Craft's digression about "colour" serves not only to garner the support of white audiences but also to "frame" Ellen's inverse racial "crossings" (Garber 283) and to initiate an inquiry into the ontological status of racial categories. Craft wants to reveal the wrongs of an institution that functioned by insisting on the "natural" inferiority of those "of African extraction," a system that was predicated on the assumption that some bodies are naturally nonpersons, utterly different from other (white) persons and so subject to their claims. He thus gives us a number of figures who contest slavery's assumption of natural binary difference and who suggest that such difference is itself a construct. If white can be taken for black, and black, for white, the notion of discrete and meaningful racial categories becomes increasingly hollow.

When Ellen "passes" across the boundaries of race and of class—at, specifically, a locus of proslavery Negrophobia no less—she reveals those boundaries to be culturally imposed, politically interested. In her multiple significations—her ability to "read" as white and/or black—Ellen takes from the hand of slavery a crucial device: the "possibility," as Gerda Lerner puts it, "of designating the group to be dominated as entirely different from the group exerting dominance" (77). The figure of Ellen Craft suggests that such a notion of "entire" difference—particularly, in the case of America, *racial* difference—is a cultural construct. And, as Ellen's "crossings" challenge the very notion of essential (and essentially different) identities on which slavery is erected, they come to signify, for William Craft, freedom.[8]

Even as Ellen contests the categories of race in her ability to pass for white, she also, *at the same time,* contests those of gender in her ability to "pass" for a man. It is notable and telling, by contrast, that Craft's exploration into the discursive quality of identity focuses in on and is specific to the issues of race / class. Indeed, it would appear that Craft feels compelled to isolate issues of gender in order to write Ellen's cross-dressing into the narrative as a kind of misconduct: in the course of the narrative, Ellen's movement across the lines of gender begins to look like a dangerous species of transgression. Despite the fact that Craft chooses to rename Ellen as his "master" and to draw our attention to that act of renaming ("my *master* (as I will now call my wife)"), the image of "my master, Mr. Johnson" has a more disturbing valence. The urbane surface of Craft's narrative is broken throughout by anxious claims, efforts to contain Ellen's unruly *gender* identity with an insistence on her "true" womanhood.

I have already noted the way in which Craft assures us that Ellen "had no ambition whatever to assume [her] disguise," that she would have avoided doing so if she could (35). My point is not to argue with the notion of Ellen's reluctance but rather to show how Craft, here and elsewhere, uses that reluctance to insist on Ellen's essential femininity. Craft maintains that there are two characters in *Running a Thousand Miles for Freedom:* one is the fictitious "Mr. Johnson," a persona born of necessity, an illusion of the "outside," and the other is the "real" Ellen, the "true" womanly self inside the male costume. While in Mr. Johnson we get a figure of agency, independence, and courage, beneath the costume is the real Ellen, a delicate, faint-hearted true woman. When, for example, the couple is about to embark on their journey, Ellen reveals the true self beneath her costume: Craft tells us that she "shrank back, in a state of trepidation" and "burst into violent sobs," "her heart almost sink[ing] within her" (40–41). This fainting female reappears periodically throughout the journey and emerges in full force at the moment of arrival in the free states. At that point, Mr. Johnson is transformed from "my master" to "my wife" (both literally and discursively transformed, in fact; Craft writes "my master—or rather my wife, as I may now say") and manifests behavior appropriate to the new role; Ellen utters a few words of thanks and "then burst into tears, leant upon me, and wept like a child. The reaction was fearful. So when we reached the house, she was in reality so weak and faint that she could scarcely stand alone" (79).[9]

Figure 1.
Engraving of Ellen Craft.
First published in the *London Illustrated News,* 19 April 1851, and used as frontispiece for *Running a Thousand Miles for Freedom.*

Thus in the narrative, William Craft makes of Ellen what Mr. Johnson is notably not, that is, an antebellum wife, a *feme covert.* On the journey north, the marital relationship has been materially inverted as Ellen becomes master, owner rather than owned, controlling subject rather than passive object. Far from being "one" with her "husband" and acting under his "wing, protection, and *cover,*" she serves as William's protection. But by reasserting the very categories of gender that Mr. Johnson has put into question, Craft restores the "natural" order; he repossesses Ellen's "very being" and rewrites it, not in his own image, but in the image of the antebellum wife who cannot "stand alone."

Craft's attempts to reinscribe Ellen as his "wife" are reflected in his narrative constructions of her character as well as, and perhaps more intriguingly, in his use of the portrait that served as the frontispiece to the narrative when it appeared in print (see figure 1).[10] The portrait shows a fine-featured young man in a top hat, cravat, and spectacles. His hair is cropped but curly, his chin has a tiny cleft, and his mouth wears the slightest trace of a smile. The first thing one sees on opening *Running a Thousand Miles for Freedom* is this portrait of Ellen in disguise. Craft understands the sensational power of Ellen's ability to assume so successfully the identity of a white man. Indeed, early in the narrative, he suggests his willingness to capitalize on Ellen's remarkable "switch." Craft writes that he has been attempting to save enough money to buy his sister out of slavery: "I am happy to say," he adds, "that, partly by lecturing occasionally, and through the sale of an engraving of my wife in the disguise in which she escaped . . . I have nearly accomplished this" (12). While the publicization of the engraving would seem to reflect Craft's willingness to acknowledge Ellen's unruly identities, it in fact operates, paradoxically, to control her representation. He captures her in a visual image as well as in the verbal images of the narrative itself, rendering her a static object available for public consumption.[11] Even if the proceeds of her "sale" go not to promote slavery but to free Craft's sister from it, Ellen becomes another sort of commodity when she is represented in the frontispiece.[12]

In *Running a Thousand Miles for Freedom*, Craft makes one other note of the portrait. Describing the details of Ellen's disguise—most notably the poultice she used to hide the "smoothness of her face"—Craft informs us that "the poultice is left off in the engraving, because the likeness could not have been taken well with it on" (35). But whose "likeness" are we seeing? The engraving is not, apparently, what Craft has earlier claimed it to be: "an engraving of my wife in the disguise in which she escaped" (12). Indeed, it is precisely *not* that, for a central element of the disguise is left out in the portrait. Thus it would appear that the purpose of the engraving is to represent not "Mr. Johnson" but Ellen herself. The portrait thus becomes another occasion to assert the opposition between Ellen's "true" womanly self and her "fictional" masculine persona. In this context, rather than a manifestation of Ellen's contestation of the categories of identity, the portrait is simply a representation of a fair-skinned fugitive slave woman who has temporarily assumed male attire to "run a thousand miles for freedom."

Craft's verbal and visual insistence on the distinct separation between his "real" wife and her "fictional" male persona serves, clearly, as a form of narrative control. This is, after all, Ellen as William Craft presents her:

it is he who grants access to Ellen, he who designates how she is to be understood, how she is to be read. While Craft may want to indict the restricting cultural "laws," both categorical and juridical, that deny him and Ellen various "inalienable rights," the narrative itself reveals his concurrent attempts to bring Ellen within the confines of another set of laws—the laws of gender and of marriage.

A clear difference exists between the act of appropriation performed by a white male slave owner such as Mr. Clements, whose claim to his black female slave triumphed so completely in the Pennsylvania case discussed above, and the effort to name a wife *as* wife made by men such as William Craft or George Stephens. And Claudia Tate has brought our attention to the ways in which marriage frequently functions as a discourse of liberation in the texts of African American women.[13] The question thus becomes one of register: How are we to read William Craft's alarm at this "slave-wife's" sudden mastery? The answer has something to do, I would argue, with Craft's own multiplicity—his doubled position as the property of a white man and as a husband who finds himself ruled by his wife/property—and with his own effort to write his way *out* of the discourse of property itself. Lerner has argued that the "invention of slavery" depended in part on the "symbolic castration" (80) of conquered men—the emphasis on the male slave's impotence within the slave relation.[14] The issue of emasculation certainly circulates in *Running a Thousand Miles for Freedom,* in which not just the slave owner but also the slave-wife poses a threat. On their run for freedom, Ellen and William play out the roles of master and slave. Their charade thus emblematizes the relations of proprietorship at work in the roles of husband and wife. In this case, however, those roles are reversed; the slave-wife becomes white "master," and the husband becomes once again a slave.

But another, related issue is at stake here, as well: Craft's move to claim Ellen as a "natural" wife suggests the ways that white legal norms underwrite the very notion of identity itself. In *The Political Theory of Possessive Individualism,* C. B. Macpherson argues that with John Locke's elaboration of a theory of natural rights and private property, the liberal subject assumed fundamentally proprietary proportions. "The individual," Macpherson writes, "was seen neither as a moral whole, nor as part of a social whole, but as an owner of himself. The relation of ownership, having become for more and more men the critically important relation determining their actual freedom and actual prospect of realizing their full potentialities, was read back into the nature of the individual" (3).

According to Macpherson, the "individual" came to be defined as an "owner of himself," the "proprietor of his own person" (3). This, as Gillian Brown notes, is "a market society's construction of self, a self aligned with market relations"—and thus aligned with white men to whom "market activities" were "generally available" (2).[15] Those who are defined not as subjects but as objects of ownership and exchange, in other words, are denied status as possessive individuals. "Of course," James Grunebaum writes in his *Private Ownership*, "if persons are themselves owned, as slaves, children, or wives, then they cannot be owners" (9); nor can they be defined as autonomous, self-owning subjects—not, at least, according to the proprietary terms of Lockean liberal culture. For property *in* the private self, Macpherson explains, must be substantiated from objects beyond or outside the ostensible limits *of* that self: "The man without property in things," Macpherson writes, "loses . . . full proprietorship in his own person" (231).

Through the lens provided by Macpherson's formulation—through the framing notion of the possessive individual—we can understand the crisis provoked in William Craft by Ellen's passage across the boundaries of identity: as she becomes owner rather than owned, she throws the very terms of Craft's emergent identity into question. Craft's journey toward selfhood is interrupted not simply by Ellen's "mastery" but by the ways that mastery challenges the very concept of identity itself. Ultimately, Craft is left with no ground from which to articulate himself; and it is this, I would suggest, that he cannot tolerate. Only by denying the implications of Mr. Johnson and owning Ellen as his wife can William Craft begin to imagine becoming a person and achieving the ostensible "freedom" that comes with "identity." In the context of an America that equates proprietorship with selfhood, selfhood with masculinity, and masculinity with whiteness, this black slave narrator stakes the only claim available to him.

Despite Craft's regulatory measures, Ellen Craft eludes inscription. The engraving that opens the "account of our escape" is not a simple representation of "my wife" dressed in male clothes. Although the poultice is removed in the portrait to make it more "like" Ellen, the plan backfires: the sex of the figure remains indeterminate, enigmatic. Although

Craft wants to assert the discontinuity between Ellen's true (feminine) self and her fictional (masculine) persona, the engraving instead reflects the continuity between these. The two "selves" underwrite each other: Mr. Johnson is—as the engraving itself confirms in its first appearance in the *London Illustrated News*—"Ellen Craft, The Fugitive Slave." It is this image that introduces the text and haunts it. Indeed, in its insistent presentation of Ellen's fluid identities—and in Craft's continuing insistence on her containment—this portrait can serve as a resonant and haunting emblem for what I would suggest is the issue this text finally foregrounds: *Running a Thousand Miles for Freedom* concerns not just the different ways "freedoms" are negotiated, achieved, or denied but also the fluid, complex, and always vexed relationship between gender and race in the American journey toward emancipation.

Notes

1. Scholars have long debated the nature and meaning of the relationship between the abolitionist and feminist movements. See, for example, Hersh; Yellin, who examines in particular the complex relationship between "antislavery feminists" and the female slave; Ellen DuBois, who contends that women borrowed strategies from the abolitionist movement but had come to an awareness of their own oppression long before their involvement in the antislavery movement; and Warbasse, who discusses abolitionism in relation to feminist agitation over women's property rights (117–32). It should also be noted that the relationship between these two "reform" movements was not an exclusive one: as Karen Sanchez-Eppler notes, "Women involved in both the abolitionist and [the] woman's rights movements also tended to advocate temperance, oppose prostitution, and reform schools, prisons, and diets; they referred to themselves as 'universal reformers'" (29).

2. For treatment of the relations of dominance at work in the relationship between white women and black (female) slaves, see Sanchez-Eppler 31 and Yellin 78–79. This dynamic has not, of course, gone away: we can see it working still, in a contemporary feminist movement that is often insensitive to the needs of those who fall outside the white (heterosexual) middle class.

3. Arguing that we have defined "freedom" in the black idiom from only a male perspective, Claudia Tate shows how, for the antebellum black woman, legal marriage became a site on which to claim freedom rather than a site on which freedoms were denied. Marriage, Tate argues, was a "sign of civilization" ("Allegories" 103),

of the ability to enter a civil contract and create a socially sanctioned family unit. While white women lacked positive-law rights to their property and their bodies, they clearly possess something that both men and women slaves do not; hence, the desirability, for the black woman, of acceding to gender discourse. Tate works out these ideas at greater length in her 1992 *Domestic Allegories of Political Desire.*

4. In one retelling of the Crafts' story, Ellen herself conceives of the plan. In a biography of her father, William Wells Brown (famed fugitive slave, abolitionist speaker, and longtime friend and colleague of the Crafts), Josephine Brown gives the following genesis of the plan of escape: " 'Now William,' said the wife, 'listen to me, and take my advice, and we shall be free in less than a month' " (76). "The wife" proceeds to counter all "the husband's" objections with clever devices and a few shaming remarks: " 'Come, William, . . . don't be a coward! Get me the clothes, and I promise you we shall both be free in a few days" (77). The discrepancy between this representation of Ellen—forceful, cunning, and active rather than reactive—and that of Craft's narrative is intriguing.

5. In his discussion of the Crafts and their escape, Starling suggests that cross-dressing was, if not common, at least not completely unique as a mode of escape (235). For other sketches of women who effect their escape from slavery by dressing as men, see Still 60–61, 177–88.

6. The narrative does not stop with the couple's arrival in Philadelphia. After a brief stay there, the Crafts are compelled to move on to the antislavery sanctum of Boston. They remain in Boston for two years; but with the passage of the Fugitive Slave Act of 1850, they have an alarming brush with slave catchers and are finally forced to "fly from under the Stars and Stripes to save our liberties and our lives" (87). At the end of the narrative, the couple is beginning a new life in England, where—to the shame of America, Craft reminds us—they are at last "free from every slavish fear" (108).

The Crafts remained in England until 1869, when they returned to America with plans to establish a cooperative farm and educational facility in Georgia. They spent the remainder of their lives struggling—and finally failing—to make their agricul-tural/educational cooperative viable. Ellen died in 1891, and William, in 1900. Blackett (86–137) provides the most exhaustive account of the Crafts' biographies, including details of their lives in England and their return to the United States. Sterling provides extensive biographical information as well, focusing, notably, on Ellen Craft (2–59; for a useful list of sources, see 160–61). Though many studies of slave narratives make reference to *Running a Thousand Miles for Freedom,* only

Doyle gives it any extended attention and this on the basis of the ways in which the narrative, despite its rhetorical "flaws," finally succeeds as an adventure tale.

7. Craft also notes that the opposite can occur: a free black can easily be taken into custody as a slave, for "in Georgia (and I believe in all the slave States,) every coloured person's complexion is *prima facie* evidence of his being a slave; and the lowest villain in the country, should he be a white man, has the legal power to arrest" him (36). The sociocultural meanings assigned to skin color are thus thrown into question: fair skin does not always guarantee "freedom," nor does dark skin always signify enslavement.

8. For a discussion of the ways feminists and abolitionists attempted to "pu[t] into question the presumption that the body can provide reliable information about the institutional and racial status of the whole person" in order to write "black and female bodies into the discourses of personhood," see Sanchez-Eppler, especially 29–31.

9. In arguing that we might question Craft's representation of the "true" Ellen Craft, I do not intend to suggest that she deliberately flouted the gender conventions of her time. By all accounts, in fact, Ellen was a "modest," "shy," and "sweet" woman, quite the model of appropriately feminine behavior (Sterling 47). These same accounts, however, stress those qualities in combination with a stoical courage, emotional strength, and clearheadedness. I would posit that the emotionally vulnerable, highly strung character Craft develops may be a rhetorical figure that serves as a (necessary) counterbalance to Mr. Johnson.

10. According to Sterling, the portrait first appeared in the *London Illustrated News* on 19 April 1851—nine years before the publication of Craft's narrative.

11. Ellen was similarly "employed" on the abolitionist lecture circuit. Blackett describes the nature of the presentations the Crafts would make in British lecture halls: "First, [William Wells] Brown spoke against American slavery, then William described their escape, and finally, in a tear-jerking scene, Ellen was invited onstage. This careful orchestration was guaranteed to provoke strong antislavery sentiments" (98). Ellen Craft existed not as a speaking subject but rather as an object of the public gaze. With her fair skin, she was used explicitly to arouse shock and dismay in the audience. Samuel May addressed the racist implications of such responses: "To think of such a woman being held as a piece of property, subject to be traded off to the highest bidder (while it is no worse or wickeder than when done to the blackest woman that ever was) does yet stir a community brought up in prejudice against color a thousand times more deeply than could be effected in different circumstances.

She was a living proof that Slavery has no prejudice about color, and is as ready to enslave the whitest and the fairest as any other" (qtd. in Blackett 98).

12. For a discussion of the ways in which the achievement of emancipation for slave narrators always involves commercial negotiation and, typically, a process of self-commodification, see Baker.

13. See note 6, above.

14. Lerner points out that this "symbolic castration" was often effected via "the rape of conquered women": "Men in patriarchal societies who cannot protect the sexual purity of wives, sisters, and children are truly impotent and dishonored" (80). Slavery on the basis of race and class is thus "invented" and "created" partly through what Lerner would argue is a preexisting system of sexual enslavement.

15. Although both Gillian Brown and I make use of C. B. Macpherson's thesis in our discussions of the logic of selfhood in nineteenth-century American literature, our conclusions ultimately differ. Brown argues that "this form of individualism comes to be associated with the feminine sphere of domesticity" (2), indeed, that domestic ideology virtually maintains possessive individualism. I argue, by contrast, that while women and slaves may be implicated in the discourse of possessive individualism, their roles in that discourse often serve to contest and challenge its structures. For a related argument about the ways antebellum feminism contested the structures of possessive individualism, see Leach.

PART II

The (Re)Construction of Race

The Autobiography of an Ex-Coloured Man: (Passing for) Black Passing for White

SAMIRA KAWASH

*I*n 1912, *The Autobiography of an Ex-Coloured Man* appeared anonymously. While neither author James Weldon Johnson nor the book's publishers actively attempted to deceive the public as to the book's status or origin, readers were left to draw their own conclusions. Some readers took it as true autobiography, the actual narrative of the anonymous author's life. Johnson's biographer Eugene Levy believes Johnson intended the work to be taken in this way. Levy points to a letter to a college friend, in which Johnson writes, "When the author is known, and known to be one who could not be the main character of the story, the book will fall flat."[1] Johnson suggests that the book's success was not only a question of anonymity but also a question of veracity. In a climate of increasing racial tensions, a confession of "true" race passing might produce a sensation in a way that a fictional account could not. In the preface to the second edition, Carl Van Vechten, one of the principal white patrons of African American writers and artists in the 1920s, recalls the initial reception of the book: "The work was hailed on every side, for the most part, as an individual's true story." Van Vechten's recollection perhaps overstates the impact of the narrative's first appearance fifteen years prior, for in fact, the book was hardly hailed at all in its first issue.

Alfred Knopf reissued the book in 1927, at the height of African American cultural productivity and visibility now known as the Harlem Renaissance. This time, Johnson's name appeared on the title page, along with an introduction written by the prestigious Van Vechten clarifying the status of this particular "autobiography": "*The Autobiography*, of course, in the matter of specific incident, has little enough to do with Mr. Johnson's own life, but it is imbued with his own personality and feeling, his *views* of the subjects discussed, so that to a person who has no previous knowledge of the author's own history, it reads like *real* autobiography. It would be truer, perhaps, to say that it reads like a composite autobiography of the Negro race in the United States in modern times" (xxxiv). Van Vechten's preface authorizes and authenticates the text, assuring the reader that it is, as Jessie Fauset wrote in *The Crisis*, "fiction based on hard fact."[2] But the terms of this authentication have the added effect of destabilizing the common sense meaning of the term *autobiography*. Autobiography is commonly supposed to be the true story of a real person's life, written or narrated by that person. Van Vechten subtly shifts the referent of autobiography from the author's life to the reader's *knowledge* of the author's life. Whether the text is actually fictional or factual matters only to the reader who is acquainted with the author's personal history; otherwise, the text "reads like real autobiography," that is, from the reader's point of view, it *is* real autobiography. The distinction between true history and fictional narrative is not in the text but in the reader.

Contemporary scholars recognize *The Autobiography of an Ex-Coloured Man* as the first *novel* written in the first person by an African American as well as one of the best known race-passing novels in the literature of the United States.[3] The history of the novel's publication and reception, however, suggests a more complicated and unstable identity. *The Autobiography*'s evasion of generic identity in Van Vechten's introduction reproduces the structure of the narrative itself: like the novel's protagonist, who passes between black and white, the text itself passes back and forth between the poles of truth and fiction, autobiography and novel. This passing plays not on shifting identities but on shifting perceptions, what the world takes the narrative, or the protagonist, to be. In effect, the passing narrative in *The Autobiography* is itself the subject of another passing narrative, this one to do with literary genre, fiction, and fact.

Six years later, in 1933, Johnson published his "real" autobiography, *Along This Way: The Autobiography of James Weldon Johnson*. In principle, the appearance of *Along This Way* settles the indeterminate relation between "fiction" and "autobiography" set into motion by the peculiar status of *The Autobiography of an Ex-Coloured Man*. Because the reader posited by Van Vechten's introduction now has access to "the author's own history," she can correctly distinguish between *The Autobiography*, which "reads *like* autobiography," and *Along This Way*, which *is* autobiography. The reader of Johnson's avowed autobiography *Along This Way* will realize, as critic Joseph Skerrett Jr. remarks, that "while some of the events related there were used in the novel, the personality and much of the life experience of the young James Weldon Johnson have little or no resemblance to the narrator's" (542). The game is up: the Ex-Coloured Man has been exposed as a purely fictional character, and *The Autobiography* can no longer pass as a "real autobiography."

Unfortunately, this orderly return to the certainties of truth and fiction is precarious at best. One can make a strong case for reading *The Autobiography*, written twenty years earlier, as the source for Johnson's own "nonfictional" account of his life. *Along This Way* frequently appears to be a revision of *The Autobiography*, lifting phrases, episodes, and descriptions virtually verbatim from the latter. Some brief examples may indicate the similarity. For instance, in *The Autobiography*, Johnson writes: "When I reached Atlanta, my steadily increasing disappointment was not lessened. I found it a big, dull, red town. . . . It was raining when I arrived and some of these unpaved streets were absolutely impassable. Wheels sank to the hubs in red mire" (52–53).[4] And in *Along This Way*, he notes that "Atlanta disappointed me. It was a larger city than Jacksonville, but did not seem to me to be nearly so attractive. Many of the thoroughfares were still red clay roads. It was a long time before I grew accustomed to the bloody aspect of Atlanta's highways" (65). The narrator's descriptions in *The Autobiography* of his relation with his millionaire patron indicate that "he treated me in every way as he dressed me, as an equal, not as a servant. In fact, I don't think anyone could have guessed that such a relation existed" (130). He adds later: "Between this peculiar man and me there had grown a very strong bond of affection, backed up by a debt which each owed to the other" (143); and "Between him and me no suggestion of racial differences had ever come up" (145). From *Along This Way*, Johnson's description of his relation with Dr. Summers, for whom he works one summer during college, is similar: "From the beginning the relation between us was on a high level. It was not that of employer to employee. Less still was it that of white employer to Negro employee. Between the two of us, as individuals, 'race' never showed its head" (95). Johnson's life experience may have been a source for some of the episodes or characters in *The Autobiography;* this would seem to grant logical priority to Johnson's actual autobiography. But the temporal priority of *The Autobiography* suggests a reciprocal relation between "true life" and "fiction." Given these two texts, it is difficult to decide which we should read as autobiography and which we should read as fiction. Which is the original, and which is the copy? In this case, the "original" autobiography, *Along This Way,* is a "copy" of *The Autobiography,* which is a "copy" of the "original" autobiography, and so on. This circle of *copy* and *original* has neither beginning nor end; the two terms are trapped in a relation of mutual undecidability. If *The Autobiography* might pass as "true" autobiography, one can also say that it passes as "fictional" auto-biography. Neither fully true nor wholly fictional, it seems it can occupy a generic identity, whether novel or autobiography, only by "passing."

In the publisher's preface to the first edition of James Weldon Johnson's *The Autobiography of an Ex-Coloured Man,* the writer nervously notes that "these pages . . . reveal the unsuspected fact that prejudice against the Negro is exerting a pressure which . . . is actually and constantly forcing an unascertainable number of fair-complexioned coloured people over into the white race" (xl). The narrator of *The Autobiography* is one of these "fair-complexioned coloured people" who, by the end of the narra-tive, is living as a white man in New York City. This is the cultural phenomenon known as *passing.* In *An American Dilemma,* sociologist Gunnar Myrdal gives a working definition: "For all practical purposes 'passing' means that a Negro becomes a white man, that is, moves from the lower to the higher caste. In the American caste order, this can be accomplished only by the deception of the white people with whom the passer comes to associate and by a conspiracy of silence on the part of other Negroes who might know about it" (683). To pass is, for Myrdal as for the author of the preface, to disguise oneself, to simulate whiteness, to conceal the truth under a false appearance—this is the "cultural logic" of passing. *The Autobiography,* the preface promises, will afford the reader "a view of the inner life of the Negro in America" (xl). The narrator, as one of these "Negroes," has access to this inner life previously hidden from white America's gaze. By implication, he has no such access to the inner life of whites in America. If the narrator of *The Autobiography* cannot see white America, it is because he is not white, even though he is living as a white man. The narrator is passing: his apparent whiteness conceals the truth of his blackness.

The assumption that passing for white conceals or obscures a true black identity has generally been the basis for reading passing novels. For me, however, the figure of passing as it is narrativized in these novels challenges the received notions of race, identity, and cultural difference that continue to inform our understanding of the politics of representation. My claim is that the passing narrative is not about the *representation* of blackness or whiteness; rather, it is about the *failure* of blackness or whiteness to provide the grounds for a stable, coherent identity. Blackness and whiteness as they emerge in the passing narrative belie the possibility of identity or authenticity that would allow one to be unequivocally black or white. Passing insists on the fallacy of identity as a *content* of social, psychological, national, or cultural attributes, whether bestowed by nature or produced by society; it forces us to pay attention to the *form* of difference itself. In the case of race in the United States, difference is named and produced on the "color line." Passing plays on this line, exposing racial difference as a continually emerging distinction empty of any essential content. Through a sustained engagement with the functioning of racial identity in *The Autobiography,* I want to argue that it is the perpetual production of the *form* of difference that sustains and determines the incommensurability and irreducibility of racial identities.

The race-passing plot of *The Autobiography of an Ex-Coloured Man* is embedded in a narrative line structured by the Ex-Coloured Man's passage through the North, the South, and Europe. As the Ex-Coloured Man tells the story of his life, from his birth in an unnamed town to his current life as an anonymous white man in New York, he lays out two trajectories of travel: a psychological journey through whiteness and blackness and a physical journey through the United States and Europe.

These two trajectories, the psychological journey of passing and the physical travel through the United States and Europe, are linked by more than narrative coincidence. *The Autobiography* does not take place in any fixed locale; rather, it traverses multiple locations. The narrator takes us on what Eugenia Collier has called "an endless journey"[5] through Savannah, Connecticut, Atlanta, Jacksonville, New York, Paris, London, Amsterdam, Berlin, Boston, Washington, D.C., Richmond, Nashville, Atlanta again, and Macon, finally concluding in New York. He is perpetually homeless, traveling light, following at a whim whatever opportunity or adventure fate brings him. He is never so much *in* a place as he is, to turn a phrase, passing through. The coincidence of the thematics of geographic mobility and race passing is not accidental. Practically, if one is to pass, one must go somewhere else, where one's identity is unknown.

Signaling a more important connection between geographic mobility and race passing is the fact that the very word *pass* contains the trace of its origins in movement. The use of the term *passing* to mean, as the *Oxford English Dictionary* puts it, "to be accepted as equivalent to; to be taken for; to be accepted, received, or held in repute as," obscures its etymological roots in the Latin noun *passus*, a "step"; in its verbal form, "the primary signification was thus 'to step, pace, walk,'" although as early as the eleventh century, "it had come to denote progression or moving on from place to place." This etymological origin in movement is recovered, in the case of race passing in the United States, in the implicit reference to a metaphoric geography of race: one crosses, or passes, over the color line dividing black and white. Here, passing regains its transitive property: "to go through, across, or over (something); to go from side to side of, or across, to cross." The Ex-Coloured Man's perpetual movement suggests that the geography of race as it emerges in the figure of passing is not just metaphoric; passing is the continual motion of crossing the color line.

Although the narrator knows he is colored, he is plagued by his inability to translate that knowledge into a feeling of being colored. His initial understanding is transitive, filtered through his knowledge of the meaning of blackness for the other children in his school: "I myself would not have so clearly understood this difference had it not been for the presence of the other coloured children at school; I had learned what their status was, and now I learned that theirs was mine" (23). Blackness is produced in this shift of perspective: he forms his idea of what it is to be colored by seeing others who are marked as colored. Learning that he also is colored, he translates that status and condition to himself. Despite his only vague understanding of his "exact relation to the world in general" as one marked as colored and his "very strong aversion to being classed with them," he realizes that in the eyes of others, he is the same as his colored classmates.

In this early encounter with his blackness, the narrator's relation to race identity is structured around two terms that I will call *spectatorship* and *specularity*. The preface has positioned the reader as a spectator who will, through the eyes of the narrator, "glimpse behind the scenes of this race drama which is being here enacted" (xl). In fact, the reader is no less a spectator than the Ex-Coloured Man. But because he too has been marked as colored, the narrator must find some term for translating the blackness he sees in others into a sense of himself. The narrator's relation to the other colored children in school is figured as an identificatory transitivity: "I had learned what their status was, and now I learned that theirs was mine" (23). This is a form of specular identification: the narrator sees blackness in others and then identifies himself with that blackness. It is only through the image of these others that Ex-Coloured Man knows himself as black.

Jacques Lacan's description of the assumption of subjectivity in what he calls the "mirror stage" emphasizes that this specular identification must also always be an alienating *mis*recognition (*Écrits* 4). Lacan suggests that the identification of the self with an image external to the self provides a basis for identity by substituting the coherent image of the other for a complex, unstable self. If identity is the product of such a specular identification, then the possibility of any authentic, essential, organic identity is foreclosed. That is, identity does not originate in some internal core of the self but rather emerges in the distance between self and other. In the case of the Ex-Coloured Man, it is not the immediacy of a common black identity ("we are the same") but an alienating distance between himself and others ("we are not the same") that is the condition for his understanding of blackness. Blackness for the Ex-Coloured Man is always predicated on this alienating disidentification.

When the time comes for him to leave his home, the narrator chooses Atlanta College, a black institution, over Harvard in part to satisfy his "peculiar fascination with the South" (51). This is his first brush with "coloured people in large numbers" (55), but he encounters them more as a tourist in search of the curious and exotic than as his own people. Atlanta disappoints; rather than the "luxuriant semi-tropical scenery which [he] had pictured in [his] mind," the narrator finds "a big, dull, red town" (52). He is repulsed by the "unkempt appearance, the shambling, slouching gait and loud talk and laughter" (56) of the colored people he encounters in the streets of Atlanta but is relieved to discover that they are "of the lower class" (55). The class distinction that the narrator insists exists between himself and these "lower classes" allows him to remain a spectator, consoled that he is not one of them.

He takes the most pleasure in the stereotypical. He is thrilled to breakfast in the boarding house of a benevolent "mammy" figure: "Scrupulously clean, in a spotless white apron and coloured head-handkerchief, her round face beaming with motherly kindness, she was picturesquely beautiful" (59). This is what the narrator had hoped for, *Uncle Tom's Cabin* come to life: "When I had finished, I felt that I had experienced the realization of, at least, one of my dreams of Southern life" (59). As the narrator's journey continues, the reader is afforded many more occasions for those "glimpse[s] behind the scenes of this race drama" promised by the preface. The descriptions are from the point of view of an objective observer, a disinterested spectator who does not consider himself a part of what is going on. In fact, it is because of the episodic character of these scenes of "race life" that *The Autobiography* is often considered a failure as a novel; character and narrative thread seem to disappear under the burden of representing the various classes of colored people, their enjoyments, public and private amusements, religion, language, and music. The narrator's presence seems to fade into a disembodied ethnographic voice of reportage.

In Atlanta, the distance between the narrator and the colored people he meets is emphasized in terms of class difference. In Jacksonville, however, he is welcomed into the cultured black middle class, with which he can more closely identify: "Through my music teaching and my not absolutely irregular attendance at church I became acquainted with the best class of coloured people in Jacksonville. This was really my entrance into the race. It was my initiation into what I have termed the freemasonry of the race. I had formulated a theory of what it was to be coloured; now I was getting the practice" (74). This entrance is the culmination of an autodidact's course in the assumption of race identity. The narrator enters into the race through an act of volition. The theory of blackness formed through studious spectatorship becomes a practice of blackness as he applies the lessons learned to himself. Blackness is almost a bodily discipline, acquired through study and repetition. The "freemasonry of the race" suggests a club with which he can, at his discretion, affiliate. This transformation into privileged insider accentuates his position as outsider; he must be initiated into the race because he is not truly of the race. The structure of specularity initially suggested by his childhood encounter with blackness is repeated here: again, it is in terms of distance as the difference between himself and other black people, not in terms of a common identity, that he encounters his own blackness.

I want to consider more carefully the status of the narrator's racial identity by examining in detail the formative scene of the narrator's first childhood encounter with his own blackness. One day in school, his teacher singles him out in class as colored. The principal enters the classroom, and "for some reason said: 'I wish all of the white scholars to stand for a moment.' I rose with the others. The teacher looked at me and, calling my name, said: 'You sit down for the present, and rise with the others'" (16). Barbara Johnson points out that here, the racial difference between the narrator and the white students is produced through textual repetition.[6] As both black and white, the narrator will "rise with the others." The difference for Barbara Johnson lies in the hierarchy of the terms *black* and *white* that the repetition veils, which gives them a false air of equality. I would add that this repetition is in fact a repetition containing difference, bound up in the play of meaning in the term *others*. When the narrator first intends to "rise with the others," we understand other to indicate other individuals conceived in opposition to the self. To this other, the narrator might say, "I am not *you*." But in the second iteration, the teacher interpellates the narrator as one of the others, where other indicates a socially delimited otherness, in this case, the otherness of blackness. As this other, the narrator must say, "I am not *white*." The marker of difference, the phrase "to rise with the others," contains even before it is repeated an irresolvable turning between self-identity and social identity.

He rushes home and gazes in the mirror, terrified to confront the signs of this "truth" as written on his face. This is the first and only view of the narrator provided the reader, and it is a striking one:

I noticed the ivory whiteness of my skin, the beauty of my mouth, the size and liquid darkness of my eyes, and how the long, black lashes that fringed and shaded them produced an effect that was strangely fascinating even to me. I noticed the softness and glossiness of my dark hair that fell in waves over my temples, making my forehead appear whiter than it really was. (17)

For Kimberly Benston, the scene represents "the fracturing of an initial cognition (or consciousness) of blackness into the desired re-cognition of whiteness: the face the hero sees (as hyperbolically 'ivory' as it is homoerotically 'beautiful') is the secret, endangered other of his suddenly activated 'I'" (102). This suddenly activated I, the black I, is one that can exist only as object; the narrator seeks to identify with the face in the mirror in a desperate attempt to preserve his sense of self as subject.

Benston wants to insist that in the Ex-Coloured Man's world, the only possibility for identity as "an authorized selfhood that is truly sameness" is whiteness; blackness is difference itself in Benston's reading.

I do not agree that this splitting of the narrator into a black consciousness and a white mirror image is the loss of a prior "selfhood that is truly sameness." Rather, the fragmented subjectivity that emerges in this scene of mirroring seems to me to demand a reconsideration of an earlier, apparently undivided self. The structure of the narrative, as a first-person account, ensures that the whiteness of the narrator before this scene is not an untroubled sameness. This whiteness is represented retrospectively; thus, the narrative knows the narrator is not white even before the narrator-as-child is marked as colored. The narrator's childhood whiteness is implicitly characterized as a condition of ironic misrecognition. When, for example, one of the black boys in school is provoked into throwing a slate at the white boys, the narrator is strongly affected: "I was very much wrought up over the affair, and went home and told my mother how one of the 'niggers' had struck a boy with a slate. I shall never forget how she turned on me. 'Don't you ever use that word again,' she said, 'and don't you ever bother the coloured children at school. You ought to be ashamed of yourself'" (15). The narrator is split between present and past, between the "I" that experiences the event and the "I" that narrates it as recollection. The original whiteness of the narrator is necessarily inauthentic because it can emerge narratively only as already contaminated by the knowledge of not-whiteness.

In "Autobiography as De-facement," Paul de Man considers this peculiar splitting of the "I" in autobiography, raising the question of the relation between the life and its representation, between the original and its copy: "We assume that life *produces* the autobiography as an act produces its consequences, but can we not suggest, with equal justice, that the autobiographical project may itself produce and determine the life. . . . [D]oes the referent determine the figure, or is it the other way round[?]" (920). De Man describes the experience of the undecidability of reference and figure as that of being caught on a "whirligig . . . capable of infinite acceleration [that is], in fact, not successive but simultaneous" (921). De Man's insistence on simultaneity rather than succession reveals that for him, this undecidability is not a question of the oscillating or shifting identity of the original. Rather, original identity is displaced altogether. The original, wherever it is located, even instantaneously, is no more original than its copy.

The narrator's face reflected in the mirror can be read as enacting this "revolving door" of referent and figure: the face prior to its specular recognition in the mirror is no more original than its image. The structure of the narrative itself repeats the splitting of the narrator in the mirror scene: the narrated "I" is white, the narrating "I" is colored, but neither is prior to, or more authentic than, the other. It is only through the mode of specular (mis)recognition, seeing himself, that the narrator forms a prior image of his whiteness. Thus, the self-consciousness of whiteness also is necessarily divided, emerging when "I see myself," whether as the immediate image in the mirror or as the image of myself recollected across time. There is no recognition without this division between "I" and "myself," between "me" and "my image." The prior whiteness that Benston wants to call "identity" can no more be authentic selfsameness than is the blackness that the narrator wants to call pure difference.

The narrator's experience of race is structured by the specular undecidability, and displacement, of original and copy. In contrast, the cultural logic of race passing, as implied by the novel's preface and articulated explicitly in the passage I have quoted from Myrdal's *An American Dilemma*, is based on a substitutive relation of selfsame original and inauthentic copy. In the cultural logic of passing, race functions as a form of embodied identity. The narrator inherits blackness from his mother; his "few drops of Negro blood" overdetermine all other aspects of his experience or sense of identity. Race is assumed to be an inescapable fact, a bundle of psychological and physical attributes transmitted from generation to generation. In this logic, the narrator's blackness, whether conceived as cultural or biological identity, originates in his body. His troubled relationship to his blackness as culture or a sense of history is therefore a tragic failing.

Concern with the tragic alienation of the narrator dominates the work of such critics as Robert Stepto or Lucinda Mackethan, who focus their readings on the narrator's failure to recognize his "proper" heritage and tradition. For these readers, the novel represents an ironic revision of key figures and forms of the African American literary tradition: we should read the narrator's opinions on class and race as ironic because they are based in his own "illiteracy," his "inability to 'read' himself in his presen-

tation of his past" (Mackethan 140). Irony serves to illuminate the "narrator's failings through presentations of his misreadings and nonreadings of
'tribal' texts and contexts" (Stepto 188). In their presumption of an authentic originary blackness from which the narrator has fallen, these
critics repeat the cultural logic of race and passing: by posing the narrator's blackness as fixed, they imply that passing for white can only be a
deviation from his real identity as black.

The narrative itself works against the simple "black passing for white"
logic of passing, however, and its attendant model of race as the expression of a prior, embodied identity. Although the narrator claims to be
"really black," the terms of blackness and whiteness as they emerge in the
narrative belie the possibility of identity or authenticity that would allow
the narrator to *be* black *or* white. As the novel unfolds, Ex-Coloured
Man's relation to blackness is shown to be as inauthentic as his relation to
whiteness; rather than being "both black and white," he is in fact neither
black nor white.

In my insistence that Ex-Coloured Man is neither black nor white, I am
explicitly disagreeing with Henry Louis Gates Jr., who argues in his
introduction to the 1989 Vintage edition of *The Autobiography* that the
narrator's movement "between black and white racial identities is intended to establish the fact that such identities are entirely socially constructed" (xvi). Socially constructed identity seems here to connote an
identity easily altered or cast off: according to Gates, the narrator is
"white *and* black, at his whim and by his will" (xviii). But whether race
identity is construed as fixed or changeable, essential or constructed,
natural or cultural, the yoking of race with identity makes the phenomenon of passing a deviation from the otherwise supposedly direct and
authentic relation between an individual and her or his assigned or assumed race. The alternative posed by this text is to view passing not as a
deviation from the "truth" of the social identity of race but as the only
way in which a subject can take up a position of identity in terms of race.
All race identity is, in this view, the product of passing.

To this point, I have maintained that race is not and cannot be embodied as an authentic expression of being. Yet the ambivalence of the Ex-
Coloured Man requires an additional consideration of the reembodiment
of race as, in this case, an undeniable, irreducible fact of blood. Despite
The Autobiography's insistence that the narrator's blackness is an empty

mark and not an expression of what he is, either naturally or culturally, he is never completely free from the structure and strictures of that blackness.

What I am calling here a "reembodiment" is not a return to some idea of race as essence; race is not a physical or psychological fact but a legal fiction. The basis of distinction is purely arbitrary. Nevertheless, once the law has defined "a few drops of Negro blood" as the line separating black from white, the cultural definition of blackness becomes a naturalized fact. The law appears to take the demarcation between black and white as given and to legislate only the rules for each side. But, in fact, it is this law that produces black and white, calling into being a distinction by naming a difference. The "few drops of Negro blood" that make the narrator, in society's eyes, a colored man, have no meaning outside this law of difference; the mark is completely arbitrary but, as it functions in terms of the law, absolutely irresistible.[7]

Despite his failure ever really to be black, blackness continues to determine the narrator's consciousness in a way whiteness does not. As he says of his experience of being singled out in school: "I did indeed pass into another world. From that time I looked out through other eyes, my thoughts were coloured, my words dictated, my actions limited by one dominating, all-pervading idea which constantly increased in force and weight until I finally realized in it a great, tangible fact" (21). The mark of race, the "great tangible fact," is irrefutable; and yet the narrator's mediated relation to that mark, his futile effort to become what the mark says he in fact is, shows that the mark is empty of any referential content. Race is itself constitutively contradictory: it is produced as a bodily marking, but it is not, and cannot be, authentically embodied.

Although Ex-Coloured Man can experience blackness only as an outsider, he never escapes the imperative to embody blackness. His final decision to pass as white is couched in passivity, a refusal to declare himself one way or the other: "I finally made up my mind that I would neither disclaim the black race nor claim the white race; but that I would change my name, raise a moustache, and let the world take me for what it would" (190). Despite his casual attitude toward this final act of crossing over, the tension between discretion at others' knowing and paranoia that others may somehow already know or find out makes the Ex-Coloured Man's whiteness a state of perpetual anxiety, in a way blackness is not.[8]

At first, passing as white and the material success it makes possible are something he has pulled over on the world. His life is a prank, one big practical joke that belies all the prejudice he encounters: "The anomaly of my social position often appealed strongly to my sense of humour . . . [M]ore than once I felt like declaiming: 'I am a coloured man. Do I not disprove the theory that one drop of Negro blood renders a man unfit?' . . . I laughed heartily over what struck me as the capital joke I was playing" (197). His joke loses its punch when he falls in love with a white woman. The possibility of consummating his "whiteness," of joining himself to "the most dazzlingly white thing I had ever seen" (198), raises the specter of exposure and discovery. What begins as a fear of being caught out of character gives way to a paranoia that something invisible to himself will give him away: "I began to doubt myself. I began even to wonder if I really was like the men I associated with; if there was not, after all, an indefinable something which marked a difference" (200).

In fact, there is an "indefinable something which mark[s] a difference," but it is not the tangible something of appearance, behavior, or character. Rather, it is the mark of difference itself, the empty signifier of race that the narrator cannot shed: "This was the only time in my life that I ever felt absolute regret at being coloured, that I cursed the drops of African blood in my veins and wished that I were really white" (205). A feeling of duty impels him to divulge his secret, but even in the moment of confession, the narrative resists naming or fixing the identity of the Ex-Coloured Man: "I told her, in what words I do not know, the truth" (204). At the very moment in which the cultural logic of passing seems most powerfully to impose its rule of identity, the specular logic of passing intervenes: in the terms of the former, the narrator must confess the truth of his real identity, his real being. However, this real being is revealed as a *not*-being: Ex-Coloured Man does not name the truth because the truth *is not*.

The Ex-Coloured Man's lack of a stable or singular race identity and his failure to embody fully either race successfully, suggests the ontological impossibility that uneasily inhabits the structure of racial identity. To say "I am white" or "I am black" locates me in relation to others, but the *being* that relates me to each of these terms of identity is in fact a *not-being*. As Jean-Paul Sartre elegantly formulates this paradox, "The nature of consciousness simultaneously is to be what it is not and not to be what it

is" (116). In this knot of being and not-being, the facticity of identity—
the mark of the law that continually produces identity as codified difference—coexists in a tangled tension with the necessary inauthenticity of
the experience of that identity. As Ex-Coloured Man discovers, authenticity can be experienced only negatively, as the mark of failure.

The intellectual and political tradition of liberal humanism equates
authenticity with freedom: freedom is the freedom to "be yourself." We
ought not forget, however, that the exhortation to "be yourself" is simultaneously a call to liberation and a command of normalization.[9] Ex-
Coloured Man's failure to be either black or white is also a failure to "be
himself," both a failure to realize himself authentically and a failure to
identify himself with blackness or whiteness. This is not, however, his
personal, subjective failure; rather, this failure reveals the not-being, the
"that which one cannot be" at the heart of racial identity. Perhaps it is the
case, then, that my identity is not what I am but what I am passing for.

Notes

This essay is based on material from Samira Kawash, *Dislocating the Color Line*
(Stanford: Stanford UP, 1996). Used with permission. No material from this essay
may be reproduced without the express written permission of Stanford University
Press.

1. Johnson to Towns, 10 August 1912, in Miles Jackson, ed., "Letters to a Friend:
Correspondence from James Weldon Johnson to George A. Towns," *Phylon* 29
(1968): 189. Quoted in Levy, *James Weldon Johnson: Black Leader, Black Voice* 126.

2. *The Crisis* 5 (1912–13): 28. *The Crisis* was the magazine of the National
Association for the Advancement of Colored People (NAACP), founded and edited
by W. E. B. Du Bois. At the urging of Du Bois, Johnson served as executive secretary
of the NAACP from 1917 to 1918 and from 1920 to 1931.

3. *The Autobiography of an Ex-Coloured Man* is one of a number of "passing
novels" authored by African Americans in the late nineteenth and early twentieth
centuries that formed an important part of the African American literary project of
imagining and exploring "blackness" and "whiteness" in the post-emancipation
United States. Some other well-known examples are Frances E. W. Harper, *Iola
Leroy; or, Shadows Uplifted* (1892); Charles Waddell Chesnutt, *The House behind the
Cedars* (1900); Sutton E. Griggs, *The Hindered Hand* (1905); Walter White, *Flight*
(1926); Jessie Fauset, *Plum Bun* (1928); and Nella Larsen, *Passing* (1929). For an

Samira Kawash

overview of the passing novel in the Harlem Renaissance, see Singh, *The Novels of the Harlem Renaissance,* esp. chapter 4, " 'Fooling Our White Folks': Color Caste in American Life."

4. All page references to the text of *The Autobiography* are from the 1989 Vintage edition.

5. I am building on Collier's reading of the novel as a story "built upon a framework of two journeys: a physical and a psychological one" (365). However, my approach to the figure of travel or movement aims to go beyond Collier's interpretation of *The Autobiography* as an exploration of the "dilemma of the light-skinned Negro" (373).

6. Barbara Johnson, "Fanon and Lacan," paper delivered at the University of North Carolina, Chapel Hill, 28 March 1991.

7. The arbitrary nature of what counts as racial difference is especially apparent when one adopts a global perspective. Although legal and social definitions of race developed asymmetrically after emancipation in the United States, resulting in what has been called the "one drop" rule, this has not been the case in other multiracial societies. For a comparatist and historicizing account of the development of racial definitions in the United States, see Frank Davis, *Who is Black? One Nation's Definition.*

8. Eve Kosofsky Sedgwick's work on the epistemology of the homosexual closet provides an important framework for my thinking on the anxiety of passing. As Sedgwick notes, "Ethnic/cultural/religious oppressions such as anti-Semitism are more analogous [to homophobia] in that the stigmatized individual has at least notionally some discretion—although, importantly, it is never to be taken for granted how much—over other people's knowledge of her or his membership in the group" (*Epistemology of the Closet* 75). An invisible race stigma, the Ex-Coloured Man's "few drops of Negro blood," raises similar questions of knowledge and exposure.

9. This ambiguity is central to the tradition of liberal humanism. For example, the collapse of discipline and freedom marked in the command to "be yourself" echoes the double edge of Rousseau's promise that the sovereign citizen of the democratic state will be "forced to be free." See Jean-Jacques Rousseau, "On the Social Contract," *The Basic Political Writings* 150.

74

Sliding Significations: Passing as a Narrative and Textual Strategy in Nella Larsen's Fiction

MARTHA J. CUTTER

"I was determined . . . to be a person and not a charity or a problem, or even a daughter of the indiscreet Ham. Then, too, I wanted things. I knew I wasn't bad-looking and that I could 'pass.'" —Larsen, *Passing*

*N*ella Larsen's heroines all want to "pass." Furthermore, as the above quotation indicates, "passing" is more than just a racial strategy: it is a strategy "to be a person." Yet how can "passing" for what one is not help an individual "to be a person"? Only when "passing" becomes a subversive strategy for *avoiding* the enclosures of a racist, classist, and sexist society does it become truly liberating. However, in Larsen's first novel, *Quicksand* (1928), Helga Crane attempts to use "passing" as a way of finding a unitary sense of identity—a sense of identity structured around *one* role, a role that somehow corresponds to her "essential self." Although Helga Crane passes for many things (an exotic Other, a committed teacher, an art object, a devout Christian, a proponent of racial uplift, a dutiful mother) she is only, at any given point in her career, *one* of these things. So, in the end, she cannot resist the enclosures of her world and becomes entrapped in one stifling and constricting role—that of wife to a poor, rural preacher. On the other hand, Clare Kendry of Larsen's second novel, *Passing* (1929), uses "passing" as a way of avoiding the enclosures of a unitary identity. Like Helga, Clare passes for many things; yet unlike Helga, Clare chooses not to be confined by any one signification, be it of race, class, or sexuality. She founds her identity not on some sense of an "essential self" but rather on a self that is composed of and created by a series of guises and masks, performances and roles. In so doing, she transcends the labeling of society, for the more she passes, the more problematic and plural her presence becomes.

Thus, in her second novel, Larsen raises "passing" to a subversive narrative strategy and to an artful method for keeping open the play of textual meaning. Clare's sliding significations within the novel create what Roland Barthes would call a "writerly text," one that makes "the reader no longer a consumer, but a producer of the text" (4). Clare's problematic passing presents the ultimate mechanism for creating "a perpetual present . . . before the infinite play of the world . . . is traversed, intersected, stopped, plasticized, by some singular system . . . which reduces the plurality of entrances, the opening of networks, the infinity of languages" (Barthes 5). In the galaxy of signs that is the novel *Passing*, Clare functions as a signifier whose meaning cannot be stabilized, fixed, confined, limited; and "passing" becomes the ultimate mechanism for creating a text that refuses to be contained, consumed, or reduced to a unitary meaning.

Many critics have noted the frequency of "passing" in Larsen's works, but most seem to see "passing" in a limited and negative light. Cheryl Wall, for example, comments that "Larsen's protagonists attempt to fashion a sense of self free of both suffocating restrictions of ladyhood and fantasies of the exotic female Other. They fail. The tragedy for these mulattoes is the impossibility of self-definition. Larsen's protagonists assume false identities that ensure social survival but result in psychological suicide" ("Passing for What?" 98).[1] I would contend that it is not the assumption of a false identity per se that causes Larsen's protagonists to fail. Rather, the assumption of only one guise or one form of passing causes Larsen's characters to become stable, static, fixed in their meaning, entrapped within social definitions. To assume a single identity in a world in which identity itself is often a performance—a mask, a public persona—is to ensure psychological suicide.

Larsen's novel *Quicksand* demonstrates the fallacy of belief in a "true self" most clearly through the character Helga Crane: Helga repeatedly attempts to find a true identity, only to learn that no such thing exists, only a variety of social roles. At Naxos, for example, Helga passes as a dignified and committed teacher; she tries to fit herself into Naxos's strict mold, even though this means curbing her own desires for colorful clothing and relegating her behavior to "the strenuous rigidity of conduct required in this huge educational community" (1). This "strenuous rigidity of conduct" at Naxos requires accepting a particular social role for the school and for African Americans in general; as a white minister says of the school, "Naxos Negroes knew what was expected of them. . . .

They knew enough to stay in their places . . . to be satisfied to the estate in which they had been called, hewers of wood and drawers of water" (3). Naxos is, in fact, a world where everyone must assume the same social identity—an identity as a "good" black who knows his or her place, an identity that stamps out individuality in favor of bland acquiescence. At Naxos, in short, everyone must "pass."

Helga pretends to support the school's mission and passes as a committed teacher, but in reality she sees the school as "a big knife with cruelly sharp edges ruthlessly cutting all to a pattern, the white man's pattern" (4). Helga does not endorse this vision of education, feeling extreme dislike for this world: "The South. Naxos. Negro education. Suddenly she hated them all" (3). Yet ultimately Helga realizes that her inability to fit in at Naxos has less to do with the role Naxos offers her and more to do with herself: "Helga . . . had never quite achieved the unmistakable Naxos mold, would never achieve it, in spite of much trying. . . . A lack somewhere. Always she had considered it a lack of understanding on the part of the community, but in her present new revolt she realized that the fault had been partly hers. A lack of acquiescence. She hadn't really wanted to be made over" (7). On the one hand, Helga has struggled desperately to pass for a true Naxonian. Yet she has also resisted this role, believing that the role itself is not entirely to her liking.

Helga's relationships with James Vayle and Robert Anderson also illuminate her desire to fit into a particular social group yet still retain her "true" identity. With Vayle, Helga feels the security that comes from having "family": "The Vayles were people of consequence. The fact that they were a 'first family' had been one of James's attractions for the obscure Helga" (8). Helga wants to have a powerful social identity and influential family connections; however she does not want to give up any of her own personality to gain this: "She had wanted social background, but—she had not imagined that it could be so stuffy" (8). While she longs to be an "insider," she also feels smothered by the prospect of adapting herself to a particular social role. Similarly, Helga longs to be an "insider" to Robert Anderson's vision of education; when Anderson tries to convince her to stay at Naxos, she feels "a mystifying yearning which sang and throbbed in her. She felt again that urge for service, not now for her people, but for this man who was talking so earnestly of his work, his plans, his hopes. An insistent need to be a part of them sprang in her" (20). Anderson offers Helga the prospect of a new social definition—she will not be a Naxos devotee but rather an Anderson devotee. However, when Anderson makes the statement that Helga is " 'a lady' " (21), Helga finds herself rejecting the role Anderson offers, realizing that it does not mesh with her sense of self. As she tells Anderson, she is no lady, no docile and demure matron who belongs at Naxos: "My father was a gambler who deserted my mother, a white immigrant. It is even uncertain that they were married. As I said at first, I don't belong here. I shall be leaving at once" (21).

Ironically enough, in this scene Helga chafes at being labeled precisely what she has been trying to become for all those years at Naxos: a "lady." Helga does not want to become confined by this unitary definition of self. As soon as she lets go of a particular social identity, however, as soon as she stops passing for something, she feels a terrifying sense of "apprehension" (10) and even vertigo: "The room whirled about her in an impish, hateful way. Familiar objects seemed suddenly unhappily distant. Faintness closed about her like a vise" (8). Throughout the novel, such moments of vertigo mark Helga's abandonment of a specific social identity— her sensation before she has located a new social role. Cut free from social restrictions, Helga experiences not liberation but fear and a sensation of falling. Indeed, she may be falling into a void of nothingness—the nothingness of identity stripped from all its social moorings. In these moments, Helga is confronting the possibility that perhaps she has no "essential self" to discover; she is glimpsing the idea that perhaps identity itself is a mask, a social and public role, rather than a reflection of some core of being. Such knowledge is terrifying to Helga, and she usually responds by fleeing to another persona.

In New York and Chicago, Helga thinks she has found "freedom" after "the cage which Naxos had been to her" (27). In fact, what she has actually found is another role. The key to this identity is provided by Mrs. Hayes-Rore, who hears Helga's tragic family history and comments: "I wouldn't mention that my people are white, if I were you. Colored people won't understand it, and after all it's your own business. . . . I'll just tell Anne that you're a friend of mine whose mother's dead. That'll place you well enough and it's all true" (41). In fact, Mrs. Hayes-Rore does "place" Helga, both literally and metaphorically: she finds Helga a place to live, but she also finds Helga a social identity. Helga is to ignore her mixed heritage and take her place firmly within the black middle-class world.

Both women are aware that this new identity involves passing. As Helga completes the recital of the facts of her life, the women resume their social personas, which according to Larsen do involve "passing," concealment behind socially acceptable masks: "During the little pause that followed Helga's recital, the faces of the two women, which had been bare, seemed to harden. It was almost as if they had slipped on masks" (39). Both Helga and Mrs. Hayes-Rore retreat into their safe, socially defined, and acceptable roles—they resume their masks. This exchange clearly demonstrates that the society Helga moves in is one in which identity itself is a socially defined public construct rather than an expression of inner or true self. Mrs. Hayes-Rore, for example, masks her true attitudes about topics such as miscegenation behind social conventions: "The woman felt that [Helga's] story, dealing as it did with race intermingling and possibly adultery, was beyond definite discussion. For among black people, as among white people, it is tacitly understood that these things are not mentioned—and therefore they do not exist" (39). What Mrs. Hayes-Rore actually feels about miscegenation is not stated; instead, her views are placed in their social context: what black and white people do and do not discuss.

Helga still clings to the idea that she can find a social identity that corresponds to her inner self. In Harlem, Helga thinks she has lost "that tantalizing oppression of loneliness and isolation which always . . . had been a part of her existence" (45). Her immersion in the social role offered by Harlem's black middle-class society is so strong that for many months she does not question this identification at all; she firmly intends, one day, to marry and have a home and children in Harlem. Helga also thinks she has found a place where she can belong: "*Again* she had that strange *transforming* experience, this time not so fleetingly, that magic sense of having come home" (43, emphasis mine). Larsen's language emphasizes that although Helga thinks she truly belongs, she is passing: once again, she finds a role that transforms her from an isolated individual into a connected member of a social network. But Helga confuses belonging to a certain social group with discovering who she is; she feels great joy "at seeming at last to belong somewhere. For she considered that she had, as she put it, 'found herself' " (44). Helga's sense of identity is clearly structured around her social and public role, yet she believes that she has "found herself"—that she has gained access to her essential identity.

Of course, this public role does not mesh completely with her perception of her inner self, and Helga's feelings of oppression return: "It was as if she were shut up, boxed up, with hundreds of her race, closed up with that something in the racial character which had always been, to her, inexplicable, alien. Why, she demanded in fierce rebellion, should she be yoked to these despised black folk?" (54–55). Helga realizes that she has been passing once again; although she has pretended to be part of this society, she knows that "she didn't, in spite of her racial markings, belong to these dark segregated people. She was different" (55).[2] Helga's feelings of fear and vertigo reappear: "For a moment everything seemed to be spinning round; even she felt that she was circling aimlessly" (58–59). Helga is indeed circling aimlessly, for she has not yet found a new identity. Abandoning her Harlem identity, she feels "a little frightened, and then shocked to discover that, for some unknown reason, it was of herself she was afraid" (47). Helga's shock stems from a glimpse of the instability and perhaps nonexistence of a self apart from social roles.

Rather than confronting the vacuum of her "essential" self, Helga makes her way to Denmark, where she believes she will find a truer identity. As when she first arrived in Harlem, she feels a sense of freedom, of having escaped; she finds "that blessed sense of belonging to herself alone and not to a race" (64). Helga wants to "belong to herself alone" but never stops to question whether it is possible to have an identity that is completely self-defined. Moreover, Helga has not abandoned her search for a public identity: "With rapture almost, she let herself drop into the blissful sensation of visualizing herself in different, strange places, among approving and admiring people, where she would be appreciated, and understood" (57). Judith Berzon argues that Helga seeks "a status that will bring with it peace, but not stagnation" (224), but as these quotes indicate, Helga also seeks a status that will bring with it status, that is, social prestige. She dreams of being "understood"—of not having to play a role that masks who she is. Yet her dreams also involve a specifically social aspect: she will be "among approving and admiring people." She dreams, in short, of a place where a powerful social identity will mesh perfectly with her essential self.

Denmark is no such place. Here Helga is again given a persona, a mask to wear, and she becomes trapped by this unitary definition of self. Helga's aunt has already "determined the role that Helga was to play" (68), that of an exotic Other: "She was incited to make an impression, a voluptuous impression. She was incited to inflame attention and admiration. She was dressed for it, subtly schooled for it. And after a little while she gave herself up wholly to the fascinating business of being seen, gaped at, desired" (74). But she allows herself to be so transformed only to find that Axel Olsen's portrait of her—which depicts her as she has created herself, as a "sensual creature" (89)—disgusts her. Olsen's portrait does not individualize Helga but assimilates her to the racist and sexist stereotype of the "jungle woman." Once again Helga has become trapped by a unitary definition of self, again passing for something she is not, as Larsen makes clear by continually referring to Helga's face as masked: "[Helga's] smile had become a fixed aching mask" (71), and "[Fru Dahl] gazed penetratingly into the masked face of her niece" (79). Soon Helga's mask begins to suffocate her; she feels "discontent, and . . . growing dissatisfaction with her peacock's life" (81).

Helga wonders if the problem might be within herself but quickly dismisses this possibility: "Was there, without her knowing it, some peculiar lack in her? Absurd" (81). Yet, while in Denmark, Helga does begin to see some of the cracks in her identity. She wonders, "Why couldn't she have two lives, or why couldn't she be satisfied in one place?" (93), seeing "the division of her life into two parts in two lands, into physical freedom in Europe and spiritual freedom in America" (96). Here, Helga consciously acknowledges for the first time that her identity may not be a seamless, unified whole—that her identity might be split, dual. Helga equates these two sides of her identity with her two races and believes that in Denmark she has abandoned her black identity. In fact, it can be argued that in Denmark, Helga feels closer to her race than she has ever felt before, speaking of the black race thus: "*These* were her people. . . . How absurd she had been to think that another country, other people could liberate her from the ties which bound her forever to these mysterious, these terrible, these fascinating, these lovable, dark hordes. Ties that were of the spirit. Ties not only superficially entangled with mere outline of features or color of skin. Deeper. Much deeper than either of these" (95). Whereas Helga has previously denied her allegiance to her race, seeing it as mere physical similarity, she now claims that her kinship with her race is much more than skin deep—it is spiritual and in fact allied with her essential self.

In Denmark, Helga believes she has been forced to ignore this part of her identity; yet in America, she has been forced to ignore the white part of her heritage—her status as a product of a mixed marriage. No wonder Helga sees herself as "moving shuttle-like from continent to continent . . . from the pale calm of Copenhagen to the colorful lure of Harlem" (96); in fact, Helga has been shuttling back and forth between white and black identities. In wishing for two lives, however, Helga reveals her ignorance of the complexity of her own search for identity. In America, Helga's "black self" has played a variety of roles: she has passed as a Naxos lady and a black bourgeois; and when she returns to New York, she takes up still another role: religious convert. Helga wishes she could have two lives and two geographical spaces within which to define her identity, when in fact, her identity seems more plural than dual. Larsen further emphasizes the plurality and instability of Helga's identity when Helga contemplates becoming Dr. Anderson's mistress. After Anderson's impetuous kiss stirs Helga's passions, she considers an affair with him, all the while knowing that she is not "after all, a rebel from society, Negro society. It did mean something to her. She had no wish to stand alone" (107). Through Anderson, Larsen emphasizes that Helga's identity is not dual but plural and even contradictory. Helga thinks of risking her place within society, even as she affirms that she is no social rebel willing to sacrifice all for passion.

Helga herself, however, does not face these conflicts; rather than realizing the plural nature of her identity, she flees again. Her vertigo returns, and she is forced to cling to the Reverend Mr. Pleasant Green: "She had been seized with a hateful feeling of vertigo and obliged to lay firm hold on his arm to keep herself from falling" (115). Literally and symbolically, Helga does lay "firm hold" onto Reverend Green; she lays a firm hold onto the identity he offers her—preacher's wife—to keep from falling into the abyss of nothingness that she now suspects is herself. Once again, Helga believes she had found "a place for herself" (118) but realizes eventually that she is still passing. Helga turns herself into the perfect preacher's wife, only to find that this role controls and confines her: "She couldn't endure it. Her suffocation and shrinking loathing were too great. Not to be borne. Again. For she had to admit that it wasn't new, this feeling of dissatisfaction, of asphyxiation. Something like it she had experienced before. In Naxos. In New York. In Copenhagen. This differed only in degree" (134). Behind her mask, Helga is suffocating: she has found no liberation in her strategy of "passing." Barbara Christian has argued that Helga is trapped and destroyed by her womb (53), and certainly, as Hazel Carby states, "The novel ends with [Helga's] fifth pregnancy which means her certain death" (169). Yet Helga ties the sense of entrapment she experiences in the South not with her biological destruction but with the suffocation she has experienced elsewhere when trapped within a role. Larsen's text thus allies Helga's destruction with both her biological capacities and her inability to find an identity that expresses her true self.

Throughout the novel, Helga wears a series of masks; through these masks, she hopes to avoid the enclosures of society and to find a role that corresponds to her sense of self. She is always seeking a role—a single persona—that can encompass and unify the various pieces of her identity. As Thadious Davis observes, Helga is "a restless, complex personality" who "seeks synthesis of self" (*Nella Larsen* 253).[3] Yet Helga is unable to find synthesis of self; instead, she finds a world that offers her only partial and limiting choices for self-definition. Rather than seeking to multiply these choices, Helga moves from identity to identity, always hoping to find a role that meshes with her essential self—a social role that will not involve passing. Helga never confronts the fact that perhaps her identity itself is both plural and social and, therefore, that she can never achieve synthesis of self, she can never stop passing. And she never confronts the fact that one is always on "quicksand"—that firm ground, a real self behind the mask, may not exist.

Helga also refuses to confront conflicts of identity that center around her sexuality. Helga will not admit the power her sexuality has over others, and although she uses it to gain roles she desires, she also denies it. With James Vayle, for example, Helga feels ashamed of her sexual appeal but knows it is what attracts him to her, what allows her to be part of his powerful family (8). Throughout the novel she consistently denies her sexual appeal and has feelings of "nausea" and shock when contemplating her own feelings of sexual desire (24). Helga uses her sexuality to get her from one role to another, but she also continually contains it and recoils from acknowledging its power.[4]

Quicksand thus stands in direct contrast with Larsen's second novel, for the protagonist of *Passing*—Clare Kendry Bellew—tries to be all things to all people at all times, and she uses her destabilizing sexuality to multiply the roles available to her. As Irene Redfield notes, Clare has a " 'having' " way (*Passing* 174): she takes what she wants, regardless of the consequences: "Clare, it seemed, still retained her ability to secure the thing that she wanted in the face of any opposition, and in utter disregard of the convenience and desire of others" (201). And what Clare wants is everything; as Irene puts it, "The trouble with Clare was, not only that she wanted to have her cake and eat it too, but that she wanted to nibble at the cakes of other folk as well" (182). Metaphorically, the trouble with Clare is that she refuses to contain her desires; she will not curtail her "having" ways. Thus for Clare, "passing" becomes a mechanism to get what she wants—which is not a singular identity, an identity that corresponds to a theoretical inner self, but an identity that can escape the enclosures of race, class, and sexuality, enclosures that would limit her "having" ways.

Through Clare, Larsen creates a character with multiple significations and a text that resists containment; one that, with its plural sexualities and identities, remains mysteriously enigmatic to the end. Unlike Helga's, Clare's identity never becomes fixed or stabilized, and unlike *Quicksand*, *Passing* never limits or constrains its own meaning, its own possible readings. *Passing* is thus a more open text than *Quicksand*, for whereas *Quicksand*'s central character and its narrative structures end by closing down the possibilities of meaning, *Passing*'s characters and narrative structures remain open and writerly. As Umberto Eco explains, some texts challenge readers' complacency and force them to construct their own solutions to enigmas. Such texts are characterized by narrative structures which are flexible and which "validat[e] . . . the widest possible range of interpretative proposals" (33).[5] Clare's presence within *Passing* creates a narrative that is unstable, flexible, open. In fact, Clare's sliding significations within the text are meant to destabilize both other characters' and the reader's sense of identity. Through Clare, readers are deliberately invited to construct their own interpretations of the text and in so doing to see the problematic plural of Clare's identity and of identity in general. Eco suggests that open texts invite their "Model Readers to reproduce their own processes of deconstruction by a plurality of free interpretive choices" (40). *Passing* is a writerly and deconstructive text in that we as readers must create our own interpretations of Clare and of other characters in the novel, and we must do so by choosing from a number of different, equally plausible interpretative scenarios. And the more problematic and plural our own interpretations of the text as a whole become, the more we reproduce the instability of our own identities.

The narrative's deconstructive processes are thus produced on an intra- and intertextual level, both between characters within the text and between text and reader. Within the novel, many characters insist on a unitary definition of identity for themselves and for others, a definition of identity that Clare destabilizes. Brian Redfield and Jack Bellew, for example, are ensconced within their social roles, yet both find that Clare destabilizes their sense of identity and of the world around them. Brian has rather reluctantly but solidly assumed his allotted place as a part of the black heterosexual middle class in America, despite the fact that he abhors his country's racism and his own profession and has no physical desire for his wife, calling sex a joke (189). He has suppressed the conflicts in his identity, the knowledge that he is in fact passing for something he does not want to be.[6] Yet in the process of the novel, his role inscription becomes destabilized, and Clare seems to be connected to Brian's discontent. Irene believes that she has "a special talent for understanding" Brian, that she "knew him as well as he knew himself, or better" (187). Only six pages later, however, Irene admits to feeling "helpless" after Clare has infiltrated their lives (193). Irene fears that she has lost control of her husband: "It was as if he had stepped out beyond her reach into some section, strange and walled, where she could not get at him" (214).

Irene's explanation for these changes is that her husband is having an affair with Clare. Of course, many critics have pointed out that Irene is an unreliable narrator who has no hard evidence for this supposition. But an omniscient narrative perspective within the novel also conveys information Irene does not know.[7] Brian's restlessness is confirmed by this omniscient narration, as well as by the overall development of the narrative. His feelings of restlessness are intensified by Clare's presence; for example, in the later parts of the novel, when Clare is around the household more often, his denouncements of the United States grow increasingly bitter and vocal. And at Clare's death, Brian speaks in a "frenzied hoarse voice, which Irene had never heard before" (241), his usual calm and emotionless demeanor having been destabilized; symbolically, Clare has shocked him out of his usual and habitual pose.

Again and again Clare seems to have this effect on people: her presence destabilizes their role inscription. Clare's husband, Jack Bellew, through his insistence on the "innate" differences between the races, emphasizes a conception of identity that is essentialistic, fixed, and unitary: one is white or black, not both of these things at once. Like Clare's aunts who "couldn't forgive the tar-brush" and who believe that "the good God . . . intended the sons and daughter of Ham to sweat" (159), Jack Bellew claims that blacks are "scrimy devils," always "robbing and killing people. And . . . worse" (172). Bellew even believes he can discern who is black and bar them from his household: "I draw the line at that. No niggers in my family. Never have been and never will be" (171). Bellew believes he can draw the color line, separate black from white, prevent the intrusion of the unwanted and savage Other. Of course, he cannot; as Irene notes, he is "sitting here surrounded by three black devils, drinking tea" (172). And before the novel ends, Bellew realizes this. Literally, he learns that Irene, Gertrude, and Clare are not "white"; he learns that his knowledge of race is not as certain as he believes it is—he cannot draw the color line. Bellew also learns that his own identity—which is so firmly founded on an opposition between himself and a black Other—is subject to erosion. Bellew bases his identity on a sense of absolute racial differences that he can know and tell. The world is very simple to him: either you are white (and therefore "good") or you are black (and therefore "bad"). Yet Clare disrupts this binarism by being both his adored wife *and* black. And, certainly, she disrupts his sense of the firmness of these divisions, for he has lived with Clare for twelve years and never discerned that she is black. Bellew's understanding of the world around him and of his own identity is thus disrupted, if not completely unhinged, by Clare.[8]

Clare's ability to disrupt an individual's role inscription is, of course, clearest in the case of Irene Redfield, for Irene is extremely committed to the persona she has achieved. Irene Redfield adheres "to her own class and kind" (166), as well as possibly repressing her homosexual desire for Clare, as Deborah McDowell has noted. Like Jack Bellew, Irene believes in the fixity of social and racial roles: she likes to be able to place people, also liking them to remain in their places. She judges Clare's smile, for example, to be "too provocative for a waiter" (152). Irene is consistently irritated by Clare's refusal to adhere to proper class distinctions and injunctions, such as one does not flirt with waiters, one does not chitchat with the maid, and one does not intrude where one is not wanted. Irene also believes in people staying in their proper racial positions; she claims to feel loyalty to "the race" and works hard to remain within her own social niche within black middle-class society. Any disruption of Irene's world frightens her greatly, and she fights off threats "to that security of place and substance which she insisted upon for her sons and in a lesser degree for herself" (190).

And yet, although she claims to be pleased with "the easy monotony" (190) of her life, contradictions within her behavior reveal that she too is "passing." Although Irene claims that she never passes (160), when she first appears in the novel she is passing at a fancy restaurant that would eject her if her racial identity was known. In fact, Irene enjoys "being wafted upward on a magic carpet to another world, pleasant, quiet, and strangely remote from the sizzling one that she had left below" (147). Irene's passing is more than just a matter of convenience: she enjoys the sensation of leaving her habitual racial niche; she enjoys passing out of the dark, black, sizzling world and into the magically pleasant, remote, and quiet white world of the Drayton Hotel. Irene's fascination with passing is also revealed when she questions Clare: "She wished to find out about this hazardous business of 'passing,' this breaking away from all that was familiar and friendly to take one's chances in another environment, not entirely strange, perhaps, but certainly not entirely friendly. What, for example, one did about background, how one accounted for oneself" (157). Irene sees passing as a problem of identity—how one accounts for oneself, defines oneself apart from all known social ties but it is a problem that clearly interests her. So despite Irene's insistence on safety, stability, and social fixity, she does have a fascination with that which transcends the limits and refuses to stay stable and fixed.

Irene usually represses this fascination; for example, she condemns Clare's passing and states that she herself has no desire to pass, that she has "everything I want" (160). Irene believes that she and Clare are "strangers in their ways and means of living. Strangers in their desires and ambitions. Strangers even in their racial consciousness. Between them the barrier was just as high, just as broad, and just as firm as if in Clare did not run that strain of black blood" (192). Still, the parallels between Clare's and Irene's lives and thoughts are all too clear; as Jonathan Little has noted, "Clare is Irene's projected psychological double. It is through Irene's descriptions of Clare that readers learn about Irene's deepest and unacknowledged impulses and desires" (177).[9] No wonder, then, that Irene fears Clare: like Helga Crane, Irene fears a confrontation with herself, with the contradictory, plural, or even absent self behind the social facade. And, like Helga, Irene refuses to confront her fear: "For an instant a recrudescence of that sensation of fear which she had had while looking into Clare's eyes that afternoon touched her. A slight shiver ran over her. 'It's nothing,' she told herself. 'Just somebody walking over my grave, as the children say'" (176). Irene reduces her feelings to a childish aphorism rather than examining them. Yet the feelings aroused by Clare do not disappear; three months later, after she has torn up Clare's letter and "dropped Clare out of her mind" (178), Irene's fear remains.

After Clare's arrival, Irene is no longer quite so content to stick to her race; in a scene that parallels Helga Crane's dislike of being boxed up with her race, Irene feels a similar sense of suffocation: "Irene Redfield wished, for the first time in her life, that she had not been born a Negro. For the first time she suffered and rebelled because she was unable to disregard the burden of race. . . . Surely, no other people so cursed as Ham's dark children" (225). Irene repeats Clare's language of being one of "Ham's dark children," also reiterating Clare's sense of the constraints that race imposes. Irene has never before questioned what her race means to her: it is merely something to adhere to, not something to think about. But race itself is a gap in this text, a mystery, something completely unfathomable. When Irene questions Brian about why people pass, he responds, "If I knew that, I'd know what race is" (185). Brian understands that race itself is difficult to define, is enigmatic.

Irene's racial identity is thus destabilized by Clare's presence, and for the first time, she begins to question what race means. Clare also destabilizes Irene's role as wife and mother. When Irene suspects that Clare and Brian are having an affair, her identity is profoundly destabilized: "She shook her head, unable to speak, for there was a choking in her throat, and the confusion in her mind was like the beating of wings. . . . The face in the mirror vanished from [Irene's] sight, blotted out by this thing which had so suddenly flashed across her groping mind" (217). Irene's face vanishes from sight; symbolically she becomes a gap, a blank, an absence. Larsen's imagery implies that without her identity as the wife of Brian and the mother of his children, Irene has no identity at all. Irene also realizes that Clare has changed her: "Life about her, apparently, went on exactly as before. . . . It was only that she had changed. Knowing, stumbling on this thing, had changed her. It was as if in a house long dim, a match had been struck, showing ghastly shapes where had been only blurred shadows" (218). We might say that Irene's identity has been "Clarified"—it has been illuminated ("a match had been struck"), but it has also been darkened, as Irene says: "Clare . . . had suddenly clouded all her days" (220).

What gives Clare the ability to disrupt so many people's role inscriptions? In a world of fixed identities, Clare is such a powerful presence because she denies all the boundaries that the other characters work so hard to establish and maintain; she denies divisions of race, class, and even sexuality. Clare's plural identity destabilizes others' sense of identity, but it also destabilizes the narrative as a whole. For Clare is the element that refuses to be contained, the open textual structure that forces the reader to be not a consumer but a producer of the text. Clare's presence within the novel requires the reader to be active in constructing the meaning of the text, for Clare herself provides no answers; to the end, she is passing, plural, and ultimately unknowable. Like Barthes's pensive text, Clare always "seems to be keeping in reserve some ultimate meaning, one [she] does not express but whose place [she] keeps free and signifying" (216). But unlike Barthes's classic text, Clare's pensiveness is not merely an "allusion" that creates "closure" but also is a product of her plural and uncontainable presence within the narrative, a refusal of closure.

From the start, Irene notices the differences between herself and Clare. Clare is uninterested in Irene's main preoccupation (safety); she does not care for the stable and sheltered life that Irene works so earnestly to maintain. Clare admits she does not have "any proper morals or sense of duty" (210) and that "to get the things I want badly enough, I'd do anything, hurt anybody, throw anything away" (210). Clare's statements emphasize a refusal to bind herself by the same scruples as does Irene, scruples about what is or is not proper conduct. Clare's attitudes clearly frighten Irene, for Irene knows they have the potential to disrupt her stable world and her stable identity: "Above everything else [Irene] had wanted, had striven, to keep undisturbed the pleasant routine of her life. And now Clare Kendry had come into it, and with her the menace of impermanence" (229). Clare represents such a menace because she refuses to play by the rules that Irene and others believe in so firmly. And a player who refuses to play by the rules calls those rules into question, suggesting that they are not permanent, fixed, and closed but changeable, unstable, and open.

The rules Clare calls into question involve race, class, and sexuality. Clare insists on having a plural identity that slides from race to race, from class to class, from one sexual orientation to another. Clare uses her sexuality, for example, in a variety of situations and with a variety of people to get what she wants. Although I do not disagree with Deborah McDowell's reading of a homosexual subtext in *Passing*, Larsen emphasizes that Clare insists on being an object of attraction to *both* sexes. Certainly Clare flirts with men and even with strange waiters in restaurants. Yet Clare also turns her sexual appeal on Irene, and Irene usually responds by doing what Clare wants: "She'd done it again. Allowed Clare Kendry to persuade her into promising to do something for which she had neither time nor any special desire. What was it about Clare's voice that was so appealing, so very seductive?" (165). As it is in other passages of the novel, Clare's voice is here a synecdoche for her presence as a whole. Seductive and appealing, Clare's voice is an instrument she uses to further her having ways. She also uses her sexuality in this way, turning her "potent" smile on Irene to calm Irene's anger, or soothing Irene's feelings of outrage by "turn[ing] on Irene her seductive caressing smile" (169).

Clare also insists on a plural and uncontainable class identity. While Clare is growing up, a certain ambiguity exists about her class position: "Clare had never been exactly one of the group, just as she'd never been merely the janitor's daughter, but the daughter of Mr. Bob Kendry, who, it was true, was a janitor, but who also, it seemed, had been in college with some of their fathers" (154). Clare is not exactly middle-class, for her father is a blue-collar worker, but she is not exactly lower-class, for she and her father are on good social terms with other educated middle-class blacks. In her youth Clare is an outsider because of this ambiguity, but as an adult she uses her ambiguous class position as a strategy of empowerment. Clare passes to lift herself out of her unfortunate class position, to get the "things" she associates with middle-class life. But she also wants to transcend a bourgeois class position; seeing the possessions of others makes Clare "all the more determined to get them, *and others*" (159, emphasis mine). When Clare marries Jack Bellew, who possesses "untold gold" (159) from South Africa, Bellew's wealth allows Clare to flaunt her position in the upper class in front of her middle-class friends. Clare often wears clothes and jewelry that indicate that her social position is *above* the bourgeois world Irene inhabits: "Around her neck hung a string of amber beads that would easily have made six or eight like one Irene owned" (220). Larsen continually associates Clare with various symbols of wealth and luxury: Clare is "golden" (203) or wearing "a little golden bowl of a hat" (220), and her eyes sparkle "like dark jewels" (203). Jack Bellew's money thus allows Clare to be gold and golden: to transcend the class position she was born into and that of her former acquaintances.

Yet Clare's newfound wealth is rewarding only in opposition to her poor and beleaguered background; in other words, her upper-class status is valuable only as a reminder of how far she has come from her obscure origins. Clare thus insists on a class position that is both upper- and lower-class at the same time; she flaunts her wealth while also making her friends remember her former status as the daughter of an itinerant, alcoholic janitor. On her way to a party at the Freeland's, for example, Clare reminds Irene and Brian of her obscure origins: "Ask 'Rene. My father was a janitor, you know, in the good old days" (236). Clare's friends are made to remember that she was once below them in the class structure but is now above them. And it is certainly no coincidence that in the final scene of the novel, Clare wears a dress of "red and gold" (239). This dress flaunts her wealth but is also meant to be a reminder of Clare's poorer days when she sat sewing a "pathetic little red frock" (143) to wear to her Sunday school picnic while her drunken father "raged threateningly up and down the shabby room" (143–44). The red and gold dress Clare wears in the final scene connects the "old" Clare with the "new" one, the poor and pathetic daughter of a janitor with the golden wife of a wealthy and influential businessman. Clare's dress, like Clare herself, emphasizes her plural and unfixable class position.

Clare maintains too, a racial identity that is plural and unstable, mysterious and enigmatic. Abandoning her race for twelve years, Clare still claims to feel "homesick" for it, as she tells Irene: "You can't know how in this pale life of mine I am all the time seeing the bright pictures of that other that I once thought I was glad to be free of. . . . It's like an ache, a pain that never ceases" (145). Whereas Helga Crane vacillates between black and white identities, Clare chooses to have both a black and white identity. Or rather, Clare chooses not to be constrained by either a black or white identity; she chooses to slide back and forth between these identities. In fact, what most disturbs Irene about Clare is precisely that she insists on moving *back and forth* between races; Irene tells Clare: "I can't help thinking that you ought not to come up here, ought not to run the risk of knowing Negroes" (194). Irene wants Clare to stay in her place, in a fixed and stable identity as the "white" wife of the racist Jack Bellew.

But Clare is interested not in a fixed and stable identity; rather she wants one that is most "having." If Clare is to have Jack Bellew's wealth, she must maintain her white identity. But if Clare is to have the ability to flaunt her wealth in front of those who knew her as a poor and miserable girl, she must also maintain her black identity. Larsen's characterization shows a brilliant nexus between Clare's racial and class concerns: Clare initially passes from the black to the white race to transcend her class position, but to flaunt this new class position, she must pass back from a white racial identity to a black one.[10] To have all she wants, Clare must maintain multiple identities—multiple subject positions—and pass back and forth between them. According to Mary Dearborn, Clare's passing is a symbol for the way she finds "freedom in her very marginality" (60). However, Larsen's text indicates that Clare demands to be central, not marginal, to a variety of different social networks, actually finding freedom in her plural and often contradictory subject positions.

When Clare initially leaves black society, she is described as having "disappeared," both literally and in terms of people's consciousness (153–54). When one of her former acquaintances sees her, Clare is completely ignored: "Once I met Margaret Hammer in Marshall Field's. I'd have spoken, was on the very point of doing it, but she cut me dead. My dear 'Rene, I assure you that from the way she looked through me, even I was uncertain whether I was actually there in the flesh or not" (154).

Clare has passed over into another world; literally and figuratively, she is a ghost to her black former acquaintances. Through this imagery, Larsen emphasizes that for Clare's friends, passing is a permanent and irrevocable act; once one passes into the white world, one's black identity dies. Yet Clare insists on passing back and forth between these separate realms; she insists on being alive in both worlds.[11]

In so doing, Clare throws into question racial divisions, as well as the idea of firm and irrevocable differences between the races. Larsen's descriptions of Clare's appearance also continually remind the reader that Clare refuses easy racial categorization and that race itself is unknowable, mysterious, and even unstable. Irene describes Clare as having "ivory skin" and "gold hair," but she also has "arresting eyes, slow and mesmeric, and with, for all their warmth, something withdrawn and secret about them. . . . They were Negro eyes! mysterious and concealing" (161). Clare's skin and hair mark her as "white," yet her eyes mark her as "black." Moreover, Clare's eyes both conceal *and* reveal her racial identity. Clare's fair skin also becomes a trope for the way her physical appearance obscures her racial identity. Jack Bellew, for example, jokingly refers to the fact that his wife is "gettin' darker and darker. I tell her if she don't look out, she'll wake up one of these days and find she's turned into a nigger" (171). These statements imply that Clare's skin, despite its fairness, its whiteness, might give away the secret of Clare's "true" racial identity, of Clare's blackness. Yet despite his jokes, Bellew is completely fooled by Clare's racial identity, which in his eyes has nothing to do with her actual skin color. A moment later Bellew comments to Clare: "I know you're no nigger, so it's all right. You can get as black as you please as far as I'm concerned, since I know you're no nigger" (171). All the references Bellew makes to Clare's skin therefore mean nothing to him, for he believes that race is not, in fact, skin deep (an odd statement for a racist who believes in biological essentialism). Clearly, then, Clare's "true" race cannot be located in her eyes, her skin, her hair. Physically, Clare transcends easy racial categorization, and Jack Bellew's comments are emblematic of the confusion and mystery that surrounds racial identity in the text as a whole.[12]

In Clare Kendry, then, Larsen has created a character who slides from race to race, class to class, and from one sexual orientation to another. Clare refuses to be fixed in one signification; she multiplies the subject positions available to her in a dizzying plethora, a plethora that confounds all who confront her. And, in fact, she is most often described in the text as a mystery, an enigma, a riddle with no solution. For example, Clare's letters are "mysterious and slightly furtive, . . . Furtive, but yet in some peculiar, determined way a little flaunting" (143). Clare's identity is contradictory and indescribable: "Catlike. Certainly that was the word which best described Clare Kendry, *if any single word could describe her.* Sometimes she was hard and apparently without feeling at all; sometimes she was affectionate and rashly impulsive" (144–45, emphasis mine). Larsen also obfuscates Clare's identity through a series of paradoxes. Irene describes Clare as "abhorrent" yet "strange and compelling" (161), "a joy" and yet "a vexation" (208), changed and yet unchanging (one of Irene's first comments to Clare is "you are changed, you know. And yet, in a way, you're just the same" [152]). Others also view Clare as a paradox: "No matter how often she came among them, she still remained someone apart, a little mysterious and strange, someone to wonder about and to admire and to pity" (209). Clare can be pitied and also admired but never completely fathomed.

Certainly, a great part of Clare's appeal and her power is that she does resist easy categorization—she is a mystery that Irene and others seek to penetrate. But Clare is ultimately unfathomable because of the secondary representations of her within the text. Not only is she a mystery, but she is also a gap or blank, a screen onto which others project their own in-stabilities. So as an enigma she cannot be penetrated, because behind the mystery there is no solution. In this sense, the characters in the novel function like the Sarrasinean (or realist) artist described by Roland Bar-thes; they try to "get *beyond, behind,* according to the idealistic principle which identifies secrecy with truth: one must thus go *into* the model, *beneath* the statue, *behind* the canvas" (122). Yet behind the canvas there is "nothing but its surface, scribbled lines, an abstract, undecipherable writ-ing, the unknown (unknowable) masterpiece" (122).

Clare's name itself may be emblematic of her status in the text as a whole: Clare is a variant of Clara, the Latin root of which means "clear" or "clear light"; Clare is also an anagram of clear. Certainly, Clare is not transparent or clear in her motivations or her demeanor. But Larsen's name for this most unclear character is more than just ironic, for Clare is a clear screen onto which others project. In the novel as a whole, Clare is often associated with light; at the Negro Welfare League dance, for example, she is described as being "fair and golden, like a sunlit day" (205). Light can illuminate and clarify, but it can also blind and obscure one's vision. Clare's name emphasizes that her "personality" itself is an absence.

Into this absence, others project their fears and desires. When she first meets Clare at the Drayton, Irene fills "in *the gap* of twelve years with talk" while Clare is "for the most part . . . silent" (155, emphasis mine). In fact, Clare is the gap, for in this conversation Irene realizes that "she hadn't asked Clare anything about her own life" (155). Later, after Irene learns more of the details of Clare's life, Clare still remains a gap. Irene puzzles over a look that crosses Clare's face, a look that she perceives as "partly mocking . . . and partly menacing. And something else for which she could find no name" (176). Irene cannot name the look: "It was unfathomable, utterly beyond any experience or comprehension of hers" (176). She never understands the gap that is Clare, and so she projects her own fears about her marriage onto Clare (and possibly her own lesbian impulses, as McDowell has argued). Larsen also uses imagery of masking to emphasize that Clare's "personality" cannot be penetrated, describing her face at one point as "an ivory mask" (157) and at another as "beautiful and caressing. Or maybe today *a little masked. Unrevealing.* Unaltered and undisturbed by any emotion within or without" (220, emphasis mine). Clare's masked face is literally a blank that does not reveal, that does not tell of the emotions within or without.

If we examine *Passing* as a language (rather than just being composed of language), what is the signification of the entity known as <Clare Kendry>? Unlike the other characters in the novel, whose meaning is easy to understand (or stabilize), Clare remains elusive. In a linguistic universe of fixed and stable realities (or significations), Clare is the element that creates the gap between signifier and signified, for she causes one to question if there is any such thing as one meaning, one signification, one "essential" identity. In a world where language is contained and controlled, Clare's voice is always just "a bit too lavish in its wordiness, a shade too unreserved in the manner of its expression. It roused again the old suspicion that Clare was acting" (182). In this passage, Clare's voice again functions synecdochically for her presence in the novel as a whole: in its unreserved, too full, and too expressive manner, her voice suggests that performance is occurring—a performance that if recognized as such destabilizes the entire galaxy of significations of those who are not "acting." Clare performs her role, she says her lines, but she does not reveal the real woman behind the actress. Clare forces her watchers to question whether the real woman behind the role can ever be known, whether she even exists.

On a narrative level Clare's presence within the text thus creates a great deal of openness. In this sense, character and discourse are complicit with each other; as Barthes would say, "The discourse creates in the character its own accomplice" (178). The discourse creates a character that cannot be known, and the character then contributes to the unfathomable quality of the discourse. When discourse creates characters, "it is not to make them play among themselves before us but to play with them, to obtain from them a complicity which assures the uninterrupted exchange of the codes: the characters are types of discourse and, conversely, the discourse is a character like the others" (Barthes 178–79). As both a figure of discourse and a character, Clare facilitates the uninterrupted exchange of codes, the text's plurality.

It is this uninterrupted exchange of codes that frightens Irene. Clare's murder by Irene at the end of *Passing* is Irene's attempt to erase the problematic signifier <Clare Kendry> that has destabilized Irene's entire universe.[13] As Thadious Davis says, "It is symbolically appropriate that Irene kills Clare, who embodies the dangerous, subversive, and willful characteristics of an individual who would risk everything for her own potential well-being, who would try on one way of being and discard it if it were found wanting" (*Nella Larsen* 320–21). Yet does Clare's death return Irene to her previous world of fixed identities, of stable significations? Does the murder contain the text's meanings? Certainly, Clare's demise removes Clare physically from Irene's life, but it also leaves open the questions Clare has raised, for she dies with her secrets intact.[14] Literally, Irene attempts to push Clare into the void of nothingness that Helga Crane feared so much; Irene attempts to force Clare to pass over permanently into another realm, the realm of the dead. Yet she does not succeed. Irene knows that Clare is not "gone": "She was utterly weary, and she was violently staggered. But her thoughts reeled on. If she could be as free of mental as she was of bodily vigour; could only put from her memory the vision of her hand on Clare's arm!" (239). Clare remains in

Irene's memory, a presence that continues to jar, that cannot be erased. And Irene herself is the one who falls into the void of nothingness, of vertigo: "Her quaking knees gave way under her. . . . Then everything was dark" (242). Clare's death does not enlighten Irene or the readers of the text; the mysteries are actually compounded and multiplied—not contained—by her death.

Many critics have faulted the ending of Larsen's novels, arguing that Larsen is unable to resolve the complexities she has raised.[15] But *Passing* seems to illustrate that Larsen is not seeking resolution but rather to create a text that remains open and uncontainable. According to Barthes, reading "does not consist in stopping the chain of systems, in establishing a truth, a legality of the text . . . [but] in coupling these systems, not according to their finite quantity, but according to their plurality" (11). Clare's removal from the novel facilitates this reading process, this plurality of interpretations, for her death leaves the systems of meaning open and plural. Thus in the scope of Larsen's narrative strategies, Clare's death at the end of *Passing* is a stroke of genius that maintains her problematic "passing" presence. Having used Clare to destabilize the universe of her other characters, Larsen removes Clare from the novel *before* she can become enclosed by one meaning. For with her death, no one will ever know the "truth" about her: what she really was, what she really wanted. To the end, Clare is passing, but truly, as Cheryl Wall has asked, "Passing for what"? Larsen's answer seems to be for everything and for nothing. "Passing" thus becomes a narrative strategy for creating a presence that can evade ideologies that usually confine the "tragic mulatto."

Yet "passing" is also a textual strategy used by Larsen to destabilize our notions of identity and textuality, returning us to a galaxy of significations, of plural and uncontainable meanings. *Quicksand* and *Passing* are inverse images of each other, as even their titles hint. Both novels concern the search for an identity and also a text that can break free from heterosexist, racist, and classist ideologies. But *Quicksand* portrays how both individuals and texts get stuck in various roles; it concerns the ways both identities and texts get confined by various "resolutions." As readers, we finish *Quicksand* with a degree of certainty: Helga has become fixed in her identity as a preacher's wife, and most likely this identity will be her last, for the role seems to be consuming her. When we finish *Quicksand*, we thus experience the same sense of suffocation that Helga does, for we cannot escape from the novel's inexorable sense of closure. *Passing*, on the other hand, concerns moving from role to role, from reading to reading; it concerns the plural and unstable nature of identities and of texts themselves. And so when we finish reading *Passing*, we are not suffocated by the text's meaning, by its closure. Rather, we are free to construct our own interpretations of the text, as Barthes says, not by giving it a stable and fixed meaning but by appreciating the *plural* it constitutes.

Notes

1. Most critical evaluations contend that Larsen's texts treat passing in a negative way; see, for example, Priscilla Ramsey's argument that Larsen associates passing with characters who "den[y] their black histories" (33), Michael Cooke's case that Larsen equates passing with "a stifling emptiness" or "death" (66–67), and Mary Helen Washington's argument that Larsen sees passing as "an obscene form of salvation" (164).

2. Hostetler suggests that Helga's hatred of the race problem "barely masks the agony of facing color as division rather than as fruitful multiplicity" and that Helga "attempts to create a spectrum rather than an opposition, a palette [of color] that will unify her life rather than leave it divided" (35). Although I agree with this line of reasoning, I also think that part of Helga's problem (for Larsen) is that she attempts to use color to *unify* her sense of identity rather than to pluralize it. Several critics have examined both Clare's and Helga's searches for unity or wholeness; see, for example, Cary 120 and 133 and Dearborn 157.

3. Davis argues that *Quicksand* is "a text of a daughter's coming to terms with her mother, an act of an enraged child's displacing a mother's intuited story with her own necessary one" (*Nella Larsen* 252).

4. For a discussion of the entrapments of sexuality, see Hortense E. Thornton, "Sexism as Quagmire: Nella Larsen's *Quicksand*."

5. Although all texts can be considered "open" in some way, certain texts contain deliberate textual and narrative strategies that facilitate their openness. According to Eco, such texts "are characterized by the invitation to *make the work* together with the author" and are open "to a continuous generation of internal relations which the addressee must uncover and select in his act of perceiving the totality of incoming stimuli" (63). Open works may seem "quite literally 'unfinished': the author seems

to hand them on to the performer more or less like the components of a construction kit" (49).

6. A recent article by David Blackmore suggests that Brian is also passing as a heterosexual when in fact this is not his true sexual orientation. See Blackmore, " 'That Unreasonable Restless Feeling': The Homosexual Subtexts of Nella Larsen's *Passing*."

7. For example, this narrative voice sometimes reveals information about Irene's motives that Irene is not aware of: "It was only that she wanted him to be happy, resenting, however, his inability to be so with things as they were, *and never acknowledging* that though she did want him to be happy, it was only in her own way. . . . *Nor did she admit* that all other plans, all other ways, she regarded as menaces" (190, emphasis mine). If Irene never acknowledges or admits these ideas, then these statements must be made by an omniscient narrator, a narrator who knows what Irene does not. Judith Butler also notes the presence of a narrator who often "supplies the words . . . Irene finds herself unable to speak" (*Bodies That Matter* 169). Jacquelyn McLendon, on the other hand, argues that although there is "no single, ultimately authoritative voice" in the text, Irene's point of view dominates (100).

8. For a reading that reaches similar conclusions using a psychoanalytical perspective, see Butler's argument that Bellew creates in Clare a fetish that allows him to constitute his own fragile racial boundaries (*Bodies That Matter* 171–72). Butler also argues that Bellew must destroy Clare "to avoid the kind of association that might destabilize the territorial boundaries of his own whiteness" (184).

9. Thadious Davis makes a similar point, arguing that Clare is "a screen upon which Irene's psyche is made visible" (*Nella Larsen* 323).

10. Jennifer DeVere Brody also sees the interconnection of racial, sexual, and class concerns in *Passing*.

11. Corinne Blackmer suggests similarly that Clare Kendry "does not internalize the sexual and racial self-divisions of the 'Veil,' but rather becomes highly adept at subverting the expectations and eluding the domination of others through selective shape-shifting and camouflage" (251). Blackmer also argues that the text as a whole "constantly explores marginal areas between clear significations" (255).

12. Butler argues that racial identity—blackness—is not primarily a visual mark in *Passing* because "what can be seen, what qualifies as a visible marking, is a matter of being able to read a marked body in relation to unmarked bodies, where unmarked bodies constitute the currency of normative whiteness" (*Bodies That Matter* 170–71). Race is determined by an association with individuals who have been socially coded as "black," rather than by physical markings.

13. Although there has been some controversy about the cause of Clare's death, most critics believe the text suggests that Irene pushes Clare out the window. See, for example, Deborah McDowell's strong argument for this reading of the ending (xxix). Other readings are certainly possible, given the deliberately open quality of the ending. It is my view that this open ending asks readers to "write" their way toward a logical conclusion, for Larsen's text remains pensive, both revealing and concealing its own meaning. But for an alternative view of the ending of *Passing,* see Thadious Davis's *Nella Larsen* (321–22).

14. As Jonathan Little comments, "While Clare's physical presence has been eliminated, the underlying impulses and desires that she represents for Irene are in no way purged or contained by Irene's final act of repression / murder" (180).

15. Thadious Davis, for example, states that Larsen is unable to "envision conclusions according to the organic, internal logic of her narrative" ("Nella Larsen" 191) and that her "narratives, like her public life, would stop abruptly, present no viable solutions, and remain dominated by dissatisfaction" (*Nella Larsen* 18). For other arguments supporting this view, see Youman 241 and McDowell xxxi. For a defense of the novel's ending and its consistently ironic logic and design, see Little.

PART III

Blackness and

the White Imagination

Spanish Masquerade and the Drama of Racial Identity in *Uncle Tom's Cabin*

JULIA STERN

*C*lassic narratives of American slavery often feature cross-dressing and the trope of disguise in their representations of the slave's passage from bondage to freedom.[1] But of all the autobiographical and fictional accounts that employ the motif of masquerade, *Uncle Tom's Cabin* offers a unique exploration of racially determined "definitional distinctions" and "original and stable" identities, terms Marjorie Garber invokes to describe the significance of the transvestite's power to interrogate cultural categories. Garber examines the most famous instance of cross-dressing in Stowe's novel: the moment when the mulatta slave Eliza Harris cuts her hair, dons the disguise of a boy, and dresses her son as a girl to facilitate her family's final escape to Canada. Eliza's flight for liberty, enabled by her assumption of male garb and a white identity, constitutes a major plot of *Uncle Tom's Cabin*.[2] Far less conventional than this episode of interracial gender crossing is another scene of "passing," George Harris's initial act of Spanish masquerade, in which makeup and costume effect a triple transformation of race, nationality, and class. This scene, occurring in chapter 11 of the novel, "In Which Property Gets into an Improper State of Mind," both complicates and provides commentary on the binary terms of the color line that organizes antebellum society, where a minute degree of blackness functions as an absolute arbiter of identity. Fascinating in its own right as a symbolic set piece, the episode also plays a crucial role in the larger narrative of *Uncle Tom's Cabin*, introducing Stowe's most subtle meditation on the history of race and domination in America.

The chapter is organized around a series of textual, visual, and verbal tableaux; specularity—both gazing and the failure of sight—structures and determines its action. Though the events of this section unfold in a decidedly social arena, as the episode proceeds and as its central characters retreat from public space into the recesses of privacy, the narrative takes on the rhythms of a dream or an extended fantasy.[3] Chapter 11 recounts the first stage of George Harris's two-part escape from the clutches of his malicious owner, Mr. Harris, who, in a fit of jealous rage, has removed George from the factory where he was acclaimed as a mechanical genius, relegating him to field labor and a vicious branding. The scene opens in a Kentucky tavern, where assorted Westerners, described in the tall-tale tradition of nineteenth-century American regionalism, gather around a posted handbill advertising for the capture of a fugitive slave who has recently escaped from the area. Details of this text-within-a-text play a crucial role in the outcome of the events that ensue:

Ran away from the subscriber, my mulatto boy, George. Said George six feet in height, a very light mulatto, brown curly hair; is very intelligent, speaks handsomely, can read and write; will probably try to pass for a white man; is deeply scarred on his back and shoulders; has been branded in his right hand with the letter H.
I will give four hundred dollars for him alive, and the same sum for satisfactory proof that he has been killed. (178)[4]

This fictive version of the antebellum advertisement for "blacks who stole themselves"[5] closely approximates nineteenth-century examples of the genre: in comparison with surviving documents from the period, Stowe's fictional handbill stands out only for its relative terseness and the unadorned nature of its descriptive information.[6] The advertisement is, nevertheless, a revealing text, less for its predictive accuracy, which will be proven false by George's Spanish masquerade, than for its exhibition of Mr. Harris's white supremacist fantasies.

Harris's handbill is most faithful to the facts of George's escape in its articulation of such unalterable physical details as the fugitive's height and, ironically, in its insistence on the intelligence of the runaway. The advertisement also reveals the master's naïve and mistaken belief in stable, manichean[7] notions of identity: Mr. Harris automatically assumes that George will orchestrate his flight according to the binary rules of a racial dynamic that delineates selfhood in black and white, despite the fact that he has identified his bondsman as a mulatto. Finally, the ad reflects the narrow scope of the master's ingenuity when it comes to predicting George's capacity for dissimulation; according to Mr. Harris's hypothetical vision of events, his slave possesses a total repertoire of one probable disguise ("he will probably try to pass as a white man"). Meant to be transparent and clinically accurate, the advertisement functions, in fact, as a narcissistic mirror, telling us less about George Harris than it does about his owner.

What is striking is the proprietary language Harris employs, itself a standard convention of slaveholders' discourse. The advertisement features the possessive pronoun "my" and indicates that such a relationship of ownership and objecthood has been literalized by the fire of the burning iron. With both the lash ("deeply scarred on his back and shoulders") and the impress of the brand, Mr. Harris inscribes his name all over George, permanently marking his most valuable slave as an appendage of the master's economic dominion. Synonymous with the term *laborer*, the concept of a "hand," metonymically the most vital part of the worker's body, eloquently expresses the slave's function as sheer instrument of toil, volitionless and without agency. Mr. Harris's brutal "writing on his hand" literalizes in flesh and blood the master's drive to colonize the intimate operations of the slave's body. Interestingly, George's price will remain the same, whether he is found dead or alive. Mr. Harris has little interest in recovering George's use value or even his worth as an object of exchange; instead, he seeks a forum for the grand display of the master's power, enacted in a spectacle of discipline and punishment.

This inscription on a black body by a white patriarch formalizes—in grotesquely ironic fashion George's unspeakable relation to another white father, the man who violated his mother and who, in characteristic masterly manner disavowed him at birth. In this regard, the brand, with its single letter standing in for Harris, takes on the resonance of an uncanny signature, a displaced and disguised facsimile of the white father's name that George is legally prohibited from bearing.[8] Denying the child the name of the father in social practice, white patriarchy inscribes the mulatto's flesh to assure an economic relation in which the ties that bind are undeniable. What is repressed and foresworn at the level of culture returns, in brutal and literal form, on the surface of the body.

Despite his heinous assertions of domination, Mr. Harris's "writing" has failed to fix the meaning of George Harris's identity, and the master's portrait of the runaway slave projects telling traces of his insecurity. Why does he mention the fact of George's mulatto heritage not once but twice? Why, in his second use of the word, does he modify the term with the phrase "very light"? Why is the "boy" of color in the first line of the ad imagined to be feigning the role of a white "man"? How do high intelligence, eloquence ("speaks handsomely"—connoting a mastery of language that borders on the aesthetic), and, most significant, literacy ("can read and write") work to transform the abject and infantilized slave ("boy") into a bonafide adult ("will try to pass for a white man"), entitled to citizenship and human dignity?

Henry Louis Gates Jr. has argued that in the eighteenth and nineteenth centuries, a slave's possession of literacy played an essential and determining role in the fight to discredit proslavery assertions that blacks lacked rationality and therefore deserved to be ranked with beasts; literate slaves, possessing the human faculty of reason, constituted living and irrefutable proof that the institution was morally untenable.[9] George Harris rehearses this classic antislavery argument when, early in the novel, before his wife Eliza, he asserts his superiority over Mr. Harris:

"I'm a better man than he is. I know more about business than he does; I am a better manager than he is; I can read better than he can; I can write a better hand,—and I've learned it all myself, and no thanks to him,—I've learned in spite of him; and now what right has he to make a dray-horse of me?—to take me from things I can do, and do better than he can, and put me to work that any horse can do." (60)

George's exceptional literacy, counterpoised against the ill-educated Harris's consistent brutality, exposes the master's bestial treatment of his slave for what it really is: the projection of his own inferiority. By taking George out of the factory and inserting him into the anonymous role of field laborer, where intellectual gifts are irrelevant, if not detrimental, to a worker's productivity, Harris forfeits valuable cash wages that only George's work can provide. The master acts without thought to the economic repercussions of his white supremacy. As George implies in the passage, only a brute would squander the resources of a man of George's talent in order to preserve the hierarchical relationship that such talent invariably calls into question. It matters little if such degradation has the reflexive effect of hurtling both perpetrator and object of oppression down the food chain in a one-way trajectory.[10] No matter how low he sinks, the master must always remain on top.

I

George Harris's intellectual aptitude arouses rage and violently repressive behavior in his owner; but simultaneously, his gifts enable him to dream of a self that transcends the manichean identity that slavery constructs for its subjects and masters. The statutes regulating the bondage of African Americans consolidate and codify American racist fantasies in the antebellum period: by reducing subtle and various shades of color into a legal fiction of black and white, miscegenation is disavowed and black blood is fetishized in wholly negative terms. In the context of such dualistic representations of racial difference, George Harris's Spanish masquerade, however ironic and mistaken in its historical implications, must be read as an important alternative vision to the manichean allegory at work in his culture.

There is no denying, of course, that Spain is associated historically with the origins and imperialist development of slavery. In fact, Spanish complicity in slavery figures centrally in Stowe's meditation on the crime of the founding of America, the subject of the end of this essay. At this juncture, however, it is important to note that in the lavish town house and courtyard of Augustine St. Clare, slave owning and things Spanish come together in the present tense of Stowe's novel. The narrator speaks of

an ancient mansion, built in that odd mixture of Spanish and French style, of which there are specimens in some parts of New Orleans. It was built in the Moorish fashion,—a square building enclosing a court-yard . . . evidently . . . arranged to gratify a picturesque and voluptuous ideality. Wide galleries ran all around the four sides, whose Moorish arches, slender pillars, and arabesque ornaments, carried the mind back, *as if in a dream*, to the reign of oriental romance in Spain. (252, emphasis mine)

While Spanish architectural influences in southern Louisiana were an actual nineteenth-century legacy that Stowe adopted as a feature of her realism,[11] Spanishness as a world elsewhere,[12] a space of ideality, functions as the narrative equivalent of a latent dream text counterposed to the waking life of slavery and racism that constitutes the manifest narrative content of *Uncle Tom's Cabin*. By expressing a fantasy of escape to a world elsewhere, a land of conquistadors and bullfighters that nineteenth-century artists aestheticized in romantic poetry and painting, George's disguise figures a self that could exist beyond the terms of nineteenth-century African American slavery.[13]

Averting the dualism of black versus white in his capacity as neither, the brown-skinned Spanish gentleman transmutes the problem of race by disrupting its rigid terms. To reject this binary, however, he must master and willfully embrace the elitism of racist, class-conscious nineteenth-century American culture. Despite the rhetoric of Jacksonian democracy that prevails in this period, the reality of slavery (as well as class difference) marks antebellum America as a deeply stratified and hierarchical society. Social critics of America from de Tocqueville to Richard Sennett have noted that the public drama of American class relations has, since the eighteenth century, played itself out in a highly theatrical form.[14] Skin color and accent provide the most obvious clues to identity, but clothing and comportment complete the picture and help one to dramatize his or her status.

Stowe is not unaware of the theatrical nature of nineteenth-century American social encounters in which disparate races and classes mix. Capturing the rhythms of a humorous travel narrative, her narrator's description of the unidentified George Harris, as he enters the Kentucky tavern disguised as a Spaniard, is structured, in fact, as a series of stage directions. Consider how Stowe's native Kentuckians encounter and remark on the advent of an "uncommon" stranger:

Here the conversation was interrupted by the approach of a small one-horse buggy to the inn. It had a genteel appearance, and a well-dressed, gentlemanly man sat on the seat, with a colored servant driving.

The whole party examined the newcomer with the interest with which a set of loafers in a rainy day usually examine every newcomer. He was very tall, with a dark, Spanish complexion, fine, expressive black eyes, and close-curling hair, also of a glossy blackness. His well formed aquiline nose, straight thin lips, and the admirable contour of his finely-formed limbs, impressed the whole company instantly with the idea of something uncommon. He walked easily in among the company, and with a nod indicated to his waiter where to place his trunk, bowed to the company, and, with his hat in his hand, walked up leisurely to the bar, and gave his name as Henry Butler, Oaklands, Shelby County. Turning, with an indifferent air, he sauntered up to the advertisement, and read it over.

"Jim," he said to his man, "seems to me we met a boy something like this, up at Bernan's, didn't we?"

"Yes, Mas'r," said Jim, "only I an't sure about the hand."

"Well, I didn't look, of course," said the stranger with a careless yawn. Then walking up to the landlord, he desired him to furnish him with a private apartment, as he had some writing to do immediately. (180–81)

Stowe has inflected this prose with a number of phrases suggesting that "uncommonness" is best understood as dramatic dissimulation. Locating the reader's vision within the collective gaze of the Kentucky loafers, Stowe invites us to watch as the mysterious figure approaches the inn by carriage. The buggy that transports him possesses a genteel *appearance;* its well-dressed occupant is of gentleman*ly* demeanor; the narrator cannot affirm that the newcomer is indeed a gentleman but simply reports the unfolding of events as they *seem*. Omniscience must bide its time; Stowe's allegiance to her audience must not come at the expense of loyalty to her own characters.

Following the script of a drama he has crafted himself, the mysterious stranger makes his grand entrance on the stage of the tavern in what is quite literally the role of his life. Most notably, the narrator remarks on the stranger's extraordinary pigmentation, describing it as "a dark, Spanish complexion." Recognition of hue is quickly followed by the narrator's registration of color as a sign of attendant ethnic or national character; the "dark" stranger is perceived as clearly Caucasian, though his skin is what will later be characterized as "genteel brown" (183) and his hair is described as being "of glossy blackness." Given the delicate nose and exquisitely thin lips, the narrator has no doubt as to the newcomer's European origins. And why should anyone question the *naturalness* of the Caucasian details that make up this countenance? After all, the stranger is in fact the son of a white father from whom he has inherited the very "fine set of European features" (182) on which we earlier remarked.

Freudian theory tells us that the *form* a fantasy takes is often more meaningful than its content, and in that vein, we must consider Spanish masquerade as a kind of wish fulfillment.[15] By *darkening* his skin rather than highlighting his own naturally *fair* complexion, George Harris rejects the obvious route of assimilation into white culture that his master had predicted in the advertisement warning that his slave would try "to pass for a white man." The genius of the Spanish disguise lies in its capacity to articulate the seemingly antithetical qualities of Europeanness and dark complexion, both of which speak the real truth about George Harris's multiracial African American identity. In effect, George puts on the accoutrements of his biological inheritance, acting out the privileged role of his father's son, all the while appearing exotic and decidedly nonwhite. The disguise inverts George's actual identity as the illegitimate white (looking) son of a Caucasian master and an enslaved mulatta. The last refuge of a fugitive slave would seem to be in *darkened* skin. Spanish masquerade obscures the legibility of white supremacist fantasies about slaves in flight, and as the obsequious reaction to George reveals, thrusts a privileged and mysterious "darkness" squarely in the face of white racist patriarchy.

In historical terms, this representation is unlikely, or at least, confused: presumably, a Spanish gentleman traveling in nineteenth-century America would hail from Castile and possess white skin. The brown tint of George's disguise is more closely associated in the white American nineteenth-century, middle-class imagination with the exotic Spaniard: bullfighters, gypsies, and flamenco dancers who are often darker in skin tone and who represent a romantic vision of the old world.[16] The image of the Spanish gentleman testifies to the equivocal nature of Stowe's knowledge of "foreign" culture as much as it foregrounds the Kentuckians' decidedly uncosmopolitan ignorance of the European other; it is just such cultural illiteracy that George so brilliantly manipulates and upon which his escape depends. In this provincial milieu, which Stowe figures as being representative of rural antebellum America, the nonblack, nonwhite other passes precisely because such otherness remains relatively unintelligible in the terms of a manichean hierarchical system.

As such, the representation must be seen as the expression of a paradoxical wish, George's desire to be both economically privileged and physically of color. At the end of the novel, George Harris will grieve over the very identic illegibility that has enabled his escape when he laments that "if I wished anything, I would wish myself two shades darker, rather than one lighter" (608). Spanish masquerade may be pure fabrication, but it is a fantasy that expresses the biological truth by rendering the reality of George's mixed racial heritage in both dark and universally visible tones.

What are we to make of a disguise that highlights the complexity of racial identity more vividly than does the unadorned self, thought by eighteenth-century philosophers to be the transparent product of nature? Such questions take on a particular resonance when we contemplate the figure of Jim, George Harris's "slave" companion who masquerades as his valet. Jim has already escaped from slavery to the freedom of Canada but returns to the United States and to the present tense of Stowe's novel to rescue his aged mother, whose master has subjected her to brutal punishment in revenge for her son's flight.

By the time he arrives on the scene at the Kentucky tavern, Jim has traced a complex geographical and identic trajectory, making the transition from slave to fugitive to freeman and back again to fugitive. *Acting* the fictional role of slave, a part he knows by heart, Jim prefigures the black characters in Melville's great "Benito Cereno" (1855), another narrative of the 1850s that features slavery and a Spanish gentleman and former bondspeople engaged in identic masquerade.[17]

Jim's masquerade as a slave raises important philosophical questions about the institution itself, exposing the fantastic nature of a system that operates by "a *fiction* of law" (446). Jim's tenure as George's "slave" illuminates the ways in which the "peculiar institution" functions at the level of culture. That a man who is technically free[18] and affecting the *caricature* of a slave could be mistaken, so unblinkingly, for an actual bondsman speaks to the ways in which antebellum American racial conflict takes the shape of tragic drama. In this scene, Stowe unveils the unnaturalness of slavery for what it truly is: not a system that derives organically and logically from the inherent differences that exist between blacks and whites but one that proceeds by the rules of a hierarchical cultural conspiracy that unfolds along the lines of a dramatic production.[19]

The figure of Jim disrupts this model of racial drama by foregrounding its inherent artificialness, its theatricality, in his burlesque rendition of the "slave" valet.[20] Jim also focuses attention on the relational, rather than the autonomous, nature of *white* racial identity under slavery. According to antebellum American law, a free black can, at any time and with no probable cause, be taken into custody as a fugitive slave, regardless of whether he or she possesses free papers: color determines status, notwithstanding the legal reality of condition. But Caucasian superiority does not declare itself in anything like the obverse way. What is needed to shore up white privilege is the visible presence of a black slave. How else are we to understand that white ("European") identity, as observed and reenacted by George Harris, must be underwritten by the presence of an African American bond servant in order to be "read" as legitimate?[21] The figure of Jim raises important questions about our notions of the fullness, the adequacy, of a white elite that, without the supplement of the slave, would fail to register its own supremacy. Working according to zero-sum principles, slavery ensures that the material privilege of one group occurs at the explicit expense and physical freedom of the other.[22]

The black supplement, the auxiliary presence of a slave that enables and solidifies white supremacy, is a crucial ingredient for making such preeminence legible. And nowhere is this fact better illustrated than in the Kentucky tavern scene. "White" dependence on the proximity of the black other, who serves to augment the precarious superiority of the master, takes multiple forms in this section of the novel. Even the false name that George Harris concocts to match his "Spanish" identity gives expression to the inextricable link between black and white lives that the logic of the supplement demands.

Consider the pseudonym with which George introduces himself to the bartender: "Henry Butler, Oaklands, Shelby County." The introduction telegraphs to the characters within the novel world that the stranger is a member of the gentry: only a gentleman would introduce himself by referring to the name of his estate in addition to his place of origin. But George's false name has an additional, ironic resonance, functioning as the linguistic analogue to the physical metamorphosis enacted by Spanish masquerade. For the individual elements of the pseudonym conjure associations to George's true identity and to his loathsome entanglement with white slave-holding culture.[23]

Significantly, the name Henry Butler is not Spanish. This suggests that the stranger's foreignness derives from his *maternal* side and that all traces of the mother's lineage will be erased from the record in keeping with the patriarchal custom that governs the transmission of identity in Anglo-American culture.[24] Henry is the formal name from which the diminutive Harry derives; Harry sounds distinctly like Harris. George has redignified his abject relation to Mr. Harris through the fiction of a more formal name, Henry. The name also evokes associations to the American

Revolution and, specifically, to the oratorical heroism of Virginia's Patrick Henry.

Butler is the title of an elite domestic servant, the highly skilled figure who manages and oversees domestic operations in a plantation household. Though George's managerial skills were actually employed in factory labor before he was recalled to the plantation and demoted to the position of field hand, he has described himself in a passage cited earlier as a someone who knows "more about business then [Mr. Harris] does; . . . [and who is] a better manager than [Harris] is" (60). Had George not possessed mechanical abilities, he might very well have served, with other elite mulattoes, as a valet or a house servant—even, perhaps, as a butler.

Finally, the choice of Shelby County as a place-name of origin communicates George's sense that his young black family—wife Eliza is owned by the Shelbys—constitutes his entire universe. Pointedly, George does not claim that he hails from "Harris County." Such a place-name would recall his brutal treatment at the hands of his master while he was a slave; his removal from the factory; and even worse, his master's assurance that George must take, and live conjugally with, another wife. Despite the fact that Shelby County as a "place" does not exist beyond slavery, it functions in the latent dream work of *Uncle Tom's Cabin* in the manner of Spanish masquerade: both fictively gesture toward a world elsewhere that holds out the (perhaps illusory) promise of a life beyond the known horrors of bondage in Kentucky at the hands of Mr. Harris.

But the world elsewhere of Spanish masquerade has roots in the reality of slavery: though George plays an exoticized version of his own father or someone very like him, "Mr. Butler," like his father, is a slave owner; and like any actual slave owner, this fictive facsimile stages his status in a public display of white power. For the benefit of the Kentucky audience, "Mr. Butler" and his "waiter" Jim play out their hierarchical relationship for dramatic effect in a stunning act of improvisation. The inspiration for their performance is taken from Mr. Harris's handbill for the fugitive George, an artifact that the latter confronts with poise and equanimity. Historical accounts of fugitives facing advertisements for themselves describe the peril with which this encounter is fraught; indeed, the reader expects such a scene to be narrated in the tones of a nightmare in which the runaway slave, undone by being forced to face the evil mirror of the master's advertisement, inadvertently exposes himself or herself to the white community and is recaptured.

Instead, George's "facing scene"[25] assumes the tone of a harmless dream, in which everything unfolds according to the protracted rhythms of fantasy. Stowe's narrator emphasizes Mr. Butler's apparent languor in her description of his approach to the handbill: he seems "indifferent"; he "saunter[s]"; he replies to his servant's comments with a "careless yawn" (180–81). As if to contrast the nightmare of slavery over against the felicitous daydream of the escape, Stowe ensures that it is whites in this section of the novel who will prove anxious, confused, and disoriented and the former slaves who will demonstrate self-assurance, lucidity, and vigilance, even as they feign disinterest and lassitude. The real facing scene occurs not between the fugitive George and the yokels in the Kentucky tavern who potentially could betray him; rather, it unfolds between two equally textual and equally fictional renditions of himself: the fantastic "boy" passing for a white "man" of Mr. Harris's fantasy, and "Mr. Butler," in Spanish masquerade.

Through the auspices of George's imaginative power, what could have been a mirror scene of enforced abjection has been transformed into what we might call an improvisational tableau of reading and writing.[26] Refusing to perform his identity in the terms of Mr. Harris's white supremacist fantasy, in which he would depend on the endowments of "nature" to enable his passing for white, George pursues the channels of culture in his flight for freedom. Borrowing the master's instrument of domination, Tzvetan Todorov's terminology for the technology of writing (252), but rejecting the violence of Harris's scriptive practices, George employs face paint and costume to create again the story of his identity, to transform himself from slave to master.

In the moment that he decides to declaim his thoughts about the advertisement—a moment of privacy that the narrator does not bring into representation precisely because the events at the tavern are recounted throughout this scene from a dramatic point of view—George Harris embarks on what Stephen Greenblatt would term a *cross-cultural improvisation*. Meditating on improvisation as an activity that enables certain kinds of cultural power, Greenblatt writes of "what we can call appropriative mimesis, imitation in the interest of acquisition. As such, it need not have entailed any grasp of the cultural reality of the other, only a willingness to make contact and to effect some kind of exchange" (99). The imaginary facing scene (cited above) is an exchange that unfolds by inspiration rather than premeditation and becomes crucial to the solidification of George's fictive identity. Without missing a beat, George refers to Mr. Harris's phantasmagoric fugitive as a "boy," thus shoring up his own manhood. Significantly, it is *Jim* who breaks character in playing the role of slave, which he should, theoretically, know by heart. Had the tavern-goers been paying attention, they would have thought it odd that Mr. Butler's slave can read the poster; according to the terms of the masquerade of slavery, a bondsperson must not appear literate, whether or not he or she can actually read.

Jim's bold expression of uncertainty about a mark as utterly legible as a brand on the right hand of a runaway slave constitutes a wonderful touch of inspiration; Stowe means this observation to arouse anxiety and sympathetic identification in the reader; both emotions further her antislavery purpose: the white audience worries collectively over how George will avoid exposing the scar that proves the key to his identity. We can only assume that, dressed as an elegant gentleman, George is wearing gloves.

From the beginning of the novel, George Harris's identity has been bound up, emblematically, with the state of his hands. George undergoes an identic journey of astounding variation, from functioning as the best hand to employing a creative hand,[27] suffering a branded hand, and, ultimately, devising a hidden hand. Only in the second, *darker* skin of Spanish masquerade, literalized in the gloved hand he wears as a fictive gentleman, can George rewrite the script of his racial identity and revise the course of his future.

That such a future could unfold in a space beyond the specular relations of American racism seems an unimaginable luxury in the present circumstances.[28] The mark of the authentic master is his propensity to *see through*, to *not see*, the slave in his presence. Speaking of his phantom fugitive self, George answers Jim's remark about spying the imaginary runaway in feigned tones of supercilious annoyance. " 'Well, I didn't look, of course,' " he irritably explains, punctuating this subtle reassertion of superiority "with a careless yawn." Jim's goal in the improvisation would seem to be to throw the report of the sighting into some confusion. George, on the other hand, must reconsolidate his own "white" power by conveying careless indifference, an obliviousness to the plight of the racial other. Who better than George Harris would know how to express this horrid truth about slavery: to the master, the slave is an invisible man.

George's retreat into a private room to do some writing is also highly emblematic. Behind closed doors, the body—apparent site of racial identity—is revealed to be a *scene of writing*. More precise, if slavery itself transforms the surface of the body of the African American other into a three-dimensional text on which white power writes its name with lash and iron, then masquerade becomes a *scene of counterwriting*. Walnut bark and black dye replace the tools of violence and become the means by which the racial other is recast into a self.

The significance of George's assumption of privacy in this scene cannot be underestimated. To be a slave is to have been robbed of the experience of solitude, never to have known privacy, the freedom that exists inside one's own mind when the body is unconstrained. Spanish masquerade affords the privilege of a locked door, control over entry and egress, and a room of one's own, however temporary. Only by seizing the space of privacy can George Harris reclaim possession of the body alienated by slavery; such reconquest of his person marks the first step in George's creation of a new destiny.

II

The final scene of chapter 11, in which "Mr. Butler" is confronted by Mr. Wilson, George's former employer, marks the climax of Stowe's meditation on racial identity and America's history of racist imperialist domination. When George insists that Mr. Wilson join him in the private apartment and, safe behind closed doors, reveals his masquerade with the assertion "so you see I don't answer to the advertisement at all" (182), we are meant to understand that such resistance bespeaks the desire to shatter the phantasmagoric expectations of racist specularity. George will not "answer" his master categorically: he rejects both Mr. Harris's fantasies about black identity and his assertion of ownership and domination.

The profound disorientation of Mr. Wilson upon seeing George, whom he does not fully recognize in masquerade, registers with symbolic force. It is only logical that benevolent white patriarchy, which has enabled the perpetuation of slavery, would be disturbed, confused, and filled with "uneasy curiosity" upon seeing a former slave blanketed in the accoutrements of privilege, which seem to be worn so *naturally*. That the "bright, dark eyes" of the elegant fugitive George Harris should meet Mr. Wilson's gaze with "such unconcerned coolness" is, according to the logic of racist domination, indeed amazing.

When George introduces himself to Wilson as Mr. Butler, asserting that " 'I see you remember me,' " and Mr. Wilson replies "like one speaking in a dream" (181), we must read the narrator's description as a cultural diagnosis. The fantasy in which Mr. Wilson finds himself caught up is the dream of Spanish masquerade, the vision of a life beyond African American slavery. Stowe's choreography of this scene is itself symbolic: in reverse of the factory hierarchy, Wilson *follows George* in the Kentucky tavern, "as one who walks in his sleep" (182). Well-intentioned white America has not assumed the lead in the battle for abolition of slavery and is indeed sleepwalking through a crisis that threatens to rend the nation. Such citizens must give up their own somnambulism and join the African American's dream, a vision of a nation without slavery.

That Stowe's dream of ending slavery in America includes the hygienic deportation of the nation's black population to Africa significantly diminishes the moral force of her vision, and we will return to this issue shortly. Before doing so, we must examine George's final appeal to Mr. Wilson, who is deeply concerned that the fugitive George is breaking the law of the land in his flight for freedom. After George undertakes a rigorous and detailed explanation of the ways in which American laws are not *his* laws and America is not *his* country, borrowing heavily from the pre-Revolution anti-Parliament rhetoric of the men who were to become the Founders, Wilson makes the case for Providence. His argument is hardly original; in fact, it is as old as the origins of Protestant America. John Winthrop made a similar appeal to the nascent Puritan community aboard the *Arabella* in 1630, when, like Mr. Wilson, he remarked: "Let everyone abide by the condition in which he is called" (184).

In response, George poses the following analogy to Mr. Wilson, making a comparison so extraordinary that it conjures in microcosm what I will call the primal scene of American race relations. Looking his former employer directly in the eye, George inquires: " 'I wonder, Mr. Wilson, if the Indians should come and take you a prisoner away from your wife and children, and want to keep you all your life hoeing corn for them, if you'd think it your duty to abide in the condition in which you were called. I rather think that you'd think the first stray horse you could find an indication of Providence—shouldn't you?'" (184). It is probable that Stowe meant this metaphor to function in one interpretive direction: to evoke white fear and loathing of Native Americans, who still posed a threat on the Western frontier and whose history of taking white captives provoked a living legacy of trauma in postcolonial New England. Such an example, in which African American slavery is likened to the Anglo-American ordeal of Indian captivity, is guaranteed to rouse racist horror in the white reading audience; simultaneously it creates in the reader a bond of sympathy with the African American, whose allegorical representative in George's parable the reader has become; through this fictive identification, the white audience can better imagine and deplore the evils of African American slavery.

In George's scenario of Caucasian captivity, the Native Americans stand in for white slaveholders, and the whites play the part of African American slaves. What goes unarticulated in this timeless vision of primitive America (which existed, temporally, at the moment of the founding of America, just as in the nineteenth century it continued to exist geographically on the Western frontier) is the earlier *Spanish* domination of the Indians during the epoch of the conquest, what we might call the triumph of "brown" over "red." In this tableau, the relationship of "red" over "white" stands in for a series of other hierarchical relationships that, while not present to Stowe's representation, nevertheless constitute the truth of the founding of the Americas: the relationship of "brown" over "red" to which we alluded; that of "brown" over "black" (for the Spanish were involved in the African slave trade by the time Columbus sailed for the "Indies"; black slaves even journeyed with him to the New World); and, most obvious, that of "white" over "black."

While it is likely to summon racist associations in the white audience, the specter of Indian captivity speaks simultaneously to the dynamics of a more subtle equation about race in America, an equation that George puts forward under the cloak of metaphor. It is here that Stowe's "simple" parable escapes the control of her conscious artistry and that a complex and paradoxical fantasy unfolds beyond the ideological reaches of romantic racialism.[29]

If Indians are standing for slaveholders in this picture, conjuring an identification of red atrocity and white inhumanity, we must also read this scene as a tableau of *revenge*. Historically, Native Americans took captives during times of war to use as pawns in negotiations, and less frequently, they kidnapped Caucasians in retaliation for white destruction of Indian lives or as punishment for Anglo-American encroachment on their lands. In George's exemplary tale, Mr. Wilson is kidnapped not for reasons of economic ambition (he becomes another laborer in the tribe, enduring equally the hardships that tribe members endure); the motivation for his kidnapping is cultural outrage, a collective indignity over wrongs suffered at the hands of the white man. That George highlights the hoeing of corn is a pointed detail: at the end of his servitude under Mr. Harris, George was made to perform a plantation economy's version of this sort of agricultural labor, the "hoeing and digging" (55) he found so destructive to his sense of self-worth after knowing the creative freedom of the factory. George's vision of hostage taking constitutes a form of vengeance for incursions against culture, a vengeance that, while brutal, is not undeserved.

The fugitive's tableau sets before both Mr. Wilson and the reader a genealogy of the unrighteous founding of America; George's masquerade, with its allusion to Spain, figures centrally in this representation of discovery, conquest, colonization, enslavement, and displacement. In George's fictive fantasy, red men stand in both for slaveholders and for the racial other who has been wronged by white patriarchy and whose impulse to exact revenge is hardly gratuitous but, in fact, utterly justified. The vengeance of red men, in other words, also expresses the insurrectionist rage of the African American slave who, unlike Nat Turner, seeks not blood but a more enduring, though less violent, form of retaliation.

Racial identity is on the move in this verbal panorama as the victims and the villains in America's tragic racial drama shift positions and *become each other*. Most fascinating is the way in which black identity is literally erased from a picture which deliberately represents Caucasians and Native Americans and which gestures toward Spain in its historical resonances as well as through George's disguise. Repressed from representation here, the missing figure in the myth of origin is, of course, the African slave. Black identity is unspeakable in part because the transitive properties released by George's allegory are fully apparent; and black identity remains an unnecessary representation because George's own

exegesis of the parable for Mr. Wilson's enlightenment provides interpretation for anyone ignorant enough to be unable to work the equation
without aid. Blackness cannot figure because to articulate African American desire in the context of identic transformation would be to conjure the
rage of Nat Turner, and Stowe, however unconscious she might be in this
passage, cannot allow George Harris to imagine a truly *violent* revolutionary scenario.[30] Nat Turner marks for Stowe what is clearly beyond the
pale.

George's invocation of the rhetoric of the American Revolution white-
washes the danger latent within the rebellious slave: the righteousness of
the cause must be seen in the reflected whiteface of the Founders, through
the ventriloquized voices of Patrick Henry and George Washington, two
figures whose very names evoke associations to Stowe's heroic mulatto.
That the ideology of the American Revolution is an exclusively white
inheritance is Stowe's guiding doctrine. In creating the figure of George
Harris, *son of a white father,* and in *identifying with this character,*[31] Stowe
simultaneously expresses her sense that slavery violates the foundational
principles of the American Republic and maintains and preserves her
hygienic racialist views about who should be allowed to bear arms and
"bring to a final phase" the uncompleted "revolution of 1776" (Sundquist, *To Wake the Nations* 34). In a marvelous detail that casts ironic
backlight on exactly this paradox, the narrator describes "a portrait of
General Washington, drawn and colored in a manner which would have
astonished that hero, if he had ever happened to meet with its like" (68)
hanging in Uncle Tom's cabin.

Christina Zwarg argues for a subversive reading of this episode of
blackfacing, connecting it to Stowe's Sambo figures, Sam and Andy, who
seem racist caricatures on first appearance but who magically elude the
control of their creator and posit a fascinating resistance to the racism
of the novel world and its author (279). Although Zwarg's reading of
Samboism is convincing, her analysis of the blackface George Washington is less so, precisely because it is not attuned to the disturbing
implications of Stowe's "raucous" minstrel-show comedy. The Founding
Father in blackface constitutes another tableau that, like Spanish masquerade, bears multiple and contradictory valences. Both the blackface portrait and George's disguise as a Spaniard pose the possibility of a world
elsewhere and simultaneously shut it down; Spanish masquerade conjures

the vista of a better Old World beyond the reaches of America, but tragically, of all the countries of that Old World, Spain is perhaps the nation most implicated in the history of European slavery. Similarly, while the blackface portrait would seem to allow Mr. Shelby's slaves to express their dreams of liberty, it also discredits such aspirations as the burlesque mimicry of ideals for which African Americans have no *natural* affinity—such an icon can only be comical. Both blackface and Spanish masquerade partake of what we might call the conservative *carnivalesque*, Mikhail Bakhtin's term for the dynamic whereby the marginal figure is allowed the temporary imaginative respite of a world turned upside down, a world that is ultimately unrealizable and fated to be repressed by the dominant culture.[32]

Using George Harris as her surrogate within *Uncle Tom's Cabin*, Stowe gives eloquent expression to her own ambivalence about racial otherness through the drama of his masquerade. That she deploys her critique of American slavery through a fictional slave figure who is utterly identified with the very ideology, crafted by the white revolutionary Founding Fathers of the new Republic, that upheld slavery and wove its protection into the fabric of their constitution is a paradox that doesn't trouble Stowe (Sundquist, *To Wake the Nations* 36). As Zwarg and others have noted, George Harris never rejects the patriarchal politics of ownership and domination that, taken to their logical conclusions, enable such structural inequities as slavery to thrive in an allegedly free society: how ironic it is that against the backdrop of the Quaker kitchen, George celebrates "possessing" his wife and child, as if he were just another property-owning white male citizen of America.[33]

Carrying his ideals of freedom to Liberia, ideals that encode hierarchy and domination into a rhetoric of liberty, George, speaking for Stowe, doesn't see that his dreams of emigration are contaminated by the ideology of the Founders that he has so thoroughly incorporated. As a world elsewhere, Liberia is to be structured as a better, purer version of America, dedicated to upholding American republican principles but committed to improving on them by outlawing the institution of slavery. What worries neither the procolonization novelist nor the Africa-bound fugitive slave through whom she speaks is the idea that the problems of hierarchy sundering antebellum America are reinscribed in Liberia's American foundations. Nor do either George or Stowe imagine that the Liberian landscape may not be the virgin ground, the space of endless possibility that fuels colonializationist dreams. That native Africans might already inhabit Liberia and possess a culture all their own, as did the peoples of the Americas at the time of the Spanish conquest, and that they might object to colonial domination never crosses the mind of the fictive émigré slave. Nor does the thought of indigenous African opposition to the African American enterprise dissuade or deter advocates of colonialization, such as Stowe.[34]

This brings us full circle to the primal scene of the founding of America that George Harris conjures in his efforts to convert Mr. Wilson to a deeper understanding of the evils of slavery. That this tiny moment should resonate so suggestively with a political and moral significance found nowhere else in Stowe's enormous novel is no surprise; for we must remember that America's most imaginative abolitionist was also a romantic racialist who believed that free blacks could make no place for themselves in an America without slavery. Despite the repugnance of her position, we must remember that it was also Stowe who contrived George Harris's Spanish masquerade and, with it, the evocative allegorical tableau of American racist domination through which Mr. Wilson is made to feel the full horrors of slavery. Without such a fable, Wilson would experience no change of heart, and without such a change of heart, the patriotic factory owner could not justify his decision to aid and abet the escape of a fugitive slave.

In the context of domination—a binary state in which authority vies to assert itself by producing subordination in the other—racial identity functions as a fluid and flexible cipher. This is the political implication of George's parable. Race tells no essential truth about identity, for race is a *sign* and, thus, interchangeable: until color is attached to structures of power, it does not and cannot *figure*, as George Harris's Spanish guise attests. The implications of Stowe's use of masquerade extend far beyond the conscious political stance she assumes in *Uncle Tom's Cabin*; although clearly at odds with her romantic racialism, the message encoded in the tableau of disguise makes its uncanny and radical presence felt in the political unconscious of her novel. There, in the dream work of Stowe's tale, its world elsewhere, the extraordinary nature of identity reveals itself in a form that would probably surprise and disturb the ultimately conservative Stowe. What the latent narrative of *Uncle Tom's Cabin* suggests is that to believe in the definitive legibility of race is a delusion, a misconception that carries with it potentially tragic ramifications. As George Harris dramatically proves, identity is not a stable fact but a fluid and reversible category.

A world without the security of firm categories such as black and white is the world of racial amalgamation—an American reality that Stowe and other supporters of colonialization seek to counteract with their program of black deportation. Such terror over racial blending constitutes one of the more ironic facts of antebellum American culture; well before 1830, when the dream of colonialization began to become a reality, Americans had long been and would continue to be a deeply mixed people. In this regard, George Harris's desire to undo the "Fall" that is miscegenation, expressed in his last speech in *Uncle Tom's Cabin*, takes on a special poignancy: " 'I have no wish to pass for an American, or to identify myself with them. It is with the oppressed, enslaved African race that I cast my lot; and, if I wished anything, I would wish myself two shades darker, rather than one lighter' " (608). Though he may wish to make his blackness fully legible, color, as he himself has shown, does not make a man. And though he may seek to mingle with the sons of Africa, his fellow Liberian compatriots will inevitably be (African) Americans. There is no getting behind the "Fall" of racist domination as long as the tyrannical categories of the color palette determine the ways in which Americans think. Such is the redemptive, if transient, value of masquerade, the third term that deconstructs the manichean allegory of race operative in *Uncle Tom's Cabin;* like the fiction for which it stands in microcosm, masquerade gestures toward freedom, a world elsewhere beyond the color line.

Notes

1. See, for example, Harriet Jacobs, *Incidents in the Life of a Slave Girl* (1861). Narrating the details of the first leg of her escape, which occurred seven years before her ultimate flight from bondage, Jacobs describes her assumption of male garb: "Betty brought me a suit of sailor's clothes,—jacket, trowsers [*sic*], and tarpaulin hat. She gave me a small bundle, saying I might need it where I was going. . . . 'Put your hand in your pockets, and walk rickety, like de sailors.' I performed to her satisfac-

tion" (111–12). Jacobs implies throughout her autobiography that for runaway slaves, it was second nature to take up such forms of disguises and to *perform* alternative identities.

2. See Garber, *Vested Interests* 16–17 and, specifically, 285–88, the section of chapter 11 devoted to Stowe's novel.

3. Using the terms of Lacanian theory, we can characterize the action of this chapter as opening in the symbolic register of language, the law of the name-of-the-father, and then shifting into the imaginary register of the mirror, the dyadic face-to-face encounter. If slavery as an institution is legislated and practiced in the realm of the symbolic, its interpsychic and interracial relations unfold, nevertheless, in the domain of the imaginary.

4. Harriet Beecher Stowe, *Uncle Tom's Cabin; or, Life among the Lowly* (1852); all references will be to the 1981 Penguin edition of the novel edited by Ann Douglas.

5. I borrow this phrase from the title of a fascinating study of advertisements for slave runaways written by two historians of early America. See Billy G. Smith and Richard Wojtowicz, *Blacks Who Stole Themselves: Advertisements for Runaways in the Pennsylvania Gazette, 1728–1790.*

6. See Smith and Wojtowicz 17–161. See also Jacobs 215. In the illustrations section of her edition of Jacobs's narrative, Jean Fagin Yellin has included a photographic reproduction of the newspaper advertisement for Jacobs's capture placed by Dr. Norcom in the *American Beacon* (daily) of Norfolk, Virginia, in June and July of 1835. Norcom's ad is considerably more detailed and idiosyncratic (filled with intimate ruminations about his runaway servant that border on the pornographic) than is Stowe's fictive handbill for the capture of George Harris.

7. The term is Abdul JanMohamed's. See his "The Economy of Manichean Allegory: The Function of Racial Difference in Colonialist Literature" 78–106.

8. It is interesting to note that George Harris's Anglo-Saxon paternity, though of no legal import, implies (in fictional terms) that Stowe's revolutionary slave protagonist is not *really* a black character at all. The narrator articulates this rather baldly: "We remark, *en passant,* that George was, by his father's side, of white descent. His mother was one of those unfortunates of her race, marked out by personal beauty to be the slave of the passions of her possessor, and the mother of children who may never know a father. From one of the proudest families in Kentucky he had inherited a set of fine European features, and a high, indomitable spirit. From his mother he had received only a slight mulatto tinge, amply compensated by its accompanying rich, dark eye" (182). If we add to this description Augustine St. Clare's response to the notion that the Anglo-Saxons are "the domi-

nant race of the world" (392), an interesting picture emerges: " 'Well, there is a pretty fair infusion of Anglo Saxon blood among our slaves, now,' said Augustine. 'There are plenty among them who have only enough of the African to give a sort of tropical warmth and fervor to our calculating firmness and foresight. If ever the San Domingo hour comes, Anglo Saxon blood will lead on the day. Sons of white fathers, with all our haughty feelings burning in their veins, will not always be bought and sold and traded. They will rise, and raise with them their mother's race' " (392). Disavowing the significance (and the difference) of an African heritage as he parses the bloodlines of mulatto "sons of white fathers," the liberal patriarch, himself a guilty slaveholder, projects his own unrealized political ideals onto the racially mixed other. George Harris perfectly embodies the figure sketched by St. Clare. Using language and expressing ideology that at every turn evoke the republican sentiments of the Founders, George Harris would seem to be a nineteenth-century Patrick Henry in "yellow"-face, a revolutionary son of a white father whose mixed blood is so fired by its Caucasian endowment that it cannot help but to burn for freedom *as if* it were pure.

9. Gates writes that literacy is a commodity that, once possessed, allows the enslaved subject to enter the world of human exchange from which, as an economic object, he or she had been barred. See Gates, *Figures in Black: Words, Signs, and the "Racial" Self* 11–14.

10. In conceptualizing the hierarchical relations of nineteenth-century America, I have adopted the notion of the *food chain*, a phrase that originates in the discourse of ecology, to describe most vividly the complex and stratified organization of social life in the antebellum period, in which race, class, and gender determine vertical status. Most crucial to my figurative use of the term is the relationship between appetite (the drive to consume) and the social and economic ambition (predation) that works itself out in racial terms in antebellum culture: the higher one dwells on the food chain, the more likely one is to be an eater and not to become someone else's food.

11. In *The Spanish Background of American Literature*, Stanley T. Williams notes that Spanish (Moorish) architecture was an important part of the heritage of southern Louisiana. Williams writes that "if we wander through the streets of old New Orleans, we shall find the Spanish influence, as in reading the romances of George Washington Cable and Grace King, real enough yet somehow elusive. . . . Perhaps the old Cabildo . . . speaks most definitely of Spanish ancestry" (1:111–12).

12. The phrase is Richard Poirier's. See Poirier, *A World Elsewhere*.

13. See Williams, particularly volume 2, which details the influence of Spain on

the careers of eight nineteenth-century American writers roughly contemporary with Stowe: Washington Irving, George Ticknor, William Hickling Prescott, William Cullen Bryant, Henry Wadsworth Longfellow, James Russell Lowell, Francis Brett Harte, and William Dean Howells. I am grateful to art historian Elizabeth Boone for recommending Williams's monumental study and for sharing her insights about nineteenth-century American representations of Spain and the Spanish, which form the subject of her work in progress on pictorial representations of Spain in nineteenth-century art.

14. Richard Sennett locates the origins of such cultural theatricality in eighteenth-century Europe, particularly in England and France. See Sennett's *The Fall of Public Man: On the Social Psychology of Capitalism.*

15. See Sigmund Freud, *The Interpretation of Dreams,* 1900, in *The Standard Edition of the Complete Psychological Works of Sigmund Freud* 4:1–338.

16. Elizabeth Boone explains that American reactions to the Spanish people during the nineteenth century are ambiguous at best. There are two kinds of representations in art: the Spanish "conquistador" who is white (Christopher Columbus, pictured with Ferdinand and Isabella, is a frequent figure in nineteenth-century American paintings of Spain), and which was particularly popular before the Civil War; and the exotic Spaniard (bullfighters, gypsies, flamenco dancers) who is darker in skin tone and was more popular in the later nineteenth century. "Simply put, light skin suggests power and dark skin suggests difference." Boone, letter to the author, August 9, 1993.

17. In the Melville novella of 1855, the black characters have revolted from their Spanish slave master aboard a transport ship and must feign the part of slaves when an American captain interferes in the progress of their revolution. More radical than Stowe's novel in its willingness to address the specter of San Domingo and Nat Turner head on, "Benito Cereno" fleshes out the questions to which Spanish masquerade in *Uncle Tom's Cabin* only alludes. Whether or not Stowe's novel had a direct influence on the creation of "Benito Cereno," it is nevertheless significant that these two important narratives of slavery written in America in the 1850s interrogate the institution of slavery in its international form.

18. Stowe's Jim prefigures another literary black Jim, the most memorable fugitive slave of late-nineteenth-century American fiction. Unlike Stowe's fugitive character, the Jim of *Huckleberry Finn* does not know, in the final chapters of that novel, that technically he has become free. Twain's tale becomes most painfully and powerfully ironic when Tom Sawyer, arriving on the scene at the eleventh hour, withholds

the crucial information that Jim's status has changed. More extensively than Stowe, but in a manner that evokes her chapter on Spanish masquerade, Twain explores what Laurence B. Holland has eloquently termed the dilemma of "how to set a free man free." See Holland 67.

19. Tzvetan Todorov writes of the imperialist dynamic in which the difference of the cultural other is read in terms of a hierarchical paradigm that inevitably leads to a program of domination and subordination. According to such a script, certain people are "cast" to play the roles of nonhuman functionaries by other peoples occupying the roles of fully human agents and masters. Such objectification produces in its victims a collective sense of abjection and degradation, for such are the qualities found to be so desirable in slaves. Abjection and degradation are then essentialized and read by slave owners as innate qualities that inhere "naturally" in the race of the other. Culture is mistaken for nature, and the manichean terms of the drama of racist domination are solidified. Todorov's work has been central to my thinking about slavery and Stowe's meditation on the racist, imperialist origins of the founding of America. See Todorov, *The Conquest of America*.

20. In "Benito Cereno," Babo, the revolutionary black who orchestrates the slave uprising and seizes control of the Spanish slave ship, must feign the part of Captain Cereno's valet to persuade Captain Delano, the dim American officer who stumbles onto the San Dominick in the immediate aftermath of the revolution, that everything is "normal." That as a slave Babo had in fact *been* Cereno's valet makes the role all the more ripe for exaggeration and exploitation.

21. A similar relationship of white master and black slave buttresses the disguise of Ellen Craft in *Running a Thousand Miles for Freedom*. See the discussion of that narrative by Ellen Weinauer, in this volume.

22. Philosophers have discussed slavery in precisely these terms since the nineteenth century. Eric Sundquist writes: "For Hegel, the master's power is hedged by his discovery that his very identity *as a master* is bound to, and mediated through, another consciousness, that of the slave. The slave, in turn, although he is in thrall to the master and lives to a degree for his enhancement, nonetheless wields power over the master by refusing to grant him autonomy and forcing him into a psychological posture of dependence" (*To Wake the Nations* 40–41). Sundquist cites Orlando Patterson's "reconceptualization of the master-slave relation as one of 'parasitism,' a relation in which the master, by various paternalistic strategies that amounted to self-deceptions rather than statements of natural relations, camouflaged his own parasitic dependence on the slave with the pretense that slaves were parasites on their

masters. For their part, slaves in turn camouflaged, or masked, their resistance to slavery—and hence the nature of their freedom through consciousness—only on occasion removing the mask and exposing the parasitic relationship of slavery as an 'ideological inversion of reality' " (42). See also Patterson, *Slavery and Social Death: A Comparative Study*.

23. I am grateful to Duke University Press's reader for pointing out that at the time of the publication of *Uncle Tom's Cabin*, "the Butlers of Georgia/Philadelphia were among the most prominent of the large-plantation slaveholders in the United States. Pierce Butler had just gone through a highly publicized divorce from Fanny Kemble."

24. Ironically, according to traditional Spanish practices, surnames are transmitted through the maternal line, and hyphenated names indicate the identity of both male and female progenitors. (It is unclear, however, if Stowe knew this.) Had George's Spanish masquerade been truly authentic, his relation to his mother would have received *legitimate* expression. But, of course, slaves, debarred from possessing property in themselves, much less material goods and symbolic privileges, *possess* no authentic surnames of their own; by convention (since by law they have no identity) bondspeople bear the names of their owners in order to indicate their relationship to white patriarchy as *possessions*: thus "Harris's George" becomes George Harris.

25. The term is Kimberly W. Benston's and comes from his important "Facing Tradition: Revisionary Scenes in African American Literature" 106. I am indebted to Benston's essay for many of my thoughts about tableaux in *Uncle Tom's Cabin*.

26. I borrow this phrase from Richard Brodhead, who uses it in a less figurative fashion than I do. See Brodhead, *Cultures of Letters: Scenes of Reading and Writing in Nineteenth-Century America*.

27. In Mr. Wilson's bagging factory, George has united brain and hand to invent a machine that cleans hemp. He has created, in effect, a mechanized hand that does the work of minions. The labor of his creation is appropriated by his owner; Mr. Harris earns the patent for George's invention, stealing the work of his hand. The irony of an invention that would enable the more efficient production of hemp is pointed: bags and ropes are made from hemp and are used to sequester animals and slaves. Dark are the implications of George's ingenuity; his creativity is co-opted by the master who, in a pique of jealousy, reduces him to the labor of a beast, thereby completing a circular drama of exploitation and domination.

28. Kimberly Benston writes: "The end of the tradition imagined in the topos of facing would be the effacement of an encounter *face-to-face*, the scene beyond the

vertiginous exchanges of master-slave and oedipal positions, where the spatial and temporal predicaments of tradition are suspended, where immediacy is no longer an illusion of scopic power but the dissolution of specular relations altogether." See "Facing Tradition" 106.

29. The term *romantic racialism* was coined by historian George Fredrickson in his important study *The Black Image in the White Mind: The Debate on Afro-American Character and Destiny, 1817–1914* 97–129. Eric Sundquist elaborates on Fredrickson's definition in his introductory essay to *New Essays on* Uncle Tom's Cabin, writing that romantic racialism is the belief that "blacks are innately inferior to whites in political and social terms, but perhaps superior to them in affections and natural Christian virtues" (32).

30. Stowe's bifurcated conception of black heroism in *Uncle Tom's Cabin* has been noted and explored by Richard Yarborough, Robert Stepto, and Eric Sundquist, some of the finest late-twentieth-century critics of the novel. These scholars show that Stowe is torn between a deeply felt Christian belief in passive resistance bequeathed to her by a ministerial family, and the compelling power of the ideals of the American Revolution, in which armed resistance to tyranny and oppression represent the cause of the just. According to these critics, Stowe is unable or unwilling to imagine the conjunction of power, intelligence, and revolutionary impulses at work in a purely black character lest she conjure Nat Turner; thus, they argue, Stowe creates both Tom and George Harris to bear the burden of her double vision. See Yarborough, "Strategies of Black Characterization in *Uncle Tom's Cabin* and the Early Afro-American Novel"; Stepto, "Sharing the Thunder: The Literary Exchanges of Harriet Beecher Stowe, Henry Bibb, and Frederick Douglass"; and Sundquist, "Introduction"; all in *New Essays on* Uncle Tom's Cabin, ed. Sundquist.

31. Marjorie Garber's observation about Stowe's use of names supports such a reading. George and Eliza name their son "Harry"; when Harry must put on the garb of a girl to expedite the family's final escape, Eliza, herself in cross-dress, announces that they will call the child "Harriet." Garber claims that it "is almost as if Stowe places herself within the narrative as the wide-eyed, 'peeping,' and disbelieving child of the primal scene—the primal scene, here, of American cultural intercourse, the imagined and unimaginable coupling of race and gender" (*Vested Interests* 286). I would argue that Stowe is more closely identified with the adult vision of "Harriet's" father George, to whom she is linked symbolically through the name of the common child they have in a sense co-created, George Harris as fictional father, and Harriet Beecher Stowe as novelist.

32. See Bakhtin, *Rabelais and His World* 196–277 and 303–67. See also Lott, *Love and Theft: Blackface Minstrelsy and the American Working Class*, especially 27–28 and 146.

33. George exclaims: "O! Eliza, if these people only knew what a blessing it is for a man to feel that his wife and child belong to *him*! I've often wondered to see men that could call their wives and children *their own* fretting and worrying about anything else" (285). See Zwarg 280. See also Ellen Weinauer's observations about William and Ellen Craft in this volume.

34. It is interesting to consider twentieth-century Liberian history in the context of the utopian representation of its founding in *Uncle Tom's Cabin*. Engaged in a civil war that pits the colonial elite—descendants of nineteenth-century African American slaves—against the descendants of the colonized indigenous African tribes of the area, late-twentieth-century Liberian factions can be seen as playing out the final act of the patriarchal, revolutionary politics at work in *Uncle Tom's Cabin*.

Blackness and the Literary Imagination:

Uncovering *The Hidden Hand*

KATHARINE NICHOLSON INGS

*F*rom 1859 through 1883, E. D. E. N. Southworth's sentimental novel *The Hidden Hand* appeared in the *New York Ledger* three times, confirming its status as the *Ledger*'s most popular serialization. Such an honor was probably quite unexpected by Southworth, who began writing solely out of a need for money. Deserted by her husband four years into their marriage and responsible for two young children, she embarked on her literary career after schoolteaching failed to provide sufficient income. Although an unassuming, introverted woman—she felt psychologically isolated after a two-year-long eye inflammation in childhood—Southworth recognized the social problems of America and ardently opposed slavery. She frequently published her early stories in *The National Era,* an abolitionist periodical, which led her to describe herself later as a "poor, obscure young public school teacher, out of favor with my friends and neighbors on account of my writing for an abolitionist paper" (qtd. in Kelley 160). She was, according to Joanne Dobson, "well acquainted with black men and women" ("Introduction" xxiv) but was a product of her age and thus "not free from the limiting prejudices of her era" (xxiv).

The great appeal of *The Hidden Hand,* no doubt, lay not only in Southworth's intricate plot twists but also in the antisentimental characterization of its heroine, Capitola Black. Sentimental fiction, largely a genre written by and for women, promoted a pious exemplar of true womanhood. The conventional heroine obeyed her guardians, followed a strict moral code, and positioned herself comfortably within the domestic sphere. In portraying Capitola, however, Southworth draws on these sentimental criteria only to subvert them: Capitola defies her guardian's authority at every turn, prefers to fight her own duels, and cross-dresses as a boy to support herself on the streets of New York. Southworth thus creates an adventurous heroine whose comic and dangerous exploits critique women's limited place in nineteenth-century society. But in Capitola Black, with her ferocious independence, dark features, and a darker surname, Southworth also explores possibilities for women by weaving "blackness" into her heroine's character and her plot.

Such an integration of blackness into the narrative reflects what Eric Sundquist identifies as the imbrication of "two conflicting yet coalescing cultural traditions—'American' and 'African'" (*To Wake the Nations* 6). This miscegenated foundation of American literature, however, has been largely unacknowledged by white scholars who may misinterpret cultural signs or disregard those elements that appear trivial or even (to use Sundquist's word) "nonsensical" to them (6). Such a reading practice contributes to the idea of textual "passing": by not recognizing or by misreading the racial influence on canonical texts, scholars can actually help a text pass as "white" literature. Textual passing thus encourages cultural blinders, allowing literary historians to perpetuate the myth of a homogeneous literary tradition.

In *The Hidden Hand*, one of Southworth's strategies is to reverse the traditional moral order in sentimental fiction by employing color symbolism to resemanticize whiteness as blackness. According to Winfried Fluck, sentimentality pivots on the tension between moral and social systems that are at odds with each other and on the threat of their being permanently separated. In *Uncle Tom's Cabin*, for example, Stowe's moral order, represented by white Christianity, conflicts with the social order, represented by slavery. To reunite the two, the "reality and the superiority of the moral order" must be reasserted (Fluck 324); in so doing, the sentimental novel becomes a "specific symbolic strategy to make an increasingly elusive order 'visible' again" (324). By the end of *Uncle Tom's Cabin*, Tom, society's invisible slave, emerges as the moral victor, realigning the two orders. But Fluck notes that because black people did not connote "genuine morality" (325), for Tom to represent the novel's "white" moral order, his blackness has to be "resemanticize[d]" as "whiteness" through his highly visible friendship with little Eva and his Christian deeds. Ironically, for Tom to be a visible black man, he must (morally) "pass" as white; the "meaning of the sign 'black'" must be moved "from one semantic field—which comprises all characters and settings linked by their lack of a genuine moral dimension—to the semantic field informed by genuine morality" (326).[1] Morality in sentimental fiction is thus contingent on attaining a "whitewashed" blackness—a moral passing.

In Capitola Black, however, Southworth creates a character who often acts in opposition to what is traditionally considered "good" in sentimental fiction. Capitola does not, for example, uphold the expected "white" moral order, one so piously and obediently illustrated by Stowe's little Eva and Susan Warner's Ellen Montgomery.[2] Instead, she engages in "naughty," morally dark acts, such as masquerading as Craven Le Noir's bride or facilitating Black Donald's escape from prison. Capitola's rebellion against the sentimental trappings, however, makes the girl immensely likable, and consequently the naughty acts she performs are represented to the reader as less "bad" than "good." Cheerfully violating the sanctity of sentimental fiction, Capitola's character destabilizes readers' expectations for a sentimental heroine: her behavior critiques the sentimental standard that only "whiteness" connotes genuine morality.

Southworth's characterization of Capitola also suggests how blackness permeates nineteenth-century literature to express rebellion against the more passive and static "true womanhood" or to represent white oppression. Such a strategy, however, leads to Southworth's appropriation of both the stereotypes and the experiences of blacks, lifting them from context to represent the white woman's freedom or captivity. In *The Hidden Hand*, blackness functions as a vehicle for communicating and critiquing white oppression. Drawing on white perceptions of black energy, such as a rebellious attitude, or a symbol of black oppression, such as a brand on the flesh, Southworth challenges society's standards and negotiates new limits for her antisentimental white heroine, although not for the black woman.

In nicknaming her heroine "Cap" Black, Southworth links her with "Old Hat" (16), a black woman who nurses Cap's dying guardian, Granny Grewell. A more grown-up version of a "Cap," Hat's name and appearance foreshadow Capitola's name and first appearance in the narrative. When visitors arrive at her "Witch's Hut" (16), for example, Hat appears to be genderless: "The door was immediately opened by a negro, whose sex from the strange anomalous costume it was difficult to guess. The tall form was rigged out first in a long, red, cloth petticoat, above which was buttoned a blue cloth surtot. A man's old black beaver hat sat upon the strange head and completed the odd attire" (16). In this chapter entitled "The Masks," Hat engages in a masquerade, one that renders her androgynous and mysterious—and perhaps appropriately so, since Hat makes a "scanty living by telling fortunes and showing the way to the [Devil's] Punch Bowl" (16). Her costume is both outrageous enough for a witch and ambiguous enough that Hat's sex is obscured: it serves as a practical uniform for work. Hat's appearance thus anticipates the gender passing that takes place in Capitola's masquerade: the unusual outfit suggests a relationship between clothes and profession, because certain jobs demand a certain "look."

Born on Halloween night to a "masked mother" (21), Cap is literally born into masquerade. As ambiguous as Hat's portrait, for Cap looks neither wholly feminine nor masculine, Southworth's first full description of her reveals "a handsome boy, too, notwithstanding the deplorable state of his wardrobe. Thick, clustering curls of jet black hair fell in tangled disorder around a forehead, white, and smooth as that of a girl; slender and quaintly-arched black eyebrows played above a pair of mischievous, dark gray eyes, that sparkled beneath the shade of long, thick, black lashes; a little turned-up nose, and red, pouting lips, completed the character of a countenance full of fun, frolic, spirit, and courage" (33). Part boy and part girl in a ragamuffin's clothes, Cap also dresses for work. But unlike Hat, whose clothes complement her profession, Cap wears a boy's garments in order to get work. While living on the streets of New York as a girl, she explains, "there seemed to be nothing but starvation or beggary before me" (44), but as a boy, her job opportunities seem limitless: she can earn money by "selling newspapers, carrying portmanteaus and packages, sweeping before doors, clearing off snow, blacking boots, and so on" (41).

Within this figure of the girlish boy, Cap's body acts as a site of both literal gender passing and symbolic racial passing. Alfred Habegger points out that her masculine counterpart "brings to life her stillborn male twin" (202), but Cap's passing also suggests a more rebellious strategy. Her actions look back to those "apolitical theatrical men" of the early nineteenth century documented by Eric Lott in *Love and Theft* who "pursued a newly available bourgeois dream of freedom and play by paradoxically coding themselves as 'black'" (51). By appropriating the "cultural forms of blackness," these white men also appropriated—for a time—the "cool, virility, humility, abandon, or *gaité de coeur* that were the prime components of white ideologies of black manhood" (52). As a boy, Cap has access to the kinds of activities that would be considered morally too "dark" for girls, such as exchanging labor for money or wearing a boy's costume, and she performs them under the double veil of *black* masculinity.

Although Capitola and Hat exhibit comparable degrees of independence and self-sufficiency, Cap the boy achieves a more unfettered, rebellious freedom. When she first introduces Hat, Southworth takes care to mention that she is "an old free negro" (16), yet this freedom may be hard-won, or qualified. Indeed, Hat's freedom may be predicated on the fact that as an old woman, she can no longer be physically capable of efficiently supporting and maintaining the slaveholder's visible prosperity. The freedom Cap achieves, however, both confirms and contradicts Gillian Brown's observation about nineteenth-century labor: "To be a working body is virtually to be a slave, to be labor value and potentially salable" (64). To pass as a worker, then, suggests that Cap also passes as black. Indeed, Lott gives compelling evidence for the shared experience of the white working body and the black one. According to Lott, many Northern working-class whites and blacks experienced similar struggles against the upper class; both were the objects of similar "racial slurs" such as "coon" or "buck," and the phrase "wage slavery" described the employment conditions of the artisan working class (68). As well, black caricatures transcended race, "culturally represent[ing] workers above all" (68). Thus, Lott argues, "blackface quickly became a sort of useful shorthand in referring to working men" (68). As a worker, Capitola participates in this "equation . . . of slaves and white workers" (Lott 68) with one important exception: instead of resenting the upper class or feeling enslaved, she achieves a degree of independence. Her working body ironically gives her freedom, making her "happy and prosperous"; her only regret "was to see what a fool I had been, not to turn a boy before, when it was so easy!" (Southworth 47). Although her female body may be salable or "awardable"—authorities eventually appoint her the ward of Old Hurricane, who returns Cap to her native Norfolk from her life on the street—her male body remains independent.

As the confident "ragged lad," Cap is identified with such "dark" characteristics as "jet black hair," "black eyebrows," and "black lashes" (33). Conversely, her feminine "forehead broad, white, and smooth" (33) suggests purity and a pampered life and, indeed, seems out of place on a streetwise newsboy. These conflicting physical characteristics link two sides of Capitola's character: the dark qualities evoke the risk-taking, bold boy, while the white girl's forehead suggests the innocent sentimental heroine. Significantly, such a configuration relates to the historical imbrication of race and gender: the "true women" in the South were white, and black men were seen as potential threats to the white woman's purity. Thus the stereotype of coding white women as "helpless" and black men as dangerous and "oversexed" (Dobson, "Introduction" xxv) functioned as a form of social control: white women dared not act unlike a lady, that is, like a black woman, and black men had to be particularly deferent to white women. Following this standard, Cap's adventurous side, swathed in darkness, is black-identified, but her pure, "feminine" side is white.[3] Southworth, however, overturns this stereotypical formulation by not limiting Capitola's exploits to her male persona, letting Cap-the-girl have all the adventures that a boy could. In doing so, Southworth uses blackness as a vehicle through which the sentimental *heroine* exercises her independence, though she does not extend this independence to the few black servant women in the novel.

Although Capitola's birth name is Le Noir, Old Hurricane calls her Black, a name that distinguishes Capitola from a conventional sentimental heroine and from her paternal ancestors. Symbolically, the name places Capitola in opposition to the second, more traditional heroine in the novel, Clara Day, who is as clear-minded and sunny in character and countenance as Cap is complex and dark. But there also appears to be a hierarchy of social prestige separating Black and Le Noir. Black, the lower-class name, connotes not only the skin color of the oppressed but also the name of a notorious bandit, Black Donald, who sold the baby Cap and Granny Grewell into slavery. In Capitola's name, the legacy of slavery and the morality of banditry are reflected. When Old Hurricane names Capitola "Black," however, his action seems more liberating than enslaving. He has learned Capitola's hidden history and knows that Cap's uncle, Gabriel Le Noir, kidnapped Cap's pregnant mother and tried to destroy her newborn girl. Because Cap's father shares a surname with Le Noir, the man who would own and dispose of her, Hurricane saves Cap from bearing her potential master's name, thus preventing her from becoming Le Noir's symbolic property.

But when her mother gains her release from long years of confinement, Cap should finally be recognized as Capitola Le Noir, daughter of Eugene and the elder Capitola, her namesake. Yet Capitola's birth name is curiously absent from the reunion scene with her mother, and on the eve of her wedding, the sheriff and warden still address Capitola as "Miss Black," the "name under which they had *first* known her" (478, emphasis mine). The past perfect tense suggests that they do know that her "real" name is Le Noir, though they do not use it, and Cap does not correct them. Capitola's symbolic and literal Black-ness becomes ironically both present and absent: she is at once (socially) "Black" and not (originally) "Black," (originally) "Le Noir" and not (socially) "Le Noir." In fact, Southworth moves her plot so rapidly from the mother and child reunion to Cap's marriage to Herbert Greyson that she literally devotes no ink to Capitola Le Noir: the girl transforms from Capitola Black into her mother's daughter and then into Capitola Greyson, a blending of white and black. Although the name change suggests that she has reconciled the male and female and black and white components of her character, it also suggests a compromise: Capitola appears newly domesticated. That "wild cat" who had been born "squalling" (21) now appears tamed; its blackness has become a muted grey.

Capitola's hidden hand, a birthmark that stains her palm, also represents the girl's "wild" side. It symbolizes what Dobson calls Cap's "dashing, even illicit, courage" ("Subversion" 235) and her "obvious parallels with the outlaw, Black Donald, whose own 'hand is red . . . with crime'" (235). The birthmark also suggests, however, that Southworth creates a parallel between oppressed white women and enslaved African American women, though its purpose is to critique the social control of white, not black, women. Outwardly, the hand boasts the creamy, white flesh of a sentimental heroine, but its underside reveals the hidden hand, symbolic of a brand. Although the mark on Capitola's hand certainly does not denote a literal brand, significantly, the birthmark does enter the novel within the context of white slavery. After Cap and Granny have been sold into slavery and left for dead on a ship transporting them to a new city, they are rescued by a second ship going to New York, where they remain for ten years. When Granny returns home to Norfolk to locate Cap's family, she informs Old Hurricane that Cap's birthmark will be the means by which he can recognize the girl—not as a symbolically marked slave, however, but as a Le Noir.

In this sense, Southworth both codes Capitola's birthmark as and distinguishes it from the bodily markings that Hortense Spillers discusses in "Mama's Baby, Papa's Maybe: An American Grammar Book." As Spillers suggests, the slave woman's flesh is a tabula rasa on which slavery's horrors are written:

These undecipherable markings on the captive body render a kind of hieroglyphics of the flesh whose severe disjunctures come to be *hidden* to the cultural seeing by skin color. We might well ask if this phenomenon of marking and branding actually "transfers" from one generation to another, finding its various symbolic substitutions in an efficacy of meanings that repeat the initiating moments? . . . This body whose flesh carries the female and the male to the frontiers of survival bears in person the marks of a cultural text whose inside has been turned outside. (67, emphasis mine)

Although the mark on Capitola's hand suggests the crimes committed on black flesh, the transfer is merely symbolic; the physical pain and the extreme social hardships accompanying black women's oppression are elided. Capitola's hidden hand may signify the gender oppression of the sentimental heroine, but it also identifies her not as a street urchin coded as black or as oppressed by the symbols of slavery but as the Le Noir heiress.

Although Old Hurricane knows that Cap's "hand" identifies her, he never looks for or mentions its existence. Cap's mark is, however, noticed thrice, and every time it is seen, it involves the generational transference of the brand, which Spillers outlines above.[4] All those who see the mark are women, suggesting that Southworth may be relying on a certain slippage between white women's oppression and slavery: the women recognize the "cultural text" (Spillers 67) that enslaved women share, but Southworth symbolically applies that text to a white woman in the narrative. The first woman to see Cap's birthmark is Granny Grewell, who describes it as being "very strange," the "perfect image of a crimson hand about half an inch in length" (Southworth 28). Acting as midwife, Granny brings Capitola into the world, and her kind hands both contrast with the cruelty represented on Capitola's palm and follow the hidden hand's example: her arms conceal the baby girl from Le Noir. The image of the potentially harmful hand thus turns into a helpful one.

Old Hat notices Capitola's mark when she reads her palm, and the birthmark transforms from a sign of legacy to a sign of prophesy. Although at the beginning of the novel, Hat was Cap's androgynous double, when the two encounter each other in the woods, Southworth has added another dimension to her character: Cap cannot determine if Hat is "man, woman, beast or demon" (271). The animal and demonic characteristics Hat has acquired suggest a stereotypical reading of the African American. Although she is free, the inhuman imagery recalls the perception of the slave woman; so here, a symbolic slave figure interprets Cap's mark as one of violence:

"Away! Begone!" she [Hat] cried, shaking her long arm at the girl. "Away! Begone! the fate pursues you! the badge of blood is stamped upon your palm!"
" 'Fee—faw—fum!' — " said Cap.
"Scorner! Beware! the curse of the crimson hand is upon you!" (273)

Hat tells Cap her hand will be bloody but does not specify whether Cap will perform the deed or be hurt; she merely says Cap is "destined to rise by the destruction of one who would shed his heart's best blood for [her]" (272).

And the prophesy does come true, for when the girl visits the Hidden House, where her mother remains captive, her mark is seen for a third time. On recognizing Cap as the elder Capitola's daughter, Dorcas Knight, the housekeeper and jailkeeper, "seized [Cap's] right hand, forcibly opened it, gazed upon the palm, and then flinging it back with a shudder," orders Cap to leave (278). Cap, however, does not go, and her overnight visit results in Clara Day's horrified discovery the next morning: Dorcas's hand is stained with the blood of Capitola's mother, spilled in a struggle with Dorcas and Le Noir. Here, the blood on Dorcas Knight's symbolically "dark-as-night" hand suggests both the captivity and the immorality of the black hand. The blood represents the crimes committed on captive black flesh but also looks to the sentimental tradition where black represents villainy; in Dorcas's situation, the red blood paints her hand morally "black." Yet Dorcas, concerned for Cap's welfare, hurries her out of the Hidden House, implying that "black" immorality is in fact forced on the housekeeper by her master.

Such contradictory readings of Dorcas's hand hearken back to the depictions of Cap's mother in childbirth and her captors. Granny Grewell remembers that the villains' faces *"were covered over with black crape"* (18) and the pregnant woman's *"right hand was sewed up in black crape, and her whole face and head completely covered with black crape, drawn down and fastened securely around her throat, leaving only a small slit at the lips and nose to breathe through!"* (20). In the first description, moral blackness seems evident: the black crape masks mark the villains as "black-headed demons" (22), establishing the woman as captive. More than a disguise, the black crape imprisoning the woman's face and head functions as symbolic flesh, evoking the black female slave's position as sexual slave to her master. The scenario Southworth paints suggests a "typical" relationship between slave woman and master—the villain who takes away the woman's child seems coextensive with a slave master unwilling to have revealed the secret of the child's paternity. The woman's vulnerable position—she is in labor—suggests the sexual indignities that slave women experienced under their masters' rule. This particular master controls the woman's sexuality by forcing her to give birth in captivity and bound in crape.

The scene also evokes the woman's maternal anonymity: her black mask conceals her face, and her covered right hand probably conceals a hidden hand birthmark; thus she cannot be identified or recognized as the mother of the twin babies. Capitola the elder's double mark of blackness—the black crape that covers her face and hand and functions as symbolic flesh, and the concealed birthmark—suggests a further link with the slave woman: neither can be legally or socially recognized as a mother. Like the master who had the right to control his slave woman's offspring, Le Noir insists on taking Capitola's newborn from her. But this mother defies her master by offering him only the stillborn or "sleeping" body of her boy twin. Her apparent willingness to turn over the baby to Le Noir without a fight suggests to the uninformed observer a weak bond between mother and child, that socially, Capitola is a "bad" mother; but secretly, she passes the surviving girl twin—both literally and figuratively—to Granny Grewell in an act of maternal sacrifice. Although she does not know if the midwife can save her child, she pleads for baby Cap's life: *"Save my child! the living one I mean! hide her! oh, hide her from him!"* (21). Her sacrifice exemplifies the ultimate gesture of maternal love: to save her daughter from the white male authority, the mother gives up her child, taking drastic measures that could lead to the baby's death.

The town minister, however, later voices the vexed nature of such a sacrifice when he demands of Old Hurricane: "But tell me, sir, of the girl's mother! Is it not astonishing; in fact, is it not perfectly incomprehensible, that so lovely a woman as you have represented her to be, should have consented to the concealment, if not to the destruction of her own legitimate offspring" (179). He does not question why a mother would turn over a stillborn child to her captor but cannot fathom that a "legitimate" mother would send her child to an unknown destination, a socially unacceptable act to the moral community depicted in sentimental fiction. His exclamation suggests that he sees Capitola's act as being more aligned with "black" morality, but it also reveals the folly of privileging "white" goodness. Old Hurricane's hasty response might describe Capitola's circumstances as well as the plight of the enslaved mother: "Sir, to me it is not incomprehensible at all! She was at once an orphan and a widow; stranger in a strange land; a poor, desolate, broken-hearted child, in the power of the cunningest and most unscrupulous villain that the Lord ever suffered to live!" (179). Captive herself, the only freedom the slave mother could offer her child was either through escape or, paradoxically, through death. As the one act that socially inscribes her as a mother under her circumstances, her sacrifice allows her to exercise control over her child's fate. In depicting Capitola's determination not to allow her baby to be placed in the hands of Le Noir, Southworth incorporates into the plot the kind of maternal sacrifice made by some slave women, but she does so to argue against the sexual subjugation of white women. Paradoxically, though whiteness typically represents power, as a visible white woman, Capitola has none. But bound in black crape as a symbolic slave mother, she can save her baby girl from the Le Noirs.

And, indeed, the sacrifice Capitola makes leads her baby to freedom but results in her own lengthy incarceration in an attic. Such a location has historically been a place of refuge or imprisonment for women denied freedom. Linda Brent hides from her master in her grandmother's "crawlspace," Cassy and Emmeline conceal themselves in Simon Legree's garret, and Bertha Rochester is confined to her husband's attic.[5] Like Cassy and Bertha, Capitola makes a ghostly descent from her attic abode to haunt an unsuspecting sleeping person. But although doctors later pronounce Capitola insane, making her the true "madcap" of the book's title,[6] she does not become a Bertha Rochester "madwoman in the attic" figure. Her madness is not real but constructed by her captors and doctors who force this identity on her in an asylum. In a chapter ironically entitled

"The Maniac's Story," her doctor patronizes her, indulging her "lunatic fancies" (443) by grudgingly calling her "Madame." Capitola desires the title because it reminds her that she had been married and has a child, but to the doctor, Capitola's attempt to pass as a married woman makes her "the maddest of the whole lot" (443). From his position of white masculine authority, he perceives Capitola's apparent passing as an illness, a misguided attempt to lay claim to marriage and children, an inappropriate desire to be perceived as a "true woman."

Capitola's maternal convictions and her insistence on the truth of her history, the purpose of her ghostly visit to her unsuspecting daughter, Cap, parallel Cassy's nighttime visit to Simon Legree. Both women are confined, willingly or not, because they are mothers, and both use their ghostly presence as the mother "who is not there" as a means or a reason to escape from captivity. But the two women also transcend their literal and symbolic blackness through their ghostly transparency, which would, if carried out successfully, ultimately negate blackness or whiteness and unite the women's bodies through their socio/maternal functions. For these mothers, passing as a ghost permits them to secure freedom or a child's legitimacy. Indeed, Cassy's feigned maternity gives birth to her freedom as a black woman, whereas Capitola's ultimately acknowledged maternity rights the social wrongs that have been done to her as a white woman.

Cassy's "authentic ghost story" (Stowe, *Uncle Tom's Cabin* 594) and Capitola's "authenticated ghost story" (Southworth 454) both succeed in making visible the invisible moral order in the sentimental novel by making present the absent mother—sentimentality's moral center—if only as a ghost. Cassy's ghostly presence is a predatory one that plays on Simon Legree's fear of his dead mother, initiated by his immense guilt over rejecting his mother's morality. Having secreted herself in Legree's attic, Cassy glides down to terrify him one night, wearing a bedsheet, whispering, "Come! come! come!" (Stowe, *Uncle Tom's Cabin* 596). Because Cassy's "partial insanity" had previously given her words and language "a strange, weird, unsettled cast" (567), disturbing Legree, her ghostly utterance commands even more power. Her words, coming from the mouth of a dead white mother but mediated by the mouth of an enslaved black mother, suggest an attempted merging of the white and black moral order, of the sane (white) and mad (black) maternal figure. But as Eva Cherniavsky notes:

For all Stowe's apparent desire to redomesticate Cassy, to position her in the reconstituted familial sphere to which the freed black women in this novel accede, the figure Cassy cuts in that white sheet is beyond recall. For as much as Stowe seeks to reinscribe Cassy's face with the tender expression of white motherhood, engineers the altogether implausible return of Cassy's children to her, Cassy stands out, apart, in the scenes of family reunion which follow, a strange, unsettled figure, marking time on a utopian clock. (136–37)

Capitola's ghost story, however, is not predatory but protective: she tells Traverse Rocke that "anxiety for the fate of my child caused me to do what nothing else on earth would have tempted me to — to creep about the halls and passages on tiptoe and under cover of the night, and listen at keyholes" (453). In essence, she becomes a ghost. One night, when her lost daughter Cap escapes a storm by sleeping in the Hidden House, she sneaks into the girl's room and kisses her. The figure Cap sees differs from the figure who visits Legree, for whereas Cassy completely covers herself with a sheet, Capitola appears in plain view as a "figure clothed in white — a beautiful, pale, spectral woman, whose large, motionless black eyes, deeply set in her death-like face, and whose long, unbound black hair, fallen upon her white raiment, were the only marks of color about her marble form" (284). Here, Cap does not realize that the "ghost" is her mother, but at the same time, Capitola secures her future visibility by taking the wedding ring engraved with her name from her daughter. Stowe and Southworth thus approach maternal visibility differently: Stowe uses the ghostly figure to resemanticize Cassy as white, though she does not completely succeed, whereas Southworth defers Capitola's visibility, using the ghost to claim the ring with which she will assert her legitimacy later on.

Capitola the younger achieves visibility as a sentimental heroine whose history bears only the trappings of sentimentality: Cap is an orphan raised by a "narrow-minded, tyrannical guardian" and the plot "takes her from puberty to marriage" (Dobson, "Subversion" 234). But Cap emerges as an antisentimental heroine, as evident in her cross-dressing, her dark coloration, her bold exploits, and her adamant dislike of sentimentality. When Craven Le Noir, "with much ardor and earnestness and much more eloquence than anyone would have credited him with, poured forth the history of his passion and his hopes" (Southworth 356), Cap, unlike a sentimental heroine such as Ellen Montgomery or Clara Day, does not respond "properly" to his plea. Instead of acting graciously in front of the prostrate suitor, Cap announces, " 'Well, I declare!' ... 'this is what is called a declaration of love and a proposal for marriage, is it!—It is downright sentimental, I suppose, if I had only the good sense to appreciate it! It is as good as a play! pity it is lost upon me!' " (356).

In a twist on Helena Michie's argument that sentimentality is a form of "*disease*," the "disturbances" and "excesses" of the female body, Cap feels ill at ease with sentimentality. In sentimental novels, Michie notes, "it is the woman or the little girl whose deathbed we as readers are invited— or forced—to attend" ("Dying" 189), and Cap, it seems, will have none of that tired old plot. Greatly preferring "fire, flood or thieves, or any- thing to stir her stagnant blood" (Southworth 213) to feminine bodily disease, Cap's bodily excesses suggest particularly masculine excesses. As she challenges Craven to a duel or works for her living in the streets, Capitola either acts or dresses as a male. But this is not to suggest that Cap is male-identified; rather, she is antisentimental, and although the con- verse of sentimental is not "traditional" female territory, it is not neces- sarily masculine. For through her antisentimental antics, Cap opens up the category of feminine bodily excesses: they need not represent only Michie's "feverish" sentimental (189) but may constitute adventure and independence. When Capitola insists she "naturally abhored sentiment" (Southworth 123), the emphasis is on natural—she is not characterized as an adventurous male but as a "naturally" adventurous young woman.

Capitola's exploits not only challenge the sentimental female body but also sentimentality's traditional morality. A young white lady was not expected to take an extended horseback ride on her own, and when Old Hurricane learns that Cap has ridden "just across the river, and through the woods and back again" (121), he lets loose his anger in a thunderous rage: "And didn't I *forbid* you to do that, minion? and how *dare* you disobey me? *You*, the creature of my bounty! *you*, the miserable little vagrant that I picked up in the alleys of New York, and tried to make a young lady of" (121). Two days later, however, Cap finds Old Hurricane coming home late at night and comically turns on him, retorting: "Didn't you know, you headstrong, reckless, desperate, frantic veteran! *didn't* you know the jeopardy in which you placed yourself by riding out alone at this hour? Suppose three or four great runaway negresses had sprung out of the bushes—and—and" (128). As Winfried Fluck notes, the "cultural semantics of blackness" (326) position "black" as a sign of immorality, but here, Southworth subverts the semantics, not by resemanticizing black as white but by mocking the apparent threat posed by blackness. In recasting the potential villains as "great runaway negresses" and not as black men, Southworth reverses the cultural stereotype to humorous effect, revealing and dismantling its construction. Furthermore, by switching the gender of the traditionally male villains, Cap aligns herself with the women: if they are out at this hour and if they are the only threats, then Cap would also be perfectly safe riding at night.

But Cap also challenges the supposed immorality of a less obviously innocent target: Black Donald. Notably, her surname, Black, suggests that she shares a kindred spirit with the outlaw, and indeed, they engage in "black" or improper activities: he disobeys the law of the land, and she disobeys the law of her surrogate father, Old Hurricane. Yet Cap's first name also links her with the outlaw through the dynamics of slavery. Shortly after meeting her young black housemaid, Pitapat, Cap decides to look under the trapdoor in her room, soothing the child's fears and establishing a kinship between them by pointing to a similarity in their names: " 'Bring the light, Pitapat, and hold it over this place, and take care you don't fall in,' said Capitola. 'Come, as I've got a "pit" in my name and you've got a "pit" in yours, we'll see if we two can't make something of this third "pit"!' " (76).

This semantic trinity of Capitola, Pitapat, and the pit opens to include Black Donald, who later finds himself trapped in the pit, thanks to Cap's (hidden) foot that springs the trapdoor. The pit connects Black Donald with immorality, both figuratively and literally. It is, on one level, the proper place for him to be sent; he has, after all, sneaked into Capitola's room with the intent to kidnap her. As a criminal, then, the morally "black" Donald deserves to suffer in the pit's "abyss," where Cap notes the "horrible darkness [is] 'visible' " (76), like the darkness of Milton's hell. But rather than a general hell for criminals, this one seems to be more specific—the pit also connotes the "hold" of the ships that made the Middle Passage from Africa to America, transporting slaves. Little Pitapat's name and race recall the horrors of being packed into the ship's pit, where indeed, as a spectacle for the white crew, only darkness was visible, and as in Cap's pit, the captives were sure to hear "the deep distant roaring as of subterraneous water" (76).

Dropping Black Donald into such a racially and historically inflected pit, then, paints him not as a criminal but as a victim who does not deserve incarceration. This second reading of the pit renders Southworth's characterization of Black Donald ambiguous: he represents the morality of a criminal and the oppression of a slave. In addressing his apparent lack of morality before tripping the trapdoor, Capitola angrily informs the outlaw: "I will not call you *Black* Donald! I will call you as your poor mother did, when your young soul was as white as your skin, before she ever dreamed her boy would grow black with crime" (389). In Cap's speech, Southworth draws on color symbolism in order to condemn Black Donald's misadventures, suggesting that he wrongly passes as an immoral man. But when she sees him rescued from the pit, lying on the floor while her companions "were all looking upon him as upon a slaughtered wild beast, Capitola alone felt compassion" (398). Capitola's ability to see Black Donald from two perspectives indicates how blackness has traditionally been used in sentimental fiction and how Southworth reworks it. Cap first feels indignation, linking Donald's name with immoral behavior, but as she sees him being categorized as a wild animal, as black people stereotypically were, her change in attitude implies that her original feelings were too hasty. This somewhat didactic moment echoes Cap's confrontation with Hurricane regarding his evening ride, suggesting that here Southworth instructs her readers against following stereotypes too readily (though she does employ them). Because of Cap's ability to be morally "good" while doing "naughty" things, she can alter her perspective before she completely succumbs to typecasting Black Donald.

Indeed, throughout the novel, Cap likes Black Donald: she finds him handsome; as an expert in masquerade, she enjoys how he fools her household with his various disguises, and she admires his sense of adventure, which rivals her own. By sharing this "good naughtiness," Capitola and Black Donald end the novel in a most unexpected manner for sentimental fiction. Although the last pages do honor the nineteenth-century reader's expectations with a wedding—in fact, a double wedding—Southworth both undercuts and enriches the happiness of the moment with the announcement that Black Donald has escaped from jail, an escape that Capitola has engineered. Her great friendship with Black Donald indicates that "bad" can be "good" and "immoral" can indeed be "moral." But it also shows that the opposite is true—that moral crimes are committed in the name of the sentimental standard: maintaining a white, homogeneous, sexually divisive hierarchy within the community. Indeed, the increasing visibility of Cap's and Black Donald's black presence makes invisible the old moral white order, thus blurring the traditional sentimental moral and bodily boundaries.

But what becomes of the hidden hand, the mark of Capitola's Le Noir's identity as well as her mark of blackness? Somewhere between Granny Grewell's confession and Capitola's visit to the Hidden House, the birthmark shifts from Cap's left to right hand and then is not mentioned again. Though its disappearance from the narrative probably results from its no longer being needed as a plot device—and Southworth's editor may not have caught the slip—it is interesting that the birthmark's last appearance immediately precedes Cap's visit to the Hidden House, where Southworth reintroduces the girl's mother into the story. With this potential for matrilineal order to be reestablished in the story, perhaps the birthmark's absence parallels the rightings of maternal wrongs that had been committed: the crimes against mothers and daughters.

Reading the birthmark in this manner alters the perspective provided by Dobson's comparison of Nathaniel Hawthorne's story "The Birthmark" and Cap's birthmark. Georgiana, Hawthorne's heroine, shares with Capitola a "crimson" hand, though it is impressed on her cheek. The hand, to Georgiana's male admirers, has a magical quality, suggesting the mark of a "fairy," but to her female rivals, the hand looks "bloody" and taints the young woman's beauty (Hawthorne 119). To Georgiana's husband, a scientist, the birthmark symbolizes "his wife's liability to sin, sorrow, decay, and death" (120), so he prepares a concoction that not only will erase the "superficial" marking but also will "go deeper" (125) to repair Georgiana's "entire physical system" (128). In "*The Hidden Hand*: Subversion of Cultural Ideology in Three Mid-Nineteenth-Century American Women's Novels," Dobson contrasts the two marks: "Unlike Georgiana, . . . there is no question of Capitola being the 'perfect woman.' Georgiana's life ends when she becomes 'perfect' with the removal of the crimson hand birthmark that 'mars' her left cheek. Cap's crimson hand is a badge of her identity; the birthmark not only stands for her outrageous individuality, it identifies her as heiress to the Le Noir fortune as well" (242 n. 32). The removal of Georgiana's birthmark constitutes a crime against the flesh, but it also represents a reversal of the evils committed against black women, on whose skin whips left their marks. For Georgiana, visibility is vexed: for her beauty to be more visible to her husband, her facial mark must be invisible against her pale whiteness. Capitola's "legitimate" life, however, seems to begin when her mother reappears and reclaims her wedding ring, an act that corresponds temporally with the birthmark's disappearance from the narrative. The absence of Cap's mark does not make her more physically "perfect" like Georgiana but may suggest the release of her flesh from a symbolic captivity.

Though it does not dissolve the white moral and social order that resolves the plots in sentimental fiction, *The Hidden Hand* does destabilize readers' expectations for a sentimental heroine: not only is Capitola Black dark, naughty, and unrepentant, but she is also delightfully, engagingly, and morally so. As Dobson notes, "Implicit in [Capitola's] creation" lies a "critique of conventional gender definitions" ("Introduction" xiv), for this heroine ignores her properly submissive role. Significantly, when Capitola exercises this appealing independence, Southworth associates her with descriptions that connote a moral darkness or situations that parallel those experienced by black women. Describing Capitola's exploits and character in terms of blackness suggests that Southworth was experimenting with strategies of characterization, especially with overturning the stock sentimental female standard. Indeed, the moral dimensions associated with "blackness" are a foil to those associated with the "whiteness" of other sentimental heroines: piety, obedience, and passivity. Resemanticizing Capitola's moral whiteness as blackness thus allows Southworth to explore possibilities of situation or character that would never have been appropriate for Ellen Montgomery or Eva St. Clare. But by appropriating the energy and experience of blacks, Southworth excludes black women from benefiting from her critique of gender limitations and the social oppression of women. Her novel thus indicates the profound impact blackness had on shaping the fiction of nineteenth-century white women writers but also suggests the limitations of the feminist literary imagination.

Notes

1. In *The Dark Center* Eualio Baltazar presents a history of color symbolism that is relevant here: he traces color symbolism's biblical roots from Genesis, where God not only provides for a physical separation of darkness and light into night and day but creates a moral dichotomy too: "Associated with the terms night and day are the terms black and white. In the scriptures, white symbolizes purity, sinlessness, grace and glory. . . . white garments are symbolic of divine favor, of the purity of one's soul. . . . In contrast to the symbolism of whiteness as positive, blackness is used as a sign of sin and damnation. . . . blackness is a symbol of hell" (11).

2. Capitola presents a marked contrast to little Eva of *Uncle Tom's Cabin* and Ellen Montgomery of *The Wide, Wide World*. The latter sentimental heroines are characterized by their obeisance to God and to their respective paternal figures. Though Ellen is occasionally "naughty," her misbehavior causes her great emotional pain, and she willingly receives moral punishment from her "brother" and future husband, John. Unable to reconcile her father's participation in the institution of slavery with her Christian beliefs, Eva dies a long, melodramatic death without having to make a choice. Capitola, however, cheerfully rejects both human and divine authority, preferring to act according to her own sense of right and wrong.

3. The title of the collection of essays, edited by Hull, Scott, and Smith, *All the Women Are White, All the Blacks Are Men, but Some of Us Are Brave*, alludes to the silencing of black women by positing white middle-class women as the norm and alludes, conversely, to the stereotyping of black men as potential criminals or sexual threats.

4. Stafford explores another type of generational transference of the birthmark in *Body Criticism*. She writes that eighteenth-century doctors considered "the illicit powers of the maternal imagination" responsible for creating birthmarks (306). The mother's depraved thoughts and desires were transferred to the child's skin. The "white negro," however, posed a problem: doctors were unsure if her complete (dis)coloration was "the result of a mental tattoo or of a maculating morbidity of the skin" (319).

5. See Harriet Jacobs, *Incidents in the Life of a Slave Girl*; Stowe, *Uncle Tom's Cabin*; and Charlotte Brontë, *Jane Eyre*. Linda, Cassy, and Emmeline are all African American slaves, but Bertha is a white Creole from Jamaica. Although her story is typically read as a psychological one—according to Sandra Gilbert and Susan Gubar's *Madwoman in the Attic*, Bertha represents the wild, uninhibited side of Jane Eyre—it seems also to be a metaphor for condoning the captivity of the colo-

nized woman. For Bertha Rochester's history, see also Jean Rhys, *The Wide Sargasso Sea*.

6. The complete title of Southworth's book is *The Hidden Hand, or, Capitola the Madcap*. Although "madcap" refers to Capitola's blatant disregard for feminine conventions, it should also ironically refer to her mother's supposed psychological illness. Indeed, the word suggests that being a "mad" Capitola is only a step away from being a delightful madcap, and it points to the small difference between judgments of women's behavior as either outrageous or insane.

"A Most Disagreeable Mirror":

Reflections on White Identity in *Black Like Me*

GAYLE WALD

Between me and the other world there is ever an unasked question: unasked by some through feelings of delicacy; by others through the difficulty of rightly framing it. All, nevertheless, flutter round it. They approach me in a half-hesitant sort of way, eye me curiously or compassionately, and then, instead of saying directly, How does it feel to be a problem? they say, I know an excellent colored man in my town; or, I fought at Mechanicsville; or, Do not these Southern outrages make your blood boil? — W. E. B. Du Bois, *The Souls of Black Folk* (1903)

*O*f the works of civil rights advocacy produced by white authors, among the most remarkable is *Black Like Me*, John Howard Griffin's autobiographical account of his ethnojournalistic experiment in racial passing. For a little over a month in late 1959—four years after Rosa Parks's refusal to cede her seat on a Montgomery bus, the year of Mack Parker's Mississippi lynching, and one year before the Greensboro lunch counter sit-ins—Griffin, a white male Texan, medically and cosmetically altered his skin color so that he could pass as a black man in some of the most segregated and impoverished regions of the deep South. *Black Like Me* consists of a series of entries from the journals Griffin kept while traveling in racial disguise through Louisiana, Alabama, Mississippi, and Georgia. In them, he expresses outrage and mortification at a variety of incidents that would have been commonplace to black Southerners living under Jim Crow: being turned away from hotels and restaurants, made the target of racial animosity and sexual objectification, denied banking privileges, rejected peremptorily from jobs, required to use segregated toilet facilities, and forced to sit at the back of the bus. Filtering these incidents through the lens of his "white" consciousness—that is, from the position of one who has been the beneficiary of the dominant racial discourse—Griffin sought to authenticate the existence of racism and thereby promote a level of white cross-racial understanding that he believed to be unavailable through more conventional modes of inquiry. Driven by liberal optimism and by Christian faith in the efficacy of moral persuasion to eradicate social injustice, Griffin hoped to turn racial impersonation—a practice with a long and frequently ignominious history in American popular culture[1]—into a tool for antiracist social critique.

From a contemporary viewpoint, *Black Like Me* poses two distinct but related challenges: to historicize Griffin's ethnojournalistic experiment within the context of the postwar civil rights movement and the discourses of white liberalism, and to account for the book's remarkably durable reputation and appeal even as it becomes increasingly fashionable to refer to "civil rights" as a historical era rather than an ongoing struggle. Initially serialized in 1960 as "Journey into Shame" in *Sepia*, a now-defunct black monthly whose white publisher funded Griffin's experiment, *Black Like Me* continues to draw new readers and inspire new imitators decades after the dismantling of de jure segregation.[2] Since its publication in book form in 1961, *Black Like Me* has sold more than twelve million copies, been translated into fourteen languages, and appeared in numerous English-language editions, including one in South Africa (Sharpe 52). By 1971, it had become enough of a staple in junior high and high school classrooms to merit its own *Cliffs Notes*, which are still in print. Even today, despite the ready availability of a range of more eloquent portrayals of racism and segregation by African American authors, from Richard Wright's "The Ethics of Living Jim Crow" to Anne Moody's *Coming of Age in Mississippi*, *Black Like Me* remains popular for teaching white students about their country's legacy of racial oppression. At my local bookstore, newly minted copies share a shelf crowded by recent titles in African American cultural studies, an arrangement which would have been unimaginable when *Black Like Me* first appeared.

Although he had previously published a bestselling novel, *The Devil Rides Outside* (1952), Griffin did not attain national celebrity until after he had crossed the color line. The remarkable notoriety of the *Sepia* series, and later of *Black Like Me*, propelled Griffin, a devout Catholic with a propensity toward monastic life, into the spotlight of 1960s civil rights activism, where he remained for eight years. Griffin's exposure of white Southerners was not universally lauded, however: in his hometown of Mansfield, Texas, Griffin's neighbors reacted to the *Sepia* series by branding him a race traitor and burning him in effigy—the mannequin painted half white and half black, with a yellow stripe down its back. Yet the response to *Black Like Me* was overwhelmingly positive. Griffin himself liked to point out that of the nearly six thousand letters he received in response to the book, most of which were from Southerners, only nine were hostile. White and black reviewers alike greeted the book with widespread, if sometimes stiff, applause, nodding approvingly at Griffin's candor in debunking the myth of harmonious race relations widely promulgated by Southern conservatives during the 1950s. In a diplomatic review for the *Saturday Review,* African American commentator Louis Lomax wrote that "it was a joy to see a white man become black for a while and then re-enter his own world screaming in the tones of Richard Wright and James Baldwin" (53). While Lomax's analogy seems farfetched, his comment suggests that he understood *Black Like Me*'s central achievement to be Griffin's emergent sense of the theatricality of his own racial identity, a point missed by most white critics. Anxiously emphasizing the stability and purity of whiteness, the reviewer for *Commonweal,* for example, commended the book's liberal social critique but complained about Griffin's unconventional methodology, writing that "it seems perverse to tamper with one's identity in this way, no matter what the motive" (Cook 129).

Riding on a wave of unanticipated public approbation, Griffin fashioned himself as a white voice for the black voiceless, an ambassador of interracial goodwill on television talk shows, on college campuses, and in local community centers. In addition to earning Griffin a reputation as a mouthpiece for civil rights causes, *Black Like Me* prompted at least two direct spin-offs: a 1964 black-and-white film adaptation directed by Carl Lerner, and a 1969 reenactment of Griffin's experiment by a white woman, Grace Halsell, whose rather more infamous account of traveling as a black woman through Mississippi and Harlem is dubbed *Soul Sister.*[3] Yet Griffin came to repudiate and even scorn his position as a white spokesman for black Americans. Such a change of heart was spurred not only by Griffin's desire to slough off the skin of his identity as an "expert" but also by political changes that affected the tenor of civil rights—in particular, the increasingly fraught place of white liberals within the movement. Griffin describes the process of disavowing this role in two 1973 *Sepia* articles, "What's Happened in America since *Black Like Me*" and "Why Black Separatism?" which were later combined and appended to the 1977 second edition of the book. Despite these late attempts to distance himself from *Black Like Me,* however, Griffin was ultimately unable to shake his reputation as the white man who had "turned" black. In what is merely the most outrageous example, rumors circulated that the cause of Griffin's death in 1980 was skin cancer, as if the disease were the fallout of, or retribution for, the earlier experiment in passing.[4]

For Griffin, a religious intellectual as well as a social activist, segregation posed a corresponding ethical dilemma, making it difficult if not impossible for most white Southerners to apprehend racism from the viewpoints of those most marginalized by race. Convinced that Jim Crow had produced what he called an "area of unknowing" between whites and blacks, Griffin believed that his project potentially could mediate new avenues of communication and mutuality across the color line. He attributed the commercial and critical success of *Black Like Me* to its strategy of undercover exposé, its unearthing of a "secret face" of white racism unknown, or so Griffin thought, to most white Southerners. Under the personalistic and psychologistic idiom of "race relations" that Griffin envisioned, racism could be eradicated through the demonstration of a common humanity, what Griffin conceived as "sameness under the skin."

Laying aside for the time being the question of the efficacy of *Black Like Me* as social critique—a question to which I will return at the conclusion of this essay—I want to argue that the enduring popularity of Griffin's book potentially owes more to the persistence of white incredulity at black peoples' interpretations of their experience—indeed, to a positing of blackness *as* pure experience—than it does to Griffin's portrait of himself as a moral crusader exposing a white conspiracy of silence and racial subterfuge. Such an argument does not contradict the apparent sincerity of Griffin's own narrative of "good intentions" but instead demonstrates the precise manner in which Griffin's self-positioning and self-authorization empower him to authenticate racism while reifying blackness and romanticizing "real" black people. Based upon a false opposition between the white researcher's theoretical apprehension and the black subject's non-thetic "experience" or non-consciousness, Griffin's ethnojournalistic experiment is unequipped to imagine black people elaborating their own ontology of blackness or voicing their own opposition to segregation.[5] As a result, whereas *Black Like Me* portrays Griffin as the white protagonist of his own "civil rights" drama, the book largely fails to represent black people acting as social and political agents. In light of these unresolved contradictions at the heart of Griffin's analysis, it is hardly surprising that he ultimately felt obliged to withdraw from the spotlight.

Griffin arrived at a determination to pass for black through the failure of his own efforts to initiate a frank dialogue about race across the color line. On returning to Texas after serving in the Army during World War II, he was struck by the similarity between white supremacy as practiced in the United States and Aryan supremacy as practiced to genocidal effect against Jews in Europe. The late 1950s found Griffin engaged in informal sociological research on what he termed the "suicide-tendency"—the apparent hopelessness—of young black men in the South, who faced (then as now) dim employment prospects, the persistent threat of police harassment, and short life expectancy relative to their white peers. Though he had sent out a research questionnaire to prominent blacks and whites, Griffin was frustrated by the uneven and inconclusive results his survey yielded. In particular, he was perplexed by the reticence of most black respondents and the defensive posturing of most whites. Convinced that no amount of dialogue could ever fully answer the question that W. E. B. Du Bois described as taboo but always tacit in conversation between whites and blacks—"How does it feel to be a problem?"—Griffin determined to find out for himself through an experiment in passing. He justifies this turn away from sociology in the inaugural journal entry of *Black Like Me*, dated 28 October 1959:

How else except by becoming a Negro could a white man hope to learn the truth? Though we lived side by side throughout the South, communication between the two races had simply ceased to exist. Neither really knew what went on with those of the other race. The Southern Negro will not tell the white man the truth. He long ago learned that if he speaks a truth unpleasing to the white, the white will make life miserable for him.

The only way I could see to bridge the gap between us was to become a Negro. (2)

At various points in this essay I will return to the troubling assumptions contained in Griffin's defense of his experiment and its methodology: his implicit perception that as a white male intellectual he is entitled to the cultural knowledge of others; his assumption that he can willfully transcend the conditions of his own social formation; his conviction that passing affords the only means of authenticating racial oppression; and his belief that he can better convey the meaning of this oppression to other whites than can African Americans. Griffin's explanation additionally belies an unacknowledged investment in a gendered construction of blackness; not only does he posit "Negro" identity as static and unitary, in other words, but he erases the possibility that a "Negro" might also be a woman. For the purposes of my own narrative, however, I would like to focus on Griffin's implicit belief in his capacity for disinterested observation. For it is by presuming his invulnerability to the kinds of passionate investments that others bring to their research on race and racism that Griffin unwittingly reveals the reliance of his project upon what might be called an essentialist construction of "whiteness." Such a construction posits the liberal white male researcher "passing" as a universal, neutral subject, the masterful interpreter of his own and another's "truths." Griffin's justification thus proposes a curious twist on the authenticating preface that was a staple of nineteenth-century slave narratives, for whereas the white abolitionists who authored these prefaces typically drew upon the conventions of sentimental writing to sanction less politically powerful black voices, Griffin's preface sentimentalizes and romanticizes "black experience" in order to authenticate the interpretive power of the white male voice.

Griffin found support for *Black Like Me*'s explicitly reformist rationale and its methodology of participant-observation within the disciplinary conventions of modernist anthropology. As modernist ethnography often presupposes a critique of prevailing "home" ideologies or institutions, as it unveils "foreign" cultures, so Griffin discerned in racial passing a strategy of social criticism that would draw its authority from the apparent authenticity of his experiences in the "field."[6] "It seemed to me," he wrote in retrospect, "that if one of us could take on the 'skin' of a black man, live whatever might happen and then share that experience with others, perhaps at the level of shared experience we might come to some understanding that was not possible at the level of pure reason" (*Time to Be Human* 24). Griffin's turn to participant-observation is anticipated in his semiautobiographical novel *Nuni* (1956). The first-person narrative of John Harper, a plane crash survivor who finds himself the sole white man on a remote South Pacific island, *Nuni* is named after the small South

Pacific island where Griffin served as an Army liaison during the war. For a year of his military service, Griffin lived on Nuni as the island's only white man and its only Westerner; like an anthropologist engaged in fieldwork after the style of Bronislaw Malinowski or Margaret Mead, he learned the native language, practiced local customs, ingratiated himself into the life of the people, and even married a Nuni woman, although the marriage was later annulled (Sharpe 46). Indeed, Griffin traverses no great representational distance in the transition from John Harper, *Nuni*'s castaway turned anthropologist, to John Howard Griffin, *Black Like Me*'s disguised-self-as-researcher engaged in more or less authentic fieldwork.

Griffin's shift from an empirical mode of inquiry (the abandoned sociological study on the tendency toward suicide of black males) to a more personalized mode based on his experience as a researcher requires him to rethink the relation between knowledge and body. In the traveling "field" of the deep South, Griffin's sweating, hungry, tired, and aching body—a body itself always on the move—becomes not merely the instrument of observation but also a source of evidence. Having taken medicine (the drug oxsoralen, usually given to sufferers of vitiligo) to alter his pigmentation, exposed his flesh to ultraviolet rays, stained his skin with vegetable dye, shaved his head, and inserted himself into the field, Griffin transforms bodily sensations such as hunger, fatigue, and pleasure into symptoms or data. When he writes in his journal (as he often does) that his feet ache after walking two miles in search of a Jim Crow toilet, he is also writing, "This is what it feels like to *be* a black man whose feet ache from walking two miles in search of a toilet. *This is how a black man's feet feel.*"

Yet moments in the journals that draw attention to Griffin's body establish an unresolved tension, one that results from Griffin's opposition of the observing self's "scientific" position of speech and the experiencing self's subjective position of speech. Here Griffin's strategy of passing deviates from traditional anthropological inquiry, which seeks to maintain the authority of the observer over the subject of scrutiny, the segregation of participation and observation. Even among contemporary anthropologists, according to James Clifford, "the ethnographer's personal experiences, especially those of participation and empathy, are recognized as central to the research *process*, but are firmly restrained by the impersonal standards of observation and 'objective' distance" (13). In the migratory field of Griffin's research—variously composed of an Atlanta bus station toilet stall, a dilapidated hotel room in Hattiesburg, Mississippi, a shoeshine stand on a busy street in New Orleans, a rickety, two-room house in the swamp country between Mobile and Montgomery, and his own writing retreat in Mansfield—Griffin reproduces himself as both the subject and the object of his anthropological fieldwork. Through repeated experiences of internalized self-division—of contradictory and overlapping identifications as subject and object, participant and observer, black and white—Griffin re-creates in himself what Du Bois at the turn of the century described as "the peculiar sensation" of "always looking at one's self through the eyes of others" (5). This "double-consciousness" born of Griffin's attempt to use self-erasure as a strategy of mastery in turn complicates his identity as a speaking and writing subject. As he traverses different temporal, spatial, and racial geographies, his journal begs the question of who occupies the shifting position of author-observer and what his position is with respect to his object of inquiry.

The vicissitudes of Griffin's identifications (As a white man passing for black? As a white man passing for white?) resound in his various and fluctuating narrative modes of address. A scene in which Griffin is pressured to relinquish his seat at the back of a segregated New Orleans bus to a white woman provides an example. At first, Griffin identifies with the African American passengers, whose facial expressions urge him to refuse to give up his place. He writes: "If the whites would not sit with us, let them stand. When they became tired enough or uncomfortable enough, they would eventually take seats beside us and soon see that it was not so poisonous after all" (*Black Like Me* 21–22). Through pronouns ("we" and "them") that effect a rhetorical distance from white identity, Griffin signals his collaboration with black people. Yet despite this participation in and identification with the black passengers' collective outrage, Griffin remains internally divided. Because the act of giving up a seat to a white woman functions as a crucial affirmation of masculine identity for the white Griffin, he also feels "tormented" by his "lack of gallantry" (21), unable to reconcile the exigencies of conventional white masculinity with the demands of racial solidarity. The scene on the bus ends with Griffin's outrage when the other white passengers confront him with a "silent onrush of hostility." Out of this experience, "I learned a strange thing," Griffin writes, shifting pronouns once again, now in a personalized and familiar appeal to readerly sympathies, "—that in a jumble of unintelligible talk, the word 'nigger' leaps out with electric clarity. *You* always hear it and always it stings" (22, emphasis mine).

Slave autobiographies, such as Frederick Douglass's widely known 1845 *Narrative,* are instructive here, because they demonstrate the variability of—and even the conflicts residing in—racial and gender identifications, as well as the dilemmas associated with the representation of psychical and physical violence. One scene in the *Narrative,* in which Douglass recalls observing the sadistic whipping of his Aunt Hester by an overseer, Mr. Plummer, provides insight into Griffin's particular ethnographic predicament:

I remember the first time I ever witnessed this horrible exhibition. I was quite a child, but I remember it well. I never shall forget it whilst I remember any thing. It was the first time of a long series of such outrages, of which *I was doomed to be a witness and a participant.* It struck me with awful force. It was the blood-stained gate, the entrance to the hell of slavery, through which I was about to pass. It was a most terrible spectacle. I wish I could commit to paper the feelings with which I beheld it. (51, emphasis mine)

Though he endures the "horrible exhibition" of the whip, not its lashes, Douglass's spectatorship of Plummer's sadism and his aunt's pain carries the weight of a physical violation, striking the narrator "with awful force." Such an account testifies to the young Douglass's empathetic identification with his aunt according to race, not gender. His description also articulates the inevitability of his voyeuristic participation in the scene of torture and thus his inability to master the scene through the activity of writing, to consummate his authority over it by assuming the identity of a disinterested or transcendent observer. In contrast to Griffin, who attributes to the white subject the privileged capacity to function simultaneously as participant and observer, Douglass's description demonstrates the imperative, for the black subject, of negotiating the same "split" subjectivity. In wishing that he could "commit" the scene "to paper" and thereby signify his authority over it (rather than its mastery over him), Douglass reveals the difficulty of ever being merely observer and not participant, participant and not observer.

As does Griffin, Douglass uses the trope of "bearing witness" to link the experiences of participant-observation to the ardent advancement of progressive social causes. Yet Griffin's journals also inscribe the impossibility of ever fully relinquishing the role of white observer. Despite his desire to use passing as a way of mobilizing and politicizing empathy, of linking individual sympathy for another's experiences with an ideological commitment to broad social change, he cannot ever resolve the two "unreconciled strivings" of his fieldwork: the desire to record his observations (to remain in a position of white mastery), and the desire to become a full "participant" by ditching his notebooks (to relinquish white privilege). Though the black Griffin attempts to lose himself in a racial masquerade, the observing Griffin never suspends his disbelief, never completely loses himself in the illusion of having "become" the other.

I have taken this route through anthropology to show how, in Griffin's experiment in passing, the position of observer inevitably bleeds into the position of participant and to demonstrate the impact of Griffin's shifting and contradictory identifications on his writing. Yet to supplement this reading, which stays within the terms of Griffin's explicit narrative of his intentions (the paragraph from the first journal entry cited above), I want to propose another narrative, one that supplements and perhaps contradicts Griffin's consciously constructed account. Although he claims to be appropriating passing as a political strategy and a way of understanding others, I want to suggest that Griffin also appropriates passing as a form of introspection and personal freedom: freedom to explore the contours of his own (racial) identity. To say that such self-referentiality is the repressed subtext of Griffin's experiment is not to say that it cannot also be governed by humanitarian impulses but merely to point out that these impulses are never free of self-interest. Griffin's compassion for the plight of black people under Jim Crow is inseparable, in other words, from a corresponding concern for his own spiritual well-being. Racial passing thus affords Griffin a way of discovering his own links (by virtue of a white racial identity) to the very system of segregation that he is attacking.

The dependency of white self-scrutiny on various concepts of "blackness" is a theme played out in the history of Western colonialism, in which African cultures are used to "revitalize" fallen white Western cultures, as well as in much of the fiction of white American authors in the nineteenth and twentieth centuries. In her examination of the "Africanist presence" in American literature, Toni Morrison has demonstrated how writers from Herman Melville and Ernest Hemingway to Willa Cather and Gertrude Stein have incorporated images of blackness into their fiction as a backdrop against which to stage dramas of white identity. Often these fictions invert the conventional symbolism of white and black, so that whiteness, usually associated with moral purity, signifies spiritual depravity and corporeal corruption in contrast to black moral rectitude and physical beauty. In his novels, William Faulkner, for example, obsessively recycled the notion that African Americans were the conscience of the South, that they "endured" (in the words of *Absalom, Absalom!* and other works) precisely through the "nobility" of black suffering. The "unspoken" presence of Africanist peoples in American fiction has often served, in Morrison's account, not only to repress the intersubjectivity of cultures and races but also to reduce black humanity to a prop for white conscience and white selfhood. Karen McCarthy Brown, a white feminist anthropologist who studies Haitian voodoo, provides another angle on the white intellectual's use of the racial "other" for her own self-enrichment. In an essay about her initiation into voodoo, she describes the process through which she exploits not only a concept of "otherness" but also a concept of "difference" for the purposes of self-discovery:

The subtext goes something like this: I am fascinated by the "other." I feel most alive in her presence. I have my best insights into myself, other people and life in general when I am in relation to her. More precisely, the clarity and energy come in the moment when I pull back from the primacy of experience and stand in the current of fresh air that pulses gently through the crack between our worlds. (67)

Griffin's project is less suited to authenticating "black experience" than it is to the task of self-exploration that Brown describes, in part because Griffin's donning of racial disguise requires him to acknowledge the ways his own white male selfhood is mediated through, and constructed by, a corresponding imagination of black masculinity.[7] As Brown argues that proximity to the "other" affords her an opportunity for self-discovery, so Griffin's ethnojournalistic enterprise authorizes him to undertake a pointed—albeit perhaps not intended—inquiry into his own self as raced. To return to the terms of my own earlier formulation, Griffin's experiment requires him simultaneously to see and be seen, to participate and observe, to theorize as well as apprehend "whiteness." His racial imposture thus serves less as a window into black experience, as he initially believes, than as a mirror that reflects back on the sources of his own social construction as a white man, including the complicity of white supremacy in white subject-formation. That Griffin was interested not only in the observation of others but also in self-observation can be inferred from the two questions he poses in the first journal entry: "If a white man became a Negro in the Deep South, what adjustments would he have to make? What is it like to experience discrimination based on skin color, *something over which one has no control?*" (*Black Like Me* 2, emphasis mine). Griffin's language in the second of these questions bespeaks a desire temporarily to relinquish mastery, to forgo the social authority of whiteness. The title of Griffin's journals as serialized in *Sepia* conveys a similar message. The "shame" into which Griffin journeys is a double or split shame born of the indignity of his experiences, as a black man, of chronic unemployment and persistent objectification, and of a mortification at (through a crucial identification with) the thoughtlessness and even cruelty of some white Southerners. Racial passing, in his account, entails not only pretending to be what one is not (black) but also discovering that one is not what one has all along pretended to be (white). Thus the deeper question underlying Griffin's experiment is not, "What does it feel like to be black?" but rather, "Am I myself a fraud?"

Although the project of white self-examination may not in and of itself seem reprehensible, much of the apprehension around white appropriations of qualities romantically ascribed to blacks descends from the fact that white people (especially white men) traditionally have enjoyed a greater liberty than others to play with racial identities and to do so in safety, without permanent loss or costs. White sanction to "pass" inevitably hinges on the structure of race itself, that is, on a system in which some racial identifications are more rigidly organized and maintained than are others. In an important essay on the social construction of whiteness, Richard Dyer has written that whiteness accrues power precisely through its ability to "pass" as universal and invisible, as at once "everything and nothing" (45). The "depth" of white male identity, which retains its social value despite conscious efforts to depreciate it, contrasts in this narrative with the "surface" of black identity, which can be put on or taken off at will. Griffin's experiment evokes anxiety because it takes for granted these conditions of freedom; his passing ensues from a sovereignty over identity rather than from the exigencies of economic necessity or personal safety. It is precisely because of the social construction of race, in other words, that Griffin can equate "becoming a Negro" with losing control. Indeed, it is by claiming a right to such *white* agency that Griffin authorizes his own experiment.

Despite these structural links to the preservation of white male privilege, however, passing has been identified with white countercultural resistance and rebellion. In the tradition of white hipsterism exemplified by Mailer's "White Negro" essay, passing for black has served as a mode through which white men in particular have symbolized their alienation from cultural norms and their pleasurable embrace of marginality and radicalism. By adopting black radical chic as a mode of self-conscious unorthodoxy, white liberals have attempted to indicate their solidarity with the struggles of marginalized African Americans, as well as their belief in basic principles of racial equality. Yet even these self-conscious attempts to stylize a self "outside" the dominant social order are fraught by the essential nature of white privilege. It is precisely the prerogative of white people to "try on" black identities that paradoxically weakens their ability to assume an oppositional identity. White experiments with "blackness" are drained of their subversive potentiality, in other words, because they will always be recognized as experiments. Here the marginality ascribed to black identity is associated not only with freedom and autonomy—precisely those qualities that would seem to be conferred by white status—but also with a disruptive power, an ability to interfere, shock, or terrorize, to play with ideas of centrality and marginality. White people who pass may be attracted to this disruptive power of marginality because they recognize and acknowledge its salience within their own experience.

Griffin's experiment in passing is informed by both tendencies that I have been describing: to use passing as a metaphor for self-examination and self-disclosure, and to use passing as a metaphor for rebellion and oppositionality. Because it is not the act of passing in and of itself but Griffin's own fantasies of passing that are important to his transformation, it doesn't matter whether his cosmetic disguise fools black people or even whether readers believe in the verisimilitude of his experiment. Because Griffin's own illusions of what it means to be black are ultimately the driving force behind his narrative, the most important drama is that which plays itself out in Griffin's own mind—and hence in his choices, actions, and behaviors.

A whole series of such productive tensions are at work in *Black Like Me*: those that materialize in the gap between illusion and reality; black mask and white skin; conscious, philanthropic intentions and subconscious, self-referential desires; as well as those between expectations and outcome. Griffin "assumed he would find racism," writes Ernest Sharpe, "but he did not expect to find it everywhere, least of all in himself" (54). Because Griffin fully expected to find racism in white people who (unlike himself) had neither the benefits of education nor the generosity of spirit that sometimes accompanies personal wealth and success, he was proportionately unprepared to discover it in himself; having assumed that he was outside of white supremacist ideology, Griffin was shocked to realize that his own "invisible" racism was merely the alter ego of a more visible and externalized racism that he associated with "inferior" white people. To the degree that Griffin had placed responsibility for racism on the shoulders of white "others," he had in effect merely displaced his own racist beliefs and emotions.

I want to examine in more depth several passages that trace the process of Griffin's self-transformation, from his initial confrontation with his own "Negro face" in a traumatic and paradigmatic mirror scene to his eventual formulation of a theory of "passing for white." Griffin affronts what he calls his "Negro self" for the first time on November 7, 1959, just before midnight. After a week of preparation, he walks into a dark bathroom, closes the door, stands before a mirror, turns on the light, and stares at his reflection. The exaggerated theatricality of Griffin's representation of this scene underscores the histrionic, performative nature of racial identities and the psychic drama inherent in "passing over." Yet what I would like to focus on in this passage is Griffin's uncanny confrontation with and misrecognition of his own mirror image.[8] Turning on the light, he stares at the reflection of "a fierce, bald, very dark Negro" who "in no way resembled me" (*Black Like Me* 11):

The transformation was total and shocking. I had expected to see myself disguised, but this was something else. I was imprisoned in the flesh of an utter stranger, an unsympathetic one with whom I felt no kinship. All traces of the John Griffin I had been were wiped from existence. Even the senses underwent a change so profound it filled me with distress. I looked into the mirror and saw reflected nothing of the white John Griffin's past. No, the reflections led back to

Africa, back to the shanty and the ghetto, back to the fruitless struggles against the mark of blackness. Suddenly, almost with no preparation, no advance hint, it became clear and it permeated my whole being. My inclination was to fight against it. I had gone too far. I knew now that there is no such thing as a disguised white man, when the black won't rub off. The black man is wholly a Negro, regardless of what he once may have been. I was a newly created Negro who must go out [the] door and live in a world unfamiliar to me.

The completeness of this transformation appalled me. It was unlike anything I had imagined. I became two men, the observing one and the one who panicked, who felt Negroid even into the depths of his entrails. (11–12)

Echoing Marlowe's fear of Kurtz—that he has "gone too far"—Griffin here identifies blackness with chaos and upheaval, shadow and blemish, poverty and disgrace. His use of "Negroid" at the end of the passage (instead of "Negro," the word he otherwise uses) marks the crescendo of a gradual movement from a vocabulary of the existential (of "stranger" and "I") to a vocabulary of the biological (of "flesh" and "entrails"). He even alludes to his own ethnographic paradigms, in writing that he feels "no kinship" with the mirror image. Griffin's need to dissociate his self immediately from what he perceives to be the symbolic connotations of "the mark of blackness" attests powerfully to the potential of racism to inflict psychological trauma, to dehumanize and depersonalize. More important, however, the scene also demonstrates Griffin's first traumatic confrontation with his own stereotypes of blackness and hence with a truer and less idealized reflection of himself. His shock before the mirror is so severe because it lays bare the cracks in Griffin's *self*-image. Speaking and writing from a white subject-position, Griffin takes no pride or pleasure in his reflection, but feels only self-loathing. Rather than submit to an identification with an "utter stranger," one who so profoundly assails his sense of his own humanity, Griffin splits in two, becoming simultaneously Dr. Frankenstein and the aberrant, half-human monster of his own mad creation.

Griffin's initial traumatic confrontation with his own whiteness functions as a primal mirror scene that organizes subsequent journal entries, which are marked by the repetition of paradigmatic moments of recognition and denial. As opposed to another moment of self-recognition from James Weldon Johnson's *Autobiography of an Ex-Coloured Man* (1912)—

in which the narrator appreciates the beauty of his own light-skinned reflection, only to be informed by his mother that this self-image is itself fraudulent—Griffin's moment before the mirror is profoundly antinarcissistic (Benston 98–109). I have argued that in his experiment, Griffin internalizes something akin to Du Boisian double-consciousness. Yet whereas Du Bois describes a condition of "twoness," of internalized self-contradiction and self-striving, Griffin, in his contempt for the "Negroid" face, relates a more literalized splitting of the self in two. As one of these selves panics, feeling perhaps something of Du Boisian double-consciousness, the other, the "observer," watches and records.

The internalization of an observer figure facilitates the rest of the narrative, which consists primarily of Griffin's self-observation. Such a self-splitting also allows Griffin simultaneously to occupy positions of detachment from and engagement with his own experience. The mirror scene illustrates Griffin's racialized construction of these positions: the observer, occupying a panoptical position of authority, is white, while the observed, the deindividualized spectacle, is black. In addition to evoking Du Bois, then, this twofold splitting of the self recalls the redoubled hierarchies of participation and observation that trouble the terms of Griffin's auto / ethnography. By racially coding the functions of observer and observed, Griffin also internalizes the larger Southern economy of spectatorship under the dominant social order. His experiment in passing proves instructive in these "invisible" laws of looking, under which spectatorship is a function of economic and social power and hence dependent on race, class, and gender. For example, he discovers that a black male passenger on a Jim Crow bus can signify his defiance of white male hegemony by meeting the gaze of the white driver, an act that recuperates the legitimacy of black masculinity. He learns that although black men are prohibited from meeting the gaze of white women, with whom eye contact is tantamount to physical contact and hence rape, white men and black men are socially sanctioned in their objectification of black women. He learns the role of spectatorship in policing, how observation is related to supervision, and how supervision is dependent on hierarchy.[9]

Using the eyes of others as a yardstick, Griffin's observing self also notes how his "Negro self" is made into a spectacle. In the journal entry of November 7, for example, as Griffin awaits a bus to take him from New Orleans to Hattiesburg, Mississippi, he describes the "hate stare" of a white man whose hostility bears a strong resemblance to Griffin's own previous self-contempt:

[The hate stare] came from a middle-age, heavy-set, well-dressed white man. He sat a few yards away, fixing his eyes on me. Nothing can describe the withering horror of this. You feel lost, sick at heart before such unmasked hatred, not so much because it threatens you as because it shows humans in such an inhuman light. You see a kind of insanity, something so obscene the very obscenity of it (rather than its threat) terrifies you. It was so new I could not take my eyes from the man's face. I felt like saying: "What in God's name are you doing to yourself?" (*Black Like Me* 54)

While the man fixes his eyes on Griffin, Griffin in turn feels himself fixed to the spot, paralyzed and transfixed by the Medusa-like horror of the spectacle of a stranger's malevolence. Instead of responding to the hate stare with anger, Griffin directs his outrage and disgust at the fact of the man's "unmasked hatred," at the sheer visibility of such malice. As opposed to the previous mirror scene, in which Griffin expresses no conscious compunction at his own visceral response to "the mark of blackness," here the nakedness of the stranger's reaction (itself a kind of mirror image) reflects clearly on Griffin himself. Whereas the previous mirror scene located "shame" in the identity of the "bald Negro," here the focus of Griffin's concern is the potential of "unmasked hatred" to shame and dishonor the white subject.

The depth of Griffin's simultaneous identification with and revulsion from the white stranger is reflected in the ambiguity of the pronoun "you." Whereas the stranger's hate stare is intended to provoke feelings of shame in the black (observed) Griffin, in the white (observing) Griffin the expression kindles both shame (at the obvious brutality of the act) and guilt (at his own complicity with the act). The narrator's use of the word "you"—in phrases such as "You see a kind of insanity"—reiterates this doubleness, at once depersonalizing and universalizing his response; in such cases, "you" both includes and excludes the speaker's "I." Out of this sense of doubleness, Griffin is able to experience the withering effects of racism on black self-realization as well as the shattering effects of the realization of racism on his own self-esteem.

Griffin's encounter with the stranger in New Orleans portends his even more traumatic arrival in Hattiesburg on November 14. On that day, before departing New Orleans, Griffin had learned of a federal grand jury's failure to hand down any indictments in the April 25 lynching of Mack Parker, a twenty-three-year-old truck driver. At the time a mob attacked him, Parker was being held in a Poplarville, Mississippi, jail on trumped-up charges of rape. Tough FBI agents, called in to assist with the investigation, had managed to obtain several admissions of guilt and had included these in a 378-page report on the lynching; the jury—composed of twenty white people and one black man—found no basis for prosecution.[10] When Griffin arrives in Hattiesburg, not far from the site of the lynching, the black population is reeling from rage and despair at the verdict. It is under these circumstances (and perhaps out of an unconscious desire to probe the limits of his own response to the lynching and jury verdict) that Griffin, now in a dilapidated Hattiesburg hotel room, decides to write a letter to his wife:

The observing self saw the Negro surrounded by the sounds and smells of the ghetto, write "Darling" to a white woman. The chains of my blackness would not allow me to go on. Though I understood and could analyze what was happening, I could not break through.
    Never look at a white woman—look down or the other way.
    What do you mean, calling a white woman "darling" like that, boy? (72)

In its staging, this scene reveals both the sexualized aspects of racism (its rootedness in sexual fear and sexual jealousy) and the attendant intractability of white taboos against the transgression of racialized sexual prohibitions. Here the observing self—now internalized as "conscience"—takes on the menacing voice of white lynchers, thereby recasting Griffin in the image of their victim, Mack Parker. The voice not only forbids look and address, but it also castrates desire, ultimately forcing Griffin to lay down his pen. Whereas in previous scenes Griffin remains ambivalent, split by the terms of his double-identification, here—in a scene explicitly concerned with the punishment of black male sexuality (even where no rape has occurred)—an "I" emerges that affiliates itself explicitly with white power. Unable to "break through" the imaginary "chains of blackness" that shackle him to a narrow conception of black subjectivity as wholly given over to shame and dishonor, Griffin succumbs to the authority of the observing self. The result is the banishment of a black "I," the eclipsing of black autonomy by the regulatory power of a masterful white other.

Black Like Me hinges on this first night in Hattiesburg, the nadir of Griffin's experiment in passing. Exhausted and frightened, he ultimately calls sympathetic white friends and spends two days recuperating in their home before returning (in the back seat of his friend's car) to New Orleans. From New Orleans, Griffin sets out on the second leg of his journey, first traveling by bus to Biloxi, Mississippi, and then hitchhiking to Mobile, Alabama. The journal entry for November 19 recounts Griffin's disgust as white man after white man stops to offer him a ride less out of kindness than a desire to interrogate Griffin about black male sexuality. In these cases, the observing (white) Griffin is able to distance himself from the white men, whose prurient interests clash with his own deep-seated sense of sexual propriety and homophobia. Yet Griffin is struck by the apparent kindness of one young man, even despite the man's interest in discussing Negroes' "lack of neuroses." "I knew," Griffin writes, "that he showed me a side of his nature that was special to the night and the situation, a side rarely brought to light in his everyday living" (95).

With this Jekyll / Hyde conceit, Griffin comes full circle from his first journal entry, which details the splitting (into night and day, spectacle and spectator, black and white) of his own subjectivity. Yet in distinction to the mirror scene, which associates the characteristics of Hyde with "the mark of blackness," here Griffin links depravity to the white subject. In so doing, Griffin not only abdicates his prior belief in an essential white goodness (of intention, if not of character) but also de-essentializes and reindividualizes black and white subject-positions (so that each is capable of becoming Hyde).

When Griffin finally arrives in Mobile, his perceptions of the city's white residents are radically changed. "The gracious Southerner, the wise Southerner, the kind Southerner was nowhere visible," he writes. "I knew that if I were white, I would find him easily, for his other face is there for whites to see. It is not a false face; it is simply different from the one the Negro sees" (107). Yet later, Griffin recuperates the image of the gracious, wise, and kind Southerner in a portrait of a black family who takes him in for the night while he is traveling through to Montgomery. Eight people—two adults and six young children—share an unpainted two-room shanty, "patched at the bottom with a rusting Dr. Pepper sign" (115). Together, they eat a meal consisting of bread and yellow beans, to which Griffin contributes several Milky Way bars for dessert:

Closed into two rooms, with only the soft light of two kerosene lamps, the atmosphere changed. The outside world, outside standards disappeared. They were somewhere beyond in the vast darkness. In here, we had all we needed for gaiety. We had shelter, some food in our bellies, the bodies and eyes and affections of children who were not yet aware of how things were. And we had treats. We cut the Milky Way bars into thin slices for dessert. (115)

Although intended to contrast his experiences of the antagonism of Southern whites with those of the hospitality of Southern blacks, this scene—with its pastoral overtones, its romanticization of suffering, its nostalgia for Southern graciousness, and its idealization of the noble nuclear family—instead serves to domesticate blackness and a black family's poverty, reinscribing them within a protective rhetorical veil of home life and even (to invoke a phrase with more recent connotations) "family values." In portraying those within the shack as washed in "warm light," whereas the outside (white) world recedes as a space of "vast darkness," Griffin merely reverses the dominant symbolism of good and evil, white and black.

The domesticating gaze that Griffin directs upon his black informants is a product, as I have been arguing, of a white liberal political discourse that posits black subjects—here the "deserving," ennobled poor—as objects of ethnographic contemplation, a positioning that serves retroactively to justify the white researcher's presumed prerogative of masterful and disinterested observation. Even under the disciplinary conventions of modernist anthropology, Griffin's position would seem to be baldly exploitative; recall that he never announces his intentions to the family and that the Milky Way bar is his contribution to dinner. Although he provides a detailed description of the decrepitude of the family's home, down to the specifics of how the shanty has been pieced together with the abandoned remnants of commodity culture (the rusting Dr. Pepper sign), Griffin does not allow any of his informants to speak, to join him in his privileged position as observer. According a voice to his informants at this point in the narrative not only would displace some of Griffin's authority as spokesman by situating his voice in critical relation to other voices, but it would also upset the whole economy of Griffin's sentimental portraiture, in which pathos depends upon passivity. If the dinner table symbolizes commonality as well as community—in its ideal political and social form, the "beloved community" imagined by Martin Luther King Jr.—then Griffin's staging of this scene in *Black Like Me* would seem to suggest that silence, or the denial of black political agency, is paradoxically the source of black political agency, insofar as it is the means by which blacks win concessions from white elites. Silent suffering and "making do"—the two dominant tropes in Griffin's description—are in this context both sources of sentimental appeal and the pretext of white liberal political alliance across the color line.

Although *Black Like Me*'s sentimental narrative reaches a climax with Griffin's description of his night with a poor Southern family, it is also during his stay with this family that Griffin's growing distrust of whiteness enters his unconscious in the form of a nightmare about his own lynching. "White men and women, their faces stern and heartless, closed in on me. The hate stare burned through me. I pressed back against a wall. I could expect no pity, no mercy. They approached slowly and I could not escape them" (*Black Like Me* 122). Griffin's imagination of his entrapment by a white mob would seem to symbolize his emerging consciousness of being bombarded by the sheer weight of evidence contradicting the lie of harmonious Southern race relations. Moreover, the dream would seem to indicate that despite the deeply flawed foundation of Griffin's ethnojournalistic experiment, his experiences exert a transformative power over Griffin's self-conception.

Later, as a white man in Montgomery, Griffin sees "smiles, benign faces, courtesies—a side of the white man I had not seen in weeks, but I remembered too well the other side. The miracle was sour" (130). Instead of relishing the return of Southern white hospitality, Griffin feels unwillingly pulled into an identification with a white "us" of which he no longer feels a part. In *The Alchemy of Race and Rights*, Patricia Williams describes the structuring of such racial affiliations as "an architecture of trust" and characterizes the act of breaking this trust through a metaphor of racial passing. "I think," she writes, "that the hard work of a nonracist sensibility is the boundary crossing, from safe circle into wilderness: the testing of boundary, the consecration of sacrilege. It is the willingness to spoil a good party and break an encompassing circle, to travel from the safe to the unsafe" (129). By recounting his experiences, Griffin crosses, in Williams's terms, the boundary that separates safety from wilderness, puncturing the protective veil that shields from consciousness a knowledge of his own fear, envy, and loathing of the "other." He refuses to remain part of the silent, invisible, and protected majority—in other words, to "pass" as white.

Not surprisingly, in the process of shedding his illusions about the South, Griffin is left feeling somewhat naked himself. In a passage that describes his rather ignominious arrival in Georgia (shame now associated with the heart of whiteness, rather than of darkness), Griffin expresses this sense of bareness rhetorically, his normally straightforward, sometimes clunky prose slipping unsubtly into irony:

I was back in the land of my forefathers, Georgia. The town of Griffin was named for one of them. [I] . . . carried the name hated by all Negroes, for former Governor Griffin (no kin that I would care to discover) devoted himself heroically to the task of keeping Negroes "in their place." Thanks in part to his efforts, this John Griffin celebrated a triumphant return to the land from which his people had sprung by seeking sanctuary in a toilet cubicle at the bus station. (140)

In the passage that follows, Griffin, his supply of oxsoralen now depleted, removes the stain from his face with cleansing cream and scrubs the rest of his body with an undershirt, until he is satisfied that he can "pass for white." For the remainder of his experiment, Griffin switches back and forth between identities, removing the dye when he wants to be white and reapplying it when he wants to become black again. In contrast to the consternation and discomfort his disguise once inspired, these more rapid transformations do not seem to faze Griffin. A *Time* magazine article about his "journey into shame" series unintentionally puns on the shift in Griffin's sensibility in the caption below a photograph of him, which reads: "After four weeks as a Negro, Griffin harbors new doubts about his own race" ("Black Like Me" 90). Whether "his own race" refers to Griffin as an individual or whites in general, in fact, the experiment in passing has proved transformative. Although Atlanta—the "New South"—promises respite from the nightmare of Mississippi, Griffin no longer needs to shield himself from the damage such discoveries inflict on his white self-image. Feeling like shit, he seeks sanctuary in a toilet stall.

In his 1973 follow-up articles to the original *Sepia* series that became *Black Like Me*, Griffin draws on the historical lessons of the preceding decade to reexamine the status of *Black Like Me* as a work of civil rights advocacy and to rethink his role as a civil rights advocate. In particular, "What's Happened since *Black Like Me*" (the name given to the epilogue of the second edition) reflects the generational shift in tactics and goals that accompanied the transition from a late-1950s-era politics of rights, which emphasized integration and interracialism, to a mid-1960s-era politics of power, which emphasized black pride, nationalism, and economic empowerment. The shift in civil rights heralded a period of misunderstanding—what Griffin calls a new "area of unknowing"—between black activists and white liberals, one with enduring repercussions. Godfrey Hodgson argues that the 1965 Watts riots are a watershed in this history, marking "the beginning of a period when the same events took on utterly different meanings for white people and for blacks" (266). The breakdown of an alliance between black and white liberals, which previously had been exemplified by moderate groups such as the NAACP, resulted in changes in the membership and the philosophy of black political organizations. In 1966, the Student Nonviolent Coordinating Committee (SNCC) became the first major black group to vote to exclude whites from membership; a year later, in their nationalist manifesto *Black Power*, Stokely Carmichael and Charles Hamilton outlined their determination to "take care of business" by "whatever means necessary" (184–85). The shift in mood can be measured in terms of the shifts in Griffin's ongoing narrative: in 1961, he published *Black Like Me* as a treatise against segregation, using the knowledge gained by racial passing to expound a liberal critique of white supremacy; yet in 1973, he critiqued white liberalism and argued that whites needed to remove themselves from the spotlight, if not the margins, of the movement.

In a brief aside to an essay on the interventions of white critics into the study of African American literary history, Michael Awkward calls *Black Like Me* "a generally selfless response to white liberal guilt" (597). Apt as Awkward's pat response might seem, it nevertheless overlooks Griffin's ultimate skepticism about guilt as a useful tool for fostering white antiracist political consciousness. Perhaps because he had come to recognize its inadequacy in the course of examining his own racism, Griffin disparaged guilt as a screen for covert or unacknowledged intolerance. "There is not necessarily any guilt attached to *having* the prejudices," he wrote, "since most of us are no more guilty of acquiring our prejudices than we are of acquiring a disfiguring pockmark from some childhood illness" (*Time* 32). If guilt was to have any relevance in the struggle against racism, it had to be reconceived along ethical lines—not in terms of blame and liability but in terms of responsibility. James Baldwin once wrote that black skin "operate[s] as a most disagreeable mirror" ("Unnameable Objects" 173) for white people, an intolerable reminder of their part in black persecution. Having discovered in himself what Baldwin had all along discerned in white people generally, Griffin fully advocated facing this reflection, not merely assuaging the anxiety associated with it. Guilt thus transformed could become a force in relations not only between blacks and whites but—as in the trope of whites confronting their mirror images—between whites and whites.

In later years, Griffin would come to reevaluate his recruitment as a spokesman for the experiences of African Americans. In the epilogue to *Black Like Me*, he writes that in the years following the book's publication, "it was my embarrassing task to sit in on meetings of whites and blacks, to serve one ridiculous but necessary function. I knew, and every black man there knew, that I, as a man now white again, could say the things that needed saying but would be rejected if black men said them" (190–91). He adds: "Often in the presence of local black men whites would ask me questions that should have been addressed to the black men present. They knew the community, I didn't. Always this was an affront to black men, one of the many affronts that white men apparently could not perceive" (194). Paradoxically and retrospectively, Griffin illustrates the refusal of whites to recognize black people as reliable witnesses to their own experience. Paradoxically, because it was Griffin's own failure to recognize such a possibility that served as the original motivation for his own ethnojournalistic enterprise. In this, his belated disavowal of white entitlement to "speak for," Griffin has in some sense come full circle, his "journey into shame" transformed into an exploration of the shameful face of "white" selfhood.

Having said this, I want to turn in conclusion to the questions and possibilities that *Black Like Me* raises for thinking about difference and its relation to political alliance, especially alliances that link the interests of individuals across boundaries of race. In its failure to transcend the domesticating gaze of ethnography, as well as its attempt to construct an authoritative white voice that would occupy the positions of "seer" as well as "seen" (to riff on the title of one of Ralph Ellison's essays), *Black Like Me* illustrates some of the pitfalls associated with Griffin's discourse of white liberalism. In a deft reading of *Black Like Me* that regards Griffin's project as continuous with that of blackface minstrelsy, Eric Lott argues that Griffin's "disguise" is nothing more—and nothing less—than an "externalization" of the "sexualized racial unconscious of American whiteness" (487), or white masculinity's repressed libidinal investment in black masculinity. I would add to Lott's account a related observation: namely, that Griffin's fidelity to a liberal thesis of "sameness under the skin" interferes with his ability to elaborate, much less to come to terms with, the difference between playing and being "Negro"—or for that matter playing and being "white"—without reinscribing race in the very essentialist terms that he seeks to redress. The black separatist rejection of white liberal voices such as Griffin's in the late 1960s is precisely a response to the sort of mimetic desire that *Black Like Me* embodies: one that wants to appropriate black "experience" without compromising a presumed white entitlement to speak for this experience, one that wants to lose itself in the "other" without losing control. To be sure, a certain degree of self-referentiality may be inevitable in the practical "deconstruction" of whiteness, and yet it is crucial, as the shortcomings of Griffin's enterprise indicate, that white self-examination not turn into an occasion for the display of white self-interest masquerading as empathy.

Griffin's own ultimate response to the problem of confronting racism was to step aside. In the epilogue to *Black Like Me*, Griffin broadens his definition of passing so that it includes not only the contrivances of disguise but also the conditions of white identity. Dismayed after hearing 1967 State of the Union address by Lyndon Johnson, whose appeal to save the California redwoods drew more applause than the appeal for black civil rights, Griffin wires the president: "AM TIRED OF BEING A LOSER. FROM NOW ON I'M GOING TO FORGET HUMANITY AND WORK FOR THE TREES" (196). (In his frustration, Griffin could not see the link between the two.) Having already been asked too many times to speak on behalf of others, he takes recourse in self-silencing. By the late 1960s, though still serving as a white "observer," he nevertheless has finished speaking. "I hardly ever opened my mouth," he writes. "The day was past when black people wanted any advice from white men" (196).

Notes

This essay is work-in-progress from a larger project titled *Crossing the Line: Racial Passing in Twentieth-Century American Literature and Culture,* forthcoming from Duke University Press. Thanks to Andrew Ross and Cornel West for their assistance and criticism. Kimberly Benston's guidance was particularly influential in my revision of an earlier draft of this essay.

1. On minstrelsy see Michael Rogin, "Blackface, White Noise: The Jewish Jazz Singer Finds His Voice" and especially Eric Lott, *Love and Theft: Blackface Minstrelsy and the American Working Class.*

2. "Journey into Shame" appeared in monthly installments between April and October 1960. Modeled after *Look* and *Ebony, Sepia* probably never attained circulation over 75,000. The most recent of Griffin's imitators is Joshua Solomon, a white male University of Maryland student. See his article "Skin Deep: Reliving 'Black Like Me': My Own Journey into the Heart of Race-Conscious America," *Washington Post* 30 October 1994: C1, C4. Thank you to Joan Korenman for bringing the article to my attention.

3. In 1968, on an impulse inspired by a single reading of *Black Like Me,* Halsell resigned from her job as a staff writer for Lyndon Johnson, flew (on Air Force One) to Texas to meet Griffin, and began drug and sun treatments to darken her skin. Halsell lives first in Harlem, where she works as a secretary in Harlem Hospital, and eventually ends up working for a wealthy white family in Jackson, Mississippi. Her experiment in passing ends when her employer attempts to rape her. Carl Lerner's film version of *Black Like Me,* while it generally follows Griffin's journals, nevertheless makes a few changes. Most notable of these is an added romantic subplot, in which Griffin goes out on a blind date with a black woman, who teaches him how to dance.

4. There is no evidence that Griffin's death after a long illness was caused by side effects from his earlier skin-darkening treatments. See his obituaries in *Jet* 25 September 1980: 59 and the *New York Times* 10 September 1980: D 21.

5. Here I am paraphrasing insights originally made by Kimberly Benston in a personal correspondence with the author.

6. On the politics of ethnography, see the essays collected in Clifford and Marcus, eds., *Writing Culture: The Poetics and Politics of Ethnography.* On the uses of anthropology as social and cultural critique, see Marcus and Fischer, *Anthropology and Cultural Critique: An Experimental Moment in the Human Sciences.* The unanticipated success of Griffin's disguise among blacks as well as whites (none of whom, according to Griffin, ever doubted his identity) prompts additional ethical problems that are less typical within mainstream modernist anthropology, in which the relationship between ethnographer and informant is made explicit through an exchange of goods for knowledge. Although he stayed in black peoples' homes, broke bread with them, and sought their companionship and advice, Griffin never disclosed his purpose or revealed that he was on assignment for *Sepia* magazine. The one exception is Sterling Brown, a black shoeshine and *Black Like Me*'s only named "informant," who knowingly serves as Griffin's intermediary when Griffin first crosses the color line in New Orleans.

7. This is an argument elaborated at greater length by Eric Lott in "White Like Me: Racial Cross-Dressing and the Construction of American Whiteness."

8. In a footnote in his definitive essay on "The Uncanny," Freud describes an experience much like Griffin's. On entering a train compartment at night, Freud mistakes his own reflection for that of an elderly "intruder": "Jumping up with the intention of putting him right, I at once realized to my dismay that the intruder was nothing but my own reflection in the looking-glass on the open door. I can still recollect that I thoroughly disliked his appearance. Instead, therefore, of being frightened by [my double] . . . I simply failed to recognize [it] as such." See Freud, "The Uncanny" 17: 248 n. 1.

9. For more on the relations between gender, race, and spectatorship, see Jane Gaines, "White Privilege and Looking Relations: Race and Gender in Feminist Film Theory."

10. On the Parker lynching, see articles during May 1959 in the *Chicago Defender*, the *Pittsburgh Courier* and the *Norfolk Journal and Guide.* See also "Mack C. Parker of Lumberton, Miss., Kidnapped and Lynched: The Story behind the Lynching," *Jet* 14 May 1959: 12–15.

PART IV

Creating

the Self

Confederate Counterfeit: The Case of

the Cross-Dressed Civil War Soldier

ELIZABETH YOUNG

I

*T*he American Civil War has been over for a long time, but its battles continue to be fought afresh, and in some surprising ways. Consider, for example, the case of Lauren Cook Burgess, a North Carolina woman whose lawsuit against the United States Department of Interior was widely reported in 1991–93. Along with her husband, Fred, Lauren is a Civil War enthusiast who enjoys the elaborate network of events held each year at Civil War battlefield sites overseen by the National Park Service. Unlike Fred, however, Lauren Cook Burgess was banned from participating in these events because she was discovered attempting to impersonate a male soldier in the 21st Georgia Infantry, one of three volunteer organizations to which she belongs (see figure 1). Although her disguise—which included binding her chest, wearing her hair short, and speaking with a husky voice—was convincing on other occasions, during a reenactment at the Antietam Battlefield Park in August 1989, Burgess was unmasked, reputedly spotted after leaving the women's bathroom. Ordered to remove her uniform or to leave the park, Burgess refused; when her protests met with a hostile response, she filed a sex discrimination suit against the National Park Service. In March 1993, she won her suit.[1]

The story of Lauren Cook Burgess has been hotly contested among Civil War devotees, who "bitterly debated," as one journalist acerbically wrote, "whether middle-aged men with beer bellies had more right than [Burgess] to portray an 18-year-old Rebel soldier." The Park Service asserted that her uniform, which was that of a fife player, was simply inappropriate for the reenactment on the day in question; said one spokesman, "We have a very serious commitment to authenticity." Similarly, the superintendent of the Antietam National Battlefield Park insisted that no cross-dressed women soldiers were present at Antietam, explaining that

Figure 1. Lauren Cook Burgess and her husband, Fred Burgess
(AP / Wide World Photos).

"if you're going to portray anything . . . you have to portray an accurate
picture." This group of opponents, in other words, held that historical
authenticity, rather than gender per se, was the problem; to the extent that
gender entered in, as one man put it, "her lack of authenticity happens to
be caused by her gender." But another male commentator revealed that
"there was no hedging about why she wasn't allowed to participate. . . . [It
was] because she was a woman." To Lauren Cook Burgess herself, the
issue was specifically sex discrimination—"a matter of principle"—and
she believed her own abilities to be not only sufficient but superior: "I
think I do a far better job than a lot of the men out there." Burgess also
argued for the authenticity of her participation, presenting in her defense
extensive research on Civil War cross-dressers present at Antietam. The
judge in the case vindicated both Burgess's claims, declaring that her

exclusion constituted "discrimination against women" and that she herself was "a devoted amateur [who] takes historical accuracy seriously."[2]

What are we to make of these explanations, which seem to mobilize the overlapping claims of "gender" and "historical authenticity" on behalf of both sides? To begin with gender, it appears on the one hand as though there could be no more "authentic" issue involved, since there was "no hedging" that what determined Burgess's expulsion was her status as a woman. Yet if Burgess's imposture illustrates the perils of sex discrimination, it also registers the problem of discriminating between the sexes, and in so doing it offers a version of gender politics from another perspective—that of cross-dressing as the cultural destabilization, rather than the legal recognition, of gender categories. In this context, media interest in Burgess becomes part of a larger celebration of cross-dressing that includes mass-market vogue about Madonna, avant-garde excitement over Jennie Livingston's film *Paris Is Burning*, and a veritable frenzy of academic enthusiasm extending from the encyclopedic catalogue of transvestite "category confusion" in Marjorie Garber's *Vested Interests* to the philosophical paradigms of subversive masquerade in Judith Butler's *Gender Trouble*.[3] Indeed, Burgess's cross-dressing appears to correspond to the theoretical model, offered by Butler and others, of the "performativity" of gender, since its setting provides a literal space for repeated performances that are not only acts but *re*enactments and whose form thus reinforces the idea of gender as a belated imitation rather than a stable original. In terms of both gender politics and gender theory, then, the story of Lauren Cook Burgess would seem to offer feminist cultural critics that rare and wonderful thing: a case of life imitating not only art but theory.

If Burgess's imposture seems to offer an exemplary case of gender as an inauthentic copy, so too does it suggest that history is itself a series of imitations. Let us return to the question of historical authenticity, the ostensible antonym and antidote to Burgess's gender oscillation. In fact, "authenticity" is a slippery term in this context, since Civil War reenactments are by definition a belated version of something else, usually a practice—a march, a firing drill, an encampment—which was itself highly ritualized at the time. What a "serious commitment to authenticity" means in this case is adherence to a model of history wherein battlefields have been sanitized as tourist sites, events are highly choreographed, and individual actors play roles that are only as genuine as their costumes. Indeed, when the superintendent at Antietam asserts that "you have to portray an accurate picture," the terms "portrayal" and "picture" inadvertently highlight the inevitable fictionality of historical representation. Instead of looking backward toward authenticity, we seem instead to be slouching forward toward the self-reflexive, decentered realm of the postmodern.[4]

In Lauren Cook Burgess's masquerade, then, the ostensible conflict between "gender" and "historical authenticity," which begins to collapse within the arguments of both sides, is ultimately self-canceling. Both gender and history are finally "inauthentic," offering imitations rather than originals. In these deracinations, too, the story of Lauren Cook Burgess might appear to provide a particularly current representation of both the female body and the body politic. Yet theatrical rites of national self-definition are hardly limited to the present era, since the very idea of nation requires a retrospective invention and consolidation of images, rituals, and traditions.[5] Nor is military cross-dressing a contemporary phenomenon: rather, the masquerading female soldier appears in so many accounts of war as to seem ubiquitous (Wheelwright 1–20). More specifically, Burgess's story is but the latest narrative of a cross-dressing in the American Civil War, since references to women soldiers have appeared with frequency in journalism, memoirs, and novels about the war from the 1860s onward.[6] Mary Livermore, Civil War nurse and relief worker, believed that at least four hundred women had cross-dressed during the war, writing that "some startling histories of these military women were current in the gossip of army life; and extravagant and unreal as were many of the narrations, one always felt that they had a foundation in fact" (120).[7] The experience of these women forms a vital part of the histories of women, gender, sexuality, and war—as well, of course, as the history of cross-dressing itself.[8]

My concern in this essay is less with the documentary recovery of the lives of women soldiers per se than with their significance as figures in the cultural imagination of Civil War America. The narratives that describe these women, I will argue, take up precisely the same issues of gender and authenticity that frame the story of Lauren Cook Burgess, transposed to the literary terrain of nineteenth-century fiction. Nowhere is this resonance stronger than in the case of *The Woman in Battle* (1876), an account of Civil War cross-dressing that presents itself as the autobiography of one Loreta Velazquez, a woman who masqueraded as a Confederate officer and spy during the war. *The Woman in Battle* is among the most well known of Civil War cross-dressing accounts, but critical discussions of it have long stalled on the question of its historical accuracy. When we treat this work as a picaresque nineteenth-century novel rather than as an evidentiary account of the Civil War, however, *The Woman in Battle* becomes a productive site for an extended inquiry into the meanings of cross-dressing, as constructed by the intersecting axes of gender, sexuality, race, region, and nation. The importance of cross-dressing in *The Woman in Battle*, I will argue, inheres in its figurative as well as literal meanings and particularly in its ability to forge fictional links between disparate ideas and images. Military masquerade functions in this text as a metaphorical point of exchange for intersections between individual bodies and the body politic in Civil War and Reconstruction America. From the phantasmatic possibilities of a "lesbian confederacy" to the cultural myths of the postwar South, *The Woman in Battle* offers important insights into the meanings of cross-dressing for identity—both individual and national—in nineteenth-century America.

II

The Woman in Battle is the supposed first-person story of Loreta Janeta Velazquez, a Cuban-born, Confederate woman whose Civil War experience, by her own account, encompassed an astonishing range of activities. The book's subtitle gives some sense of its scope:

A Narrative of the Exploits, Adventures, and Travels of Madame Loreta Janeta Velazquez, otherwise known as Lieutenant Harry T. Buford, Confederate States Army. In which is given Full Descriptions of the numerous Battles in which she participated as a Confederate Officer; of her Perilous Performances as a Spy, as a Bearer of Despatches, as a Secret-Service Agent, and as a Blockade-Runner; of her Adventures Behind the Scenes at Washington, including the Bond Swindle; of her Career as a Bounty and Substitute Broker in New York: of her Travels in Europe and South America; her Mining Adventures on the Pacific Slope; her Residence among the Mormons; her Love Affairs, Courtships, Marriages, &c., &c.[9]

Figure 2.
Loreta Velazquez
as herself (*top*)
and in disguise (*below*)
as Lt. Harry Buford
(from *The Woman
in Battle*).

As the length of this subtitle suggests, the book's overall size (six hundred pages, fifty-two chapters) is massive; its structure ("&c., &c."), energetically episodic; and its tone ("Exploits, Adventures, and Travels"), sensational. Edited by a Union Army veteran, C. J. Worthington, the book narrates Velazquez's adventures while disguised as an officer of her own invention, Lieutenant Harry T. Buford (see figure 2). As Buford, Velazquez fights in a number of early battles, including Bull Run, Fort Donelson, and Shiloh, and is wounded twice, escaping detection the first time but not the second. Switching from the role of soldier to that of spy, she then engages in a dizzying round of disguises in both North and South, appearing as a Southern woman abolitionist, a train conductor, a Confederate private soldier, a Confederate woman, a Union woman fleeing from the Confederacy, a Spanish widow spying for the Union army, a Northern war widow, and a Spanish-speaking servant girl in the North. Later in the war, she also engages in blockade-running, counterfeiting, bounty-jumping, and other activities in support of the Confederacy. *The Woman in Battle* frames these activities with additional material about Velazquez's life, beginning with her childhood and continuing after the war to her travels and business ventures in Europe, South America, the Caribbean, and the American West. In the course of this account, Velazquez also marries four times and gives birth to several children; the final chapter remarks the birth of her only surviving child, a boy. The text as a whole is introduced by notes from both author and editor, assuring readers of Velazquez's authenticity and propriety. *The Woman in Battle* concludes with Velazquez's own self-deprecating appeal to her readers: "Perhaps my story was worth the telling, perhaps not—the great public, to whom I have ventured to a confide a plain and unpretentious account of my adventuresome career, will be a better judge of that than I am" (606).[10]

Such instructions to the public, however, have been dramatically at odds with the book's reception from the start. Accusations of inauthenticity have surrounded *The Woman in Battle* since its publication in 1876 and continue to inform contemporary treatments of it. In 1878, a former Confederate general, Jubal Early, argued in an eleven-page letter to a Southern congressman that the book was filled with inaccuracies, improbabilities, impossibilities, suspicious omissions, and many statements that are "simply incredible."[11] Twentieth-century discussions of the work center almost exclusively on this issue of veracity, concluding that Velaz-quez's career, in its range and successes, is simply in excess of verisimil-itude. The book appears so resistant to any definitive pronouncements on its accuracy that even an apparently authentic piece of evidence, a nineteenth-century letter written in support of Velazquez, was later re-vealed to have been written by a perjurer and forger (Hoffert 31). As with the story of Lauren Cook Burgess, then, a narrative of gender indeter-minacy is inseparable from the question of historical authenticity.

In this case, moreover, what emerges in the absence of authenticity is the presence of the literary and, particularly, literary fiction. Early writes: "The book . . . cannot be a truthful narrative of the adventures of any person. If intended as a work of fiction, then it is one which ought not to be patronized by Southern men or women, for it is a libel on both" (Letter to Slemons). In a less impassioned echo of this same opposition, a Civil War historian declares: "If Madame Velasquez's account be true, her career was indeed a phenomenal one; if it be false, she deserves high rating as a fictionist" (Wiley 335). This opposition between truth and fiction can only be a stagnant one if it focuses on the issue of the book's empirical truth-value, but what happens if we embrace rather than ward off the label of fiction for this text? To begin with, Velazquez herself repeatedly invokes fictional frames of reference. Of her courtship with her second husband, for example, she notes, "It was like a romance, and it was in the scenes of a romance . . . that I alone could find any similitude to it" (319); later, she remarks, "What a strange career I had gone through—stranger far than that of many a heroine of romance whose adventures had fascinated my girlish fancy!" (560). "Romance" may be Velazquez's self-described fictional reference point, but the restlessness of her pro-tagonist suggests another literary genre: "It was an absolute necessity for me to be in motion, to be doing something" (126). With its episodic structure, its protagonist on the road, and its breathless movement from adventure to adventure, *The Woman in the Bottle* takes on the fictional form of the picaresque.

Reading the text as a picaresque novel, we can now return to its presentation of cross-dressing, interpreting the literary as well as histor-ical pressures that the Civil War places on its narrative of gender impos-ture. First, Velazquez's text responds metaphorically to the enlarged spec-trum of possibility for Southern white women during wartime. The Civil

War altered conventional gender behavior for Southern white women in numerous ways. The needs of the Confederacy authorized a variety of activities for white women, including sewing flags and uniforms, raising money for the militia, forming relief societies, nursing, and teaching. The war years also brought Southern white women into the public sphere, in angry mass gatherings including bread riots. Some women participated in the military effort itself, as cooks, nurses, and camp-followers but also, in smaller numbers, as spies, scouts, and soldiers. Finally, Confederate women wrote about the Civil War in unprecedented numbers. From Mary Chesnut's diaries to Augusta Jane Evans's novels, Southern women narrated their experience of a war in which the boundary between battle-front and homefront had eroded significantly.[12] Given this blurred boundary, Velazquez's textual mobility evidences, if not the actual realization of power for women during wartime, then the war's catalytic role in creating the *fantasy* of such power. Her masquerade is testament to the ways in which the demands of war could so transform the ideology of separate spheres that a fantasy of gender masquerade might be voiced in the name of Confederate nationalism.

If the Civil War functions as a psychic space of release even in its most literal register—as the historical setting for *The Woman in Battle*—then its thematic of internal conflict is even more inseparable from the fictional biography of Loreta Velazquez herself. From the start, questions of nationhood implicitly shape questions of individual identity in *The Woman in Battle*. In the book's first chapter, Velazquez describes her family history in terms of a series of geographic splittings, displacements, and margins. Claiming to be from a family of Spanish noblemen headed by Don Diego Velazquez, she notes that the Velazquez family name is highly honored "both in Spain and in the Spanish dominions on this side of the Atlantic" (39), and she frames her own identity in relation to the heritage of this family name: "If in assuming the garments of a man . . . I transgressed against the conventionalities of modern society, the reader will, I am sure, charitably attribute some of the blame to the adventure-some blood of old Governor Don Diego" (39). Velazquez's biography of her parents marks a series of geographic displacements: her mother is the daughter of a French naval officer and an American woman, and her father, a diplomat, was born in Cartagena, educated in Madrid and Paris, and appointed to a diplomatic position in Cuba. Velazquez, in turn, bears the traces of this mobility, now focused on locations near United States borders: she was born in Cuba, raised in Texas (then part of Mexico), moved to St. Lucia in the Caribbean, educated by an English governess, and then sent to New Orleans. Calling attention to her foreignness in the introduction, she declares: "My adopted country people will have to decide for themselves whether the writing of it was worth the while or not" (6). An "adopted" citizen rather than an "authentic" one, she stands metaphorically at the margins of the United States, just outside its boundaries in her youth and just inside in her adulthood.

Velazquez's first marriage symbolically maps national boundaries onto individual identities, bringing into view the question of territorial conflict as engaged by the Mexican War. Her father, an ardent supporter of Mexico and a bitter opponent of the United States government, disapproves of her first husband, a United States citizen, on nationalist grounds. The two lovers must marry without his permission: "When I met [my father] for the first time after my marriage, he turned his cheek to me, saying, 'You can never impress a kiss on my lips after a union with my country's enemy,'—from which I concluded that it was not so much my marriage without his consent, as my alliance with an American soldier that imbittered him" (50). Here, a father's accusation—a version of "sleeping with the enemy"—combines national and sexual registers, with the marital "alliance" of Velazquez and her husband literalizing the blasphemous geographic "union" of disputed areas of Mexico with the United States. The father's condemnation is both an explicit invocation of paternal authority and an implicit rejection of his own half-American wife. Conversely, to Velazquez, her marriage offers a revolution against patriarchal authority that metaphorically echoes, even as it literally contradicts, the terms of her father's own rebellion against the American government.[13] The passage as a whole exemplifies what Margaret Higonnet has described as a characteristic connection in novels of civil war "between political struggles to realign the national 'family' and social struggles to realign the relationships between men and women" (80). In the battle between Velazquez and her father are the first notes of what will sound throughout *The Woman in Battle:* the way in which, as Higonnet argues, "civil war serves as emblem and catalyst of change in the social prescription of sexual roles" (81).

If Velazquez's relationship to her father transgresses one version of regional authority, her marriage embroils her in the politics of another geographical struggle: the Civil War itself. As the war begins, Velazquez, an adopted Southerner, passionately supports the Confederacy, while her husband, William, is reluctant to leave the Union: "When my husband's State determined to secede, I brought all my influence to bear to induce him to resign his commission in the United States army. . . . I was resolved to forsake him if he raised his sword against the South" (*Woman in Battle* 50–51). This passage offers a relay of rebellions in which Velazquez's secession from the national union is both cause and effect of her rebellion against the terms of marital union. Although her husband eventually agrees to fight for the Confederacy, their détente is as unstable as the relation between regions. Her initial cross-dressing plan is "to appear at the head of my little army before my husband, and to offer him the command" (70), but military leadership on behalf of the South cannot be sustained in tandem with marital subservience: "My desire was to serve with him, if possible; but if this could not be done, I intended to play my part in the war in my own way, without his assistance" (70–71). Finally, the South's regional secession from the North brings about a decisive marital separation: the death of her husband almost immediately after assuming his military commission. In a double divorce, Loreta retains her maiden name—indeed, we never even learn William's surname—while the rebellious South sheds the name, as it were, of "Mrs. United States."

After this episode, the Civil War continues to frame Velazquez's own civil wars, but from gender conflict between men and women to gender conflict within one individual. The birth of the Confederacy symbolizes as well as sparks the birth of Velazquez's identity as a man. These two developments are conjoined when she first wears the costume of her alter ego, Buford, in public and then makes a toast at a saloon: " 'Gentlemen, here's to the success of our young Confederacy' " (54). Her training as Buford, meanwhile, educates her to assume the duties of masculinity as well as those of the militia: "[I] prepared a lot of recruiting papers on the model of some genuine ones . . . and procured a manual of tactics, and before the day was over, was pretty nearly ready to commence active operations" (68). When Velazquez puts her training to work, the battles of the Civil War both symbolize and provide a setting for her gender disguise. A key early victory for the South is also a triumph for her impersonated masculinity: "No man on the field that day fought with more energy or determination than the woman who figured as Lieutenant Harry T. Buford" (105). On the suggestively named battlegrounds of "Bull Run" and "Ball's Bluff," both Velazquez and the Confederacy prove their "manhood."

When Velazquez becomes a Confederate spy, her geographic movements provide a metaphorical gloss on her oscillation between genders. Such a linkage is hinted at from the first, when her debut performance as Buford involves acting as an expert on the Yankees, "just returned from the North" (67); since she has in fact just come from the state of femininity, her words provisionally align gender and geography. This connection between femininity and the Yankees is realized when she does go North, since Velazquez then returns to female dress, or as she puts it, "Here, in the enemy's country . . . I passed for exactly what I was" (136) since "it would be safer . . . for me to attempt no disguise, but to figure as myself" (137). Later, she declares, "I had made a goodly number of trips in different directions, sometimes with passes and sometimes without, and consequently knew exactly how to proceed" (265). Velazquez's "different directions" point toward male and female as well as North and South, and here as elsewhere, the vocabulary of espionage captures the highly constructed presentation of gender in the text. In the world of the spy as Velazquez inhabits it—what she calls "playing a double game" (392)—imposture characterizes both the pretense of masculinity and the assumption of femininity, described as "passing for exactly what I was." Although Velazquez may be "sometimes with passes and sometimes without," *all* gender identity involves her in some form of passing.

Velazquez's double agency as a spy has implications for the story's presentation of sexuality as well. Presenting herself to Northern officials as a pro-Union woman, she is able to outwit them with her femininity. Such political deceptions are implicitly framed as sexual seductions, as in the case of a Northern lieutenant who "let out many things that he ought to have kept quiet about" (363). In the case of Colonel Lafayette C. Baker, head of the Union Secret Service, her success hinges on her personal seductiveness: "I am convinced that my intimate relations with Baker . . . and the confidence in me which I succeeded in inspiring in his mind, alone saved me from detection" (468). Combining gender masquerade with heterosexual seduction, such episodes signal her manipulation as well as impersonation of manhood.

Yet in the course of Velazquez's narrative, her absolute control over gender masquerade becomes a more mobile and uncontrollable blur of border crossings and border states. Velazquez's deceptions for both armies involve passage through a series of literal border states—that region of the upper South that could not decide how to affiliate in the war because it was "facing both ways."[14] These border states correspond to an ambiguity of gender identification, as in one Northern adventure in which she crawls back to Confederate lines so bedraggled that she "was not by any means so masculine in appearance as I had been at one time" (308). If her participation in the Civil War at first appears a clear-cut case of revolutionary insurrection, it also involves a much more unstable battle within as well as between geographies and genders.

This double-edged state of gender confusion corresponds, in turn, to a blurring of the lines of heterosexual seduction. Although the overt sexual narrative of this text privileges marriage—Velazquez weds four times— her husbands have an extraordinarily enervated presence in her life and text. Her first husband, William, dies early and ingloriously in the war, when he "undertook to explain the use of the carbine to one of the sergeants, and the weapon exploded in his hands" (87). Her second husband, Captain de Caulp, sickens immediately after their marriage and dies, in a chapter entitled "Again a Wife and Again a Widow." Her third husband, whom she meets while preparing for a postwar trip to South America, rates only three paragraphs of discussion; six pages later, she reports succinctly that he is "taken ill with the black vomit and [dies]" (545). Finally, she accounts for her fourth husband, an unnamed "gentleman who paid me attention," in only two sentences (585). Despite the many husbands in the text, then, their impact is in inverse proportion to their quantity. It is as though heterosexual relations, like masculinity, have so tenuous an ideological hold in this text that they must be rehearsed repeatedly. The performance of what Adrienne Rich has named *compulsory heterosexuality*—or what Judith Butler, in a different theoretical frame, has more recently termed the *heterosexual matrix*—is so lackluster in this text that its visibility serves only to call its very existence into question.[15]

In contrast to these enervated marriages, the romances on which the text lavishes its most overt, abundant, and enthusiastic narrative attention are those between figures who, beneath their costumes, are both women.

From the moment she first cross-dresses, Velazquez causes—as a chapter subhead terms it—"a sensation among the women" (73). In a military world of exaggerated masculinity, the prowess of the Southern soldier is inseparable from Velazquez's own success in after-hours romance: "After the battle of Bull Run I . . . swaggered about in fine style, sporting my uniform for the admiration of the ladies, and making myself agreeable to them in a manner that excited the envy of the men, and raised me immensely in my own esteem; for I began to pride myself as much upon being a successful lady's man as upon being a valiant soldier" (109). Throughout her narrative, as Early himself notes, "The women, especially the young and pretty ones, are ever ready to throw themselves into the arms of the dashing 'Lieutenant Harry J. Buford,' and surrender without waiting to be asked, all that is dear to women of virtue" (Letter to Slemons).

How are we to read these "unconditional surrenders" between women? Historians of sexuality have emphasized the role of the military in the twentieth century in facilitating lesbian relations; the Civil War, too, provided a setting for women to live as lesbians, in a period just before the sexological "invention" of this category. Recent scholarship has also greatly expanded the definition of a lesbian text, focusing on a work's relation to woman readers or spectators in such contexts as eighteenth-century theater, contemporary cross-dressing films, and women's autobiography. Situating *The Woman in Battle* in these enlarged genealogies of lesbian history and culture, we can see the text as one in which the literary as well as literal resonances of Civil War cross-dressing enable protolesbian plots of same-sex seduction to appear under cover of military adventure.[16]

As "lady's man," Velazquez notes that she "had some curiosity to know how love-making went from the masculine standpoint" (75). Her assumption of this role results in a series of detailed picaresque seduction narratives, of which the story of "Miss E." of Leesburg, Virginia, provides an exemplary case. In high spirits after fighting in Virginia, Velazquez, dressed as Buford, happily engages in "winning the regards of the members of my own sex" (110). By accident Buford meets "Miss E.," who falls in love with "him"; her parents mistrust him, and he stays away from them. Finally, to prevent her from becoming too attached, he shows her a photograph of a woman whom he falsely claims is his fiancée, and he breaks her heart. "So ended my Leesburg flirtation," Velazquez writes, "and a desire to avoid meeting Miss E. again, at least until she had had time to recover her equanimity . . . induced me to leave the town as soon as possible" (114). Afterward, Velazquez is remorseful but pleased: "It afforded me some amusements . . . to carry on a bit of a flirtation with a nice girl; and I was very much tempted to entertain myself in this manner, without reflecting very deeply as to the consequences. I am very willing to admit that I ought not to have acted as I did" (111). Confident and charismatic, Velazquez seduces local women and leaves them behind, playing Don Juan as well as Don Quixote in her book's picaresque plots.

These dynamics of female seduction in turn characterize Velazquez's relationship with groups of women, both within and outside the text. At one point, she describes the public mayhem that ensues when she is arrested in Richmond "on the charge of being a woman in disguise, and supposedly [*sic*] a Federal spy" (278). Velazquez purports to be irritated by "the gaze of the impertinently curious people, who watched my every motion" (287), but what her account more powerfully suggests is her pleasure at seduction on a grand scale: "Everybody—the women in particular—evinced the most eager desire to see the heroine of innumerable bloody conflicts. . . . [W]hile it was generally believed I was a woman . . . my visitors were none of them quite sure which sex I belonged to, and all their efforts were directed to solving the mystery" (284). Here, Velazquez effects a kind of striptease with "the women in particular" as audience. Ostensibly the object of the gaze, she also has power over her viewers, her public "readers," as seducing object and subject. To her actual female readers as well, Velazquez is a powerful seducer: "My error in allowing myself to indulge in flirtations with my own sex, arose from thoughtlessness . . . I am sure my readers will forgive me, as I hope the young ladies, whom I induced to indulge false expectations, will, when the publication of this narrative makes known to the world the whole truth about the identity of Lieutenant Harry T. Buford, C.S.A." (111).

In *The Woman in Battle*, then, Loreta Velazquez's story transforms the Confederacy into a confederacy of female bodies, one that extends from Velazquez to her secondary characters to her female readers. This particular "lesbian confederacy" serves to expand traditional accounts of relations between women in nineteenth-century America. The most influential discussion of this topic presents this period as a "female world of love and ritual," in which women's bonds of "sisterly" friendship shaded over into love, affection, and emotional passion, if not necessarily into sexual contact per se (Smith-Rosenberg 53–76). More recent lesbian theory has reinvestigated such models of a "lesbian continuum" for a variety of reasons—among them, the need to bring into view the physicality of lesbian sexuality, the dynamics of power between women, and the pleasures, erotic and political, of such practices as butch-femme role-playing.[17] *The Woman in Battle* can be read as proleptically contributing to this critique, for the text constructs desire between women as inextricable from masquerade, performance, and the power dynamics of seduction. Expanding the narration of Confederate nationalism to include a protolesbian plot, Velazquez's text also functions as a contemporary critique of a model of lesbianism that might translate nineteenth-century desire between women into a domesticated version of domestic feminism.

Before leaving this account of the book's protolesbian Civil War story, however, we should note the severe constraints Velazquez places on such an apparently mobile textual fantasy. The positionalities of same-sex seduction are neither completely pleasurable nor completely mobile in this text. Velazquez is comfortable only in the role of *desiring* seducer, and she intensely dislikes women who assert their desire for her. Of one female pursuer, for example, she declares, "To tell the truth, I was not particularly pleased with the decidedly unfeminine advances that were made towards me" (88), and later, "I was a little bit disgusted with her very evident desire to capture me" (92). The only acceptable agent of desire in this text is Velazquez herself in her disguise *as a man*, experiencing "love-making . . . from the masculine standpoint." Paradoxically, then, even though the text translates the gender "male" into the positionality of "masculinity," it still requires that position to act as the catalyst for desire—even when the two participants in a narrative of seduction are women.

Moreover, if the text opens some spaces for reconfigurations of lesbian sexuality, it closes off others. We can chart this closure by examining a scene late in the book when Velazquez, traveling through the American West after the war, encounters another woman on the road. Occupying a carriage with this woman, she is repelled by her profanity and drunkenness; that night, forced to share a bed with her, she reports, "I did not obtain much satisfaction from my couch, for, independently of its unpleasant human occupant, it was fairly alive with vermin" (579). Here, then, is Velazquez in bed with another woman, and the result is revulsion. This moment stands as an end point on a larger spectrum of Velazquez's ambivalence toward other women, such as those with whom she must spend an evening while in disguise: "The society of these girls was no pleasure to me whatever, especially as I had things of much more importance to think of than their love affairs" (447). As if in a reversal of the "lesbian continuum," Velazquez, too, has a unified spectrum of attitudes toward women, but hers is marked by antipathy rather than affection. What is entirely absent from the text—and what, by contrast, is basic to the "lesbian continuum" model—is any sense of her interest in "the society of these girls." In short, *The Woman in Battle* firmly expels any conception of *sisterhood* from its lesbian plot.

Consistent with such "sororophobia," Velazquez is not only anti-woman but antifeminist.[18] *The Woman in Battle* stands in stark contrast to contemporary novels of domestic feminism such as Louisa May Alcott's *Work* (1873), which extend sisterly bonds between women into feminist activism. In Velazquez's text, feminism's one mention rates condemnation, in a section entitled "A Woman's Advantages and Disadvantages":

A woman labors under some disadvantages in an attempt to fight her own way in the world, and at the same time, from the mere fact that she is a woman, she can often do things that a man cannot. I have no hesitation in saying that I wish I had been created a man instead of a woman. This is what is the matter with nearly all the women who go about complaining of the wrongs of our sex. But being a woman, I was bent on making the best of it. (130)

The passage is muddled: it first invokes an exaggerated gender binary in which women have greater abilities than men, then moves to a vision of women divorced from biological femininity altogether, and finally collapses into complaint, in which feminists are reduced to women who "go about complaining." We might account for such conservatism as a Southerner's perception of feminism as primarily a Northern movement, a function of Velazquez's class privilege, or an individualist "bootstrap" rejection of the political struggles of others.[19] Each reason, however, underscores a similar point: that Velazquez's pleasure in seducing individual women corresponds to her antipathy toward any possible feminist body politic. Her most radical notions about gender and sexuality remain at the level of fantasy, divorced not only from authorial intention but also from the social referents—lesbianism and feminism—to which their structuring terms might seem to belong.

What can we conclude from this paradox? That the bonds of woman-hood chafe rather than unite in this text is not, of course, a determining pronouncement about the political immutabilities of a rhetoric of seduc-tion between women. Quite the reverse: the sororophobia in Velazquez's text is at least in part a result of nineteenth-century social conditions that might make "the ladies," confined to a round of domestic duties and pursuits, seem like far less admirable companions to her than male adven-turers. What the story of the "lady's man" does suggest, however, is the importance and the volatility of metaphor as a mode for the construction of bodies. As we shall now see, such bodies are regional as well as individual.

III

I have been tracing the ways in which *The Woman in Battle* maps the outlines of national Civil War onto a set of "civil wars" surrounding Loreta Velazquez. The Civil War provides not only setting but also symbol for the cross-dressing plot of *The Woman in Battle*, intersecting with the book's narratives of gender insurrection and of same-sex seduc-tion. Yet as the war gives new form to Velazquez's adventures, so too, I will now argue, does *The Woman in Battle* metaphorically engage the regional identity of the postwar South. In its covert narratives of sexuality and race as well as its overt focus on gender, the cross-dressing plot of *The Woman in Battle* enacts the consequences of Southern feminization. Paradoxically, Velazquez's story threatens even as it celebrates the mem-ory of the Confederacy for white Southerners facing the legacy of defeat.

The immediate results of the Civil War for white Southerners included the formal end of the slave labor system, the destruction of the Con-federacy as a political entity, and the devastation of the physical landscape of the South—along with the death of a generation of young white men. This loss of manhood was both symbolic and literal; as one Mississippi man described the defeated South, " 'His Comb was cut,' or as you say his manhood was emasculated" (qtd. in Foster 29). Combined with this self-perception of emasculation was a barrage of Northern representations in which weak Southern men were paired with fierce Southern women. Having secured their own "manhood," Northerners could project onto the defeated South what Nina Silber has characterized as an imagery of "intemperate men" and "spiteful women" (13–38). In response to such self-perceptions and attacks, many white Southerners commemorated the Confederacy in the writings, illustrations, songs, rituals, household artifacts, and other cultural texts collectively known as the ideology of the "Lost Cause." Most popular in the last two decades of the century, Lost Cause imagery praised the valor and value of the Confederacy and consequently of white Southern manhood. Rather than playing the role of quiescent "wife" in Northern-designed plots of sectional reunion, white Southerners could pride themselves on their once and would-be manhood.[20]

White women were indispensable to the creation of the Lost Cause, both literally and metaphorically. Active creators of such commemorative organizations as the Ladies' Memorial Association and the United Daughters of the Confederacy, they also served crucial symbolic functions. As one man noted shortly after the war: "The remnants of survivors [were] subjugated to every influence from without, which can be malignantly devised to sap the foundation of their manhood, and degrade them into fit material for slaves. If our women do not sustain them, they will sink" (qtd. in Foster 29). To rejuvenate Southern manhood, white women were to function as passive iconic repositories of the tragic glory of the Confederacy. Such female imagery included the representation of specific women as devoted Confederate wives, selfless mothers, or—as in the case of Winnie Davis, a beloved cultural icon—patriotic daughters. More abstract, Lost Cause femininity also involved the allegorization of unnamed feminine figures to represent the nobility of the wartime South as a whole.[21]

This continuum of female iconography had various implications for race and gender relations in the postwar South. Images of white womanhood were an important weapon in the postwar assault against freed African American men, for they provided a rallying cry of defense against fantasized African American rapists. Moreover, icons of female devotion worked to keep white women in their proper place, privileging femininity as the defining feature of white female behavior. The valorization of femininity, too, shifted attention away from feminization—the pejorative mark of regional degradation—and thus formed an essential part of a larger strategy of what Susan Jeffords, analyzing the American response to defeat in Vietnam, has termed "remasculinization." Mythologizing a war in which Southern aspirations were so closely linked to the metaphorical achievement of "manhood," diehard Confederate followers created the promise—at once regional, racial, and sexual—that the white male South would "rise again."

Despite its enthusiastic embrace of such ideologies, however, *The Woman in Battle* troubles the restorative iconography of Southern femininity. We may begin to gauge this contradiction by returning in some detail to the response of former Confederate general Jubal Early, whose biography exemplifies a militant posture of "unreconstructed" postwar devotion to the Confederacy. Early refused to accept Confederate surrender, fleeing the United States for Canada and Mexico; when he reluctantly returned, he devoted himself to the memory of the Confederacy, writing the history of the war, continuing to defend slavery and secession, and serving as first president of the Southern Historical Association.[22] In 1878, after Velazquez learned that he planned a public attack on her book, she wrote to Early:

Now General if you have any suggestions to make please let me hear from you for my Book and Correspondence with the Press is my entire support of my self and little Son (My health is failing,) and my whole soul's devotion is the education of him who is to live after I have passed away. . . . [M]y labors and devotion this winter has been to him and the prosperity of our Glorious Sunny south. No one man or a section of men can deter me from my duty to her (May god Bless her and her people). . . . [A]ll I now ask from you is Justice to my *Child*. I live for him and him alone.[23]

Velazquez draws on common postwar rhetoric in this passage. As with many wars, narratives of maternal sacrifice and self-sacrifice were essential to the ideological construction of the Confederacy. After the war, images of maternal devotion continued to signify importantly, especially in relation to Southern rituals of mourning in which the death of a son or husband was seen as symbolic of the loss of the Confederacy as a whole.[24] Sharing in this imagery, Velazquez's plea for her son works to reconfirm her underlying allegiance to feminine norms. Like the struggling South hoping to support "her people," Velazquez wants only to provide for her son: "I live for him and him alone." Literally dedicated to the Confederate army, her book registers her devotion to South and to son.

This appeal, however, came too late for Early:

Madame Velazquez herself is no true type of a Southern woman, and the women she describes are not fair specimens of the pure devoted women who followed with their prayers the armies of the Confederate States through all their struggles and trials. . . . I have no disposition to injure the alleged author of that book, and still less to deprive her of the means of training and educating her child; but I cherish most devotedly the character and fame of the Confederate armies, and of the people of the South, especially of the women of the South, and when a book affecting all these is [sought? ms unclear] to be [palmed? ms unclear] on the public as true, and bears on its face the evidence of its want of authenticity, then I have the right to speak my opinion and will speak it, whether the author be man or woman. (Letter to Slemons)

While Early here concedes that "I have no disposition to . . . deprive her of the means of training and educating her child," he cannot accept Velazquez's appeal to motherhood. What supersedes this appeal is her story's defamation of the "character and fame of the Confederate armies, and of the people of the South." For him, the book is a large-scale counterfeit operation in which a story that "bears on its face the evidence of its want of authenticity" is passed off on the public as a true self-representation—and with such authority that the gender of its author is itself thrown into doubt. To the outraged Early, *The Woman in Battle* must be stopped "whether the author is man or woman," for that person libels the Confederate legacy.

In particular, Early's condemnation suggests that Velazquez's crimes are directly linked to her fraudulent depiction of the "women of the South." During the war, Early had severely punished two women who were discovered to be cross-dressing as soldiers; their captain condemned them as prostitutes, and Early had them sent to prison (Hall 103). More than a decade later, his vehement response to *The Woman in Battle* reprises the terms of this condemnation. Collapsing femininity and fakery, Early objects to Velazquez's account because she is "no true type" and her book does not provide a "fair specimen" of the "pure devoted women who followed with their prayers [the struggles and trials of the

Southern armies]"—those women featured as heroic martyrs in Lost Cause imagery. With its emphasis on "pure" and "true" women, Early's rhetoric links Confederate glory with true womanhood, and true womanhood with sexual purity.

Under these criteria, Early considers Velazquez to be a counterfeit Southern woman, a condemnation Velazquez herself prefigures in her account of wartime counterfeit. Late in the war, she becomes involved with a group in Washington producing counterfeit bills and securities. In her description of this operation, inauthentic money is intimately connected with immoral women, for two of the counterfeiters, corrupt government officials, "had several abandoned women employed under them, at large salaries, and with whom they were in the habit of carousing in their offices at midnight" (477). Women's involvement in this project veers perilously close to prostitution, as in the case of one man's mistress who performs various services for the counterfeiters, "for which she was paid handsomely" (480). In these examples, the sexual circulation of women is not only intertwined with but paid for by the circulation of false money. Velazquez's story brings together inauthenticity, immorality, and money—precisely the grounds on which Early condemns her, when he refuses to allow her to earn money from so false and immoral a book. For readers like Early, Velazquez's text raises a disturbing question: What is the Confederacy worth, if its women are worthless?

Just as she destabilizes the currency of Southern femininity, so too does Velazquez disturb the symbolic economy of masculinity in the postwar South. If she is the quintessential "painted woman," then her alter ego, Lt. Harry Buford—who is such false coin that his very gender is unreal—is the ultimate "confidence man." Indeed, in a conflation of the traditional roles of nineteenth-century duplicity, Buford is a painted man literally put together by a confidence woman.[25] This narrative of masculine disguise has disastrous repercussions for the allegorical "manhood" of the Confederacy as a whole, for since Velazquez's text twins Buford and the Confederacy as newly born "men," when Buford suffers, the Confederacy metaphorically declines as well. When Velazquez is wounded in her foot and arm, exposed as female, and arrested, her loss of "masculinity" serves to emblematize the South's declining fortunes in the war. As she moves closer to abandoning her disguise, the South moves closer to defeat, in a mutually reinforcing convergence of masculinities in decline.

Finally, when Velazquez resumes female dress, the disappearance of her masculine persona may quell some gender anxieties, but given the South's loss in the war, it raises others. Even as Velazquez returns to her "proper" gender, she also literalizes the rhetoric of Confederate feminization, wherein losing a war means becoming a woman.

The metaphorical inseparability of Velazquez and the Confederacy not only emphasizes the South's loss of "manhood" through military defeat but also raises the question of whether that manhood had ever existed at all. For Southerners, the memory of Confederate valor in the war served to counter two sets of Northern images of a feminized South: the antebellum image of the weak, indecisive "Southern Hamlet" as well as the postwar figure of the emasculated soldier.[26] Symbolically speaking, Southerners used the memory of the Civil War both to make a man out of the boyish South and to prove that the region was a boy and not a girl in the first place. But because Velazquez *is* a girl in the first place, she inadvertently affirms this characterization; despite her own passionate support of the Confederacy, her very adoption of its gendered rhetoric not only feminizes the tenuously "masculine" South, but also returns it to its initial condition—like her own—of femininity. It is not, then, that Velazquez contradicts the Southern desire for a myth of masculinization but that she occupies this myth so literally that she brings its defensive underpinnings clearly into view. By literalizing a gender iconography that is supposed to remain only metaphorical, Velazquez's cross-dressing plot threatens the male anatomy of regional fantasy.[27]

If *The Woman in Battle* threatens Confederate masculinity with the prospect of gender transformation, so too does it hint at the specifically sexual dimensions of Confederate loss. When the Confederate army, aided by Buford, is triumphant, the imagery of military success is that of rape. At the falsely optimistic beginning of the battle of Shiloh, for example, Velazquez announces proudly, "We took possession of their camp . . . almost without resistance" (203), and "Our assaults upon the enemy were made with irresistible fury, and we rushed through their lines" (208). Conversely, when the South loses the war, its sexual relation to the North is that of female rape victim, as in Velazquez's reluctant concession to the North: "I love the South and its people with a greater intensity than ever, while at the same time many of my prejudices against the North had been beaten down by my intercourse with its people"

(517). Elsewhere, however, the gender valences of such "intercourse" are not at all clear. For if the South is in the symbolic position of emerging from the war as a "woman," it also assumes a posture of defeat as a feminized man. Meanwhile, the North takes on yet more masculinity through its victory in the war. Hence the South risks being assaulted by the remasculinized North both heterosexually and homosexually. In a process of cultural feminization that addresses two sides of the male body, what the Confederacy faces in remembering its defeat is both losing its phallic potency and being raped from behind.[28]

Velazquez's text does not, to be sure, speak explicitly about the South as a victim of male rape. But it nonetheless raises this figurative possibility in displaced form, through a strand of imagery that constructs Southern military aggression as anal penetration. In a chapter entitled in part "Preparations for an Attack on the Federal Rear," Velazquez discusses a plan for the Confederate army to attack the Union army by entering Federal lines through Canada; the plan fails because one Confederate soldier is captured by the Union army and, to Velazquez's disgust, confesses everything about the plan—he acts, that is, in an "unmanly" fashion. After this, "The failure of the contemplated raid in the rear . . . put an end to all expectations" of successful Southern strategy, and "there was nothing to be done but to fight the thing out to the bitter end" (432). Since the eventual conclusion to this fight is, of course, Southern defeat, the story provides a metaphoric circuit whereby an original plan to raid the Northern "rear," undone by one man's lack of masculinity, results in the South's own "bitter end"—that is, its metaphorical violation at the hands of the North. Commenting on this chapter, editor Worthington defends the Confederacy: "Admitting that they were belligerents, they were justified . . . in doing all in their power to defeat their enemies . . . by demoralizing them by insidious attacks in the rear" (8). Yet his remarks, for all that they overtly name Southern military prowess, inadvertently highlight its converse, since their context is a postwar vantage point from which the defeated Confederacy exists at all only in hindsight. In this reversible imagery of anal rape and raid—as with the narrative of phallic potency and castration—Velazquez's cross-dressed body again exposes the compensatory faultlines of Confederate symbolism precisely by virtue of inhabiting that symbolism too fully. Vanishing at a moment's notice from her persona as Buford, Velazquez literalizes a model of regional masculinity that is so permeable to assault—both frontal and dorsal—as to disappear entirely.

An important set of postwar images helps to clarify this set of symbolic relations among Confederate defeat, male bodies, and male costumes. Immediately after the war, in response to a rumor that Jefferson Davis, the Confederate commander in chief, had fled Union capture while dressed in his wife's clothing, Northern artists depicted the Confederate leader in drag (see figures 3 and 4). These examples not only link the South's defeat with feminization but show the sexual ambiguity of that feminization as well. On the one hand, as Silber argues, such images convey the South's defeat as its vulnerability to heterosexual rape (29–37). Seeking "petticoat protection," Davis ends up instead an "unprotected female"— as many captions proclaimed him—open to Northern male assault. On the other hand, cartoons such as "Jeff's Last Skedaddle" and "Finding the Last Ditch" also suggest the same-sex possibilities of Davis in drag. The pun on Davis's "ram-parts" highlights the *maleness* of the body at risk, while the prominence of his backside in the "last ditch" cartoons suggests the specific part of the male body most vulnerable to assault. Doubly metaphoric, Davis's "ram-parts" are both the phallus he could lose and the bulwark he can no longer defend. For the male Confederate body politic, that is, defeat promises to bring not only an attack against femininity, but an implicitly homosexual "raid on the rear." The cultural work of transvestism in both cases—as in Velazquez's story—is to act as a hinge, at once literal and metaphoric, between two mutually dependent and similarly vulnerable regions: the male body politic that suffers military humiliation and the male body that faces physical conquests such as castration and rape. As with *The Woman in Battle*, the transvestite depiction of Jefferson Davis suggests the intrinsic difficulties of mobilizing narratives of masculine potency in the service of narratives of national power, when masculinity is itself such a vulnerable fiction.

Despite her professed dedication to the memory of the Confederacy, then, Velazquez devalues by making visible the gender mythologies of the postwar South. Her story of wartime cross-dressing illuminates a series of cultural fears that move in two figurative directions: metaphorically, between bodies and costumes; and metonymically, from counterfeit women to counterfeit men, from femininity to feminization, and from gender inversion to homosexual invasion. The result is a text that upends rather

Figures 3 and 4. Jefferson Davis in drag, in *Jeff's Last Skedaddle* (ca. 1865), and *Finding the Last Ditch* (1865).

Finding the Last Ditch.

than buttresses Southern claims to masculinity and indeed seems to render the metaphorical gendering of the Confederacy as a whole a "lost cause." For if Velazquez is insufficiently passive while dressed as a woman, she is also inadequately active while dressed as a man, and the very action that quells her transgressions against femininity—abandoning male costume—is what threatens her "masculinity" most directly. Her masquerade inadvertently exposes the contradictions of a symbolic system that demands the maintenance of femininity as a contrast to Confederate masculinity but is so unable to sustain this contrast that femininity invades and usurps the domain of the masculine itself.

As Velazquez's text suggests the sexual fault lines of Lost Cause iconography, so too does it implicate defensive constructions of race in the postwar South. Not surprisingly, given its Confederate sympathies, *The Woman in Battle* endorses Southern racism in a variety of ways. Velazquez never mentions slavery in her account of the war, but she has an African American servant, Bob, on the battlefield, whom she treats as her slave: "I told him that if he ran off and left me, I would kill him if I ever caught him again; which threat had its desired effect, for he stuck to me through thick and thin" (96). Her comments about the Reconstruction South typify the racist belief that former slaves had seized political power from white men, as she laments "the pitiable state of things. The men of intellect, and the true representatives of Southern interests, were disfranchised and impoverished, while the management of affairs was in the hands of ignorant negroes, just relieved from slavery, and white 'carpet-baggers'" (535). Finally, summarizing her postwar Southern trip, she comments that "the negroes, Indians, and half-breeds seem to be incapable of doing anything to advance their own condition, or to promote the interests of the country" (552).

When situated against the text's imagery of masculine loss, these racist comments highlight the imperiled construction of Southern whiteness after the war. Published at the end of radical Reconstruction, *The Woman in Battle* brings together characteristic anxieties of the period about figures who threaten white authority with an unusually revealing narrative of masculinity under siege. Despite Velazquez's imperious commands to Bob, the success of her disguise depends on his constancy. Since she fears that his departure will make her too vulnerable in battle, she needs Bob to "stick to her" for her male costume to stick as well.[30] As Velazquez's assumption of masculinity is authenticated only by the racial subordination of others, so too is her loss of "manhood" accompanied by an increasing paranoia about African American empowerment. After the war, when Velazquez is once again a woman, white men are "disfranchised and impoverished," while former slaves control the "management of affairs." The juxtaposition of these racial and gender narratives suggests that fears about the loss of masculinity, which are already frightening *within* the white world, are even more so in conjunction with the volatile postwar relation *between* races. In other words, Velazquez's story suggests that the postwar South experiences a feminization of whiteness.

Velazquez's own ambiguous ethnic origins also link the specter of female misrule with the coloration of racial difference in the Americas more broadly conceived. Although her Hispanic name marks her ethnic divergence from conventional Anglo-American "whiteness," Velazquez's self-proclaimed status as a Cuban-born American immigrant descended from Spanish aristocrats leaves the specific implications of that divergence unclear. Her Cuban origins, for example, have a complex relation to Southern ideals of manhood. Later in the century, Cuba—a kindred slaveholding country—would take on triumphant symbolic associations for Southern adherents of the Lost Cause, with participation in the Spanish-American War offering an opportunity for the vindication of Southern manhood. When Velazquez's book is published, however, this war is still in the future; in 1876, her Cubanness may also mark her as a part of a foreign world, a Caribbean "dark continent" distinct from the United States. In the metaphoric logic of *The Woman in Battle*, Velazquez's "mother country"—like her original gender—may signify a region of uncontrolled femininity as much as a sister state. In an extension of ethnic and racial difference from the United States to the Americas as a whole, her Cuban origins symbolically combine the hazards of femininity and the implicitly racial "otherness" of Cuba in relation to the United States.[31]

Returning to the comments of Early one last time, we can see that Velazquez's ethnic markings are unsettling not only because they are foreign but also because their very foreignness—like her masculinity—may be, in the end, yet another masquerade. In his letter to Slemons, Early declares his belief that "Madame Velasquez [*sic*] is not of Spanish birth or origin, but is an American and probably from the North," an assessment that refights the Civil War by imagining Velazquez as a Northerner. Later, he elaborates: "The solecisms in grammar contained in her letter do not result from the broken English of a foreigner, but are the blunders of an American whose education is imperfect. Her appearance and voice are those of an American woman, and has no resemblance to those of a cultivated Spanish lady. If she is really Spanish in origin, then her associations with camp life have thoroughly Americanized her." Velazquez is not "really Spanish in origin," or if so, she is "thoroughly Americanized"; her speech is not that of a "cultivated Spanish lady" but the result of "imperfect" education. These uncertainties both blur the boundary between not-American and American and reverse the traditional narrative by which an immigrant moves from a condition of original ethnicity to one of self-made "Americanness." In Velazquez's case, by contrast, ethnic otherness may be donned as well as discarded, and the making of an American—like the making of a man—is a process without clear foundation. Velazquez once again literalizes the fears of the postwar South, for she translates the image of the "self-made man" into a vision of masculinity literally self-made by a woman, of Southernness constructed by a Northerner, and of Spanishness mimicked by an American. In ethnic as well as racial terms, her text implicitly points the way toward Southern life after the Confederacy as a carnivalesque social field occupied by figures black and white, Northern and Southern, American and un-American. In this eruption of "otherness," gender masquerade is both its own form of revolt and a protean metaphor for myriad forms of misrule.[32]

In the conflict between Loreta Velazquez and Jubal Early, then, the battles of the Civil War are refought on the terrain of Confederate metaphor. *The Woman in Battle* debases the value of Confederate iconography by literalizing its terms, turning Confederate masculinity into femininity and femininity into fakery. These narratives of gender and sexuality, in turn, inadvertently unmask the whiteness that both Velazquez and Early defend, such that the former slave—and the racial "other" more broadly conceived—stand alongside the white woman as the South's Medusa. In the losing metaphors of the Lost Cause, even the stories created in defense of the Confederacy open its boundaries to multiple penetration.

IV

From the "Lost Cause" to the "lady's man," *The Woman in Battle* suggests that the metaphors of military masquerade are reciprocal and contradictory ones. As the Civil War symbolically transforms Velazquez's story of cross-dressing, so too does her masquerade alter the postwar meanings of the memory of the Confederacy. Yet at the same time as cross-dressing forges a range of connections among bodies large and small, it also subjects those connections to constant reversal. In this text, radical notions of gender do not secure radical gender politics, any more than a conservative use of gender symbolism, as in the writings of Jubal Early, necessarily secures reactionary politics. For Early, as we have seen, the masculine body politic of the postwar South is all too easily literalized in the form of a woman. Similarly, in the world of *The Woman in Battle*, capacious fantasies of sexual mobility refuse to remain in flexibly metaphoric form, since Velazquez's enthusiasm for the performance of masculinity translates into a literal hostility to other women. Even in this world of female plenitude, it turns out that ladies lack, and when women unite, they—like the Confederacy—cannot seem to secede.

All of which would seem to suggest a contrast to Lauren Cook Burgess, contemporary Civil War reenactor, whose story is a vindication of the rights of women to cross-dress, as secured through a legal system response, in this case, to feminism. Or is it a contrast? In fact, the outlines of the scandal of cross-dressing are remarkably similar. What emerges in this comparison is not simply that Burgess, like Velazquez, is a scandalous figure but that the terms of scandal are the same in each case. Like Velazquez, Burgess brings the figure of an unruly woman into a world of men. As with Velazquez's arrest, too, Burgess's exposure extends the threat of unruly femininity to its most dangerous form: male feminization. In Burgess's vision of performing maleness to excess—"I think I do a better job than a lot of the men out there"—to *out*man becomes, by implication, to *un*man. Further, the accusations of inauthenticity so inseparable from Velazquez's story provide insight into the scandal of Burgess, because those accusations suggest that gender indeterminacy and historical inauthenticity—the charges leveled against Burgess—are not simply analogous but interdependent anxieties. As the fictive quality of the reenactment helps to call Burgess's gender into question, so too does her gender masquerade unsettle the historical foundations of the reenact-ment. In equal measure, her gender is caused by her inauthenticity, and "her inauthenticity happens to be caused by her gender." Indeed, given the similarities between the two stories, it seems only fitting that Burgess has herself recently edited a collection of letters by an original Civil War cross-dresser.[33] In reprising the terms of nineteenth-century scandal, she has also become an historian of it.

As Velazquez's story brings into sharper focus the scandal of Burgess's masquerade in gender terms, it also makes visible a form of "inauthen-ticity" not immediately as apparent in the contemporary case: that of heterosexuality. What Loreta Velazquez's story accomplishes through its literary form, Lauren Cook Burgess's story evokes iconographically, for both women expose a set of sexual instabilities implicit within the military itself. In the photograph accompanying the *New York Times* story, for example, Burgess's visual image disrupts the written text of the caption, which identifies her marital status: "Lauren Cook, left, who has sued the Interior Department . . . [w]ith her was her husband, Fred Burgess." With the hand of Fred Burgess resting on the costumed body of the soldier boy, the image is first of all available for a reading of male homoeroticism, for it brings together the homosocial domain of the male military with the theatricality of gay camp. Meanwhile, if we focus on only the image of Burgess, the photograph is sexually suggestive in another direction, as much "butch lesbian" as "Butch Cassidy." Reading against the grain, we can see the insouciance of her look and posture as offering a parodic version of the twentieth-century figure of the "mannish lesbian"—here, as if in mocking fulfillment of cultural fantasy, complete with phallic gun. Burgess's refusal to be a female camp-follower in the male world of the military, that is, implicitly turns her into a figure of camp, both gay male and lesbian.[34] This link is nowhere named in the news coverage of the story and may have no relation to Burgess's own experience. Yet the camp pleasures of the photograph are nonetheless available, such that—as with Loreta Velazquez—lesbian and gay readings may emerge in the relation between text and reader.

In the relation between sexual and regional bodies, moreover, the terms of Burgess's imposture reprise those of Velazquez. Although she was raised hearing stories of a relative who fought for the North, Burgess herself lives in the South, is a member of Confederate regiments, displays

Confederate flags in her home, and was married in a Confederate-style wedding ceremony.[35] Like Velazquez's self-made Southernness, Burgess's deliberate construction of Southern identity is an important feature of her story. As in the nineteenth century, the rituals in which Burgess participates rely on attempted narratives of Confederate remasculinization. For their many Southern participants, the promised outcome of such rituals is an illusory moment of eternal present-tense possibility for the South, one in which—as the February 1992 cover of *Civil War Times Illustrated* put it—"Confederates rally again!" Similarly, now as then, the scandal of Civil War cross-dressing is particularly explosive when combined with the mythology of a region whose "manhood" had been threatened by military defeat. Destroying the metaphoric manhood of both soldier and region, Burgess renders her uniform and the Confederate flag behind her in the photograph equally counterfeit. Indeed, since the Confederate flag in its most familiar form became popular only in the 1950s, these two forms of counterfeit are not only homologous but coterminous.[36] Just as Velazquez became Buford at the moment when the South was named the Confederacy, so too were the Burgess and the contemporary Confederate flag born at roughly the same time.

Finally, Velazquez's text also helps us to see that the story of Burgess, for all its inauthenticities, has fiercely authentic—albeit divergent—political implications for region and nation. On the one hand, for example, camp sensibility has long provided, and continues to provide, a vital oppositional strategy for countering dominant heterosexual norms, and activists have brought its features to the streets as well.[37] On the other hand, the iconography of the Confederacy, and of the Confederate flag in particular, bears an intimate relation to the history and practice of racial bigotry. Despite some efforts by white Southerners to separate the issue of regional pride from racism, the Confederate flag remains inseparable from the history of slavery.[38] Such racist icons are, moreover, easily available for the campaigns of right-wing groups such as neo-Nazis, since they offer a symbolic opportunity for white people to take on the mantle of victimization by identifying with the defeated South. This paranoid narrative of white martyrdom is in turn continuous with the imperialist quest, in the wake of Vietnam, to remasculinize America in the world at large.[39]

Yet even to pose the political meanings of Civil War masquerade in this way—as a contrast between sexual radicalism and racial conservatism—is itself an insufficient account of the political implications of Burgess's story, which remain internally contradictory. A high-camp appropriation of the Confederate flag, for example, cannot negate that flag's racist symbolism. And while Burgess fights discrimination against equal rights as "a matter of principle," the role of feminism is no more fixed by her story than by *The Woman in Battle*. For white Southern women, the combination of regional pride and female self-assertion has unpredictable results. In Burgess's story, this confluence reinforces the rebelliousness of women with the metaphor of regional revolt. Historically, however, women have more often put Confederate devotion in the service of conservative politics—as in the case of the United Daughters of the Confederacy, who have long stood at the forefront of efforts to commemorate the flag.[40] In the case of Burgess as well as that of Velazquez, Confederate cross-dressing is simultaneously and inseparably a question of gender, sexuality, race, region, and nation, and the constitutive presence of metaphor in each of these realms can have both reactionary and radical consequences. In this conflict of metaphor against itself—as in many other battles declared and undeclared—the Civil War continues to be fought, today no less than a hundred years ago.

Notes

1. Cook v. Babbitt, Civ. No. 91-0338, D.D.C. (1993). Journalistic accounts of the case include "Woman Sues over Exclusion from Events at National Park," *New York Times* 25 February 1991: A7; "Morning Edition," National Public Radio, 23 August 1991; Lynda Robinson, "It's a Man's Job: A Woman's Fight to Be a Civil War 'Soldier,'" *San Francisco Chronicle and Examiner* 13 October 1991, *Sunday Punch* 2; Eugene Meyer, "A Civil War of the Sexes: Park Service Wanted Male Cast at Antietam," *Washington Post* 9 June 1992: A1, A7; "Not Just Whistling Dixie: Lauren Cook Burgess Fights for a Woman's Right to Play Civil War," *People* 5 October 1992: 103; and Eugene Meyer, "Judge Admits Women to the Antietam Armies," *Washington Post* 18 March 1993: B1, B3. For an overview of the reenactment world, see Lawliss, *Civil War Sourcebook*, 286–98; for analyses, see Turner, "Bloodless Battles: The Civil War Reenacted," and esp. Jim Cullen, *The Civil War in Popular Culture*, 179–99, which focuses on another cross-dressing woman soldier in the reenactment world. According to James McPherson, there are some 40,000 Civil

War reenactors, and 250,000 people belong to Civil War societies, subscribe to Civil War magazines, or collect war memorabilia. See McPherson, *Battle Cry of Freedom* and "A War That Never Goes Away."

2. Quotation sources, respectively: "whether middle-aged men" in Meyer, "Judge Admits Women" B3; "We have a very serious commitment" in Robinson, "It's a Man's Job"; "If you're going to portray" in "Woman Sues" A7; "her lack of authenticity" in "Morning Edition"; "There was no hedging" in Robinson, "It's a Man's Job"; "a matter of principle" and "I think I do a far better job" in "Woman Sues" A7; and judge's comments in Meyer, "Judge Admits Women" B1.

3. For overviews of cross-dressing, see also Epstein and Straub, eds., *Body Guards*, and Tyler, "Boys Will Be Girls: The Politics of Gay Drag."

4. See, for example, Fredric Jameson's characterization of postmodernism and history in *Postmodernism, or, The Cultural Logic of Late Capitalism*: "We are condemned to seek History by way of our own pop images and simulacra of that history, which itself remains forever out of reach" (25).

5. Important works on this topic include Anderson, *Imagined Communities*; Bhabha, ed., *Nation and Narration*; and Hobsbawm and Ranger, eds., *The Invention of Tradition*; and on the particular constructedness of American identity, Bercovitch, *The American Jeremiad*.

6. Apart from Loreta Velazquez's *The Woman in Battle*, the most detailed memoir of Civil War cross-dressing is S. Emma E. Edmonds, *Nurse and Spy in the Union Army* (1864). Contemporary histories of the war that mention cross-dressing include L. P. Brockett, *The Camp, the Battle Field, and the Hospital; or, Lights and Shadows of the Great Rebellion* (Chicago, 1866), 67–72, 100–30; Frazar Kirkland [Richard Millar Devens], *The Pictorial Book of Anecdotes of the Rebellion* (St. Louis, 1889); Frank Moore, *The Rebellion Record* (New York: 1864–68), 4:70, 7:87, and 8:37–58, 554, and Moore, *Women of the War: Their Heroism and Self-Sacrifice* (Hartford, 1867), 529–32; Albert D. Richardson, *The Secret Service: The Field, the Dungeon, and the Escape* (Hartford, 1865), 175; and Philip Sheridan, *The Personal Memoirs of Philip H. Sheridan* (1888), rpt. in Katz, *Gay American History*, 345–46. Nineteenth-century fiction involving Civil War cross-dressing includes John Esten Cooke, *Hilt to Hilt* (New York, 1868); Edward Edgeville, *Castine* (Raleigh, 1865); Justin Jones [Harry Hazel], *Virginia Graham, the Spy of the Grand Army* (Boston, 1868); Rachel Longstreet, *Remy St. Remy; or, The Boy in Blue* (New York, 1866); Madeline Moore, *The Lady Lieutenant* (Philadelphia, 1862); and J. Perkins Tracy, *The Heart of Virginia* (New York, 1896).

7. About estimating numbers, Livermore wrote: "Some one has stated the num-

ber of women soldiers known to the service as little less than four hundred. I cannot vouch for this estimate, but I am convinced that a larger number of women disguised themselves and enlisted in the service, for one cause or another, than was dreamed of" (119). Discussions of this statistic may be found in Schultz, "Women at the Front: A Study in Gender and Genre," and Larson, "Bonny Yank and Ginny Reb," who "would estimate it to be in the thousands" (38).

8. For descriptions of Civil War women soldiers, see De Grave, *Swindler, Spy, Rebel*; Hall, *Patriots in Disguise*; Kaufman, " 'Under the Petticoat Flag': Women Soldiers in the Confederate Army"; King, *Clad in Uniform*; Larson, "Bonny Yank and Ginny Reb," and "Bonny Yank and Ginny Reb Revisited"; Massey, *Bonnet Brigades*; Samuelson, "Employment of Female Spies in the American Civil War"; Schultz, "Women at the Front"; Sizer, "Narratives of Union Women Spies"; and Wheelwright, *Amazons and Military Maids*.

9. Dustin, Gilman (Richmond, 1876); rpt. New York: Arno, 1972. All subsequent quotations are taken from this edition and are cited parenthetically in the text.

10. Discussions of Velazquez may be found in Hall 107–53, 189–94; Hoffert 24–31; Kaufman 367–74; King, 16–17; Massey, 82–84, 195; Larson, "Bonny Yank and Ginny Reb" 43–44; and Wheelwright, esp. 172. The most detailed analyses of *The Woman in Battle* are provided by De Grave, 108–57, and Schultz, "Women at the Front" chapter 5.

11. General Jubal Early, letter to W. F. Slemons, 22 May 1878, Tucker Family Papers, Collection #2605, Folder 41, Southern Historical Collection, Library of the University of North Carolina at Chapel Hill; hereafter cited as "Letter to Slemons."

12. Relevant discussions of Southern white women in the Civil War include Bynum, *Unruly Women*; Clinton and Silber, eds., *Divided Houses*; Faust, *Southern Stories*; Massey, *Bonnet Brigades*; Rable, *Civil Wars*; Schultz, "Mute Fury" and "Women at the Front."

13. I borrow the phrase "revolution against patriarchal authority" from Jay Fliegelman, *Prodigals and Pilgrims*. In *The Woman in Battle*, the Mexican War fills the symbolic position that was more commonly occupied for Southerners by the American Revolution: that of an earlier war in which a maligned power justifiably fought for its independence. To be sure, many supporters of the Confederacy had fought *against* Mexico in the earlier war. But the symbolic resonances of the Mexican War register differently for Velazquez's father, since his "native" loyalties are with the Mexican side. On the legacy of the American Revolution to supporters of the Confederacy, see Faust, *The Creation of Confederate Nationalism* 14–15.

14. This is James McPherson's title for a chapter on the upper South in *Battle Cry of Freedom* 276.

15. See Rich, "Compulsory Heterosexuality and Lesbian Existence," and Butler, *Gender Trouble* (the term is defined on 151).

16. On lesbian history, see Faderman, *Surpassing the Love of Men,* and d'Emilio and Freedman, *Intimate Matters*; on lesbian texts, see Straub, "The Guilty Pleasures of Female Theatrical Cross-Dressing and the Autobiography of Charlotte Charke," and Straayer, "Redressing the 'Natural.'" Since the term *lesbian* emerged late in the nineteenth century, I will be using *protolesbian* to characterize same-sex relations in *The Woman in Battle.*

17. See, for example, Case and Nestle.

18. I borrow this term from Michie, *Sororophobia.*

19. On the antipathy of Southern women to feminism, see Rable, *Civil Wars* 285–88.

20. On the history of the "Lost Cause," see Foster, *Ghosts of the Confederacy*; Kammen, *Mystic Chords of Memory,* esp. 101–31; Neely, Holzer, and Boritt, *The Confederate Image*; and Wilson, *Baptized in Blood.*

21. On women's activities and female iconography in the Lost Cause, see Foster, *Ghosts of the Confederacy,* 38–45, 172–79; Rable, *Civil Wars* 236–39; Wilson, *Baptized in Blood* 32–33, 46–48; and esp. Faust, *Southern Stories* 148–59.

22. See Osborne, *Jubal.*

23. Velazquez to Early, 18 May 1878, Tucker Family Papers, Collection #2605, Folder 41, Southern Historical Collection, Library of the University of North Carolina at Chapel Hill.

24. For discussion of the ethos of female sacrifice, see Faust, *Southern Stories.* See also Huston 119–38.

25. See De Grave and Halttunen, *Confidence Men and Painted Women,* for discussion of these figures as indexes of anxiety in nineteenth-century America.

26. On the antebellum feminization of the South, see Porter, "Social Discourse and Nonfictional Prose," and Taylor, *Cavalier and Yankee* 160–62, who discusses the figure of the "Southern Hamlet."

27. I adapt this phrase from Berlant, *The Anatomy of National Fantasy.*

28. For discussion of the homophobic construction of nationhood in other American contexts, see Goldberg, "Bradford's 'Ancient Members' and 'A Case of Buggery . . . Amongst Them,'" and Edelman, "Tearooms and Sympathy, or, The Epistemology of the Water Closet," both in *Nationalisms and Sexualities,* ed. Parker et al.

29. For discussion and further examples of this imagery, see Silber, *The Romance*

of Reunion; Foster, *Ghosts of the Confederacy*; and esp. Neely, Holzer, and Boritt, *The Confederate Image,* who cite thirty-two such images.

30. Velazquez's need for Bob to authenticate and protect her disguise may be compared with the ways that the disguises of Ellen Craft as a white man and George Harris as a Spanish slave owner are authenticated through the accompaniment of "slaves" who attend them. See the essays by Weinauer and Stern in this collection.

31. On the Spanish-American War as an opportunity for Southern remasculinization, see Foster, *Ghosts of the Confederacy* 163.

32. For discussion of the ways gender symbolism obscured racial and ethnic conflict in nineteenth-century America, see Ryan, *Women in Public,* esp. 52–57.

33. See Burgess, *An Uncommon Soldier.*

34. On the figure of the "mannish lesbian," see Faderman, *Odd Girls and Twilight Lovers,* and Newton, "The Mythic Mannish Lesbian."

35. These details are taken from "Not Just Whistling Dixie."

36. See Allen Cabiniss, "Rebel Flag."

37. On the political implications of camp, see Berlant and Freeman, "Queer Nationality."

38. For an overview of contemporary struggles over the Confederate flag, see Bates, "Look Away." On the flag controversy in Georgia, see Ronald Smothers, "Georgia Governor Acts to End Confederate Symbol," *New York Times* 29 May 1992: A8, and Smothers, "Georgia Leader Ends Flag Campaign," *New York Times* 10 March 1993: A10; and on a battle over the flag involving Senators Jesse Helms and Carol Moseley-Braun, see Adam Clymer, "A Daughter of Slavery Makes the Senate Listen," *New York Times* 23 July 1993: A10.

39. On the gendering of America in relation to the world at large, see Jeffords, *The Remasculinization of America,* and Boose, "Techno-Muscularity and the 'Boy Eternal'" 67 68.

40. On the current involvement of the United Daughters of the Confederacy in flag controversies, see Clymer, "A Daughter of Slavery Makes the Senate Listen."

Displacing Desire:

Passing, Nostalgia, and *Giovanni's Room*

VALERIE ROHY

"*A*merica is my country and Paris is my hometown," writes Gertrude Stein in "An American in France" (61). Placing in question the very notion of place, this transatlantic crossing relies on the terms—origin and identity—that it will expose as most unreliable. In the American expatriate tradition, the trope of nationality comes unfixed from its geographical moorings to become an emblem of other, more arbitrary identifications, producing a rhetoric of displacement that extends from national identity to ideology, subjectivity, sexual desire, and, in this case, "home." Stein's "Paris is my hometown" sets the scene for a performance of identity in which trappings of nationality and culture are put on by the expatriate in an act that becomes more "real" than the "real" and in which the fact of the matter—that Gertrude Stein, for example, was born in Allegheny, Pennsylvania—itself comes to seem a piece of stage scenery, a pretext for her Parisian "hometown."

Questions of origin and identity are central to James Baldwin's *Giovanni's Room,* a text which not only participates in the tradition of the American expatriate novel exemplified by Stein and, especially, by Henry James but which does so in relation to the African American idiom of passing and the genre of the passing novel. As such, *Giovanni's Room* poses questions of nationalism, nostalgia, and the constitution of racial and sexual subjects in terms that are especially resonant for contemporary identity politics. After all, the trope of "home" which Stein invokes and which proves central for Baldwin as well can hardly escape political inflection in a culture that, today as in Baldwin's 1950s, champions the white, heterosexual, bourgeois home as icon of a mythical and sentimentalized family whose "values" reflect those of the dominant culture. And at a time when attempts to intervene in the imposition of such values frequently present themselves under the rubric of "identity politics," the intersection of notions of "home" with nationalism, identity, and essentialism has taken on a particular urgency. In addressing the question of identity through the metaphorics of "passing," *Giovanni's Room* articulates the ways in which identities, including "nationality," "race," and "sexuality," are retrospective, indeed nostalgic, constructions, subject to a pathos of lost origins and demanding, on the part of the dominant culture, the violent disavowal and projection of its own contingent identity. The logics of homophobia and racism, Baldwin suggests, are each rooted in the nostalgia of an impossible essentialism whose desire for coherent identity is barred by an ineluctable passing.

The term *passing* designates a performance in which one presents oneself as what one is not, a performance commonly imagined along the axis of race, class, gender, or sexuality. Although the American passing novel typically concerns an African American who successfully presents herself or himself as white to escape the virulent effects of racism or to enter into exclusively white social circles, *passing* means, in addition, the impersonation of one sex by another. In American literature, passing across race and across gender are thoroughly imbricated—most famously, perhaps, in the narrative of William and Ellen Craft (1860), who escaped from slavery, she dressed as a white man and he posing as her servant, and in Harriet Beecher Stowe's *Uncle Tom's Cabin* (1852), when Eliza, traveling to Canada, disguises herself as a white man and her young son as a girl. In the twentieth century, novels such as Nella Larsen's *Passing* and James Weldon Johnson's *Autobiography of an Ex-Coloured Man* add to the discourse of racial passing a third important sense of passing: the appearance of "homosexual" as "heterosexual." *Giovanni's Room* may be read as a passing novel in both racial and sexual senses: appearing a generation after the Harlem Renaissance, it restages the doubling of disguises performed in earlier African American novels—*The Autobiography of an Ex-Coloured Man* and *Passing* in particular—which allows racial passing to figure (homo)sexual passing.[1] Yet how does the vocabulary of passing make it possible to set tropes of racial identity alongside and against those of sexual identity? What would it mean to read *Giovanni's Room* "as" a passing novel or through the tropology that passing provides? Although race and sexuality by no means function in identical ways, in Baldwin's novel as in other texts, passing names a crucial nexus: a site of the relation between notions of racial and sexual identity whose intersection becomes a productive space in which to interrogate identity itself.

In America, Baldwin has said, "the sexual question and the racial question have always been intertwined" (qtd. in Goldstein 178), and in

Giovanni's Room these questions are most clearly articulated through the discourse of nationality and nationalism. Not only does nationality stand in for race in the novel—as Giovanni's darker coloring and lower-class status contrast with David's blondness and privilege—but perhaps more important, the rhetoric that would equate "race" with "blackness" is suppressed, and the "whiteness" of the stereotypically Anglo-Saxon hero, foregrounded. In this text's extraordinary beginning, David's reflection on his own image signifies "white" with indelible quotation marks and invites, even insists on, a reading of his race in the context of his homosexuality and his homophobia: "My reflection is tall, perhaps rather like an arrow, my blond hair gleams. My face is like a face you have seen many times. My ancestors conquered a continent, pushing across death-laden plains, until they came to an ocean which faced away from Europe into a darker past."[2] Producing the narrator as a representative of white American dominant culture—its history of colonial conquest, its arrow-straight posture, even the banality of its familiarity—this meditation on culture and identity takes shape in terms of history and temporality. It is appropriate enough that a novel so committed to a reading of nostalgia and retrospection should present its own narrative as retrospection by beginning at the story's end, with Giovanni condemned to death and David about to leave home once again. But the terms in which the novel first frames race and sexuality—through the introduction of its narrator— themselves perform a kind of metaleptic reversal: in attempting to push back the frontier that emblematizes American futurity, David's ancestors have traveled not back to the future, but forward into the past. And for white America to confront its "darker past" is here, one suspects, to come face to face with the darkness or difference that its own light face—the face of an ideology we have all, in one way or another, "seen many times"—seeks to deny.

"The whole American optic in terms of reality," Baldwin has said, "is based on the necessity of keeping black people out of it. We are nonexistent. Except according to their terms, and their terms are unacceptable" (qtd. in Troupe 210). Yet Baldwin will appropriate passing, a trope that seems to literalize that "nonexistence" or invisibility, as a means of reading and resisting dominant constructions of race, gender, sexuality, and identity as such. Although no figure in *Giovanni's Room* passes across the color line, David produces himself as heterosexual with Hella and as gay with Giovanni, who is himself passing, for the moment, as a gay man. Even Hella, as Baldwin makes clear, performs the rigorously scripted role of the heterosexual woman, passing as feminine through the gender performance that Joan Riviere has termed "masquerade."[3] While Baldwin as author does not attempt to pass for white, he may, outfitted in what some readers have persistently construed as a sort of Henry James drag, pass into the white literary tradition, whose conventions of first-person narrative require that an author always pass as his or her protagonist, as Baldwin does when he speaks in David's voice the "I" that is the novel's first word.[4]

These displacements of identity, the hallmark of passing, are juxtaposed in *Giovanni's Room* with a desire for placement seen as the retrograde movement of a nostalgia that remembers and longs for "home." In imagining nostalgia, Baldwin calls on both spatial and temporal metaphors: notions of "going back" to a place of origin on the one hand, and to a historical past on the other. I want to return to the relation between nostalgia and passing to suggest the ways in which spatial and temporal figures describe what amounts to the same logic of return, but let me begin by examining Baldwin's rhetoric of distance and placement and his figures of home, homeland, and nationality. If nationality, in *Giovanni's Room*, is an allegory of sexual and racial identity, "home" comes to represent sexual orthodoxy: when David finds himself "at home" neither in Paris nor in the United States, neither with his Italian lover nor with his American fiancée, his distance from father and fatherland suggests his venture into a space outside American bourgeois heterosexuality. When his father attempts to return the expatriate to his ideological, if not literal, homeland by recuperating for him the heterosexual masculine roles of wage earner, father, and married man, David has to admit that he "never felt at home" in the place where his father, reading a newspaper, would assume the stereotypical pose of the bourgeois American male. What is at stake in the return to, or resistance to, all things "American" is clear: "Dear Butch," his father writes, "aren't you ever coming home?" Yet only after he is brought "home" to heterosexual masculinity, here phobically opposed to homosexual effeminacy, can David be "Butch" (*GR* 119–20).

More persistently than his father's nagging letters, David's own homophobia pulls him back toward the America that constitutes his nostalgic ideal of secure gender and sexual identity. Prompted not only by his relocation in Paris but by the possibility of relocation in what he imagines to be a homosexual space, his nostalgia for home and homeland is a desire for an imagined site of heterosexual meaning. It is, after all, while break-fasting with Giovanni that David experiences his first bout of homesick-ness and "ache[s] abruptly, intolerably" with the desire to go "home across the ocean, to things and people I knew and understood . . . which I would always, helplessly, and in whatever bitterness of spirit, love above all else" (*GR* 84). In that moment the strangeness of the city, of Giovanni, and of their love seems to reanimate the promise of epistemological security that "home" holds out. David's knowledge of the knowability of American "things and people," however, depends on a denial of differ-ence, as his admission of "bitterness of spirit" suggests. His "bitterness" toward America marks the difference *within* the American "homeland"— a difference that is, for David, his own homosexual desire. Homosexuality is understood here, as in Freud, as the *unheimlich* return of a desire that gives the lie to homesickness and to the hope of a return to American orthodoxy; like the uncanny, that is, homosexuality appears as the return of something familiar that has been repressed—in David's case his ado-lescent love for Joey, which is all the more *unheimlich* for being, in fact, so close to home.

The note of "bitterness" in this discussion of differences between American and European "things and people" points to two distinct sys-tems of difference that operate simultaneously in *Giovanni's Room*. Al-though the text conspicuously compares David as American with Gio-vanni as European, the more telling differences are those within "the American," within David himself, and within the always permeable boundaries of identity. Lacan's notion of the split subject bears repeating here: "In any case man cannot aim at being whole . . . once the play of displacement and condensation to which he is committed in the exercise of his functions, marks his relation as subject to the signifier" (*Feminine Sexuality* 81–82). Because subjectivity is lacking or divided within the symbolic, the effect of coherence depends on the expulsion of difference, yet efforts to police boundaries can produce *only* the effect of "inside" and "outside"—an effect that nonetheless makes itself felt as a continual tension between the claustrophobic "inside" of identity and its dangerous "outside." Thus David both hates to be labeled an American and is horrified by the possibility of being anything else. When Giovanni calls him a *"vrai américain,"* David responds, "I resented this: resented being called an American (and resented resenting it) because it seemed to make me nothing more than that, whatever that was; and I resented being called *not* an American because it seemed to make me nothing" (*GR* 117). Outside the putative safety of "America" is a territory so phobically overdetermined that it appears wholly evacuated, a "nothing." Producing this cipher as placeholder for a famously unspeakable love, David is as unwilling to imagine being anything other than a heterosexual as he is unwilling to imagine being anything other than an American. Yet "America," of course, is itself "nothing": it emerges as a locus of identification only by distinguishing itself from the foreign—or the perverse. In the narrative of *Giovanni's Room*, the space of that "nothing," alternately emptied out and filled up by representation, will also become, in the service of defining "America," an all too substantial abjected "something." Even so, being an American, "whatever that was," is never certain; indeed, there is perhaps no better illustration of the difference within, or impossibility of, identity than the way "nothing" haunts the phrase "nothing more than" an American.

Biddy Martin and Chandra Talpade Mohanty read "home" and identity in terms that usefully describe this mapping of culture's "outside" as a "nothing" or "nowhere":

When the alternatives would seem to be either the enclosing, encircling, constraining circle of home, or nowhere to go, the risk is enormous. The assumption of, or desire for, another safe place like "home" is challenged by the realization that "unity"—interpersonal as well as political—is itself necessarily fragmentary, itself that which is struggled for, chosen, and hence unstable by definition; it is not based on "sameness," and there is no perfect fit. (209)

Just so, Baldwin acknowledges the uncertainty of "home"—that is, of identity as such—yet admits its persistent attraction in David's reluctance to "risk" locating himself elsewhere. Of course, risk is not only found outside those encircling walls; home is always as uncanny as the foreign, for it is itself the foreign. For dominant ideology to produce itself as the natural, not the *unheimlich*, it must repudiate its other as "nothing"; the coherence of "home" is thus purchased at great cost—a cost literalized, in Baldwin's novel, as David's repudiation of Giovanni, Guillaume's murder, Giovanni's flight and execution, and David's own homelessness.

But while the violence demanded by, and inherent in, the identity formation of the dominant culture may suggest the need for a gay "home" or community, the maid's room that David shares with Giovanni feels like a prison to him for most of the novel and seems an "Eden" only after it is lost. Though Guillaume's bar functions as a kind of gay "household" of which Guillaume is himself the founding father, the possibility of gay community and of essential gay identity is largely foreclosed in the novel. When the men who openly identify as gay, like Guillaume and Jacques, are called "disgusting old fairies" and worse, one hardly wonders why the only "homosexual" relationship validated here takes place between two bisexual men whose masculinity is continually and anxiously affirmed. But if *Giovanni's Room* implies that the best gay man is, in effect, a straight man—or at least one who mimics "straightness" impeccably—the novel also recognizes that something like gay identity, if not self-chosen, can be homophobically imposed. That is, though David is sickened by the barroom queens who legibly signify their desire, he is himself read as gay on the street by a sailor who gives him a look of obscene contempt, "some brutal variation of *Look, baby, I know you*" (*GR* 122). This knowing gaze, seeming to recognize in David the identity he has so assiduously denied, engenders in him what Eve Kosofsky Sedgwick has termed "homosexual panic" at his inability to contain the public signification of his body (*Between Men* 83–96).[5] This fixation of homophobic fantasy and anxiety on the supposed legibility of the gay body recalls the "I know you" of the racial gaze represented in African American passing novels in scenes of recognition and exposure. In Larsen's *Passing*, for example, when Clare and Irene meet accidentally at Drayton's restaurant, the phantasmatic epistemology of passing is all too clear: to see is to know. This is equally true in *Giovanni's Room*, where even the object of the gaze is enjoined to "look," as if only by looking at himself being looked at can he fully be interpellated as the other whom this scene labors to produce.

In reading the relation of race and sexuality in *Giovanni's Room*, it may be useful to consider the somewhat different ways Baldwin frames sexuality and race elsewhere. Although his observation on the blindness of the "American optic"—as a discourse "based on the necessity of keeping black people out" except on "their terms"—remains true if the word "gay" is substituted for "black," Baldwin does not, for the most part, imagine sexual identity as symmetrical with racial identity. Race is essential, communal, and public, whereas sexuality is contingent, individual, and private. Asked in a 1984 interview with Richard Goldstein about the meaning of writing homosexuality "publicly," Baldwin said, "I made a public announcement that we're private, if you see what I mean" (175). The act of publicly announcing one's privacy, something of a contradiction in terms, suits Baldwin's vision of homosexuality as an identity that is not properly an identity, a "we" that cannot be adequately named. Saying of the term *gay*, that "I was never at home in it," Baldwin echoes David's confession that he was "never at home" in his father's house (qtd. in Goldstein 174). His response construes homosexuality, however "private," as that which can only aspire to the status of "home" and, associating homosexuality with the failure of "home" and the failure of identity, seems to return "gay" to the "unacceptable terms" of dominant representation.

Giovanni's Room and other passing narratives, however, counter Baldwin's published remarks on race and sexuality; they suggest instead that both racial identity and sexual identity always rest on "passing," and they reveal the often brutalizing consequences of attempts by the dominant culture to deny identity's contingency. In the world of the novel, "true" identity is radically inaccessible: one can never not pass, just as one can never go home, for both homeland and identity are revealed as retrospectively constructed fantasies. Like the binary logic of "coming out," passing can suggest an hypostatized opposition, but it also marks "race" and "sexuality" as fictions of identity. As Henry Louis Gates Jr. writes, "Race has become the trope of ultimate, irreducible difference . . . because it is so very arbitrary in its application" ("Writing 'Race'" 5). Race is, however, not the only trope of difference: despite the ways in which racial and sexual identities are differently constituted, policed, and performed, both homosexuality and heterosexuality are themselves tropes of difference that, not despite but because of their arbitrariness, wield enormous social power. If difference is a trope and if the distinction that is supposed to exist before comes into being only after the naming of identity, passing is not a false copy of true identity but an imitation of which, to borrow Judith Butler's account of gender, "there is no original" (*Gender Trouble* 25).

To unfold more fully the relation of identity to passing and nostalgia, I'd like to return to some ways in which the tropes of passing in *Giovanni's Room,* as in Johnson's *The Autobiography of an Ex-Coloured Man,* Jessie Redmon Fauset's *Plum Bun,* and Larsen's *Passing,* speak to identity's essential difference from itself. Such novels, clearly engaged with issues of race, community, and what we would now call identity politics, have to varying degrees been read as denouncing imposture and defending "original" or "true" identity. In Larsen's novel, Mary Helen Washington writes, " 'Passing' is an obscene form of salvation" (164). If passing, that is, for Larsen provides no "salvation" at all, it appears "obscene" in threatening the negation of identity and in transgressing the boundaries that constitute "truth" or meaning in opposition to the abject, the meaningless. As a figure, passing insists that the "truth" of racial identity, indeed of identity as such, relies on the presence or possibility of the false. Yet passing is not simply performance or theatricality, the pervasive tropes of recent work on sex and gender identity, nor is it parody or pastiche, for it seeks to erase, rather than expose, its own dissimulation.[6] Passing, in other words, is only successful passing: unlike drag, its "performance" so impeccably mimics "reality" that it goes undetected as performance, framing its resistance to essentialism in the very rhetoric of essence and origin.[7]

To *pass* for is, according to the *OED,* "to be taken for, to be accepted, received, or held in repute as. Often with the implication of being something else." This formulation, flat and uninflected as it is, executes a sort of turn in a phrase that sounds like a redundancy: "Often with the implication of being something else." Here "being" or essence, the stuff of "true" identity, is reduced to, or endowed with, the status of "something else." Passing, however, must be understood as double: the gesture that can uncannily make what we think we know of "race" and "sexuality" into "something else" also represents the reversal of "being" and seeming that causes the dominant culture's self-presentation to be "accepted" as the natural. Passing, then, exerts rhetorical or political force not primarily as the betrayal that must be disavowed for an oppressed group to claim its own essential identity but as a betrayal of "identity" that offers one way of reading the production of the dominant culture's own identifications.

In matters of race as well as sexuality, passing both invokes and unravels the logic of primary and secondary, authenticity and inauthenticity, candor and duplicity, by placing in question the priority of what is claimed as "true" identity. The discourse of racial passing reveals the arbitrary foundation of the categories "black" and "white," just as passing across gender and sexuality places in question the meaning of "masculine" and "feminine," "straight" and "gay." Racial passing is thus subject to an epistemological ambiguity; from the beginning, the discourse of passing contains an implicit critique of "identity" precisely because what constitutes "the beginning" of identity remains in question. Born into passing, Frances Harper's mulatto heroine in *Iola Leroy* is raised as a white child without the knowledge that her mother is black or that she is, in the eyes of the law, a slave of her father, whereas Johnson's *Autobiography of an Ex-Coloured Man* relates the disjunction between the narrator's childhood experience of himself as white and the eventual revelation of his "true" race, whose definition is enforced by white juridical authority.[8] Such texts' most salient question is the possibility or impossibility of predicating both identity and "politics" on a racial subject who stands before culture, before community, and before a relation to passing. But they also ask whether the law is not itself passing when it plays the role of authority so effectively that its own dissimulation or contingency is erased.

To recognize the masquerade of "natural" identity is also to reveal the unnaturalness of what the dominant culture would have us most take for granted: the ontological status of heterosexuality and whiteness. The rhetoric of passing brings into relief the inauthenticity of "authentic" identity by bringing to the fore the passing of heterosexuality and of whiteness as themselves—which is to say, the contingency at the heart of identity that engenders, in the dominant culture, endless attempts to naturalize its own position by positing the inauthenticity or secondariness of what it will construe as its others.[9] As Baldwin himself has suggested in a published conversation, the constitution of the deviant or marginal subject is the paradigmatic gesture through which the subject position of the dominant culture is defined: "People invent categories in order to feel safe: White people invented black people to give white people identity. . . . Straight cats invented faggots so they could sleep with them without becoming faggots themselves" (Baldwin and Giovanni 88–89). That is, the white or straight world invents its other in order to recognize itself, making the "inauthentic" define the authentic. The instability of heterosexuality and whiteness is projected onto, and reified in, the passing subject, people of color, and gay men and lesbians, all of whom constitute what Judith Butler, in her reading of homosexuality and miscegenation in Larsen's *Passing*, calls the "constitutive outside" of regimes of sexual and racial purity (*Bodies That Matter* 167).

If passing, then, invokes origins only to displace origins, the passing of the law itself is manifest in its nostalgia for a point of origin that, in fact, it has never known. This nostalgia takes shape, both in *Giovanni's Room* and in other discourses of race and sexuality, not only in terms of home and displacement but in terms of retrospection and the past. Like David's nationalistic fantasy of his American homeland, subjectivity—and the various identificatory mechanisms by which we recognize ourselves as subjects—is always a story told from the vantage point of the present and projected into the past, where it gains the status of an origin. In order to think further about nostalgia, I'd like to return to some ways in which metalepsis, the displacement of the secondary into the site of the primary, has been imagined in recent criticism. While the deconstructive logic of these readings is no doubt familiar, they make it possible to trace more clearly the politics of a certain cultural nostalgia in relation to the retroactive construction of individual subjectivity.

Judith Butler has persuasively described the construction of the subject "before the law" by the very agency of the law, whose part in that history is retroactively erased: "the law produces and then conceals the notion of a 'subject before the law' in order to invoke that discursive formation as a naturalized foundational premise that subsequently legitimates the law's own regulatory hegemony" (*Gender Trouble* 2).[10] As in Kafka's story of the same name, Butler's "before the law" at once suggests a space prior to juridical discipline and the very space organized under that discipline. To recognize such retrospective projections of the dominant culture, Butler cautions, is not enough if oppositional projects will also subscribe to a politics of representation that assumes a priori an essential sameness among its constituents; nor is it productive for coalitional or "representational" politics to decide in advance what the contours of their coalitions will be and thus to invent, through "description," the constituency they come to represent.[11] Metalepsis is thus centrally a part of the ways we imagine politics as such and the ways that both hegemonic and oppositional institutions take shape; but no less "political" is the nostalgia of the subject within the symbolic—indeed, nostalgia articulates the relationship of social law to psychological subject.

Insofar as it is anchored by proleptic and retrospective projections, political "identity" comes to resemble subjectivity as Lacan understands it. Having suffered a splitting of self or loss of a presence-to-himself as a result of his entrance into the symbolic order, the subject confronts a "radical fissure, and a subjective impasse, because the subject is called on to face in it the lack through which he is constituted" (*Feminine Sexuality* 116). Unable ever to face its own constitutive lack, culture itself, not unlike the Lacanian subject, attempts to "cover over" or deny lack by positing an origin, a "before." Thus the pre-Oedipal state is produced as a site of wholeness, multiplicity, or indifferentiation—as the outside of the symbolic—only within the symbolic order, by whose agency we are able retrospectively to posit the pre-Oedipal as the prediscursive realm. And yet, for Lacan, the subject owes as much to anticipation as to retrospection: the mirror stage depends on the projected image in which the child misrecognizes himself in a proleptic fantasy of his future bodily wholeness and assumes, as "the armour of an alienating identity," the template or "rigid structure" that determines subjectivity ever after (*Écrits* 4).

Just as the image of the fragmented body that precedes the mirror stage can be only metaleptically imagined, even beyond the mirror stage, as Jane Gallop notes, individual subjectivity is thoroughly indebted to projections into the past and future: it is "a succession of future perfects, pasts of a future, moments twice removed from 'present reality' by the combined action of an anticipation and a retroaction" (82). That is, the effect of identity's coherence is generated in part by endless reference to an irrecoverable origin, an *elsewhere*. If nostalgia, like passing, gestures toward an absent "something else," it does so not to displace but to locate and confirm individual or institutional "identity." Thus what Susan Stewart has called "the social disease of nostalgia" designates not an aberration in society but the disease of the social as such, the enabling "disease" or condition that, by looking backward, allows culture to progress or persist (23).

The nostalgia of the social works to vivify, and is in turn represented by, the particular desires of individuals: in *Giovanni's Room*, David's longed-for home in American heterosexual ideology is, like identity itself, revealed to be deeply nostalgic, retroactively produced as an origin from a position of belatedness and lack. The object of David's desire exists only in fantasy, as Giovanni recognizes: "you will go home and then you will find that home is not home anymore. Then you will really be in trouble. As long as you stay here, you can always think: One day I will go home" (*GR* 154–55). "Home" becomes possible only after identity and the possibility of meaning are recognized as lost, when the contingency of the origin is erased by nostalgia and "home" is naturalized as an object of desire. As a condition of desire that, as Gallop says of the image of "the body in bits and pieces," the *corps morcelé* "comes after . . . so as to represent what came before*" (80), the nostalgia designated in Baldwin's novel by "homesickness" does not so much represent a disturbance of desire as the fate of all subjects within the symbolic order. Nostalgia, "a desire constitutively unsatisfied and unsatisfiable because its 'object' simply cannot ever be defined," becomes a fundamental condition of subjectivity— and of culture (Gallop 151). More than a retroactive effect, nostalgia is an effect which, unable to name what it experiences as lost, can only misrecognize the object it desires, for although its etymology refers back to *nostos*, or return, Gallop notes, nostalgia is a "transgression of return: a desire ungrounded in a past, desire for an object that has never been 'known'" (151). In racist and homophobic discourse, the "desire for an object that has never been known" is the desire for the coherence of whiteness or heterosexuality, an impossible ideal that nevertheless must be sustained if dominant culture is to "reproduce" itself, as Butler recognizes, as distinct from its "constitutive outside."

To name this effect "nostalgia" is to suggest as well the pathos that colors its backward glance—a pathos that may mean the masking or misrecognition of the more coercive aspects of the ideology "home" represents. It means, too, the misrecognition of identity as such figured not only in Lacan's mirror stage but in Baldwin's: when David examines his reflection in the first page of *Giovanni's Room*, his misrecognition of himself *as* self, however problematic his whiteness and straightness have and will become, seems the precondition of speech, even the precondition of narrative. David's desire to return to America is insistent and deeply felt, but as the novel's brutal conclusion suggests, nostalgia and violence go hand in hand as inseparable aspects of the positing and policing of identity. That is, nostalgia's inevitability in no way means its effects are symmetrical, for it is precisely the nonidentity of the white, bourgeois, heterosexual culture that David represents in *Giovanni's Room* that must be phobically projected onto an other who, like Giovanni, will bear the burden of that nostalgia even to his death.

Baldwin's ambivalent revision of the passing novel both exposes, through David, the operations of nostalgia and trades on a pathos of lost origins. As Baldwin observes in *Giovanni's Room*, agency and self-consciousness are never fully ours: the effect of identity continually and repetitively produced by the subject to recognize itself as a subject is imbued with the pathos of David's misrecognition of his own agency and subjectivity. "Nobody can stay in the garden of Eden," Jacques says, after the news of Giovanni's sentencing, "I wonder why." David thinks: "Perhaps everybody has a garden of Eden, I don't know; but they have scarcely seen their garden before they see the flaming sword. Then, perhaps, life offers only the choice of remembering the garden or forgetting it. Either, or: it takes strength to remember, it takes another kind of strength to forget, it takes a hero to do both" (35–36). The allusion to prelapsarian bliss appropriately represents the subject prior to the imposition of the law and the symbolic order; indeed, as Gallop has noted, Lacan's account of the mirror stage is the story of a "paradise lost" (85).[12] Just as we can understand Eden only in the language of exile, we can imagine pre-Oedipal presence only in the Oedipalized language of lack. If Eden, in this particular myth of origin, is a paradigmatic home, whether the original heterosexual household or the short-lived pleasures of Giovanni's room, it is, Baldwin suggests, always already lost. The "either, or"—to remember Eden or to forget—is, as *Giovanni's Room* makes clear, no choice at all, for to remember is to engage in a nostalgic gesture that, to posit home as the originary site of identity, must simultaneously erase its retrospective construction, and to forget is to accept the nonexistence of this Eden—or, if you will, identity—a renunciation the subject can never wholly make. Thus each decision, and each performance of identity, is necessarily a double bind: David is condemned never to remember or forget Giovanni, never to get "home" or give it up.

It is easy enough, perhaps all too easy, to say that the answer to the question of identity politics is a politics of identity that insists on the contingency of identity. Such a politics, taking its cue from the discourse of passing, might seek to de-essentialize "identity" so as not to impose, through anticipation or retrospection, an illusionary and exclusionary coherence on those it "represents" and in order not to accede in its own right to the logic of the dominant culture. Yet what Baldwin's novel brings home to us most forcefully and most poignantly is the danger not only of the exercise of nostalgia but also of the fantasy that one can ever escape it. No less than the desire for an impossible return, the denial of nostalgia is itself nostalgic, for the ending of nostalgia and the accomplishment of placement is precisely the impossible object that nostalgia forever pursues. No politics, then, can ever fully overcome the passing or impersonation of its own identity or disavow the nostalgia that sustains subjectivity in the imaginary. Instead, a "politics"—which is to say, a reading—of "race" and "sexuality" might work to uncover the constitutive nostalgia of the dominant culture, for about the notions of passing, nostalgia, and desire whose effects *Giovanni's Room* traces, there is still a great deal to be said.

Notes

Parts of this essay were presented, in substantially different forms, at Tufts University in 1990 and at the Fifth Annual Lesbian and Gay Studies Conference at Rutgers University in 1991. I would like to thank Bonnie Burns, Lee Edelman, and Annamaria Formichella for their generous advice and support.

1. For a reading of racial and sexual passing in Larsen, see the essay by Cutter in this collection. See also Deborah McDowell's "Introduction" to *Quicksand* and *Passing* and Blackmore, " 'That Unreasonable Restless Feeling': The Homosexual Subtexts of Nella Larsen's *Passing*." Cheryl Wall discusses passing in relation to gender in "Passing for What? Aspects of Identity in Nella Larsen's Novels."

2. Baldwin, *Giovanni's Room* 7. All further quotations from this novel will be from the Dell edition (1988) and will be cited in the text as *GR*.

3. See Riviere, "Womanliness as Masquerade," and Judith Butler's discussion of Riviere and the performance of gender in *Gender Trouble* 24–25, 50–57.

4. On Baldwin and Henry James, see Newman, "The Lesson of the Master: Henry James and James Baldwin."

5. See also Sedgwick's *Epistemology of the Closet*. For further discussion of the legibility of the gay male body, see Edelman, *Homographesis* 5–6.

6. In addition to Butler's work on performativity in *Gender Trouble*, see also Sedgwick's "Queer Performativity: Henry James's *The Art of the Novel*."

7. Marjorie Garber describes gender passing as "a social and sartorial inscription which encodes (as treason does) its own erasure" (234). For a concise formulation of the relation of drag to passing, see also Robinson, "It Takes One to Know One" 727.

8. The title of *The Autobiography of an Ex-Coloured Man* suggests that the man in question is originally "coloured," although the narrative begins with his perception of himself as a white child. See the discussion of this novel by Kawash in this collection.

9. For a useful discussion of the construction of racial hegemony, in which passing figures as "a model for the cultural production of whiteness," see Mullen, "Optic White" 72–74.

10. Whether the "nonhistorical 'before'" is invoked by the dominant culture or by feminists, Butler argues, its effect is conservative.

11. See Butler, *Gender Trouble*, on the contingency of gender (38) and the anticipatory logic of political coalitions (14).

12. On nostalgia and the prelapsarian, see also Stewart, *On Longing* 23. Lee Edelman offers an incisive reading of identity, narcissism, and *Paradise Lost* in *Homographesis* 101–04.

Passing for White, Passing for Black

ADRIAN PIPER

*J*t was the new graduate student reception for my class, the first social event of my first semester in the best graduate department in my field in the country. I was full of myself, as we all were, full of pride at having made the final cut, full of arrogance at our newly recorded membership among the privileged few, the intellectual elite—this country's real aristocracy, my parents told me—full of confidence in our intellectual ability to prevail, to fashion original and powerful views about some topic we represented to ourselves only vaguely. I was a bit late and noticed that many turned to look at—no, scrutinize—me as I entered the room. I congratulated myself on having selected for wear my black velvet, bell-bottom pants suit (yes, it was that long ago) with the cream silk blouse and crimson vest. One of the secretaries who'd earlier helped me find an apartment came forward to greet me and proceeded to introduce me to various members of the faculty, eminent and honorable faculty, with names I knew from books I'd studied intensely and heard discussed with awe and reverence by my undergraduate teachers. To be in the presence of these men and attach faces to names was delirium enough. But actually to enter into casual social conversation with them took every bit of poise I had. As often happens in such situations, I went on automatic pilot. I don't remember what I said; I suppose I managed not to make a fool of myself. The most famous and highly respected member of the faculty observed me for awhile from a distance and then came forward. Without introduction or preamble he said to me with a triumphant smirk, "Miss Piper, you're about as black as I am."

One of the benefits of automatic pilot in social situations is that insults take longer to make themselves felt. The meaning of the words simply don't register right away, particularly if the person who utters them is smiling. You reflexively respond to the social context and the smile rather than to the words. And so I automatically returned the smile and said something like, "Really? I hadn't known that about you"—something that sounded both innocent and impertinent, even though that was not what I felt. What I felt was numb, and then shocked and terrified, disoriented, as though I'd been awakened from a sweet dream of unconditional support and approval and plunged into a nightmare of jeering contempt. Later those feelings turned into wrenching grief and anger that one of my intellectual heroes had sullied himself in my presence and destroyed my illusion that these privileged surroundings were benevolent and safe; then guilt and remorse at having provided him the occasion for doing so.

Finally, there was the groundless shame of the inadvertent impostor, exposed to public ridicule or accusation. For this kind of shame, you don't actually need to have done anything wrong. All you need to do is care about others' image of you, and fail in your actions to reinforce their positive image of themselves. Their ridicule and accusations then function to both disown and degrade you from their status, to mark you not as having *done* wrong but as *being* wrong. This turns you into something bogus relative to their criterion of worth, and false relative to their criterion of authenticity. Once exposed as a fraud of this kind, you can never regain your legitimacy. For the violated criterion of legitimacy implicitly presumes an absolute incompatibility between the person you appeared to be and the person you are now revealed to be; and no fraud has the authority to convince her accusers that they merely imagine an incompatibility where there is none in fact. The devaluation of status consequent on such exposure is, then, absolute, and the suspicion of fraudulence spreads to all areas of interaction.

> Mr. S. looked sternly at Mrs. P., and with an imperious air said, "You a colored woman? You're no negro. Where did you come from? If you're a negro, where are your free papers to show it?" . . . As he went away he looked at Mr. Hill and said, "She's no negro." — The Rev. H. Mattison, *Louisa Picquet, The Octoroon Slave and Concubine: A Tale of Southern Slave Life*

The accusation was one I had heard before, but more typically from other blacks. My family was one of the very last middle-class, light-skinned black families left in our Harlem neighborhood after most had fled to the suburbs; visibly black working-class kids my age yanked my braids and called me "paleface." Many of them thought I was white, and treated me accordingly. As an undergraduate in the late 1960s and early

1970s, I attended an urban university to which I walked daily through a primarily black working-class neighborhood. Once a black teenage youth called to me, "Hey, white girl! Give me a quarter!" I was feeling strong that day, so I retorted, "I'm not white and I don't have a quarter!" He answered skeptically, "You sure look white! You sure act white!" And I have sometimes met blacks socially who, as a condition of social acceptance of me, require me to prove my blackness by passing the Suffering Test: They recount at length their recent experiences of racism and then wait expectantly, skeptically, for me to match theirs with mine. Mistaking these situations for a different one in which an exchange of shared experiences is part of the bonding process, I instinctively used to comply. But I stopped when I realized that I was in fact being put through a third degree. I would share some equally nightmarish experience along similar lines, and would then have it explained to me why that wasn't really so bad, why it wasn't the same thing at all, or why I was stupid for allowing it to happen to me. So the aim of these conversations clearly was not mutual support or commiseration. That came only after I managed to prove myself by passing the Suffering Test of blackness (if I did), usually by shouting down or destroying my acquaintance's objections with logic.

> The white kids would call me a Clorox coon baby and all kinds of names I don't want to repeat. And the black kids hated me. "Look at her," they'd say. "She think she white. She think she cute."—Elaine Perry, *Another Present Era*

These exchanges are extremely alienating and demoralizing, and make me feel humiliated to have presumed a sense of connectedness between us. They also give me insight into the way whites feel when they are made the circumstantial target of blacks' justified and deep-seated anger. Because the anger is justified, one instinctively feels guilty. But because the target is circumstantial and sometimes arbitrary, one's sense of fairness is violated. One feels both unjustly accused or harassed, and also remorseful and ashamed at having been the sort of person who could have provoked the accusation.

As is true for blacks' encounters with white racism, there are at least two directions in which one's reactions can take one here. One can react defensively and angrily, and distill the encounter into slow-burning fuel for one's racist stereotypes. Or one can detach oneself emotionally and distance oneself physically from the aggressors, from this perspective their personal flaws and failures of vision, insight, and sensitivity loom larger, making it easier to forgive them for their human imperfections but harder to relate to them as equals. Neither reaction is fully adequate to the situation, since the first projects exaggerated fantasies onto the aggressor, while the second diminishes his responsibility. I have experienced both, toward both blacks and whites. I believe that the perceptual and cognitive distortions that characterize any form of racism begin here, in the failure to see any act of racist aggression as a defensive response to one's own perceived attack on the aggressor's physical or psychological property, or conception of himself or of the world. Once you see this, you may feel helpless to be anything other than who you are, anything or anyone who could resolve the discord. But at least it restores a sense of balance and mutually flawed humanity to the interaction.

My maternal cousin, who resembles Michelle Pfeiffer, went through adolescence in the late 1960s and had a terrible time. She tried perming her hair into an Afro; it didn't prevent attacks and ridicule from her black peers for not being "black enough." She adopted a black working-class dialect that made her almost unintelligible to her very proper, very middle-class parents, and counted among her friends young people who criticized high scholastic achievers for "acting white." That is, she ran the same gauntlet I did, but of a more intense variety and at a much younger age. But she emerged intact, with a sharp and practical intellect, an endearing attachment to stating difficult truths bluntly, a dry sense of humor, and little tolerance for those blacks who, she feels, forgo the hard work of self-improvement and initiative for the imagined benefits of victim status. Now married to a WASP musician from Iowa, she is one tough cookie, leavened by the rejection she experienced from those with whom she has always proudly identified.

In my experience, these rejections almost always occur with blacks of working-class background who do not have extended personal experience with the very wide range of variation in skin color, hair texture, and facial features that in fact has always existed among African Americans, particularly in the middle class. Because light-skinned blacks often received some education or training apprenticeships during slavery, there tend to be more of us in the middle class now. Until my family moved out of Harlem when I was fourteen, my social contacts were almost exclusively with upper-middle-class white schoolmates and working-class black neighborhood playmates, both of whom made me feel equally alienated from both races. It wasn't until college and after that I reencountered the middle- and upper-middle-class blacks who were as comfortable with my appearance as my family had been, and who made me feel as comfortable and accepted by them as my family had.

So Suffering Test exchanges almost never occur with middle-class blacks, who are more likely to protest, on the contrary, that "we always knew you were black!"—as though there were some mysterious and inchoate essence of blackness that only other blacks have the antennae to detect.

> "There are niggers who are as white as I am, but the taint of blood is there and we always exclude it."
> "How do you know it is there?" asked Dr. Gresham.
> "Oh, there are tricks of blood which always betray them. My eyes are more practiced than yours. I can always tell them."
> —Frances E. W. Harper, *Iola Leroy, or Shadows Uplifted*

When made by other blacks, these remarks function on some occasions to reassure me of my acceptance within the black community, and on others to rebuke me for pretending to indistinguishability from whiteness. But in either case they wrongly presuppose, as did my eminent professor's accusation, an essentializing stereotype into which all blacks must fit. In fact no blacks, and particularly no African American blacks, fit any such stereotype.

My eminent professor was one of only two whites I have ever met who questioned my designated racial identity to my face. The other was a white woman junior professor, relatively new to the department, who, when I went on the job market at the end of graduate school, summoned me to her office and grilled me as to why I identified myself as black and exactly what fraction of African ancestry I had. The implicit accusation behind both my professors' remarks was, of course, that I had fraudulently posed as black in order to take advantage of the department's commitment to affirmative action. It's an extraordinary idea, when you think about it: as though someone would willingly shoulder the stigma of being black in a racist society for the sake of a little extra professional consideration that guarantees nothing but suspicions of foul play and accusations of cheating. But it demonstrates just how irrationally far the suspicion of fraudulence can extend.

In fact I had always identified myself as black (or "colored" as we said before 1967). But fully comprehending what it meant to be black took a long time. My acculturation into the white upper-middle class started with nursery school when I was four, and was largely uneventful. For my primary and secondary schooling my parents sent me to a progressive prep school, one of the first to take the goal of integration seriously as more than an ideal. They gave me ballet lessons, piano lessons, art lessons, tennis lessons. In the 1950s and early 1960s they sent me to integrated summer camps where we sang "We Shall Overcome" around the campfire long before it became the theme song of the civil rights movement.

Of course there were occasional, usually veiled incidents, such as the time in preadolescence when the son of a prominent union leader (and my classmate) asked me to go steady and I began to receive phone calls from his mother, drunk, telling me how charming she thought it that her son was going out with a little colored girl. And the time the daughter of a well-known playwright, also a classmate, brought me home to her family and asked them to guess whether I was black or white, and shared a good laugh with them when they guessed wrong. But I was an only child in a family of four adults devoted to creating for me an environment in which my essential worth and competence never came into question. I used to think my parents sheltered me in this way because they believed, idealistically, that my education and achievements would then protect me from the effects of racism. I now know that they did so to provide me with an invincible armor of self-worth with which to fight it. It almost worked. I grew up not quite grasping the fact that my racial identity was a disadvantage. This lent heat to my emerging political conviction that of course it shouldn't be a disadvantage, for me or anyone else, and finally fueled my resolution not to allow it to be a disadvantage if I had anything at all to say about it.

> I will live down the prejudice, I will crush it out . . . the thoughts of the
> ignorant and prejudiced will not concern me. . . . I will show to the world

that a man may spring from a race of slaves, yet far excel many of the boasted ruling race. — Charles W. Chesnutt, *Journals*

But the truth in my professors' accusations was that I had, in fact, resisted my parents' suggestion that, just this once, for admission to this most prestigious of graduate programs, I decline to identify my racial classification on the graduate admissions application, so that it could be said with certainty that I'd been admitted on the basis of merit alone. "But that would be passing," I protested. Although both of my parents had watched many of their relatives disappear permanently into the white community, passing for white was unthinkable within the branches of my father's and mother's families to which I belonged. That would have been a really, authentically shameful thing to do.

> "It seems as if the prejudice pursues us through every avenue of life, and assigns us the lowest places. . . . And yet I am determined," said Iola, "to win for myself a place in the fields of labor. I have heard of a place in New England, and I mean to try for it, even if I only stay a few months."
>
> "Well, if you will go, say nothing about your color."
>
> "Uncle Robert, I see no necessity for proclaiming that fact on the house-top. Yet I am resolved that nothing shall tempt me to deny it. The best blood in my veins is African blood, and I am not ashamed of it."
> — Harper, *Iola Leroy*

And besides, I reasoned to myself, to be admitted under the supposition that I was white would *not* be to be admitted on the basis of merit alone. Why undermine my chances of admission by sacrificing my one competitive advantage when I already lacked not only the traditionally acceptable race and gender attributes, but also alumni legacy status, an Ivy League undergraduate pedigree, the ability to pay full tuition or endow the university, war veteran status, professional sports potential, and a distinguished family name? I knew I could ace the program if I could just get my foot in the damn door.

Later, when I experienced the full force of the racism of the academy, one of my graduate advisors, who had remained a continuing source of support and advice after I took my first job, consoled me by informing me that the year I completed the program I had, in fact, tied one other student for the highest grade point average in my class. He was a private and dignified man of great integrity and subtle intellect, someone who I had always felt was quietly rooting for me. It was not until after his death that I began to appreciate what a compassionate and radical gesture he had made in telling me this. For by this time, I very much needed to be reminded that neither was I incompetent nor my work worthless, that I could achieve the potential I felt myself to have. My choice not to pass for white in order to gain entry to the academy, originally made out of naiveté, had resulted in more punishment than I would have imagined possible.

It wasn't only the overt sexual and racial harassment, each of which exacerbated the other, or the gratuitous snipes about my person, my life-style, or my work. What was even more insulting were the peculiar strategies deployed to make me feel accepted and understood despite the anomalies of my appearance, by individuals whose racism was so profound that this would have been an impossible task: the WASP colleague who attempted to establish rapport with me by making anti-Semitic jokes about the prevalence of Jews in the neighborhood of the university; the colleague who first inquired in detail into my marital status, and then attempted to demonstrate his understanding of my decision not to have children by speculating that I was probably concerned that they would turn out darker than I was; the colleague who consulted me on the analysis of envy and resentment, reasoning that since I was black I must know all about it; the colleague who, in my first department faculty meeting, made a speech to his colleagues discussing the research that proved that a person could be black without looking it.

These incidents and others like them had a peculiar cognitive feel to them, as though the individuals involved felt driven to make special efforts to situate me in their conceptual mapping of the world, not only by naming or indicating the niche in which they felt I belonged, but by seeking my verbal confirmation of it. I have learned to detect advance warnings that these incidents are imminent. The person looks at me with a fixed stare, her tension level visibly rising. Like a thermostat, when the tension reaches a certain level, the mechanism switches on: out comes some comment or action, often of an offensive personal nature, that attempts to locate me within the rigid confines of her stereotype of black people. I have not experienced this phenomenon outside the academic context. Perhaps it's a degenerate form of hypothesis testing, an unfortunate side effect of the quest for knowledge.

> She walked away. . . . The man followed her and tapped her shoulder.
> "Listen, I'd really like to get to know you," he said, smiling. He paused, as if expecting thanks from her. She didn't say anything. Flustered, he said, "A friend of mine says you're black. I told him I had to get a close-up look and see for myself."
> —Perry, *Another Present Era*

The irony was that I could have taken an easier entry route into this privileged world. In fact, on my graduate admissions application I could have claimed alumni legacy status and the distinguished family name of my paternal great uncle, who not only had attended that university and sent his sons there, but had endowed one of its buildings and was commemorated with an auditorium in his name. I did not because he belonged to a branch of the family from which we had been estranged for decades, even before my grandfather—his brother—divorced my grandmother, moved to another part of the country, and started another family. My father wanted nothing more to do with my grandfather or any of his relatives. He rejected his inheritance and never discussed them while he was alive. For me to have invoked his uncle's name in order to gain a professional advantage would have been out of the question. But it would have nullified my eminent professor's need to tell me who and what he thought I was.

Recently I saw my great uncle's portrait on an airmail stamp honoring him as a captain of industry. He looked so much like family photos of my grandfather and father that I went out and bought two sheets worth of these stamps. He had my father's and grandfather's aquiline nose and their determined set of the chin. Looking at his face made me want to recover my father's estranged family, particularly my grandfather, for my own. I had a special lead: A few years previously in the South, I'd included a photo-text work containing a fictionalized narrative about my father's family—a history chock-full of romance and psychopathology—in an exhibition of my work. After seeing the show, a white woman with blue eyes, my father's transparent rosy skin and auburn-brown hair, and that dominant family nose walked up to me and told me that we were related. The next day she brought photographs of her family, and information about a relative who kept extensive genealogical records on every family member he could locate. I was very moved, and also astounded that a white person would voluntarily acknowledge blood relation to a black. She was so free and unconflicted about this, I just couldn't fathom it. We corresponded and exchanged family photos. And when I was ready to start delving in earnest, I contacted the relative she had mentioned for information about my grandfather, and initiated correspondence or communication with kin I hadn't known existed and who hadn't known that I existed, or that they or any part of their family was black. I embarked on this with great trepidation, anticipating with anxiety their reaction to the racial identity of these long-lost relatives, picturing in advance the withdrawal of warmth and interest, the quickly assumed impersonality and the suggestion that there must be some mistake.

> The dread that I might lose her took possession of me each time I sought to speak, and rendered it impossible for me to do so. That moral courage requires more than physical courage is no mere poetic fancy. I am sure I should have found it easier to take the place of a gladiator, no matter how fierce the Numidian lion, than to tell that slender girl that I had Negro blood in my veins.—James Weldon Johnson, *The Autobiography of an Ex-Coloured Man*

These fears were not unfounded. My father's sister had, in her youth, been the first black woman at a Seven Sisters undergraduate college and the first at an Ivy League medical school; had married into a white family who became socially, politically, and academically prominent; and then, after taking some family mementos my grandmother had given my father for me, had proceeded to sever all connections with her brothers and their families, even when the death of each of her siblings was imminent. She raised her children (now equally prominent socially and politically) as though they had no maternal relatives at all. We had all been so very proud of her achievements that her repudiation of us was devastating. Yet I frequently encounter mutual friends and colleagues in the circles in which we both travel, and I dread the day we might find ourselves in the same room at the same time. To read or hear about or see on television her or any member of her immediate family is a source of personal pain for all of us. I did not want to subject myself to that again with yet another set of relatives.

> Those who pass have a severe dilemma before they decide to do so, since a person must give up all family ties and loyalties to the black community in order to gain economic and other opportunities.—F. James Davis, *Who Is Black? One Nation's Definition*

Trying to forgive and understand those of my relatives who have chosen to pass for white has been one of the most difficult ethical challenges of my life, and I don't consider myself to have made very much progress. At the most superficial level, this decision can be understood in terms of a cost-benefit analysis: Obviously, they believe they will be happier in the white community than in the black one, all things considered. For me to make sense of this requires that I understand—or at least accept—their conception of happiness as involving higher social status, entrenchment within the white community and corresponding isolation from the black one, and greater access to the rights, liberties, and privileges the white community takes for granted. What is harder for me to grasp is how they could want these things enough to sacrifice the history, wisdom, connectedness, and moral solidarity with their family and community in order to get them. It seems to require so much severing and forgetting, so much disowning and distancing, not simply from one's shared past, but from one's former self—as though one had cauterized one's long-term memory at the moment of entry into the white community.

But there is, I think, more to it than that. Once you realize what is denied you as an African American simply because of your race, your sense of the unfairness of it may be so overwhelming that you may simply be incapable of accepting it. And if you are not inclined toward any form of overt political advocacy, passing in order to get the benefits you know you deserve may seem the only way to defy the system. Indeed, many of my more prominent relatives who are passing have chosen altruistic professions that benefit society on many fronts. They have chosen to use their assumed social status to make returns to the black community indirectly, in effect compensating for the personal advantages they have gained by rejecting their family.

Moreover, your sense of injustice may be compounded by the daily humiliation you experience as the result of identifying with those African Americans who, for demanding their rights, are punished and degraded as a warning to others. In these cases, the decision to pass may be more than the rejection of a black identity. It may be the rejection of a black identification that brings too much pain to be tolerated.

> All the while I understood that it was not discouragement or fear or search for a larger field of action and opportunity that was driving me out of the Negro race. I knew that it was shame, unbearable shame. Shame at being identified with a people that could with impunity be treated worse than animals.—Johnson, *The Autobiography of an Ex-Coloured Man*

The oppressive treatment of African Americans facilitates this distancing response by requiring every African American to draw a sharp distinction between the person he is and the person society perceives him to be—that is, between who he is as an individual, and the way he is designated and treated by others.

> The Negro's only salvation from complete despair lies in his belief, the old belief of his forefathers, that these things are not directed against him personally, but against his race, his pigmentation. His mother or aunt or teacher long ago carefully prepared him, explaining that he as an individual can live in dignity, even though he as a Negro cannot.—John Howard Griffin, *Black Like Me*

This condition encourages a level of impersonality, a sense that white reactions to one have little or nothing to do with one as a person and an individual. Whites often mistake this impersonality for aloofness or unfriendliness. It is just one of the factors that make genuine intimacy between blacks and whites so difficult. Because I have occasionally encountered equally stereotypical treatment from other blacks and have felt compelled to draw the same distinction there between who I am and how I am perceived, my sense of impersonality pervades most social situations in which I find myself. Because I do not enjoy impersonal interactions with others, my solution is to limit my social interactions as far as possible to those in which this restraint is not required. So perhaps it is not entirely surprising that many white-looking individuals of African ancestry are able to jettison this doubly alienated and alienating social identity entirely, as irrelevant to the fully mature and complex individuals they know themselves to be. I take the fervent affirmation and embrace of black identity to be a countermeasure to, and thus evidence of, this alienation, rather than as incompatible with it. My family contains many instances of both attitudes.

There are no proper names mentioned in this account of my family. This is because in the African American community, we do not "out" people who are passing as white in the European-American community. Publicly to expose the African ancestry of someone who claims to have none is not done. There are many reasons for this, and different individuals cite different ones. For one thing, there is the vicarious enjoyment of watching one of our own infiltrate and achieve in a context largely defined by institutionalized attempts to exclude blacks from it. Then there is the question of self-respect: If someone wants to exit the African American community, there are few blacks who would consider it worth their while to prevent her. And then there is the possibility of retaliation: not merely the loss of credibility consequent on the denials by a putatively white person who, in virtue of his racial status, automatically has greater credibility than the black person who calls it into question, but perhaps more deliberate attempts to discredit or undermine the messenger of misfortune. There is also the instinctive impulse to protect the well-being of a fellow traveler embarked on a particularly dangerous and risky course. And finally—the most salient consideration for me, in thinking about those many members of my own family who have chosen to pass for white—a person who desires personal and social advantage and acceptance within the white community so much that she is willing to repudiate her family, past, history, and her personal connections within the African American community in order to get them is someone who is already in so much pain that it's just not possible to do something that you know is going to cause her any more.

Many colored Creoles protect others who are trying to pass, to the point of feigning ignorance of certain branches of their families. Elicited genealogies often seem strangely skewed. In the case of one very good informant, a year passed before he confided in me that his own mother's sister and her children had passed into the white community. With tears in his eyes, he described the painful experience of learning about his aunt's death on the obituary page of the *New Orleans Times-Picayune*. His cousin failed to inform the abandoned side of the family of the death, for fear that they might show up at the wake or the funeral and thereby destroy the image of whiteness. Total separation was necessary for secrecy — Virginia R. Domínguez, *White by Definition: Social Classification in Creole Louisiana*

She said: "It's funny about 'passing.' We disapprove of it and at the same time condone it. It excites our contempt and yet we rather admire it. We shy away from it with an odd kind of revulsion, but we protect it."

"Instinct of the race to survive and expand."

"Rot! Everything can't be explained by some general biological phrase."

"Absolutely everything can. Look at the so-called whites, who've left bastards all over the known earth. Same thing in them. Instinct of the race to survive and expand."

—Nella Larsen, *Passing*

Those of my grandfather's estranged relatives who welcomed me into dialogue instead of freezing me out brought tears of gratitude and astonishment to my eyes. They seemed so kind and interested, so willing to help. At first I couldn't accept for what it was their easy acceptance and willingness to help me puzzle out where exactly we each were located in our sprawling family tree. It is an ongoing endeavor, full of guesswork, false leads, blank spots, and mysteries. For just as white Americans are largely ignorant of their African — usually maternal — ancestry, we blacks are often ignorant of our European — usually paternal — ancestry. That's the way our slave-master forebears wanted it, and that's the way it is. Our names are systematically missing from the genealogies and public records of most white families, and crucial information — for example, the family name or name of the child's father — is often missing from our black ancestors' birth certificates, when they exist at all.

A realistic appreciation of the conditions which exist when women are the property of men makes the conclusion inevitable that there were many children born of mixed parentage.—Joe Gray Taylor, *Negro Slavery in Louisiana*

Ownership of the female slave on the plantations generally came to include owning her sex life. Large numbers of white boys were socialized to associate physical and emotional pleasure with the black women who nursed and raised them, and then to deny any deep feelings for them. From other white males they learned to see black girls and women as legitimate objects of sexual desire. Rapes occurred, and many slave women were forced to submit regularly to white males or suffer harsh consequences. . . . As early as the time of the American Revolution there were plantation slaves who appeared to be completely white, as many of the founding fathers enslaved their own mixed children and grandchildren. —Davis, *Who Is Black?*

So tracing the history of my family is detective work as well as historical research. To date, what I *think* I know is that our first European-American ancestor landed in Ipswich, Massachusetts, in 1620 from Sussex; another in Jamestown, Virginia, in 1675 from London; and another in Philadelphia, Pennsylvania, in 1751, from Hamburg. Yet another was the first in our family to graduate from my own graduate institution in 1778. My great-great-grandmother from Madagascar, by way of Louisiana, is the known African ancestor on my father's side, as my great-great-grandfather from the Ibo of Nigeria is the known African ancestor on my mother's, whose family has resided in Jamaica for three centuries.

I relate these facts and it doesn't seem to bother my newly discovered relatives. At first I had to wonder whether this ease of acceptance was not predicated on their mentally bracketing the implications of these facts and restricting their own immediate family ancestry to the European side. But when they remarked unselfconsciously on the family resemblances between us, I had to abandon that supposition. I still marvel at their enlightened and uncomplicated friendliness, and there is a part of me that still can't trust their acceptance of me. But that is a part of me I want neither to trust nor to accept in this context. I want to reserve my vigilance for its context of origin: the other white Americans I have encountered—even

the bravest and most conscientious white scholars—for whom the suggestion that they might have significant African ancestry as the result of this
country's long history of miscegenation is almost impossible to consider
seriously.

> She's heard the arguments, most astonishingly that, statistically, . . . the
> average white American is 6 percent black. Or, put another way, 95 percent
> of white Americans are 5 to 80 percent black. Her Aunt Tyler has told her
> stories about these whites researching their roots in the National Archives
> and finding they've got an African-American or two in the family, some
> becoming so hysterical they have to be carried out by paramedics.—Perry,
> *Another Present Era*

> Estimates ranging up to 5 percent, and suggestions that up to one-fifth of
> the white population have some genes from black ancestors, are probably
> far too high. If these last figures were correct, the majority of Americans
> with some black ancestry would be known and counted as whites!—Davis,
> *Who is Black?*

The detailed biological and genetic data can be gleaned from a careful
review of *Genetic Abstracts* from about 1950 on. In response to my request
for information about this, a white biological anthropologist once performed detailed calculations on the African admixture of five different
genes, comparing British whites, American whites, and American blacks.
The results ranged from 2 percent in one gene to 81.6 percent in another.
About these results he commented, "I continue to believe five percent to
be a reasonable estimate, but the matter is obviously complex. As you can
see, it depends entirely on which genes you decide to use as racial 'markers' that are supposedly subject to little or no relevant selective pressure."
Clearly, white resistance to the idea that most American whites have a
significant percentage of African ancestry increases with the percentage
suggested.

> "Why, Doctor," said Dr. Latimer, "you Southerners began this absorption
> before the war. I'understand that in one decade the mixed bloods rose
> from one-ninth to one-eighth of the population, and that as early as 1663 a
> law was passed in Maryland to prevent English women from intermarry-

ing with slaves; and, even now, your laws against miscegenation presuppose that you apprehend danger from that source."—Harper, *Iola Leroy*

(That legislators and judges paid increasing attention to the regulation and punishment of miscegenation at this time does not mean that interracial sex and marriage as social practices actually increased in frequency; the centrality of these practices to legal discourse was instead a sign that their relation to power was changing. The extent of uncoerced miscegenation before this period is a debated issue.)—Eva Saks, "Representing Miscegenation Law," *Raritan*

The fact is, however, that the longer a person's family has lived in this country, the higher the probable percentage of African ancestry that person's family is likely to have—bad news for the DAR, I'm afraid. And the proximity to the continent of Africa of the country of origin from which one's forebears emigrated, as well as the colonization of a part of Africa by that country, are two further variables that increase the probability of African ancestry within that family. It would appear that only the Lapps of Norway are safe.

In Jamaica, my mother tells me, that everyone is of mixed ancestry is taken for granted. There are a few who vociferously proclaim themselves to be "Jamaican whites" having no African ancestry at all, but no one among the old and respected families takes them seriously. Indeed, they are assumed to be a bit unbalanced, and are regarded with amusement. In this country, by contrast, the fact of African ancestry among whites ranks up there with family incest, murder, and suicide as one of the bitterest and most difficult pills for white Americans to swallow.

"I had a friend who had two beautiful daughters whom he had educated in the North. They were cultured, and really belles in society. They were entirely ignorant of their lineage, but when their father died it was discovered that their mother had been a slave. It was a fearful blow. They would have faced poverty, but the knowledge of their tainted blood was more than they could bear."—Harper, *Iola Leroy*

There was much apprehension about the unknown amount of black ancestry in the white population of the South, and this was fanned into an unreasoning fear of invisible blackness. For instance, white laundries and cleaners would not accommodate blacks because whites were afraid they would be "contaminated" by the clothing of invisible blacks.—Davis, *Who Is Black?*

Suspicion is part of everyday life in Louisiana. Whites often grow up afraid to know their own genealogies. Many admit that as children they often stared at the skin below their fingernails and through a mirror at the white of their eyes to see if there was any "touch of the tarbrush." Not finding written records of birth, baptism, marriage, or death for any one ancestor exacerbates suspicions of foul play. Such a discovery brings glee to a political enemy or economic rival and may traumatize the individual concerned.—Domínguez, *White by Definition*

A number of years ago I was doing research on a video installation on the subject of racial identity and miscegenation, and came across the Phipps case of Louisiana in the early 1980s. Susie Guillory Phipps had identified herself as white and, according to her own testimony (but not that of some of her black relatives), had believed that she was white, until she applied for a passport, when she discovered that she was identified on her birth records as black by virtue of having one thirty-second African ancestry. She brought suit against the state of Louisiana to have her racial classification changed. She lost the suit but effected the overthrow of the law identifying individuals as black if they had one thirty-second African ancestry, leaving on the books a prior law identifying an individual as black who had any African ancestry—the "one-drop" rule that uniquely characterizes the classification of blacks in the United States in fact even where no longer in law. So according to this long-standing convention of racial classification, a white who acknowledges any African ancestry implicitly acknowledges being black—a social condition, more than an identity, that no white person would voluntarily assume, even in imagination. This is one reason that whites, educated and uneducated alike, are so resistant to considering the probable extent of racial miscegenation.

This "one-drop" convention of classification of blacks is unique not only relative to the treatment of blacks in other countries but also unique relative to the treatment of other ethnic groups in this country. It goes without saying that no one, either white or black, is identified as, for example, English by virtue of having some small fraction of English ancestry. Nor is anyone free, as a matter of social convention, to do so by virtue of that fraction, although many whites do. But even in the case of other disadvantaged groups in this country, the convention is different. Whereas any proportion of African ancestry is sufficient to identify a person as black, an individual must have *at least* one-eighth Native American ancestry in order to identify legally as Native American.

Why the asymmetry of treatment? Clearly, the reason is economic. A legally certifiable Native American is entitled to financial benefits from the government, so obtaining this certification is difficult. A legally certifiable black person is *disentitled* to financial, social, and inheritance benefits from his white family of origin, so obtaining this certification is not just easy but automatic. Racial classification in this country functions to restrict the distribution of goods, entitlements, and status as narrowly as possible to those whose power is already entrenched. Of course this institutionalized disentitlement presupposes that two persons of different racial classifications cannot be biologically related, which is absurd.

> This [one-drop] definition of who is black was crucial to maintaining the social system of white domination in which widespread miscegenation, not racial purity, prevailed. White womanhood was the highly charged emotional symbol, but the system protected white economic, political, legal, education and other institutional advantages for whites. . . . American slave owners wanted to keep all racially mixed children born to slave women under their control, for economic and sexual gains. . . . It was intolerable for white women to have mixed children, so the one-drop rule favored the sexual freedom of white males, protecting the double standard of sexual morality as well as slavery. . . . By defining all mixed children as black and compelling them to live in the black community, the rule made possible the incredible myth among whites that miscegenation had not occurred, that the races had been kept pure in the South. —Davis, *Who Is Black?*

But the issues of family entitlements and inheritance rights are not uppermost in the minds of most white Americans, who wince at the mere suggestion that they might have some fraction of African ancestry and therefore be, according to this country's entrenched convention of racial classification, black. The primary issue for them is not what they might have to give away by admitting that they are in fact black, but rather what they have to lose. What they have to lose, of course, is social status—and, insofar as their self-esteem is based on their social status as whites, self-esteem as well.

> "I think," said Dr. Latrobe, proudly, "that we belong to the highest race on earth and the negro to the lowest."
>
> "And yet," said Dr. Latimer, "you have consorted with them till you have bleached their faces to the whiteness of your own. Your children nestle in their bosoms; they are around you as body servants, and yet if one of them should attempt to associate with you your bitterest scorn and indignation would be visited upon them."
>
> —Harper, *Iola Leroy*

No reflective and well-intentioned white person who is consciously concerned to end racism wants to admit to instinctively recoiling at the thought of being identified as black herself. But if you want to see such a white person do this, just peer at the person's facial features and tell her, in a complimentary tone of voice, that she looks as though she might have some black ancestry, and watch her reaction. It's not a test I or any black person finds particularly pleasant to apply (that is, unless one dislikes the person and wants to inflict pain deliberately), and having once done so inadvertently, I will never do it again. The ultimate test of a person's repudiation of racism is not what she can contemplate *doing* for or on behalf of black people, but whether she herself can contemplate calmly the likelihood of *being* black. If racial hatred has not manifested itself in any other context, it will do so here if it exists, in hatred of the self as identified with the other—that is, as self-hatred projected onto the other.

> Since Harry had come North he had learned to feel profound pity for the slave. But there is difference between looking on a man as an object of pity and protecting him as such, and being identified with him and forced to share his lot. —Harper, *Iola Leroy*

> Let me tell you how I'd get those white devil convicts and the guards, too, to do anything I wanted. I'd whisper to them, "If you don't, I'll start a rumor that you're really a light Negro just passing as white." That shows

you what the white devil thinks about the black man. He'd rather die than be thought a Negro!—Malcolm X, *The Autobiography of Malcolm X*

When I was an undergraduate minoring in medieval and Renaissance musicology, I worked with a fellow music student—white—in the music library. I remember his reaction when I relayed to him an article I'd recently read arguing that Beethoven had African ancestry. Beethoven was one of his heroes, and his vehement derision was completely out of proportion to the scholarly worth of the hypothesis. But when I suggested that he wouldn't be so skeptical if the claim were that Beethoven had some Danish ancestry, he fell silent. In those days we were very conscious of covert racism, as our campus was exploding all around us because of it. More recently I premiered at a gallery a video installation exploring the issue of African ancestry among white Americans. A white male viewer commenced to kick the furniture, mutter audibly that he was white and was going to stay that way, and start a fistfight with my dealer. Either we are less conscious of covert racism twenty years later, or we care less to contain it.

Among politically committed and enlightened whites, the inability to acknowledge their probable African ancestry is the last outpost of racism. It is the litmus test that separates those who have the courage of their convictions from those who merely subscribe to them and that measures the depth of our dependence on a presumed superiority (of any kind, anything will do) to other human beings—anyone, anywhere—to bolster our fragile self-worth. Many blacks are equally unwilling to explore their white ancestry—approximately 25 percent on average for the majority of blacks—for this reason. For some, of course, acknowledgment of this fact evokes only bitter reminders of rape, disinheritance, enslavement, and exploitation, and their distaste is justifiable. But for others, it is the mere idea of blackness as an essentialized source of self-worth and self-affirmation that forecloses the acknowledgment of mixed ancestry. This, too, is understandable: Having struggled so long and hard to carve a sense of wholeness and value for ourselves out of our ancient connection with Africa after having been actively denied any in America, many of us are extremely resistant to once again casting ourselves into the same chaos of ethnic and psychological ambiguity that our diaspora to this country originally inflicted on us.

Thus blacks and whites alike seem to be unable to accord worth to others outside their in-group affiliations without feeling that they are taking it away from themselves. We may have the concept of intrinsic self-worth, but by and large we do not understand what it means. We need someone else whom we can regard as inferior, to whom we can compare ourselves favorably, and if no such individual or group exists, we invent one. For without this, we seem to have no basis, no standard of comparison, for conceiving of ourselves favorably at all. We seem, for example, truly unable to grasp or take seriously the alternative possibility of measuring ourselves or our performances against our own past novice-hood at one end and our own future potential at the other. I think this is in part the result of our collective fear of memory as a nation, our profound unwillingness to confront the painful truths about our history and our origins, and in part the result of our individual fear of the memory of our own pasts—not only of our individual origins and the traumas of social-ization we each suffered before we could control what was done to us, but the pasts of our own adult behavior—the painful truths of our own derelictions, betrayals, and failures to respect our individual ideals and convictions.

When I turned forty a few years ago, I gave myself the present of rereading the personal journals I have been keeping since age eleven. I was astounded at the chasm between my present conception of my own past, which is being continually revised and updated to suit present cir-cumstances, and the actual past events, behavior, and emotions I recorded as faithfully as I could as they happened. My derelictions, mistakes, and failures of responsibility are much more evident in those journals than they are in my present, sanitized, and virtually blameless image of my past behavior. It was quite a shock to encounter in those pages the person I actually have been rather than the person I now conceive myself to have been. My memory is always under the control of the person I now want and strive to be, and so rarely under the control of the facts. If the personal facts of one's past are this difficult for other people to face too, then perhaps it is no wonder that we must cast about outside ourselves for someone to feel superior to, even though there are so many blunders and misdeeds in our own personal histories that might serve that function.

For whites to acknowledge their blackness is, then, much the same as for men to acknowledge their femininity and for Christians to acknowledge their Judaic heritage. It is to reinternalize the external scapegoat through attention to which they have sought to escape their own sense of inferiority.

> Now the white man leaned in the window, looking at the impenetrable face with its definite strain of white blood, the same blood which ran in his own veins, which had not only come to the negro through male descent while it had come to him from a woman, but had reached the negro a generation sooner—a face composed, inscrutable, even a little haughty, shaped even in expression in the pattern of his great-grandfather McCaslin's face. . . . He thought, and not for the first time: *I am not only looking at a face older than mine and which has seen and winnowed more, but at a man most of whose blood was pure ten thousand years when my own anonymous beginnings became mixed enough to produce me.*—William Faulkner, *Go Down, Moses*

> I said . . . that the guilt of American whites included their knowledge that in hating Negroes, they were hating, they were rejecting, they were denying, their own blood.—Malcolm X, *The Autobiography of Malcolm X*

It is to bring ourselves face to face with our obliterated collective past and to confront the continuities of responsibility that link the criminal acts of extermination and enslavement committed by our forefathers with our own personal crimes of avoidance, neglect, disengagement, passive complicity, and active exploitation of the inherited injustices from which we have profited. Uppermost among these is that covert sense of superiority a white person feels over a black person which buttresses his enjoyment of those unjust benefits as being no more or less than he deserves. To be deprived of that sense of superiority to the extent that acknowledgment of common ancestry would effect is clearly difficult for most white people. But to lose the social regard and respect that accompanies it is practically unbearable. I know—not only because of what I have read and observed of the pathology of racism in white people, but because I have often experienced the withdrawal of that social regard firsthand.

For most of my life I did not understand that I needed to identify my racial identity publicly and that if I did not I would be inevitably mistaken for white. I simply didn't think about it. But since I also made no special effort to hide my racial identity, I often experienced the shocked and / or hostile reactions of whites who discovered it after the fact. I always knew when it had happened, even when the person declined to confront me directly: the startled look, the searching stare that would fix itself on my facial features, one by one, looking for the telltale "negroid" feature, the sudden, sometimes permanent withdrawal of good feeling or regular contact—all alerted me to what had transpired. Uh-oh, I would think to myself helplessly, and watch another blossoming friendship wilt.

> In thus travelling about through the country I was sometimes amused on arriving at some little railroad-station town to be taken for and treated as a white man, and six hours later, when it was learned that I was stopping at the house of the coloured preacher or school-teacher, to note the attitude of the whole town change.—Johnson, *The Autobiography of an Ex-Coloured Man*

Sometimes this revelation would elicit a response of the most twisted and punitive sort: for example, from the colleague who glared at me and hissed, "Oh, so you want to be black, do you? Good! Then we'll treat you like one!" The ensuing harassment had a furious, retaliatory quality that I find difficult to understand even now: as though I'd delivered a deliberate and crushing insult to her self-esteem by choosing not to identify with her racial group.

> You feel lost, sick at heart before such unmasked hatred, not so much because it threatens you as because it shows humans in such an inhuman light. You see a kind of insanity, something so obscene the very obscenity of it (rather than its threat) terrifies you.—Griffin, *Black Like Me*

And I experienced that same groundless shame not only in response to those who accused me of passing for black but also in response to those who accused me of passing for white. This was the shame caused by people who conveyed to me that I was underhanded or manipulative, trying to hide something, pretending to be something I was not by not telling them I was black—like the art critic in the early 1970s who had treated me with the respect she gave emerging white women artists in the early days of second-wave feminism until my work turned to issues of racial identity; she then called me to verify that I was black, reproached me for not telling her, and finally disappeared from my professional life altogether. And there were the colleagues who discovered after hiring me for my first job that I was black, and revised their evaluations of my work accordingly. It was the groundless shame caused by people who, having discovered my racial identity, let me know that I was not comporting myself as befitted their conception of a black person: the grammar school teacher who called my parents to inquire whether I was aware that I was black, and made a special effort to put me in my place by restricting me from participating in certain class activities and assigning me to remedial classes in anticipation of low achievement; and the graduate school classmate who complimented me on my English; and the potential employer who, having offered me a tenure-track job in an outstanding graduate department (which I declined) when he thought I was white, called me back much later after I'd received tenure and he'd found out I was black to offer me a two-year visiting position teaching undergraduates only, explaining to a colleague of mine that he was being pressured by his university administration to integrate his department. And the art critic who made elaborate suggestions in print about the kind of art it would be appropriate for someone with my concerns to make; and the colleague who journeyed from another university and interviewed me for four and a half hours in order to ascertain that I was smart enough to hold the position I had, and actually congratulated me afterwards on my performance. And there was the colleague who, when I begged to differ with his views, shouted (in a crowded restaurant) that if I wasn't going to take his advice, why was I wasting his time?

> I looked up to see the frowns of disapproval that can speak so plainly and so loudly without words. The Negro learns this silent language fluently. He knows by the white man's look of disapproval and petulance that he is being told to get on his way, that he is "stepping out of line." —Griffin, *Black Like Me*

When such contacts occurred, the interaction had to follow a strict pattern of interracial etiquette. The white person had to be clearly in charge at all times, and the black person clearly subordinate, so that each kept his or her place. It was a master-servant etiquette, in which blacks had to act out their inferior social position, much the way slaves had done. The black had to be deferential in tone and body language, . . . and never bring up a delicate topic or contradict the white. . . . This master-servant ritual had to be acted out carefully lest the black person be accused of "getting" out of his or her subordinate "place." Especially for violations of the etiquette, but also for challenges to other aspects of the system, blacks were warned, threatened, and finally subjected to extralegal violence. —Davis, *Who Is Black?*

In a way this abbreviated history of occasions on which whites have tried to "put me in my place" upon discovering my racial identity was the legacy of my father who, despite his own similar experiences as a youth, refused to submit to such treatment. He grew up in a Southern city where his family was well known and highly respected. When he was thirteen, he went to a movie theater and bought a seat in the orchestra section. In the middle of the feature, the projectionist stopped the film and turned up the lights. The manager strode onto the stage and, in front of the entire audience, called out my father's name, loudly reprimanded him for sitting in the orchestra, and ordered him up to the balcony, where he "belonged." My father fled the theater, and, not long after, the South. My grandmother then sent him to a private prep school up North, but it was no better. In his senior year of high school, after having distinguished himself academically and in sports, he invited a white girl classmate on a date. She refused, and her parents complained to the principal, who publicly rebuked him. He was ostracized by his classmates for the rest of the year and made no effort to speak to any of them.

My mother, being upper-middle-class Jamaican, had no experience of this kind of thing. When she first got a job in this country in the 1930s, she chastised her white supervisor for failing to say, "Thank you," after she'd graciously brought him back a soda from her lunch hour. He was prop erly apologetic. And when her brother first came to this country, he sat in a restaurant in Manhattan for an hour waiting to be served, it simply not occurring to him that he was being ignored because of his color, until a waitress came up to him and said, "I can see you're not from these parts. We don't serve colored people here." My father, who had plenty of experiences of this sort, knew that I would have them, too. But he de clined to accustom me to them in advance. He never hit me, disparaged me, or pulled rank in our frequent intellectual and philosophical disagree ments. Trained as a Jesuit and a lawyer, he argued for the joy of it, and felt proud rather than insulted when I made my point well. "Fresh," he'd murmur to my mother with mock annoyance, indicating me with his thumb, when I used his own assumptions to trounce him in argument. It is because of his refusal to prepare me for my subordinate role as a black woman in a racist and misogynistic society that my instinctive reaction to such insults is not resignation, depression, or passive aggression, but rather the disbelief, outrage, sense of injustice, and impulse to fight back actively that white males often exhibit as unexpected affronts to their dignity. Blacks who manifest these responses to white racism reveal their caregivers' generationally transmitted underground resistance to schooling them for victimhood.

A benefit and a disadvantage of looking white is that most people treat you as though you were white. And so, because of how you've been treated, you come to expect this sort of treatment, not perhaps, realizing that you're being treated this way because people think you're white, but rather falsely supposing that you're being treated this way because people think you are a valuable person. So, for example, you come to expect a certain level of respect, a certain degree of attention to your voice and opinions, certain liberties of action and self-expression to which you falsely suppose yourself to be entitled because your voice, your opinion, and your conduct are valuable in themselves. To those who in fact believe (even though they would never voice this belief to themselves) that black people are not entitled to this degree of respect, attention, and liberty, the sight of a black person behaving as though she were can, indeed, look very much like arrogance. It may not occur to them that she simply does not realize that her blackness should make any difference.

> Only one-sixteenth of her was black, and that sixteenth did not show. . . . Her complexion was very fair, with the rosy glow of vigorous health in the cheeks, . . . her eyes were brown and liquid, and she had a heavy suit of fine soft hair which was also brown. . . . She had an easy, independent carriage—when she was among her own caste—and a high and "sassy" way, withal; but of course she was meek and humble enough where white people were.—Mark Twain, *Pudd'nhead Wilson*

But there may be more involved than this. I've been thinking about Ida B. Wells, who had the temerity to suggest in print that white males who worried about preserving the purity of Southern white womanhood were really worried about the sexual attraction of Southern white womanhood to handsome and virile black men; and Rosa Parks, who refused to move to the back of the bus; and Eartha Kitt, who scolded President Lyndon Johnson about the Vietnam War when he received her at a White House dinner; and Mrs. Alice Frazier, who gave the queen of England a big hug and invited her to stay for lunch when the queen came to tour Mrs. Frazier's housing project on a recent visit to the United States; and Congresswoman Maxine Waters, who, after the L.A. rebellion, showed up at the White House uninvited, and gave George Bush her unsolicited recommendations as to how he should handle the plight of the inner cities. I've also been thinking about the legions of African American women whose survival has depended on their submission to the intimate interpersonal roles, traditional for black women in this culture, of nurse-maid, housekeeper, concubine, cleaning lady, cook; and what they have been required to witness of the whites they have served in those capacities. And I've been thinking about the many white people I've admired and respected, who have lost my admiration and respect by revealing in personal interactions a side of themselves that other whites rarely get a chance to see: the brand of racism that surfaces only in one-on-one or intimate interpersonal circumstances, the kind a white person lets you see because he doesn't care what you think and knows you are powerless to do anything about it.

> When we shined their shoes we talked. The whites, especially the tourists, had no reticence before us, and no shame since we were Negroes. Some wanted to know where they could find girls, wanted us to get Negro girls for them. . . . Though not all, by any means, were so open about their purposes, all of them showed us how they felt about the Negro, the idea that we were people of such low morality that nothing could offend us. . . . In these matters, the Negro has seen the backside of the white man too long to be shocked. He feels an indulgent superiority whenever he sees these evidences of the white man's frailty. This is one of the sources of his chafing at being considered inferior. He cannot understand how the white man can show the most demeaning aspects of his nature and at the same time delude himself into thinking he is inherently superior. — Griffin, *Black Like Me*

It may indeed be that we African American women as a group have special difficulties in learning our place and observing the proprieties because of that particular side of white America to which, because of our traditional roles, we have had special access—a side of white America that hardly commands one's respect and could not possibly command one's deference.

To someone like myself, who was raised to think that my racial identity was, in fact, irrelevant to the way I should be treated, there are few revelations more painful than the experience of social metamorphosis that transforms former friends, colleagues, or teachers who have extended their trust, goodwill, and support into accusers or strangers who withdraw them when they discover that I am black. To look visibly black, or always to announce in advance that one is black is, I submit, never to experience this kind of camaraderie with white people—the relaxed, unguarded, but respectful camaraderie that white people reserve for those whom they believe are like them—those who can be trusted, who are intrinsically worthy of value, respect, and attention. Eddie Murphy portrays this in comic form in a wonderful routine in which he disguises himself in whiteface, then boards a bus on which there is only one visibly black passenger. As long as that passenger is on the bus, all of them sit silently and impersonally ignoring one another. But as soon as the visibly black passenger gets off, the other passengers get up and turn to one another, engaging in friendly banter, and the driver breaks open a bottle of champagne for a party. A joke, perhaps, but not entirely. A visibly black person may, in time, experience something very much like this unguarded friendship with a white person, if the black person has proven herself trustworthy and worthy of respect, or has been a friend since long before either was taught that vigilance between the races was appropriate. But I have only rarely met adult whites who have extended this degree of trust and acceptance at the outset to a new acquaintance they knew to be black. And to have extended it to someone who then *turns out* to be black is instinctively felt as a betrayal, a violation. It is as though one had been seduced into dropping one's drawers in the presence of the enemy. So a white person who accuses me of deceit for not having alerted her that I am black is not merely complaining that I have been hiding something about myself that is important for her to know. The complaint goes much deeper. It is that she has been lured under false pretenses into dropping her guard with me, into revealing certain intimacies and vulnerabilities that are simply unthinkable to expose in the presence of someone of another race (that's why it's important for her to know my race). She feels betrayed because I have failed to warn her to present the face she thinks she needs to present to someone who might choose to take advantage of the weaknesses that lie behind that public face. She may feel it merely a matter of luck that I have not taken advantage of those weaknesses already.

As the accused, I feel as though a trusted friend has just turned on me. I experience the social reality that previously defined our relationship as having metamorphosed into something ugly and threatening, in which the accusation is not that I have *done* something wrong, but that I *am* wrong for being who I am: for having aped the white person she thought I was, and for being the devalued black person she discovers I am. I feel a withdrawal of good will, a psychological distancing, a new wariness and suspicion, a care in choosing words, and—worst of all—a denial that anything has changed. This last injects an element of insensitivity—or bad faith—that makes our previous relationship extremely difficult to recapture. It forces me either to name unpleasant realities that the white person is clearly unable to confront or to comply with the fiction that there are no such realities, which renders our interactions systematically inauthentic. This is why I always feel discouraged when well-intentioned white people deny to me that a person's race makes any difference to them, even though I understand that this is part of the public face whites instinctively believe they need to present; I know, firsthand, how white people behave toward me when they believe racial difference is absent. And there are very few white people who are able to behave that way toward me once they know it is present.

But there are risks that accompany that unguarded camaraderie among whites who believe they are among themselves, and ultimately those risks proved too much for me. I have found that often a concomitant of that unguarded camaraderie is explicit and unadorned verbal racism of a kind that is violently at odds with the gentility and cultivation of the social setting, and that would never appear if that setting were visibly integrated.

> I will tell you that, without any question, the *most* bitter anti-white di-
> atribes that I have ever heard have come from "passing" Negroes, living as
> whites, among whites, exposed every day to what white people say among
> themselves regarding Negroes—things that a recognized Negro never
> would hear. Why, if there was a racial showdown, these Negroes "pass-
> ing" within white circles would become the black side's most valuable
> "spy" and ally.—Malcolm X, *The Autobiography of Malcolm X*

I have heard an educated white woman refer to her husband's black
physical education student as a "big, black buck"; I have heard university
professors refer to black working-class music as "jungle music"; and I
have heard a respected museum director refer to an actress as a "big, black
momma." These remarks are different in kind from those uttered in
expressions of black racism toward whites. When we are among ourselves
we may vent our frustration by castigating whites as ignorant, stupid,
dishonest, or vicious. That is, we deploy stereotyped white *attitudes* and
motives. We do not, as these remarks do, dehumanize and animalize whites
themselves. From these cases and others like them I have learned that the
side of themselves some whites reveal when they believe themselves to be
among themselves is just as demeaning as the side of themselves they
reveal privately to blacks. This is, I suspect, the weakness whites rightly
want concealed behind the public face; and the possibility that I might
witness—or might have witnessed—it is the source of their anger at me
for having "tricked" them. For part of the tragedy is that the racism I
witness when their guard is down is often behavior they genuinely do not
understand to be racist. So the revelation is not only of racism but of
ignorance and insensitivity. The point of adopting the public face when
whites are warned that a black person is among them is to suppress any
nonneutral expression of the self that might be interpreted as racist.

Of course this brand of self-monitoring damage control cannot possibly work, since it cannot eliminate those very manifestations of racism
that the person sees, rather, as neutral or innocuous. No one person can
transcend the constraints of his own assumptions about what constitutes
respectful behavior in order to identify and critique his own racism from
an objective, "politically correct" standpoint when it appears. We need
trusted others, before whom we can acknowledge our insufficiencies without fear of ridicule or retaliation, to do that for us, so as to genuinely ex-

tend our conceptions of ourselves and our understanding of what constitutes appropriate behavior toward another who is different. The fact of the matter is that if racism is present—which it is in *all* of us, black as well as white, who have been acculturated into this racist society—it will emerge despite our best efforts at concealment. The question should not be whether any individual is racist; that we all are to some extent should be a given. The question should be, rather, how we handle it once it appears. I believe our energy would be better spent on creating structured, personalized community forums for naming, confronting, owning, and resolving these feelings rather than trying to evade, deny, or suppress them. But there are many whites who believe that these matters are best left in silence, in the hope that they will die out of their own accord, and that we must focus on right actions, not the character or motivations behind them. To my way of thinking, this is a conceptual impossibility. But relative to this agenda, my involuntary snooping thwarts their good intentions.

My instinctive revulsion at these unsought revelations is undergirded by strong role modeling from my parents. I never heard my parents utter a prejudicial remark against any group. But my paternal grandmother was of that generation of very light-skinned, upper-middle-class blacks who believed themselves superior both to whites and to darker-skinned blacks. When I was young I wore my hair in two long braids, but I recall my mother once braiding it into three or four, in a simplified cornrow style. When my grandmother visited, she took one look at my new hairstyle and immediately began berating my mother for making me look like a "little nigger pickaninny." When my father heard her say these words he silently grasped her by the shoulders, picked her up, put her outside the front door, and closed it firmly in her face. Having passed for white during the Great Depression to get a job, and during World War II to see combat, his exposure to and intolerance for racist language was so complete that no benefits were worth the offense to his sensibilities, and he saw to it that he never knowingly placed himself in that situation again.

> "Doctor, were I your wife, . . . mistaken for a white woman, I should hear things alleged against the race at which my blood would boil. No, Doctor, I am not willing to live under a shadow of concealment which I thoroughly hate as if the blood in my veins were an undetected crime of my soul."
> —Harper, *Iola Leroy*

My father is a very tough act to follow. But ultimately I did, because I had to. I finally came to the same point of finding these sudden and unwanted revelations intolerable. Although I valued the unguarded camaraderie and closeness I'd experienced with whites, it was ultimately not worth the risk that racist behavior might surface. I seem to have become more thin-skinned about this with age. But for years I'd wrestled with different ways of forestalling these unwanted discoveries. When I was younger I was too flustered to say anything (which still sometimes happens when my guard is down), and I would be left feeling compromised and cowardly for not standing up for myself. Or I'd express my objections in an abstract form, without making reference to my own racial identity, and watch the discussion degenerate into an academic squabble about the meaning of certain words, whether a certain epithet is really racist, the role of good intentions, whether to refer to someone as a "jungle bunny" might not be a backhanded compliment, and so forth. Or I'd express my objections in a personal form, using that most unfortunate moment to let the speaker know I was black, thus traumatizing myself and everyone else present and ruining the occasion. Finally I felt I had no choice but to do everything I could, either verbally or through trusted friends or through my work, to confront this matter head-on and issue advance warning to new white acquaintances, both actual and potential, that I identify myself as black—in effect, to "proclaim that fact from the house-top" (forgive me, Malcolm, for blowing my cover).

"I tell Mr. Leroy," said Miss Delany, "that . . . he must put a label on himself, saying 'I am a colored man,' to prevent annoyance."—Harper, *Iola Leroy*

Of course, this method is not foolproof. Among its benefits is that it puts the burden of vigilance on the white person rather than on me—the same vigilance she exercises in the presence of a visibly black person (but even this doesn't always work: some whites simply can't take my avowed racial affiliation at face value, and react to what they see rather than what I say). And because my public avowal of my racial identity almost invariably elicits all the stereotypically racist behavior that visibly black people always confront, some blacks feel less of a need to administer the Suffering Test of blackness. Among the costs is that I've lost other white friends who are antagonized by what they see as my manipulating their liberal guilt or goodwill, or turning my racial identity into an exploitable profession, or advertising myself in an unseemly manner, or making a big to-do about nothing. They are among those who would prefer to leave the whole matter of race—and, by implication, the racism of their own behavior—shrouded in silence.

But I've learned that there is no "right" way of managing the issue of my racial identity, no way that will not offend or alienate someone, because my designated racial identity itself exposes the very concept of racial classification as the offensive and irrational instrument of racism it is. We see this in the history of the classifying terms variously used to designate those brought as slaves to this country and their offspring: first "blacks," then "darkies," then "Negroes," then "colored people," then "blacks" again, then "Afro-Americans," then "people of color," now "African Americans." Why is it that we can't seem to get it right, once and for all? The reason, I think, is that it doesn't really matter what term we use to designate those who have inferior and disadvantaged status, because whatever term is used will eventually turn into a term of derision and disparagement by virtue of its reference to those who are derided and disparaged, and so will need to be discarded for an unsullied one. My personal favorite is "colored" because of its syntactical simplicity and aesthetic connotations. But cooking up new ways to classify those whom we degrade ultimately changes nothing but the vocabulary of degradation.

What joins me to other blacks, then, and other blacks to another, is not a set of shared physical characteristics, for there is none that all blacks share. Rather, it is the shared experience of being visually or cognitively *identified* as black by a white racist society, and the punitive and damaging effects of that identification. This is the shared experience the Suffering Test tries to, and often does, elicit.

But then, of course, I have white friends who fit the prevailing stereotype of a black person and have similar experiences, even though they insist they are "pure" white.

> It cannot be so embarrassing for a coloured man to be taken for white as
> for a white man to be taken for coloured; and I have heard of several cases
> of the latter kind.—Johnson, *The Autobiography of an Ex-Coloured Man*

The fact is that the racial categories that purport to designate any of us are too rigid and oversimplified to fit anyone accurately. But then, accuracy was never their purpose. Since we are almost all in fact racial hybrids, the "one drop" rule of black racial designation, if consistently applied, would either narrow the scope of ancestral legitimacy so far that it would exclude most of those so-called whites whose social power is most deeply entrenched, or widen it to include most of those who have been most severely disadvantaged by racism. Once we get clear about the subtleties of who in fact we are, we then may be better able to see just what our ancestral entitlements actually are, and whether or to what extent they may need to be supplemented with additional social and legal means for implementing a just distribution of rights and benefits for everyone. Not until that point, I think, when we have faced the full human and personal consequences of self-serving, historically entrenched social and legal conventions that in fact undermine the privileged interests they were designed to protect, will we be in a position to decide whether the very idea of racial classification is a viable one in the first place.

She really thought everyone would be like her some day, neither black nor white, but something in between. It might take decades or even centuries, but it would happen. And sooner than that, racism and the concept of race itself would become completely obsolete. — Perry, *Another Present Era*

Yet it was not that Lucas made capital of his white or even his McCaslin blood, but the contrary. It was as if he were not only impervious to that blood, he was indifferent to it. He didn't even need to strive with it. He didn't even have to bother to defy it. He resisted it simply by being the composite of the two races which made him, simply by possessing it. Instead of being at once the battleground and victim of the two strains, he was a vessel, durable, ancestryless, nonconductive, in which the toxin and its anti stalemated one another, seetheless, unrumored in the outside air. — Faulkner, *Go Down, Moses*

These are frightening suggestions for those whose self-worth depends on their racial and social status within the white community. But no more frightening, really, than the thought of welcoming long-lost relatives back into the family fold and making adjustments for their well-being accordingly. One always has a choice as to whether to regard oneself as having lost something—status, if one's long-lost relatives are disreputable, or economic resources, if they are greedy; or as having gained something—status, if one's long-lost relatives are wise and interesting, or economic resources, if they are able-bodied and eager to work. Only for those whose self-worth strictly requires the exclusion of others viewed as inferior will these psychologically and emotionally difficult choices be impossible. This, I think, is part of why some whites feel so uneasy in my presence: Condescension or disregard seems inappropriate in light of my demeanor, whereas a hearty invitation into the exclusive inner circle seems equally inappropriate in light of my designated race. Someone who has no further social resources for dealing with other people besides condescension or disregard on the one hand and clubbish familiarity on the other is bound to feel at a loss when race provides no excuse for the former because of demeanor, whereas demeanor provides no excuse for the latter because of race. So no matter what I do or do not do about my racial identity, someone is bound to feel uncomfortable. But I have resolved that it is no longer going to be me.

Note

This essay previously was published in *Transition*, issue 58 (1992): 4–32.

Works Cited

Abel, Elizabeth, and Emily K. Abel, eds. *The Signs Reader: Women, Gender, and Scholarship.* Chicago: U of Chicago P, 1983.

Amin, Samir. *Eurocentrism.* Trans. Russell Moore. New York: Monthly Review, 1989.

Anderson, Benedict. *Imagined Communities: Reflections on the Origin and Spread of Nationalism.* 1983. Rev. ed. London: Verso, 1991.

Ash, Juliet, and Elizabeth Wilson, eds. *Chic Thrills: A Fashion Reader.* Berkeley: U of California P, 1993.

Awkward, Michael. "Negotiations of Power: White Critics, Black Texts, and the Self-Referential Impulse." *American Literary History* 2.4 (1990): 581–606.

Baker, Houston. *Blues, Ideology, and Afro-American Literature: A Vernacular Theory.* Chicago: U of Chicago P, 1984.

Bakhtin, Mikhail. *Rabelais and His World.* Trans. Helen Iswolsky. Bloomington: Indiana UP, 1984.

Baldwin, James. *Giovanni's Room.* 1956. New York: Dell, 1988.

——. "Unnameable Objects, Unspeakable Crimes." *The White Problem in America.* By the editors of *Ebony.* Chicago: Johnson, 1966. 173–81.

Baldwin, James, and Nikki Giovanni. *A Dialogue.* Philadelphia: Lippincott, 1975.

Baltazar, Eulalio. *The Dark Center.* New York: Paulist, 1973.

Barthes, Roland, *S/Z.* New York: Hill, 1974.

Bartlett, Katharine T., and Rosanne Kennedy, eds. *Feminist Legal Theory: Readings in Law and Gender.* Boulder, CO: Westview, 1991.

Basch, Norma. *In the Eyes of the Law: Women, Marriage, and Property in Nineteenth-Century New York.* Ithaca: Cornell UP, 1982.

Bates, Eric. "Look Away." *Southern Exposure* 18 (1990): 35–37.

Benston, Kimberly W. "Facing Tradition: Revisionary Scenes in African American Literature." *PMLA* 105 (1990): 98–109.

Bercovitch, Sacvan. *The American Jeremiad.* Madison: U of Wisconsin P, 1978.

Berlant, Lauren. *The Anatomy of National Fantasy: Hawthorne, Utopia, and Everyday Life.* Chicago: U of Chicago P, 1991.

Berlant, Lauren, and Elizabeth Freeman. "Queer Nationality." *boundary 2* 19 (1992): 149–80.

Berzon, Judith R. *Neither White nor Black: The Mulatto Character in American Fiction.* New York: New York UP, 1978.

Bhabha, Homi, ed. *Nation and Narration.* New York: Routledge, 1991.

Blackett, R. J. M. *Beating against the Barriers: Biographical Essays in Nineteenth-Century Afro-American History.* Baton Rouge: Louisiana State UP, 1986.

"Black Like Me." *Time* 28 March 1960: 90.

Blackmer, Corinne E. "African Masks and the Arts of Passing in Gertrude Stein's 'Melanctha' and Nella Larsen's *Passing." Journal of the History of Sexuality* 4 (1993): 230–63.

Blackmore, David L. "'That Unreasonable Restless Feeling': The Homosexual Subtexts of Nella Larsen's *Passing." African American Review* 26 (1992): 475–84.

Blackstone, William. *Commentaries on the Laws of England.* 1765. Vol. 1. Chicago: U of Chicago P, 1979. 4 vols.

Boose, Lynda. "Techno-Muscularity and the 'Boy Eternal': From the Quagmire to the Gulf." *Gendering War Talk.* Ed. Cooke and Woollacott. 67–106.

Brantlinger, Patrick. "Victorians and Africans: The Genealogy and Myth of the Dark Continent." *"Race," Writing, and Difference.* Ed. Gates, 185–222.

Brodhead, Richard. *Cultures of Letters: Scenes of Reading and Writing in Nineteenth-Century America.* Chicago: U of Chicago P, 1993.

Brody, Jennifer DeVere. "Clare Kendry's 'True' Colors: Race and Class Conflict in Nella Larsen's *Passing." Callaloo* 15 (1992): 1053–65.

Brodzki, Bella, and Celeste Schenck, eds. *Life/Lines: Theorizing Women's Autobiography.* Ithaca: Cornell UP, 1988.

Brontë, Charlotte. *Jane Eyre.* 1847. New York: Penguin, 1987.

Brown, Gillian. *Domestic Individualism: Imagining Self in Nineteenth-Century America.* Berkeley: U of California P, 1990.

Brown, Josephine. *Biography of an American Bondman, by His Daughter.* 1856. *Two Biographies by African-American Women.* Ed. William L. Andrews. New York: Oxford UP, 1991. 3–104.

Brown, Karen McCarthy. "Plenty Confidence in Myself: The Initiation of a White Woman Scholar into Haitian Voudou." *Journal of Feminist Studies of Religion* 3 (1987): 67–76.

Bullough, Vern L., and Bonnie Bullough. *Cross Dressing, Sex, and Gender.* Philadelphia: U of Pennsylvania Press, 1991.

Burgess, Lauren Cook, ed. *An Uncommon Soldier: The Civil War Letters of Sarah Rosetta Wakeman, 153rd Regiment, New York State Volunteers.* Pasadena, MD: Minerva, 1994.

Butler, Judith. *Bodies That Matter: On the Discursive Limits of "Sex."* New York: Routledge, 1993.

———. *Gender Trouble: Feminism and the Subversion of Identity.* New York: Routledge, 1990.

Bynum, Victoria. *Unruly Women: The Politics of Social and Sexual Control in the Old South.* Chapel Hill: U of North Carolina P, 1992.

Works Cited

Cabiniss, Allen. "Rebel Flag." *Encyclopedia of Southern Culture.* Ed. Wilson and Ferris. 685.

Carby, Hazel V. *Reconstructing Womanhood: The Emergence of the Afro-American Woman Novelist.* New York: Oxford UP, 1987.

Carmichael, Stokely, and Charles V. Hamilton. *Black Power: The Politics of Liberation in America.* New York: Random, 1967.

Cary, Meredith. *Different Drummers: A Study of Cultural Alternatives in Fiction.* Metuchen, NJ: Scarecrow, 1984.

Case, Sue-Ellen. "Toward a Butch-Femme Aesthetic." *Discourse* 11 (1988–89): 57–73.

Cherniavsky, Eva. "Poe and Stowe: Revivification vs. Reanimation." *The American Face of Edgar Allan Poe.* Ed. Rosenheim and Rochman. 121–38.

Chesnutt, Charles Waddell. *Journals.* Ed. Richard H. Brodhead. Durham, NC: Duke UP, 1993.

Christian, Barbara. *Black Women Novelists: The Development of a Tradition, 1892–1976.* Westport, CT: Greenwood, 1980.

Clifford, James, and George Marcus, eds. *Writing Culture: The Poetics and Politics of Ethnography.* Berkeley: U of California P, 1986.

Clinton, Catherine, and Nina Silber, eds. *Divided Houses: Gender and the Civil War.* New York: Oxford UP, 1992.

Collier, Eugenia. "The Endless Journey of an Ex-Coloured Man." *Phylon* 32 (Winter 1971): 365–73.

Cook, Bruce A. "What Is It Like to Be a Negro?" *Commonweal* 27 October 1961: 129.

Cooke, Michael G. *Afro-American Literature in the Twentieth Century.* New Haven: Yale UP, 1984.

Cooke, Miriam, and Angela Woollacott. *Gendering War Talk.* Princeton: Princeton UP, 1993.

Cooper, Helen M., Adrienne Munich, and Susan Squier, eds. *Arms and the Woman: War, Gender, and Literary Representation.* Chapel Hill: U of North Carolina P, 1989.

Craft, William. *Running a Thousand Miles for Freedom; or, The Escape of William and Ellen Craft from Slavery.* 1860. Miami: Mnemosyne, 1969.

Crenshaw, Kimberle. "Demarginalizing the Intersection of Race and Sex: A Black Feminist Critique of Antidiscrimination Doctrine, Feminist Theory, and Antiracist Politics." *Feminist Legal Theory: Readings in Law and Gender.* Ed. Bartlett and Kennedy. 57–80.

Cullen, Jim. *The Civil War in Popular Culture: A Reusable Past.* Washington, D.C.: Smithsonian, 1995.

Davis, Arthur P. *From the Dark Tower: Afro-American Writers, 1900–1960.* Washington, D.C.: Howard UP, 1974.

Davis, Charles T., and Henry Louis Gates Jr., eds. *The Slave's Narrative.* Oxford: Oxford UP, 1985.

Davis, F. James. *Who Is Black? One Nation's Definition*. University Park: Pennsylvania State UP, 1991.

Davis, Thadious M. "Nella Larsen." *Afro-American Writers from the Harlem Renaissance to 1940*. Ed. Trudier Harris. Vol. 51 of *Dictionary of Literary Biography*. Detroit: Bruccoli, 1987. 182–92.

——. *Nella Larsen: Novelist of the Harlem Renaissance*. Baton Rouge: Louisiana State UP, 1994.

Dearborn, Mary V. *Pocahontas's Daughters: Gender and Ethnicity in American Culture*. New York: Oxford UP, 1986.

De Grave, Kathleen. *Swindler, Spy, Rebel: The Confidence Woman in Nineteenth-Century America*. Columbia: U of Missouri P, 1995.

de Lauretis, Teresa, ed. *Feminist Studies / Critical Studies*. Bloomington: Indiana UP, 1986.

——. *Technologies of Gender*. Bloomington: Indiana UP, 1987.

de Man, Paul. "Autobiography as De-facement." *MLN* 94 (1979): 919–30.

d'Emilio, John, and Estelle Freedman, eds. *Intimate Matters: A History of Sexuality in America*. New York: Harper, 1988.

Dobson, Joanne. "*The Hidden Hand:* Subversion of Cultural Ideology in Three Mid-Nineteenth-Century American Women's Novels." *American Quarterly* 38 (1986): 223–42.

——. "Introduction." *The Hidden Hand, or, Capitola the Madcap*. By E. D. E. N. Southworth. New Brunswick: Rutgers UP, 1988.

Domínguez, Virginia R. *White by Definition: Social Classification in Creole Louisiana*. New Brunswick, NJ: Rutgers UP, 1986.

Douglas, Ann. "Introduction." *Uncle Tom's Cabin; or, Life among the Lowly*. By Harriet Beecher Stowe. Harmondsworth: Penguin, 1981.

Douglass, Frederick. *Narrative of the Life of Frederick Douglass*. 1845. New York: Penguin, 1982.

Doyle, Mary Ellen, S.C.N. "The Slave Narratives as Rhetorical Art." *The Art of Slave Narrative*. Ed. Sekora and Turner. 83–95.

DuBois, Ellen. "Women's Rights and Abolition: The Nature of the Connection." *Antislavery Reconsidered*. Ed. Perry and Fellman. 238–51.

Du Bois, W. E. B. *The Souls of Black Folk*. 1903. New York: Penguin, 1989.

Dyer, Richard. "White." *Screen* 29.3 (1988): 44–64.

Eagleton, Terry. *The Significance of Theory*. Oxford: Blackwell, 1990.

Eco, Umberto. *The Role of the Reader: Explorations in the Semiotics of Texts*. Bloomington: Indiana UP, 1979.

Edelman, Lee. *Homographesis: Essays in Gay Literary and Cultural Theory*. New York: Routledge, 1994.

Elliott, Emory, ed. *The Columbia Literary History of the United States*. New York: Columbia UP, 1988.

Works Cited

Epstein, Julia, and Kristina Straub, eds. *Body Guards: The Cultural Politics of Gender Ambiguity.* New York: Routledge, 1991.

Equiano, Olaudah. *The Interesting Narrative of the Life of Olaudah Equiano, or Gustavus Vassa, the African.* 1789. *The Classic Slave Narratives.* Ed. and Intro. Henry Louis Gates Jr. New York: Penguin, 1987. 1–182.

Faderman, Lillian. *Odd Girls and Twilight Lovers: A History of Lesbian Life in Twentieth-Century America.* New York: Columbia UP, 1991.

——. *Surpassing the Love of Men: Romantic Friendship and Love between Women from the Renaissance to the Present.* New York: Morrow, 1981.

Fanon, Frantz. *Black Skin, White Masks.* Trans. Charles Markmann. New York: Grove, 1967.

Faulkner, William. *Go Down, Moses.* New York: Random House, 1942.

Fauset, Jessie. Review of *The Autobiography of an Ex-Coloured Man. The Crisis* 5 (1912–13): 28.

Faust, Drew Gilpin. *The Creation of Confederate Nationalism.* Baton Rouge: Louisiana State UP, 1986.

——. *Southern Stories: Slaveholders in Peace and War.* Columbia: U of Missouri P, 1992.

Fliegelman, Jay. *Prodigals and Pilgrims: The American Revolution against Patriarchal Authority, 1750–1800.* Cambridge: Cambridge UP, 1982.

Fluck, Winfried. "The Power and Failure of Representation in Harriet Beecher Stowe's *Uncle Tom's Cabin." New Literary History* 23.2 (Spring 1992): 319–38.

Foster, Gaines M. *Ghosts of the Confederacy: Defeat, the Lost Cause, and the Emergence of the New South, 1865–1913.* New York: Oxford UP, 1987.

Fredrickson, George M. *The Arrogance of Race: Historical Perspectives on Slavery, Racism, and Social Inequality.* Middletown, CT: Wesleyan UP, 1988.

——. *The Black Image in the White Mind: The Debate on Afro-American Character and Destiny, 1817–1914.* New York: Harper, 1971.

Freud, Sigmund. *The Standard Edition of the Complete Psychological Works of Sigmund Freud.* Trans. James Strachey et al. 24 vols. London: Hogarth, 1953–74.

Friedli, Lynne. " 'Passing Women': A Study of Gender Boundaries in the Eighteenth Century." *Sexual Underworlds of the Enlightenment.* Ed. Rousseau and Porter. 234–60.

Fuss, Diana. *Essentially Speaking: Feminism, Nature, and Difference.* New York: Routledge, 1989.

——, ed. *Inside/Out: Lesbian Theories, Gay Theories.* New York: Routledge, 1991.

Gaines, Jane. "White Privilege and Looking Relations: Race and Gender in Feminist Film Theory." *Screen* 29 (1988): 12–27.

Gallop, Jane. *Reading Lacan.* Ithaca: Cornell UP, 1985.

Garber, Marjorie. *Vested Interests: Cross-Dressing and Cultural Anxiety.* New York: Routledge, 1992.

Gates, Henry Louis, Jr. *Figures in Black: Words, Signs, and the "Racial" Self.* New York: Oxford UP, 1987.

——. "Introduction." *The Classic Slave Narratives.* Ed. Gates. New York: Penguin, 1987. ix–xviii.

——, ed. *"Race," Writing, and Difference.* Chicago: U of Chicago P, 1986.

——. "Writing 'Race' and the Difference it Makes." *"Race," Writing, and Difference.* Ed. Gates. 1–20.

Gilbert, Sandra M., and Susan Gubar. *The Madwoman in the Attic: The Woman Writer and the Nineteenth-Century Literary Imagination.* New Haven: Yale UP, 1979.

Goldberg, David Theo, ed. *Anatomy of Racism.* Minneapolis: U of Minnesota P, 1990.

Goldstein, Richard. " 'Go the Way Your Blood Beats': An Interview with James Baldwin." *James Baldwin: The Legacy.* Ed. Troupe. 173–85.

Gossett, Thomas F. *Race: The History of an Idea in America.* Dallas: Southern Methodist UP, 1963.

Greenblatt, Stephen. *Marvelous Possessions: The Wonder of the New World.* Chicago: U of Chicago P, 1991.

Griffin, John Howard. *Black Like Me.* 1961. Boston: Houghton, 1977.

——. *A Time to Be Human.* New York: Macmillan, 1977.

Grossberg, Michael. *Governing the Hearth: Law and the Family in Nineteenth-Century America.* Chapel Hill: U of North Carolina P, 1985.

Grunebaum, James. *Private Ownership.* New York: Routledge, 1987.

Guillaumin, Colette. "The Idea of Race and Its Elevation to Autonomous, Scientific, and Legal Status." *Sociological Theories: Race and Colonialism.* New York: UNESCO, 1980. 37–67.

Habegger, Alfred. "A Well-Hidden Hand." *Novel* 14 (1981): 197–212.

Hall, Richard. *Patriots in Disguise: Women Warriors of the Civil War.* New York: Paragon, 1993.

Halsell, Grace. *Soul Sister.* Greenwich, CT: Fawcett, 1969.

Halttunen, Karen. *Confidence Men and Painted Women: A Study of Middle-Class Culture in America, 1830–70.* New Haven: Yale UP, 1982.

Harper, Frances E. W. *Iola Leroy, or Shadows Uplifted.* 1892. NY: Oxford UP, 1988.

Harris, Cheryl I. "Whiteness as Property." *Harvard Law Review* 106.8 (1993): 1706–91.

Hawthorne, Nathaniel. "The Birthmark." *The Scarlet Letter and Other Tales of the Puritans.* Boston: Houghton, 1961. 118–31.

Hersh, Blanche Glassman. *The Slavery of Sex: Feminist-Abolitionists in America.* Urbana: U of Illinois P, 1978.

Higonnet, Margaret. "Civil Wars and Sexual Territories." *Arms and the Woman.* Ed. Cooper, Munich, and Squier. 80–96.

Works Cited

Hobsbawm, Eric, and Terrence Ranger, eds. *The Invention of Tradition*. New York: Cambridge UP, 1983.

Hodgson, Godfrey. *America in Our Time*. New York: Vintage, 1976.

Hoffert, Sylvia D. "Loreta Velazquez, Questionable Heroine." *Civil War Times Illustrated* 17.3 (1978): 24–31.

Holland, Laurence B. "A 'Raft of Trouble': Word and Deed in *Huckleberry Finn*." *American Realism: New Essays*. Ed. Sundquist. 66–81.

Hostetler, Ann E. "The Aesthetics of Race and Gender in Nella Larsen's *Quicksand*." *PMLA* 105 (1990): 35–46.

Hull, Gloria T., Patricia Bell Scott, and Barbara Smith, eds. *All the Women Are White, All the Blacks Are Men, but Some of Us Are Brave*. Old Westbury, NY: Feminist, 1982.

Huston, Nancy. "The Matrix of War: Mothers and Heroes." *The Female Body in Western Culture*. Ed. Suleiman. 119–38.

Jacobs, Harriet. *Incidents in the Life of a Slave Girl*. 1861. Ed. Jean Fagin Yellin. Cambridge: Harvard UP, 1987.

Jameson, Fredric. *Postmodernism, or, The Cultural Logic of Late Capitalism*. Durham, NC: Duke UP, 1990.

JanMohamed, Abdul. "The Economy of Manichean Allegory: The Function of Racial Difference in Colonialist Literature." *"Race," Writing, and Difference*. Ed. Gates. 78–106.

Jeffords, Susan. *The Remasculinization of America: Gender and the Vietnam War*. Bloomington: Indiana UP, 1989.

Johnson, Barbara. "Fanon and Lacan." Paper delivered at University of North Carolina, Chapel Hill. 18 March 1991.

Johnson, James Weldon. *The Autobiography of an Ex-Coloured Man*. New York: Sherman, 1912. Rpt. as *The Autobiography of an Ex-Coloured Man* with an Introduction by Carl Van Vechten. New York: Knopf, 1927. Rpt. with an Introduction by Henry Louis Gates Jr. New York: Vintage, 1989.

——. *Along This Way: The Autobiography of James Weldon Johnson*. New York: Viking, 1933.

Jordan, Winthrop. *White over Black: American Attitudes toward the Negro, 1550–1812*. Chapel Hill: U of North Carolina P, 1968.

Kahn, Madeline. *Narrative Transvestism: Rhetoric and Gender in the Eighteenth-Century English Novel*. Ithaca: Cornell UP, 1991.

Kammen, Michael. *Mystic Chords of Memory: The Transformation of Tradition in American Culture*. New York: Vintage, 1993.

Kaplan, Amy and Donald Pease, eds. *Cultures of United States Imperialism*. Durham, NC: Duke UP, 1993.

Katz, Jonathan. *Gay American History*. New York: Avon, 1976.

Kaufman, Janet E. " 'Under the Petticoat Flag': Women Soldiers in the Confederate Army." *Southern Studies* 23 (1984): 363–75.

Kelley, Mary. *Private Woman, Public Stage*. Oxford: Oxford UP, 1984.

King, Wendy A. *Clad in Uniform: Women Soldiers of the Civil War*. Collingswood, NJ: C. W. Historicals, 1992.

Kinnamon, Kenneth, ed. *James Baldwin: A Collection of Critical Essays*. Englewood Cliffs, NJ: Prentice, 1974.

Lacan, Jacques. *Écrits: A Selection*. Trans. Alan Sheridan. New York: Norton, 1977.

———. *Feminine Sexuality*. Trans. Jacqueline Rose. Ed. Juliet Mitchell and Jacqueline Rose. New York: Norton, 1982.

Laqueur, Thomas. *Making Sex: Body and Gender from the Greeks to Freud*. Cambridge: Harvard UP, 1990.

Larsen, Nella. *Quicksand* and *Passing*. Ed. and Intro. Deborah McDowell. New Brunswick: Rutgers UP, 1986.

Larson, C. Kay. "Bonnie Yank and Ginny Reb." *Minerva* 8.1 (1990): 33–48.

———. "Bonnie Yank and Ginny Reb Revisited." *Minerva* 10.2 (1992): 35–61.

Lawliss, Chuck. *The Civil War Sourcebook: A Traveler's Guide*. New York: Harmony, 1991.

Leach, William. *True Love and Perfect Union: The Feminist Reform of Sex and Society*. New York: Basic, 1980.

Lerner, Gerda. *The Creation of Patriarchy*. New York: Oxford UP, 1986.

Levy, Eugene. *James Weldon Johnson: Black Leader, Black Voice*. Chicago: U of Chicago P, 1973.

"Life's a Drag." *Elle* March 1992: 33–38.

Little, Jonathan. "Nella Larsen's *Passing:* Irony and the Critics." *African American Review* 26 (1992): 173–82.

Livermore, Mary A. *My Story of the War*. Hartford: Worthington, 1889.

Lomax, Louis E. "It's Like This." *Saturday Review* 9 December 1961: 53.

Lott, Eric. *Love and Theft: Blackface Minstrelsy and the American Working Class*. New York: Oxford UP, 1993.

———. "White Like Me: Racial Cross-Dressing and the Construction of American Whiteness." *Cultures of United States Imperialism*. Ed. Kaplan and Pease. 474–95.

Luck, Kate. "Trouble in Eden, Trouble with Eve." *Chic Thrills*. Ed. Ash and Wilson. 200–12.

Mackethan, Lucinda H. "*Black Boy* and *Ex-Coloured Man:* Version and Inversion of the Slave Narrator's Quest for Voice." *CLA Journal* 32 (1988): 123–47.

Macpherson, C. B. *The Political Theory of Possessive Individualism: Hobbes to Locke*. London: Oxford UP, 1962.

Madigan, Mark. "Miscegenation and 'The Dicta of Race and Class': The Rhinelander Case and Nella Larsen's *Passing*." *Modern Fiction Studies* 36.4 (Winter 1990): 523–28.

Works Cited

Mailer, Norman. *The White Negro.* San Francisco: City Lights, 1957.

Malcolm X. *The Autobiography of Malcolm X.* New York: Grove, 1965.

Marcus, George E. and Michael M. J. Fischer. *Anthropology and Cultural Critique: An Experimental Moment in the Human Sciences.* Chicago: U of Chicago P, 1986.

Martin, Biddy, and Chandra Talpade Mohanty. "Feminist Politics: What's Home Got to Do with It?" *Feminist Studies / Critical Studies.* Ed. de Lauretis. 191–212.

Massey, Mary Elizabeth. *Bonnet Brigades.* New York: Knopf, 1966. Rpt. as *Women in the Civil War.* Intro. Jean V. Berlin. Lincoln: U of Nebraska P, 1994.

Mattison, Rev. H. *Louisa Picquet, The Octoroon Slave and Concubine: A Tale of Southern Life.* In *Collected Black Women's Narratives.* Intro. Anthony G. Barthelemy. New York, Oxford UP, 1988.

Mbiti, John S. *African Religions and Philosophy.* New York: Praeger, 1969.

McDowell, Deborah. Introduction. *Quicksand* and *Passing.* By Nella Larsen. New Brunswick: Rutgers UP, 1986. ix–xxxv.

McLendon, Jacquelyn Y. *The Politics of Color in the Fiction of Jessie Fauset and Nella Larsen.* Charlottesville: UP of Virginia, 1995.

McPherson, James. *Battle Cry of Freedom: The Civil War Era.* New York: Ballantine, 1989.

——. "A War That Never Goes Away." *American Heritage* 41.2 (March 1990): 41–49.

Mercer, Kobena. "Welcome to the Jungle: Identity and Diversity in Postmodern Politics." *Identity: Community, Culture, Difference.* Ed. Rutherford.

Michie, Helena. " 'Dying between Two Laws': Girl Heroines, Their Gods, and Their Fathers in *Uncle Tom's Cabin* and the *Elsie Dinsmore* Series." *Refiguring the Father.* Ed. Yaeger and Kowaleski-Wallace. 188–206.

——. *Sororophobia: Differences among Women in Literature and Culture.* New York: Oxford UP, 1992.

Morrison, Toni. *Playing in the Dark: Whiteness and the Literary Imagination.* Cambridge: Harvard UP, 1992.

Mudimbe, V. Y. *The Invention of Africa: Gnosis, Philosophy, and the Order of Knowledge.* Bloomington: Indiana UP, 1988.

Mullen, Harryette. "Optic White: Blackness and the Production of Whiteness." *diacritics* 24 (1994): 71–89.

Myrdal, Gunnar. *An American Dilemma: The Negro Problem and Modern Democracy.* With Richard Sterner and Arnold Rose. 1944. New York: Harper and Row, 1962.

Neely, Mark E., Jr., Harold Holzer, and Gabor S. Boritt. *The Confederate Image: Prints of the Lost Cause.* Chapel Hill: U of North Carolina P, 1987.

Nelson, Cary, and Lawrence Grossberg, eds. *Marxism and the Interpretation of Culture.* Urbana: U of Illinois P, 1988.

Nestle, Joan, ed. *The Persistent Desire: A Femme / Butch Reader.* Boston: Alyson, 1992.

Newman, Charles. "The Lesson of the Master: Henry James and James Baldwin." *James Baldwin*. Ed. Kinnamon. 52–65.

Newton, Esther. *Mother Camp: Female Impersonators in America*. Englewood Cliffs, NJ: Prentice, 1972.

——. "The Mythic Mannish Lesbian: Radclyffe Hall and the New Woman." *Signs* 9 (1984): 557–75.

Nicholson, Linda. "Interpreting *Gender*." *Signs* 19.1 (Autumn 1994): 79–105.

Olney, James. " 'I Was Born': Slave Narratives, Their Status as Autobiography and as Literature." *The Slave's Narrative*. Ed. Davis and Gates. 148–75.

Osborne, Charles C. *Jubal: The Life and Times of General Jubal A. Early, C.S.A., Defender of the Lost Cause*. Chapel Hill, NC: Algonquin, 1992.

Outlaw, Lucius. "Toward a Critical Theory of 'Race.' " *Anatomy of Racism*. Ed. Goldberg. 58–82.

Parker, Andrew, et al., eds. *Nationalisms and Sexualities*. New York: Routledge, 1992.

Patterson, Orlando. *Slavery and Social Death: A Comparative Study*. Cambridge: Harvard UP, 1982.

Perry, Elaine. *Another Present Era*. New York: Farrar, Straus and Giroux, 1990.

Perry, Lewis, and Michael Fellman, eds. *Antislavery Reconsidered: New Perspectives on the Abolitionists*. Baton Rouge: Louisiana State UP, 1979.

Poirier, Richard. *A World Elsewhere: The Place of Style in American Literature*. New York: Oxford UP, 1966.

Porter, Carolyn. "Social Discourse and Nonfictional Prose." *The Columbia Literary History of the United States*. Ed. Elliott. 345–63.

Powers, Ann. "Queer in the Streets, Straight in the Sheets." *Village Voice* 29 June 1993. Rpt. *Utne Reader* November/December 1993: 74–80.

Rable, George. *Civil Wars: Women and the Crisis of Southern Nationalism*. Urbana: U of Illinois P, 1989.

Ramsey, Priscilla. "Freeze the Day: A Feminist Reading of Nella Larsen's *Quicksand* and *Passing*." *Afro-Americans in New York Life and History* 9 (January 1985): 27–41.

Rhys, Jean. *The Wide Sargasso Sea*. London: Deutsch, 1966.

Rich, Adrienne. "Compulsory Heterosexuality and Lesbian Existence." *The Signs Reader*. Ed. Abel and Abel. 139–68.

Riviere, Joan. "Womanliness as Masquerade." *The International Journal of Psychoanalysis* 10 (1929): 303–13. Rpt. in *Formations of Fantasy*. Ed. Victor Burgin, James Donald, and Cora Kaplan. London: Methuen, 1986. 35–44.

Robinson, Amy. "It Takes One to Know One: Passing and Communities of Common Interest." *Critical Inquiry* 20 (1994): 715–36.

Rogin, Michael. "Blackface, White Noise: The Jewish Jazz Singer Finds His Voice." *Critical Inquiry* 18 (1992): 417–53.

Works Cited

Root, Maria P. P., ed. *Racially Mixed People in America*. Newbury Park, CA: Sage, 1992.

Rosenheim, Shawn, and Stephen Rochman, eds. *The American Face of Edgar Allan Poe*. Baltimore: Johns Hopkins UP, 1995.

Rousseau, G. S., and Roy Porter, eds. *Sexual Underworlds of the Enlightenment*. Chapel Hill: U of North Carolina P, 1988.

Rousseau, Jean-Jacques. "On the Social Contract." *The Basic Political Writings*. Trans. Donald A. Cress. Indianapolis: Hackett, 1987.

Rutherford, Jonathan, ed. *Identity: Community, Culture, Difference*. London: Lawrence, 1990.

Ryan, Mary. *Women in Public: Between Banners and Ballots, 1825–1880*. Baltimore: Johns Hopkins UP, 1990.

Saks, Eva. "Representing Miscegenation Law." *Raritan* 8 (Fall 1988): 39–69.

Samuelson, Nancy B. "Employment of Female Spies in the American Civil War." *Minerva* 7.3–4 (1989): 57–66.

Sanchez-Eppler, Karen. "Bodily Bonds: The Intersecting Rhetorics of Feminism and Abolition." *Representations* 24 (1988): 28–59.

Sartre, Jean-Paul. *Being and Nothingness*. Trans. Hazel E. Barnes. New York: Washington Square, 1966.

Schultz, Jane. "Mute Fury: Southern Women's Diaries of Sherman's March to the Sea, 1864–65." *Arms and the Woman*. Ed. Cooper, Munich, and Squier. 59–79.

———. "Women at the Front: A Study in Gender and Genre." Diss. U of Michigan, 1988.

Sedgwick, Eve Kosofsky. *Between Men: English Literature and Male Homosocial Desire*. New York: Columbia UP, 1985.

———. *Epistemology of the Closet*. Berkeley: U of California P, 1990.

———. "Queer Performativity: Henry James's *The Art of the Novel*." *GLQ: A Journal of Lesbian and Gay Studies* 1 (1993): 1–16.

Sekora, John, and Darwin T. Turner, eds. *The Art of Slave Narrative: Original Essays in Criticism and Theory*. Macomb: Western Illinois UP, 1982.

Sennett, Richard. *The Fall of Public Man: On the Social Psychology of Capitalism*. New York: Vintage, 1977.

Sharpe, Ernest J., Jr. "The Man Who Changed His Skin." *American Heritage* 40.1 (1989): 44–55.

Silber, Nina. *The Romance of Reunion: Northerners and the South, 1865–1900*. Chapel Hill: U of North Carolina P, 1993.

Singh, Amritjit. *The Novels of the Harlem Renaissance*. University Park: Pennsylvania State UP, 1976.

Sizer, Lyde Cullen. "Narratives of Union Women Spies." *Divided Houses*. Ed. Clinton and Silber. 114–33.

Skerrett, Joseph T., Jr. "Irony and Symbolic Action in James Weldon Johnson's *The

Autobiography of an Ex-Coloured Man." *American Quarterly* 32 (Winter 1980): 540–58.

Smith, Billy G., and Richard Wojtowicz. *Blacks Who Stole Themselves: Advertisements for Runaways in the* Pennsylvania Gazette, *1728–1790*. Philadelphia: U of Pennsylvania P, 1989.

Smith-Rosenberg, Carroll. *Disorderly Conduct: Visions of Gender in Victorian America*. New York: Oxford UP, 1985.

Southworth, E. D. E. N. *The Hidden Hand, or, Capitola the Madcap*. 1888. Ed. Joanne Dobson. New Brunswick: Rutgers UP, 1988.

Spickard, Paul R. "The Illogic of American Racial Categories." *Racially Mixed People in America*. Ed. Root. 12–23.

Spillers, Hortense. "Mama's Baby, Papa's Maybe: An American Grammar Book." *diacritics* 17.2 (Summer 1987): 65–81.

Spivak, Gayatri Chakravorty. "Can the Subaltern Speak?" *Marxism and the Interpretation of Culture*. Ed. Nelson and Grossberg. 271–313.

Stafford, Barbara. *Body Criticism*. Cambridge: MIT P, 1991.

Stanton, Elizabeth Cady, Susan B. Anthony, and Matilda Joslyn Gage, eds. *History of Woman Suffrage, Volume 1: 1848–1861*. 1881. New York: Arno, 1969. 6 vols.

Starling, Marion Wilson. *The Slave Narrative: Its Place in American History*. Boston: Hall, 1981.

Stein, Gertrude. "An American in France." *What Are Masterpieces?* New York: Pitman, 1970.

Stepan, Nancy. *The Idea of Race in Science: Great Britain, 1800–1960*. Hamden: Archon, 1982.

Stepto, Robert B. *From behind the Veil: A Study of Afro-American Narrative*. Urbana: U of Illinois P, 1979.

——. "Sharing the Thunder: The Literary Exchanges of Harriet Beecher Stowe, Henry Bibb, and Frederick Douglass." *New Essays on* Uncle Tom's Cabin. Ed. Sundquist. 135–54.

Sterling, Dorothy. *Black Foremothers: Three Lives*. Old Westbury, NY: Feminist, 1979.

Stewart, Susan. *On Longing: Narratives of the Miniature, the Gigantic, the Souvenir, the Collection*. Durham, NC: Duke UP, 1993.

Still, William. *The Underground Rail Road*. 1872. New York: Arno, 1968.

Stowe, Harriet Beecher. *A Key to* Uncle Tom's Cabin; *Presenting the Original Facts and Documents upon Which the Story is Founded*. 1853. Port Washington: Kennikat, 1968.

——. *Uncle Tom's Cabin; or, Life among the Lowly*. 1852. Ed. and Introd. Ann Douglas. Harmondsworth: Penguin, 1981.

Straayer, Chris. "Redressing the 'Natural': The Temporary Transvestite Film." *Wide Angle* 14 (1992): 36–55.

Works Cited

Straub, Kristina. "The Guilty Pleasures of Female Theatrical Cross-Dressing and the Autobiography of Charlotte Charke." *Body Guards*. Ed. Epstein and Straub. 142–66.

Suleiman, Susan, ed. *The Female Body in Western Culture*. Cambridge: Harvard UP, 1986.

Sundquist, Eric J., ed. *American Realism: New Essays*. Baltimore: Johns Hopkins UP, 1982.

——, ed. and intro. *New Essays on* Uncle Tom's Cabin. New York: Cambridge UP, 1986.

——. *To Wake the Nations: Race in the Making of American Literature*. Cambridge: Harvard UP, 1993.

Tate, Claudia. "Allegories of Black Female Desire; or, Rereading Nineteenth-Century Sentimental Narratives of Black Female Authority." *Changing Our Own Words*. Ed. Wall. 98–126.

——. *Domestic Allegories of Political Desire: The Black Heroine's Text at the Turn of the Century*. New York: Oxford UP, 1992.

Taylor, Joe Gray. *Negro Slavery in Louisiana*. Baton Rouge: Louisiana Historical Association, 1963.

Taylor, William R. *Cavalier and Yankee: The Old South and American National Character*. New York: Braziller, 1961.

Thornton, Hortense E. "Sexism as Quagmire: Nella Larsen's *Quicksand*." *CLA Journal* 16 (1973): 285–301.

Tocqueville, Alexis de. *Democracy in America*. Trans. Henry Reeve. Ed. and Intro. Philips Bradley. 2 vols. New York: Vintage, 1990.

Todorov, Tzvetan. *The Conquest of America*. Trans. Richard Howard. New York: Harper, 1984.

Troupe, Quincy, ed. *James Baldwin: The Legacy*. New York: Simon, 1989.

Tucker Family Papers. Southern Historical Collection. Library of the University of North Carolina, Chapel Hill.

Turner, Rory. "Bloodless Battles: The Civil War Reenacted." *Drama Review* 34.4 (1990): 123–36.

Twain, Mark. *The Tragedy of Pudd'nhead Wilson*. Hartford, CT: American Publishing, 1894.

Tyler, Carole-Anne. "Boys Will Be Girls: The Politics of Gay Drag." *Inside/Out*. Ed. Fuss. 32–70.

Velazquez, Loreta. *The Woman in Battle*. 1876. Ed. C. J. Worthington. New York: Arno, 1972.

Wall, Cheryl A., ed. *Changing Our Own Words: Essays on Criticism, Theory, and Writing by Black Women*. New Brunswick: Rutgers UP, 1989.

——. "Passing for What? Aspects of Identity in Nella Larsen's Novels." *Black American Literature Forum* 20 (1986): 97–111.

Warbasse, Elizabeth Bowles. *The Changing Legal Rights of Married Women, 1800–1861*. New York: Garland, 1987.

Warner, Susan. *The Wide, Wide World*. 1850. Ed. Jane Tompkins. Old Westbury, NY: Feminist, 1987.

Washington, Mary Helen, ed. and intro. *Invented Lives: Narratives of Black Women, 1860–1960*. New York: Doubleday / Anchor, 1987.

Wheelwright, Julie. *Amazons and Military Maids: Women Who Dressed as Men in the Pursuit of Life, Liberty, and Happiness*. London: Pandora, 1989.

Wiley, Bell Irvin. *The Life of Johnny Reb: The Common Soldier of the Confederacy*. Indianapolis: Bobbs, 1943.

Williams, Patricia. *The Alchemy of Race and Rights*. Cambridge: Harvard UP, 1991.

Williams, Stanley T. *The Spanish Background of American Literature*. 2 vols. New Haven: Yale UP, 1955.

Williamson, Joel. *New People: Miscegenation and Mulattoes in the United States*. New York: Free, 1980.

Wilson, Charles Reagan. *Baptized in Blood: The Religion of the Lost Cause, 1865–1920*. Athens: U of Georgia P, 1980.

Wilson, Charles Reagan, and William Ferris, eds. *The Encyclopedia of Southern Culture*. Chapel Hill: U of North Carolina P, 1989.

Wright, Lawrence. "One Drop of Blood." *New Yorker* 25 July 1994: 46–55.

Yaeger, Patricia, and Beth Kowaleski-Wallace, eds. *Refiguring the Father: New Feminist Readings of Patriarchy*. Carbondale: Southern Illinois UP, 1989.

Yarborough, Richard. "Strategies of Black Characterization in *Uncle Tom's Cabin* and the Early Afro-American Novel." *New Essays on* Uncle Tom's Cabin. Ed. Sundquist. 45–84.

Yellin, Jean Fagan. *Women and Sisters: The Antislavery Feminists in American Culture*. New Haven: Yale UP, 1989.

Youman, Mary Mabel. "Nella Larsen's *Passing:* A Study in Irony." *CLA Journal* 18 (1974): 235–41.

Žižek, Slavoj. *The Sublime Object of Ideology*. New York: Verso, 1989.

Zwarg, Christina. "Fathering and Blackface in *Uncle Tom's Cabin*." *Novel* 22.3 (1989): 274–87.

Index

Abolitionism: Ellen Craft's, 50, 55 n.11; and feminism, 39–40, 53 n.1, 55 n.8; and imperialism, 21, 25, 27–28, 35; and slave narratives, 156; South-worth's, 131; Stowe's, 122

Absalom, Absalom! (Faulkner), 161

The Adventures of Huckleberry Finn (Twain), 126 n.18

Affirmative action, 238–40

African Americans: ancestry of, 7, 234–69; female, 53 n.2, 137, 166, 261–62; hopelessness among, 155, 157; passing for white of, 1, 2–5, 7, 9, 12–13, 17 n.8, 37–56, 59–100, 103, 219, 221, 243–47, 265; white appearance of some, 1, 3–4, 15, 37–38, 44, 46–47, 50, 55 nn.7, 11, 62, 68, 234–69; and white males, 5, 15, 166, 260–61, whites passing for, 3, 134–35, 151–77, 176 n.2; white spokespersons for, 153–56, 174, 175–76; whites' use of, in writings, 133, 134–36, 148, 162. *See also* Miscegenation; Racial identity; Racism; Slaves

The Alchemy of Race and Rights (Williams), 171–72

Alcott, Louisa May, 197

Along This Way: The Autobiography of James Weldon Johnson, 60–62

An American Dilemma (Myrdal), 69

"An American in Paris" (Stein), 218

American Revolution, 14, 117, 120, 129 n.30, 215 n.13

Amin, Samir, 25, 26

Anderson, Benedict, 33–34

Another Present Era (Perry), 236, 242, 249, 268

Anthropology, 161, 177 n.6, 249; influence of, on *Black Like Me*, 151, 152, 154, 156–60, 166, 170, 174, 175

Antietam Battlefield, 181, 182, 184

Antislavery movement. *See* Abolitionism

Atlanta College, 65

"Autobiography as De-facement" (de Man), 68

The Autobiography of an Ex-Coloured Man (Johnson), 10, 11, 59–74, 165–66, 219, 226, 227, 243, 245, 257, 267

The Autobiography of Malcolm X, 254, 256, 264

Awkward, Michael, 173

Baker, Colonel Lafayette C., 192

Bakhtin, Mikhail, 121

Baldwin, James, 10, 11, 174, 218–33

Ball's Bluff Battle, 192

Barthes, Roland, 76, 89, 94, 96, 98

Basch, Norma, 41

Beethoven, Ludwig von, 254

"Before the Law" (Kafka), 228

"Benito Cereno" (Melville), 111, 127 n.20

Benjamin, Walter, 36

Benston, Kimberly, 67–69

Berzon, Judith, 80

"The Birthmark" (Hawthorne), 147–48

Birthmarks. *See* Hand imagery

Blackface, 135; in *Black Like Me*, 152, 175; George Washington in, 120–21. *See also* Minstrelsy

Black Like Me (Griffin), 9, 151–77, 245, 258, 261

"Blackness": defined in opposition to "whiteness," 7–8, 72–73; discovering one's own, 64–71, 253–56; gendered construction of, 156; in *Hidden Hand*, 131–50; not an intrinsic quality, 10, 63, 69–71; "Suffering Test" of, 236, 238, 266, 267; used to define "whiteness," 160–61. *See also* Color symbolism; Racial identity; "Whiteness"

Black Power (Carmichael and Hamilton), 173

Blackstone, William, 41

Bloomer, Amelia, 18 n.14

Body: alleged legibility of gay, 224; intersection between body politic and individual, 185, 198–210; as site of identity categories, 4–5, 37, 55 n.8, 69, 71, 157–58. *See also* Hand imagery; Specularity

Boundary crossing, 2–4, 12–13, 171–72. *See also* Color line; Passing

Branding. *See* Hand imagery

Brandon, Teena. *See* Teena, Brandon

Brantlinger, Patrick, 21, 28, 31

Brent, Linda. *See* Jacobs, Harriet

Brown, Gillian, 52, 135

Brown, Josephine, 54 n.4

Brown, Karen McCarthy, 161

Brown, William Wells, 54 n.4, 55 n.11

"Buford, Lt. Harry T.," 15, 185, 187, 191–92, 194, 195, 202, 212. *See also* Velazquez, Loreta

Bull Run Battle, 187, 192, 194

Burgess, Fred, 181, 211

Burgess, Lauren Cook, 15, 181–84, 188, 210–13

Bush, George, 261

Butler, Judith, 37, 183, 226, 230; on "heterosexual matrix," 193; on passing, 23, 36 n.2, 228

Butler, Pierce, 128 n.23

"Camp," 16 n.2, 211–13

Captivity narratives, 32

Carby, Hazel, 83

Carmichael, Stokely, 173

Carnivalesque, 121, 209

Caste system (U.S.), 62

Castration. *See* "Maleness"

"Category crisis," 8, 13, 183

Cather, Willa, 160

Cherniavsky, Eva, 143

Chestnut, Mary, 189

Chesnutt, Charles, 12, 17 n.12, 73 n.3, 239–40

Chopin, Kate, 12

Christian, Barbara, 83

Civil War, 14–15, 181–213; cross-dressed soldiers in, 3, 14–15, 182, 211, 214 n.6; reenactments of, 15, 181–84, 210–13, 213 n.1

Civil War Times Illustrated, 212

Class: in *Autobiography of an Ex-Coloured Man*, 65–66; differences in, among African Americans, 235–38; in *Giovanni's Room*, 10; in nineteenth-century, 135; and "passing," 3, 4, 11–12, 37–38, 45–48, 62, 258–59; in *Passing*, 84, 86–87, 90–92, 97; Stowe's handling of, 108–9; in *Uncle Tom's Cabin*, 11–12, 103. *See also* Status; "Whiteness": privileges associated with

Clements, Mr. (slave owner), 42, 51

Clifford, James, 157

Collier, Eugenia, 63

"Colonial imperialism," 26–27, 34. *See also* Imperialism

Color line, 23, 63–64, 86, 103, 123; Griffin's crossing of, 152, 154. *See also* Boundary crossing; Passing

Color symbolism, 9, 132–50, 160–61, 165, 169–70. *See also* "Blackness"; "Whiteness"

Columbus, Christopher, 118

Index

Coming of Age in Mississippi (Moody), 152

Commentaries on the Laws of England (Blackstone), 41

Commonweal, 153

"Compulsive heterosexuality," 193

Comraderie, 262–64

Confederate flag, 212, 213

Conrad, Joseph, 165

Cook, Lauren. *See* Burgess, Lauren Cook

Coverture, 41–42, 49

Craft, Ellen, 7, 12–13, 37–38, 43–53, 219

Craft, William, 8, 12–13, 37–56, 219

Crenshaw, Kimberle, 43

The Crisis (NAACP magazine), 60

"Cross-cultural improvisation," 114–15

Cross-dressing: in Civil War reenactments, 181–84, 210–13; among Civil War soldiers, 3, 14–15, 182, 211, 214 n.6; to escape from slavery, 12, 37–56, 103, 219; among males, 14, 37; as part of gender passing, 3, 13–14, 37–56, 103, 131, 134–35, 143, 144, 181–217; punishment for Civil War, 201; rumors about Jefferson Davis's, 205, 206. *See also* "Drag"

The Crying Game (film), 18 n.16

Cuba, 208

Cutter, Martha, 11, 75–100

Daughters of the American Revolution (DAR), 250

Davis, F. James, 244, 248–52, 259

Davis, Jefferson, 205

Davis, Thadious, 83, 96

Davis, Winnie, 199

Dearborn, Mary, 92

Democracy in America (de Tocqueville), 41

"Désirée's Baby" (Chopin), 12

The Devil Rides Outside (Griffin), 152

Difference ("Otherness"), 5, 12; as construct, 46–47, 63, 69–71; Jubal Early on Loreta Velazquez's, 208–9; and political alliance, 175–76; in *Quicksand*, 81–82; self-referential examinations of, 161, 171–73, 175; tropes of, 8, 10, 13, 67, 72, 88, 115–16, 225–26. *See also* Gender identity; Racial identity

Disguise. *See* Cross-dressing; Passing

Dobson, Joanne, 131, 137, 147–48

Domínguez, Virginia R., 247, 251

"Double consciousness." *See* Subjectivity: fragmented

Douglass, Frederick, 159

"Drag," 14, 16 n.2, 22, 226. *See also* Passing

Dream text, 103, 107–10, 113–15, 117, 122

Du Bois, W. E. B., 151, 155, 158, 166

Dyer, Richard, 162

Eagleton, Terry, 36

Early, Jubal: on the "Lost Cause," 200–202, 210; on *Woman in Battle*, 187–88, 194, 208–9

Eco, Umberto, 84–85

Eden, 224, 231

Elle magazine, 37

Ellison, Ralph, 175

Emasculation. *See* "Maleness"

Equiano, Olaudah, 6, 21–36

Essentialism: expressed by transvestites, 14, 37; in Griffin's construction of race, 156, 169, 175; and identity categories, 4, 10–11, 37, 38, 69–71, 122–23, 238; identity politics' challenge to, 16, 38, 43–44, 46–47, 218–19; in Larsen's works, 75–84, 86, 95–96; and "passing," 16 n.2, 23, 35, 62–63, 226

"The Ethics of Living Jim Crow" (Wright), 152

"Ethnic intensifiers," 6

Ethnicity: Loreta Velazquez's, 189–90, 208–9; passing and, 3; performative aspects of, 4. *See also* Difference; Nationality; Racial identity

Ethnography. *See* Anthropology

Evans, Augusta Jane, 189

"Facing scenes," 113–15

Fanon, Frantz, 4

Faulkner, William, 161, 256, 268

Fauset, Jessie Redmon, 17 n.12, 60, 73 n.3, 226

The Female Review, or, Memoirs of an American Young Lady (Mann), 14

Feminism, 39–40, 53 nn.1, 2, 55 n.8, 56 n.15; Velazquez's opposition to, 197–98

Fiction (sentimental), 9, 131–50, 156. *See also* Passing: literary genres dealing with

"Finding the Last Ditch" (cartoon), 205, 206

Flight (White), 73 n.3

Fluck, Winfried, 132, 145

Food chain imagery, 106, 125 n.10

Fort Donelson Battle, 187

Founding Fathers (United States), 117–21, 124 n.8

Frazier, Mrs. Alice, 261

French Guyana, 30

Freud, Sigmund, 177 n.8, 222

Gallop, Jane, 229–31

Garber, Marjorie: on cross-dressing, 38–39, 44, 103, 183; on difference, 5, 8, 13

Gates, Henry Louis, Jr., 31, 70, 106; on race as metaphor, 8, 13, 225

Gender identity, 2; arbitrariness of, 13; body's role in, 4–5; Craft's insistence on essentialism of, 38, 48–53; performative aspects of, 2, 4, 13, 44, 46, 181–217, 220–21; social and legal construction of, 2, 13–16; women's usurpation of men's, as threat, 2, 13, 14, 18 n.14, 210. *See also* Cross-dressing; Difference; Essentialism; "Maleness"; Passing

Gender Trouble (Butler), 183

Genealogy, 7, 243, 247–49

Genetic Abstracts, 249

Ghost stories, 142–43

Ginsberg, Elaine K., 1–18

Giovanni's Room (Baldwin), 10, 11, 218–33

Gnosis, 26

Go Down, Moses (Faulkner), 256, 268

Goldstein, Richard, 225

Greenblatt, Stephen, 114–15

Griffin, John Howard, 3, 9, 151–77, 245, 257, 258, 261

Griggs, Sutton E., 73 n.3

Grossberg, Michael, 41

Grunebaum, James, 52

Guilt, 173–74

Habegger, Alfred, 134

Halsell, Grace, 3, 153

Hamilton, Charles, 173

Hand imagery: in Hawthorne's "Birthmark," 147–48; in *The Hidden Hand,* 137–40, 147–48; in *Uncle Tom's Cabin,* 104, 105, 115

Harper, Frances E. W., 73 n.3, 227, 238, 240, 250, 253, 265, 266

Harris, Cheryl, 6–7

Hawthorne, Nathaniel, 147–48

Heart of Darkness (Conrad), 165

Hemingway, Ernest, 160

Henry, Patrick, 113, 120, 124 n.8

Heterosexuality. *See* Sexual orientation

"Heterosexual matrix," 193

The Hidden Hand, or, Capitola the Madcap (Southworth), 8–9, 131–50

Higgonet, Margaret, 190

Index

The Hindered Hand (Griggs), 73 n.3
Historical authenticity, 181–84, 210–11; and Woman in Battle, 185, 187–88, 201
Hodgson, Godfrey, 173
"Home," 10–11, 218, 221–25, 230–31
Homosexuality. See Sexual orientation
"Homosexual panic," 224
The House behind the Cedars (Chesnutt), 12, 73 n.3

Identity: in Autobiography of an Ex-Coloured Man, 64–66; construction of, 4, 16; fraud in, 227–28; multiplicity of, 4, 11, 35, 110–11; multiplicity of, in Larsen's works, 75–100; multiplicity of Ellen Craft's, 43–47, 52–53; multiplicity of William Craft's, 51–52; passing as challenge to, 226–28; performative aspects of, 76, 95–96, 218, 226. See also Essentialism; Gender identity; Passing, Racial identity; Subjectivity
Ideology (internalization of), 6, 9, 21–36
Igbo people, 21, 24, 25–26, 33
Illusion: in Black Like Me, 163–64; in "drag," 14, 16 n.2, 37, 226; Ellen Craft's, 48–50. See also Cross-dressing; Historical authenticity; Passing
Imperialism, 6, 21–36, 127 n.19, 212
Impersonality, 245–46
Impersonation. See Passing
Incidents in the Life of a Slave Girl (Jacobs), 12
Ings, Katharine Nicholson, 8–9, 131–50
The Interesting Narrative of the Life of Olaudah Equiano . . . , 21–36
The Invention of Africa (Mudimbe), 26, 29
Iola Leroy; or, Shadows Uplifted

(Harper), 73 n.3, 227, 238, 240, 250, 253, 265, 266
Irony: in Autobiography of an Ex-Coloured Man, 69–70; in Uncle Tom's Cabin, 121

Jacobs, Harriet (Linda Brent), 12, 141
James, Henry, 218, 221
Jane Eyre (Brontë), 141
Jeffords, Susan, 200
"Jeff's Last Skedaddle" (cartoon), 205, 206
Jews, 155
Jim Crow practices, 151, 154, 158, 160, 166
Johnson, Barbara, 67
Johnson, James Weldon, 243, 245, 267; passing in works of, 3, 10, 11, 59–74, 219, 226, 227, 257; racial heritage of, 17 n.12. See also Autobiography of an Ex-Coloured Man
Johnson, Lyndon, 175, 176 n.3, 261
Jordan, Winthrop, 6
"Journey into Shame" (Griffin), 152, 173

Kafka, Franz, 228
Kahn, Madeline, 14
Kawash, Samira, 9–10, 59–74
Kelley, Abby, 40
Kenney, Edmund, 1, 2, 7
The Key to Uncle Tom's Cabin (Stowe), 8
King, Martin Luther, Jr., 171
Kitt, Eartha, 261
Knopf, Alfred, 59

Lacan, Jacques, 65, 222, 229–31
Ladies' Memorial Association, 199
Larsen, Nella, 23, 224; identity in works by, 11, 228; passing in works by, 3, 9, 11, 73 n.3, 75–100, 219, 226, 247; racial heritage of, 17 n.12

289

Law, 227, 228; conflict between slavery and marriage, 40–43; and gender identity, 2; and race, 6–7, 29–31, 39–44. *See also* Jim Crow practices

Lerner, Carl, 153

Lerner, Gerda, 47, 51

"Lesbian confederacy," 185, 195–96

Lesbians. *See* Sexual orientation

Levy, Eugene, 59

Liberal humanism, 73

Liberia, 121–23, 130 n.34

"Life's a Drag" (*Elle* magazine), 37

Literacy, 106, 115; tableaux of, 114–16

Little, Jonathan, 88

Livermore, Mary, 184

Livingston, Jennie, 14, 183

Locke, John, 51–52

Lomax, Louis, 153

London Illustrated News, 53

Loss (associated with passing), 22–23. *See also* Nostalgia

"Lost Cause," 199–210

Lott, Eric, 134, 135, 175

Louisa Picquet, The Octoroon Slave and Concubine: A Tale of Southern Slave Life (Mattison), 235

Love and Theft (Lott), 134, 135

Lynching, 151, 168, 171, 199

McDowell, Deborah, 86, 90, 95

Mackethan, Lucinda, 69–70

Macpherson, C. B., 51–52

Madness, 141–42, 150 n.6

Madonna (singer), 183

Mailer, Norman, 163

Malcolm X, 254, 256, 264

"Maleness": associations with, 5, 52, 158, 194–96; and emasculation, 51, 198–208; privileges associated with, 4–5, 13, 14; Southern, 15, 198–207; white, defined in opposition to black, 161–62, 175; women's gender passing as threat to, 2, 13, 14, 18 n.14, 210;

women's role in defining, 13, 15, 38–39. *See also* Cross-dressing: as part of gender passing; Gender identity

"Mama's Baby, Papa's Maybe" (Spillers), 138

Man, Paul de, 68–69

Mann, Herman, 14

Mansfield, Texas, 152–53

Manumission: Craft's attempts at, 50; Equiano's, 25, 26–27, 29, 30

Marginality, 29, 163

Marriage: antebellum African American women on, 51, 53 n.3; conflict between slavery and, 40–43; Loreta Velazquez's, 190–91, 193; unequal roles in, 13; women's property rights under, 39–40, 49

Martin, Biddy, 223

Marx, Karl, 25

Masculinity. *See* "Maleness"

Mask(s): in *The Hidden Hand,* 133–34, 139–40; identity as, in Larsen's works, 75, 76, 78, 79, 81, 83, 95

Masquerade. *See* Passing

Mattison, H., 235

Mbiti, John, 24

Melville, Herman, 111, 127 n.20, 160

Memory, 255

Mercer, Kobena, 8

Metalepsis, 228–29

Mexican War, 190

Michie, Helena, 144

Minstrelsy, 16 n.2, 134. *See also* Blackface

Mirror scenes: in *Autobiography of an Ex-Coloured Man,* 67–69, 165–66; in *Black Like Me,* 164–67, 169; in *Giovanni's Room,* 220, 230; in *Passing,* 89

"Mirror stage" (Lacan's), 65, 229–31

Miscegenation, 5, 7, 105, 123, 124 n.8, 247–52, 254, 256; in *Autobiography of an Ex-Coloured Man,* 10, 72

Index

Mohanty, Chandra Talpade, 223
Montserrat, 30
Moody, Anne, 152
Morrison, Toni, 8, 160–61
Mother Camp (Newton), 37
Mothers: in *The Hidden Hand*, 139–43, 147–48; in *Uncle Tom's Cabin*, 142
Mudimbe, V. Y., 26, 28, 29
Murphy, Eddie, 262
Myrdal, Gunnar, 62, 69

NAACP, 173
Names: in *The Hidden Hand*, 136–37; in *Passing*, 94–95; in *Uncle Tom's Cabin*, 112–13, 129 n.31
Narrative of the Life of Frederick Douglass, 159
The National Era, 131
Nationality: and identity construction, 5, 10, 34, 103, 107–16, 189–90, 208–9; and racial categories, 6, 11–12, 33; as stand-in for race, 218–21. *See also* Ethnicity
Native Americans, 117–19, 207, 252
Negro Slavery In Louisiana (Taylor), 248
Newton, Esther, 37
New York Ledger, 131
New York State Legislature, 39
New York Times, 211
Nostalgia, 10, 11, 34, 218–33
Nuni (Griffin), 156–57

Olney, James, 39
"One drop of blood" criterion (for racial identity), 17 nn.6, 9, 69, 71, 72, 74 n.7, 103, 251–52, 268
Open texts, 11, 75–76, 84–85, 89, 96–98, 98 n.5
"Otherness." *See* Difference
Oxford English Dictionary (*OED*), 16 n.2, 64, 226

Paris Is Burning (film), 14, 183
Parker, Mack, 151, 168
Parks, Rosa, 151, 261
Passing: abolitionist's, as imperialist, 21–36; African Americans', for Spanish, 3, 11–12, 103–30; all identity as, 70, 73, 225–26; alternatives to binaries in, 11–12, 103, 104, 107–8, 123, 227; anxiety involved in, 71–72, 74 n.8; attitudes toward, 9–11, 240, 257–58; blacks', for white, 1, 2–5, 7, 9, 12–13, 17 n.8, 37–56, 59–100, 103, 219, 221; dating of phrase and phenomenon of, 36 n.1; decisions against, 3–4, 15–16, 234–69; decisions for, 71, 243–47, 265; definitions of, 16 n.2, 64, 219, 226–27; as fraudulent action, 3, 8, 62, 181–84, 235, 238–39, 257–59, 263, 264; geographical movement as part of, 3, 23–24, 38, 63; homosexuals', as heterosexuals, 4, 85, 99 n.6, 219; issues involved in, 2–3, 35, 62, 69–70, 87, 226, 240, 243–47; as journey to self-knowledge, 9, 160–73; literary genres dealing with, 59, 62, 66, 73 n.3; motivations for, 3, 13–14, 265; and status, 4–5, 11–12, 37–56, 62, 103, 253, 256, 258–59, 268–69; as subversive strategy, 11–12, 16, 75–100; "textual," 132, 221; as transgression of legal and cultural boundaries, 1, 8; of whites for African Americans, 3, 134–35, 151–77, 176 n.2; of women as men, 1–3, 12–14, 37–56, 103, 131, 134, 143, 144, 181–217. *See also* Boundary crossing; Color line; Cross-dressing
Passing (Larsen), 9, 23, 75–76, 84–98, 224, 228; homosexual subtext of, 10, 85, 86, 90, 95, 97, 99 n.6; passing as theme in, 11, 73 n.3, 219, 226, 247
Pennsylvania Supreme Court, 42, 51

Perry, Elaine, 236, 242, 249, 268
Phipps, Susie Guillory, 251
Picaresque, 185, 188, 194
Pilgrimages, 33, 34
Piper, Adrian, 3–4, 15–16, 234–69
Plessy v. Ferguson, 7
Plum Bun (Fauset), 73 n.3, 226
Point of view: in *Passing*, 85, 99 n.7; in
    Uncle Tom's Cabin, 109
*The Political Theory of Possessive Indi-
    vidualism* (Macpherson), 51–52
Postmodernism, 184
Powers, Ann, 4
Private Ownership (Grunebaum), 52
Property rights, 1, 39–40, 51–52
Providence, 117–18
Pudd'nhead Wilson (Twain), 260

Quicksand (Larsen), 10, 11, 75–84, 88,
    97–98

Racial identity, 2, 88; arbitrariness of,
    7–10, 69–73, 90, 92–93, 225, 234–
    69; Baldwin's depiction of, 224–25;
    body's role in construction of, 4–6,
    69, 71, 99 n.12; fluidity of, 103–23;
    "one drop of blood" criterion for,
    17 nn.6, 9, 69, 71, 72, 74 n.7, 103,
    251–52, 268; performative aspects
    of, 2, 4, 13, 44, 46, 76, 95–96, 108–
    14, 123 n.1, 153, 164; political pur-
    poses of, 252; social and legal con-
    struction of, 1–2, 6–13, 15–16, 69–
    73. *See also* African Americans;
    "Blackness"; Difference; Essential-
    ism; Ethnicity; Passing; Slaves;
    "Whiteness"; Whites
Racism: assumptions of, 47, 267–68;
    of blacks toward whites, 264, 265;
    effects of, 8–9, 165, 168–69, 171–
    74, 234–69; Equiano's experience
    with, 29–31; exposure of, 154, 164;
    icons of, 212–13; in oneself, 164–

67, 174, 253–54; similarities in
    American and Nazi, 155; and slav-
    ery, 5; strategies to subvert, 11, 75–
    100; verbal, 263–64; in *Woman in
    Battle*, 207–9
Rape: of black slaves by white
    slaveowners, 5, 105; imagery of, in
    military description, 203–5
Raritan, 250
Reading. *See* Literacy
Religion, 6
Revenge tableaux, 119
Rich, Adrienne, 193
Richmond (Virginia) *Whig*, 1
Riviere, Joan, 221
Robinson, Amy, 4
Rohy, Valerie, 10, 218–33
Rose, Ernestine, 39–40
Running a Thousand Miles for Freedom
    (Craft), 8, 12–13, 37–56, 219
RuPaul, 37, 38
Rust, Marion, 6, 21–36

Saks, Eva, 250
Sampson, Deborah, 14
Sanchez, Salvador, 14
Sanchez-Eppler, Karen, 41
Sartre, Jean-Paul, 72–73
Saturday Review, 153
Sedgwick, Eve Kosofsky, 224
Seduction, 192–98
Self. *See* Essentialism; Identity; Subjec-
    tivity
Sennett, Richard, 108
Sentimental fiction, 9, 131–50, 156
Sepia (magazine), 152, 153, 162, 173
Sex discrimination suits, 15, 181–83,
    213
Sexuality: "home" as stand-in for,
    221–25; implications about, in gen-
    der ambiguity, 14, 211–13; in
    Larsen's works, 83–84, 90; Loreta
    Velazquez's, 192–98; and passing, 3;

racialized, 168–69, 175; white male's control over others', 5

Sexual orientation: in case of homosexuals passing for heterosexuals, 4, 10, 219–21; in *Giovanni's Room*, 219–25; instability of concept of, 227–28, 230; in *Passing*, 10, 85, 86, 90, 95, 97, 99 n.6; questions about, in gender ambiguity, 14, 211–13; in *Woman in Battle*, 15, 193–96

Sexual roles. *See* Gender identity

Sharpe, Ernest, 164

Shiloh Battle, 187, 203

Silber, Nina, 199, 205

Silence: and *Black Like Me*, 170–71, 176; as form of speech, 24–36

Skerrett, Joseph, Jr., 60–61

Slave narratives, 6, 9, 12, 21–36, 156, 159; Olaudah Equiano's, 21–36; William Craft's, 37–56

Slavery: conflict between marriage and, 40–43; Craft's opposition to, 38; Equiano's opposition to British, 21, 25, 27–28, 35; in *The Hidden Hand*, 137–41; linking of race, sex and gender in, 5, 12–13; passing as strategy to escape, 12–13, 37–56, 103, 219; Spain's role in, 107, 118; symbolic emasculation under, 51–52; in the United States, 6–7, 108, 111, 120; white children sold into, 8, 46–47. *See also* Abolitionism; Manumission; Racism; Slaves

Slaves: African treatment of, 26, 29–31; British, 21–36; fugitive, 1, 37–56, 103–30; mothers among, 139–43; owners of, 1, 23–24, 41, 42, 51, 104–5, 109, 113, 114, 247–48, 252; as property, 1; as prop for passing, 12, 15, 38, 44–46, 108–9, 111–14, 207–8; sexual exploitation of black female, 5, 105; Stowe on recolonization of Africa by, 12, 117, 121–23;

Velazquez on, 207; white appearance of, 46–47, 55 nn. 7, 11; white women likened to, 39–40; wives of, 40–43, 49–51. *See also* Miscegenation; Racial identity; Slave narratives; Slavery

Soldiers (women as), 14–15, 181–217; number of, in Civil War, 184, 214 n.7, 215 n.8; punishment for, 201

"Sororophobia," 197, 198

Soul Sister (Halsell), 153

South (feminization of), 191, 198–209

Southern Historical Association, 200

Southworth, E. D. E. N., 8–9, 131–50

Spain, 107, 118, 119, 121, 125 n.13, 126 n.16

Spanish-American War, 208

Spectatorship: in *Black Like Me*, 9, 165–67; and racial identification, 10, 64, 65–66

Specularity: in *Black Like Me*, 166–67; in *Giovanni's Room*, 224; in *The Hidden Hand*, 9, 131–50; as issue in passing, 2, 10, 13, 64, 65–69, 103; in racial identification, 257. *See also* Mirror scenes

Spillers, Hortense, 138

Spivak, Gayatri Chakravorty, 21, 22, 25, 34, 35

Stanton, Elizabeth Cady, 40

Status (and passing), 4–5, 11–12, 62, 253, 256, 258–59, 268–69. *See also* Class; "Whiteness": privileges associated with

Stein, Gertrude, 161, 218

Stephens, George, 42, 51

Stephens, Mrs. George, 42–44

Stepto, Robert, 69–70

Stern, Julia, 11–12, 103–30

Stewart, Susan, 229

Still, William, 44

Stone, Lucy, 40

Stowe, Harriet Beecher: on black deportation to Africa, 12, 117, 121–23; moral order in works by, 132, 133; on race and domination, 11–12, 103, 107, 116–23; on white children sold into slavery, 8. See also *Key to Uncle Tom's Cabin; Uncle Tom's Cabin*
Student Nonviolent Coordinating Committee (SNCC), 173
Subalternity, 21–36
Subjectivity: in antebellum America, 39, 40–43; fragmented ("split"), 67–69, 158–62, 166, 168–69, 222, 229, 230; Lacan on, 65
"Suffering Test" (of "blackness"), 236, 238, 266, 267
Sundquist, Eric, 120, 127 n.22, 132

Tate, Claudia, 51, 53 n.3
Taylor, Joe Gray, 248
Teena, Brandon, 1, 13
Texts: dream, 103, 107–10, 113–15, 117, 122; open, 11, 75–76, 84–85, 89, 96–98, 98 n.5; which "pass" in the canon, 132, 221. See also Fiction
Time magazine, 172
Tipton, Billy, 3, 14
Tocqueville, Alexis de, 41, 43, 108
Todorov, Tzvetan, 114
Transsexuals, 16 n.2
Transvestites. See Cross-dressing; "Drag"
Turner, Nat, 119, 120, 126 n.17, 129 n.30
Twain, Mark, 126 n.18, 260

"The Uncanny" (Freud), 177 n.8
Uncle Tom's Cabin (Stowe), 66, 141; cross-dressing and race-passing associated with Eliza Harris in, 12, 103, 219; "facing scenes" in, 113–15; moral order in, 132; mothers in, 142–43; "Spanish masquerade" of George Harris in, 3, 11–12, 103–30

The Underground Rail Road (Still), 44
United Daughters of the Confederacy, 199, 213
U.S. Department of Interior, 181
U.S. National Park Service, 181
U.S. Supreme Court, 7

Van Vechten, Carl, 59–60
Velazquez, Don Diego, 189
Velazquez, Loreta, 3, 15, 184–213
Vested Interests (Garber), 183
Village Voice, 1, 4

Wald, Gayle, 9, 151–77
Wall, Cheryl, 76, 97
Wallon, Henri, 41
Warner, Susan, 133
Washington, George, 120–21
Washington, Mary Helen, 226
Water imagery, 23–24
Waters, Maxine, 261
Watts riot (1965), 173
Weinauer, Ellen, 12, 37–56
Wells, Ida B., 260–61
West Indies, 30, 33
"What's Happened in America since *Black Like Me*" (Griffin), 153–54, 173
White, Walter, 73 n.3
White by Definition (Domínguez), 247, 251
"The White Negro" (Mailer), 163
"Whiteness": associations with, 52; defined in opposition to "blackness," 7–8, 68–70, 72–73, 111–12; in *Giovanni's Room*, 220; instability of concept of, 227–28, 230; not an intrinsic quality, 10, 63; post-Civil War feminization of, 207–9; privileges associated with, 4–5, 7, 15, 62, 162–63, 253, 256, 258–59, 268–69; social construction of, 162–63. See also "Blackness"; Color symbolism; Racial identity

Index

Whites: African Americans passing as, 1, 2–5, 7, 9, 12–13, 17 n.8, 37–56, 59–100, 103, 219, 221, 243–47, 265; children of, sold into slavery, 8, 46–47; comraderie among, 262–64; effects of Civil War on women among, 188–89, 213; Olaudah Equiano on, 32–36; passing of, for African Americans, 3, 134–35, 151–77, 176 n.2; relations between black women and women among, 53 n.2, 137; sexual control among, 5, 15, 260–61; as slaveowners, 1, 5, 23–24, 41, 42, 51, 104–5, 109, 113, 114, 247–48, 252; stereotypic coding of women among, 133, 136; use of blacks in writings by, 39–40, 133, 134–36, 148, 162; women among, and the "Lost Cause," 199–200. *See also* Miscegenation; Racial Identity; Racism; "Whiteness"

Who Is Black? One Nation's Definition (Davis), 244, 248, 249, 251, 252, 259

"Why Black Separatism?" (Griffin), 153–54

The Wide, Wide World (Warner), 133

Williams, Patricia, 171–72

Williamson, Joel, 8

Winthrop, John, 117

The Woman in Battle (Velazquez), 3, 15, 194–213

Women: African American, 5, 40–43, 49–51, 53 n.2, 105, 137, 139–43, 166, 261–62; as Civil War soldiers, 14–15, 181–217; Craft's insistence on essentialism of, 38, 48–53; Loreta Velazquez's ambivalence toward, 193–98, 210; marital property rights of, 39–40; ownership of, by husbands, 121; relations between black and white, 53 n.2, 137; role of, in defining "maleness," 13, 15, 38–39; Southern white, 15, 188–89, 199–200, 213; stereotypic coding of white, 133, 136; use of blacks to represent freedom or captivity of white, 39–40, 133–36, 148

Work (Alcott), 197

Worthington, C. J., 187, 204

Wright, Richard, 152

Writing. *See* Literacy

Xtravaganza, Venus, 14

Young, Elizabeth, 14–15, 181–217

Zwarg, Christina, 120, 121

Contributors

Martha J. Cutter is Assistant Professor of English at Kent State University where she teaches courses in ethnic literatures, African American fiction, and women's writing. She has published essays in *American Literature, Callaloo,* and *Women's Studies,* and is at work on a book about Anglo-American and African American women's fiction.

Elaine K. Ginsberg, Professor of English at West Virginia University, teaches courses in American literature, literary criticism, and women's studies. Her current project is a study of race and gender in early American narrative.

Katharine Nicholson Ings is a doctoral candidate at Indiana University. A recipient of a fellowship from the Social Sciences and Humanities Research Council of Canada, she is writing her dissertation on the miscegenated imagination of white women writers in nineteenth-century America.

Samira Kawash is Assistant Professor of English at Rutgers University. Her book, *Dislocating the Color Line,* is forthcoming from Stanford University Press.

Adrian M. S. Piper is Professor of Philosophy at Wellesley College and a conceptual artist. She is the author of a two-volume collection *Out of Order, Out of Sight. Selected Writings in Meta Art and Art Criticism 1967–1992* (MIT Press, 1996), and her three-volume study in Kantian metaethics, "Rationality and the Structure of the Self," is nearing completion.

Valerie Rohy is a doctoral candidate at Tufts University. Her dissertation considers lesbianism and representation in nineteenth- and twentieth-century American literature.

Marion Rust is a doctoral candidate in the program on Modern Thought and Literature at Stanford University. She is the recipient of a Whiting Foundation fellowship, and her dissertation, "Measuring Pleasure: Agency and Anxiety in Early American Narrative," focuses on Susannah Rowson.

Julia Stern is Assistant Professor of English at Northwestern University. She has published articles in *Arizona Quarterly, ESQ,* and *American Literature,* and is completing a book on gender, sympathy, and dissent in eighteenth-century American fiction, tentatively titled "The Plight of Feeling: From Sympathy to Dissent in the Early American Novel."

Gayle Wald is Assistant Professor of English at George Washington University. Her book *Crossing the Line: Racial Passing in Twentieth-Century American Literature and Culture* is forthcoming from Duke University Press.

Ellen M. Weinauer is Assistant Professor of English at the University of Southern Mississippi. She is currently at work on a book that treats the relationship between property law and authorial identity in the American nineteenth century.

Elizabeth Young is Assistant Professor of English at Mount Holyoke College where she teaches American literature, feminist theory, and film. She has published essays in *American Literature, Feminist Studies*, and *Camera Obscura*, and is writing a book on women writers and the Civil War, from which this essay is taken.

Library of Congress Cataloging-in-Publication Data

Passing and the fictions of identity / edited by Elaine K. Ginsberg.
p. cm. — (New Americanists)
Includes bibliographical references and index.
ISBN 0-8223-1755-9 (cloth : alk. paper). — ISBN 0-8223-1764-8 (pbk. : alk. paper)
1. American literature—History and criticism. 2. Passing (Identity) in literature.
3. Difference (Psychology) in literature. 4. Gender identity in literature. 5. Afro-
Americans—Race identity. 6. Afro-Americans in literature. 7. Group identity in
literature. 8. United States—Civilization. I. Ginsberg, Elaine K., 1936- . II. Series.
PS169.P35P37 1996
810.9'353—dc20   95-40106   CIP